Janet Frame was born in Dunedin, New Zealand, in 1924. She has won many prizes and awards for her writing, including the Commonwealth Literature Prize, has been a Burns Scholar and a Sargeson Fellow, and in 1983 was awarded the CBE. She is an honorary foreign member of the American Academy of Arts and Letters.

Janet Frame has written a number of novels including *Faces in the Water* (1980), *Living in the Maniototo* (1981), *Owls Do Cry* (1985), *The Lagoon* and *The Carpathians*. She has also published short stories, including her collection *You Are Now Entering the Human Heart* (1984), and one volume of poetry, *The Pocket Mirror* (1992).

This three-volume autobiography consisting of *To the Is-Land*, *An Angel at my Table* and *The Envoy from the Mirror City* was made into the film *An Angel at my Table* by Jane Campion.

JANET FRAME

an angel
at my table

the complete autobiography

First published in Great Britain under the title *Janet Frame:*
An Autobiography by The Women's Press Ltd, 1990
A member of the Namara Group
34 Great Sutton Street, London EC1V 0LQ
www.the-womens-press.com

First published in New Zealand by Century Hutchinson New Zealand Ltd, 1989

Reprinted 1991, 1998, 1999

This edition entitled *An Angel at My Table:*
The Complete Autobiography published 2001

Reprinted 2002

To the Is-land first published 1982
Published in Great Britain by The Women's Press Ltd, 1983

An Angel at My Table first published 1984
Published in Great Britain by The Women's Press Ltd, 1984

The Envoy from Mirror City first published 1985
Published in Great Britain by The Women's Press Ltd, 1985

British Library Cataloguing-in-Publication Data
A catalogue record for this book is available from the British Library.

ISBN 0 7043 4693 1

Printed and bound in Great Britain by Cox & Wyman Ltd, Reading, Berkshire

VOLUME ONE

To the Is-Land

This first volume
is dedicated to my parents
and brother and sisters

CONTENTS

1 In the Second Place

From the first place of liquid darkness, within the second place of air and light, I set down the following record with its mixture of fact and truths and memories of truths and its direction always toward the Third Place, where the starting point is myth.

2 Toward the Is-Land

The Ancestors — who were they, the myth and the reality? As a child, I used to boast that the Frames 'came over with William of Orange'. I have since learned that this may have been so, for Frame is a version of Fleming, Flamand, from the Flemish weavers who settled in the lowlands of Scotland in the fourteenth century. I strengthen the reality or the myth of those ancestors each time I recall that Grandma Frame began working in a Paisley cotton mill when she was eight years old; that her daughters Polly, Isy, Maggie spent their working lives as dressmakers and in their leisure produced exquisite embroidery, knitting, tatting, crochet; and that her son George Samuel, my father, had a range of skills that included embroidery (or 'fancy-work', as it was known), rug making, leatherwork, painting in oils on canvas and on velvet. The Frames had a passion for making things. Like his father, our Grandad Frame, a blacksmith who made our fire pokers, the boot-last, and even the wooden spurtle smoothed with stirring the morning porridge, my father survives as a presence in such objects as a leather workbag, a pair of ribbed butter pats, a handful of salmon spoons.

As children, we heard little of our father's ancestors, the Frames and the Patersons, only that most had immigrated to the United States of America and to Canada, where 'Cousin Peg' became a schoolteacher. And none remains now of that Frame family of eight sons — John, Alex, Thomas, Robert, William Francis, Walter Henry, George Samuel, Charles Allan — and four daughters — Margaret, Mary, Isabella Woods. The fourth, my namesake, died at thirteen months.

Mother's family, the Godfreys, had long been established in Wairau and Blenheim and Picton, where Mother, Lottie Clarice, was born and brought up in a family of three brothers — Charles, Lance, William — and five sisters — May, Elsie, Joy, Grace, Jessie (who died in her twenty-first year). Mother's father, Alfred Godfrey, also a blacksmith, was the son of John Godfrey, a political character known as 'The Duke', who owned the Sheepskin Tavern in Wairau Valley and was later editor of the *Marlborough Press*. We heard from Mother of John Godfrey's brother Henry and of their father, an Oxford doctor, whose 'Godfrey's Elixir' was known in Great Britain in the early nineteenth century; of Mother's mother, Jessie Joyce, from a Jersey Islands family of French origin, and her mother, Charlotte, formerly Charlotte Nash, author of the poems in a small book with an engraved cover and sweet-pea-coloured pages, written at eighteen, before her emigration from Harbledown, Kent, to New Zealand — Charlotte, whose second marriage was to James or 'Worser' Heberley, of Worser Bay, Wellington, given to him by the tribe of his first wife (Te Ati Awa).

Mother and Father, then. Mother leaving school early to become a dental nurse at Mr Stocker's rooms in Picton, later to be a housemaid in various homes in Picton and Wellington — the Beauchamps, the Loughnins — and, during the Great War, in the early years of her marriage, in the home of Wili Fels in Dunedin; Mother, a rememberer and talker, partly exiled from her family through her marriage out of the Christadelphian faith and her distance from Marlborough, remembering her past as an exile remembers her homeland; Mother in a constant state of family immersion even to the material evidence of the wet patch in front of her dress where she leaned over the sink, washing dishes, or over the copper and washtub, or, kneeling, wiped the floor with oddly shaped floorcloths — old pyjama legs, arms and tails of worn shirts — or, to keep at bay the headache and tiredness of the hot summer, the vinegar-soaked rag she wrapped around her forehead: an immersion so deep that it achieved the opposite effect of making her seem to be seldom at home, in the present tense, or like an unreal person with her real self washed away. Perhaps we were jealous of the space that another world and another time occupied in our mother's life; and although, perhaps fearing immersion in this foreign world, we struggled to escape, we were haunted by her tales of the Guards, the Heberleys, Dieffenbach, shipwrecks in the Sounds, life in Waikawa Road and down the Maori pa, family life at the Godfreys, remembered as paradisal. We came to know by heart incidents reported with exact conversations at school, at home, in the dentist's rooms, and in the homes where Mother worked — from her excitement on her first day at school at seeing a weta crawling on brother Willy's knee ('Oooh, look on Willy's knee!') to the words of Mr Loughnin the magistrate as he (in nightshirt and nightcap) lured his wife to his bed with 'Letty, I want you . . .'

When Mother talked of the present, however, bringing her sense of wondrous contemplation to the ordinary world we knew, we listened, feeling the mystery and the magic. She had only to say of any commonplace object, 'Look, kiddies, a stone' to fill that stone with a wonder as if it were a holy object. She was able to imbue every insect, blade of grass, flower, the dangers and grandeurs of weather and the seasons, with a memorable importance along with a kind of uncertainty and humility that led us to ponder and try to discover the heart of everything. Mother, fond of poetry and reading, writing, and reciting it, communicated to us that same feeling about the world of the written and spoken word.

Father, known to us as 'Dad', was inclined to dourness with a strong sense of formal behaviour that did not allow him the luxury of reminiscence. One of the few exceptions was his tales of 'the time we had the monkey', told with remembered delight and some longing. When his family left Oamaru, where he was born, to live in Port Chalmers (where his mother, Grandma Frame, became known as midwife), Grandad Frame brought home from the pub a monkey left by one of the sailors. 'Tell us,' we used to say to Dad, 'about the time you had a pet monkey.'

Dad, too, left school early, although he was a good student, as the class photos of 'Good Workers at Albany Street School' testify. His first job was making sound effects (horses galloping and wild storm sounds) at the local theatre, and his first adventure was his attempt to fly from the roof of the family house in Dunedin. Later he began work on the railway as a cleaner, progressing to fireman, second-class engine-driver, which was his occupation when I first met him, later to first-class engine driver, following the example of his brothers who spent their lives with engines and movement — Alex, who became a taxi driver; Wattie, a sea captain, later a harbour master in Newport, Melbourne; Charlie, who was for a time a motor mechanic and chauffeur to Sir Truby King. Brother Bob became a baker in Mosgiel.

Mum and Dad (Mother was known as 'Mum' until I considered myself grown up enough to acknowledge her as a separate personality) were married at the Registry Office in Picton three weeks before Dad sailed to the Great War. When Dad returned from the war, he and Mother set up house in Richardson Street, St Kilda, Dunedin, helped by a rehabilitation loan of twenty-five pounds, with which they bought one wooden kerb, one hearth rug, two Morris dining chairs, one duchesse, one oval dining table, one iron bedstead and flock mattress, one kitchen mat, these items being listed on the document of loan with a chilling reminder that while the loan remained unpaid, the King's representative (the agreement was between 'His Majesty the King and George Samuel Frame') had the right to enter the Frame household to inspect and report on the condition of the 'said furniture and fittings'. The loan was repaid after a few years, and the document of discharge kept by my parents in their most hallowed keeping place — the top right-hand drawer of the King's duchesse — where were also kept my sister Isabel's caul, Mother's wedding ring, which did not fit, her upper false teeth, which also did not fit, Myrtle's twenty-two-carat gold locket engraved with her name, and Dad's foreign coins, mostly Egyptian, brought home from the war.

There were the ancestors, then, given as mythical possessions — your great-grandmother, your great-grandfather, did this, was this, lived and died there and there — and the living parents, accumulating memories we had not shared. Then on 15 December 1920 a daughter, Myrtle, was born, and on 20 April 1922 a son, Robert, or Bruddie; in 1923 another son, stillborn, unnamed, was buried, and on 28 August 1924 I was born, named Janet Paterson Frame, with ready-made parents and a sister and brother who had already begun their store of experience, inaccessible to me except through their language and the record, always slightly different, of our mother and father, and as each member of the family was born, each, in a sense with memories on loan, began to supply the individual furnishings of each Was-Land, each Is-Land, and the hopes and dreams of the Future.

3 In Velvet Gown

I was delivered by Dr Emily Seideberg McKinnon at St Helens Hospital, Dunedin, where I was known as 'the baby who was always hungry'. I had a twin, which did not develop beyond a few weeks. Twins were hereditary in Mother's family, and she would often quote the poem written by (I think) her grandmother, whose two sets of twins died in infancy: 'Four little locks of gold'. Mother's memory of my birth always had two repeated references — her boast that I was delivered by the first woman medical graduate in New Zealand and her pride in the abundance of milk that enabled her to feed myself and other babies.

'My milk was drawn off,' she'd say, making a liberal giving motion toward and away from her 'titties', in one of her many gestures that we, the ancestors ever alert beside us, assigned to the 'French' side of the family. With similar drama Mother spoke of *Dr Emily Seideberg McKinnon*, which must have impressed me even during my first few days of being, for her lifelong repetition of names important to her — Henry Wadsworth Longfellow, Harriet Beecher Stowe, John Greenleaf Whittier, William Pember Reeves (*The Passing of the Forest*), Michael Joseph Savage — never failed to awaken a sense of magic.

I was born into a town that had lately known two historic events and was preparing for others. In 1923 the low-lying parts of Dunedin and St Kilda, where we lived, were severely flooded by the Leith, while a few years earlier the Prince of Wales had visited Dunedin. My earliest recollections, therefore, are of the talk of the prince and the flood and of the inaccessibility of the talk, so far above me, to and fro, to and fro between tall, tall people. When I was three weeks old, the family shifted to Outram, where we had a house with a big walnut tree at the back and a cow byre with a red and white branchy-horned Ayrshire cow named Betty; and when I was six weeks old, I was in the cow byre with Mother while she milked Betty. My earliest memories are fragmentary and apart from the talking of the adults are all set outside — in the cow byre, in the neighbour's orchard, under the walnut tree where, as I grew, I was put in a huge kerosene box to play and where I learned to walk, first holding on to the rim of the box. I was told that my first words were 'Pick walnut up, Mummy', pronouncing *walnut* as 'warnut'. My pronunciation was usually incorrect and apparently amused everyone. A sty in my eye was cured by the 'pitties', not, as I was told, by the *pixies*. I sang, 'God Save our Gracious *Tin*'. I drank 'mook'. The new baby that came when I was twenty months old and was named Isabel became, for me, 'Iddabull'.

It was while Mother was busy with the new baby that Grandma Frame, who lived with us, became my companion and friend. It was she who told me about the 'pitties'. I remember her first as a tall woman in a long, black dress and later, when her diabetes forced the amputation of one of her legs, in her wheelchair. Her skin was dark, her black hair frizzy, and although she talked in Scottish, the songs she sang were of the American Deep South. She'd be going silently about the house when suddenly her voice would come out in a singing that filled me with the kind of feeling I learned much later to identify as sadness. 'Carry me back to ole Virginny . . .', Grandma sang, pausing after the first line as if she were almost there but needed a natural delay to transport her whole being. I know I could see it in the way she looked around the room as if she were suddenly a stranger and might even remark, as strangers did, 'Oh, you've got one of these, Lottie. I didn't know you had one of these. They're nice to have, aren't they?' But Grandma was away in the song, 'That's where the cotton and corn and taters grow . . .' She sang of 'Labouring hard for Ole Massa'. I assumed that Grandma Frame was African and had been a slave in

America, that her real home was 'Virginny', where she longed to return; for you see I knew about slaves.

The book that everyone was talking about in our house was *Uncle Tom's Cabin*, by Harriet Beecher Stowe, and I was being called Topsy because my hair was frizzy. 'Who are you?' they'd ask me, and I learned to reply, 'I'm the girl that never was born pras I grew up among the corn. Golly. Ain't I wicked!' Mother talked, too, of Eliza crossing the ice as if it had really happened, like the pioneers and the visit of the prince and the flood. She talked of wicked Simon Legree. There was much talk of ice, of sheet ice and pack ice and icebergs, for the *Titanic* disaster was often mentioned, still uppermost in people's minds.

Those Outram days until my third birthday give isolated memories and feelings: of the hours I spent watching Betty the cow with her skin-covered machinery working at both ends — all the smells and colours and diversity of solids (turnips and apples) and liquids, taken in at one end and let out the other. I'd stand in front of the bail, feeding her the big, red apples, and from time to time she'd open her mouth and yawn, flooding her potato-and-turnip-and-apple-and-grass-smelling breath into my face and showing her big, worn-down teeth. I remember the Snows and their orchard, my small friend Bobby Little, who taught me to say *bugger*, which I called 'budda'. I remember the terrible magazine, which was not to be approached — at the back of the drill hall (or wi'hall, as I called it) — and the shining silver kerosene tin, which was my only toy, which I pulled on a length of string after me wherever I went, while it clanged and rattled and sometimes dented in one side then popped or dinked, returning to its old shape, making the sound the rain made inside the water tank. I remember Topsy and Simon Legree and Eliza on the ice and the bogies (or 'bodies'), who came after dark when the candles were pinched out and the wick turned down on the kerosene lamp, and I remember, as my earliest memory, something that could not have happened: a tall woman wearing a clothes peg on her nose peered into the bedroom from a small window high in the wall and, looking down at me in my wooden cot, said sharply, 'You're a nosey-parker.'

My most vivid memory of that time is the long, white dusty road outside the gate, the swamp (which I called the 'womp'), which filled me with terror, for I had been warned never to go near it, and the strange unnaturally bright green grass growing around it and the weeds like the inside of the India rubber ball growing along its surface and the golden beastie in a velvet coat grazing near the fence — and of myself wearing my most treasured possession, a golden velvet dress, which I named my 'beastie' dress. I remember a grey day when I stood by the gate and listened to the wind in the telegraph wires. I had my first conscious feeling of an outside sadness, or it seemed to come from outside, from the sound of the wind moaning in the wires. I looked up and down the white dusty road and saw no one. The wind was blowing from place to place past us, and I was there, in between, listening. I felt a burden of sadness and loneliness as if something had happened or begun and I knew about it. I don't think I had yet thought of myself as a person looking out at the world; until then, I felt I *was* the world. In listening to the wind and its sad song, I knew I was listening to a sadness that had no relation to me, which belonged to the world.

I don't attempt to search for the commonplace origins of such a feeling. When you bring home a shell treasure from the beach, you shake free the sand and the mesh of seaweed and the other crumbled pieces of shell and perhaps even the tiny dead black-eyed inhabitant. I may have polished this shell of memory with the application of time but only because it is constantly with me, not because I have varnished it for display.

I was learning words, believing from the beginning that words meant what they said. I was slightly puzzled that there should be a railway magazine in the house when we children were forbidden to go near the magazine. And when I sang 'God Save Our Gracious Tin', I believed that I was singing about my cherished kerosene tin. In the Outram days, when many relatives lived near, there was much coming and going and talking and laughing, with words travelling like the wind along invisible wires, words full of meaning and importance describing the Great Dunedin and South Seas Exhibition and the visit of the Duke of York and naming places. The relatives who visited were mostly the Frames, an excitable family with a passion for detail and a love of home and hearth that helped to make the smallest expedition beyond the home an occasion to recall in minute detail all the meetings, conversations, news, rumours, and actual events, and when the events were as important as royal visits and great exhibitions and floods and the sinking of unsinkable ships, mixed with dramatic details of books being read and poems remembered as if they, too, had been present occasions, then I can explain the sense of excitement I felt but could not understand as it moved to and fro in the travelling network of words.

But we were railway people. And when I was three, we shifted house to Glenham in Southland.

4 The Railway People

My memory is once again of the colours and spaces and natural features of the outside world. On our first week in our Glenham house on the hill, I discovered a place, *my place*. Exploring by myself, I found a secret place among old, fallen trees by a tiny creek, with a moss-covered log to sit on while the new-leaved branches of the silver birch tree formed a roof shutting out the sky except for the patterned holes of sunlight. The ground was covered with masses of old, used leaves, squelchy, slippery, wet. I sat on the log and looked around myself. I was overcome by a delicious feeling of discovery, of gratitude, of possession. I knew that this place was entirely *mine*; mine the moss, the creek, the log, the secrecy. It was a new kind of possession quite different from my beastie dress or from the new baby Isabel, over whom Myrtle and Bruddie and I argued so often (for Mother had said that Isabel was *my* baby, just as Bruddie was Myrtle's baby) that it seemed to me that owning people was too hard to manage if you had to keep fighting over possession.

I remembered my overwhelming sense of anticipation and excitement at the world — the world being My Place by the fallen birch log, with the grass, the insects in the grass, the sky, the sheep and cows and rabbits, the wax-eyes and the hawks — everything Outside. I remember my special feeling for the sky, its faraway aboveness, up there where my mother and father lived, and the way I was filled with longing for it, a kind of nostalgia shared by my brother and sisters some years later when we discovered an old schoolbook with a poem that began:

> On his back in the meadow a little boy lay
> with his face turned up to the sky
> and he watched the clouds as one by one
> they lazily floated by . . .

We lay together in the long summer grass, looking up at the clouds, reciting the poem, and knowing that each was feeling the same homesickness and longing for the sky.

This passion for the outside world was strengthened by the many journeys we made in Dad's grey Lizzie Ford to rivers and seas in the south, for Dad was a keen fisherman, and while he fished, we played and picnicked and told stories, following the example of Mother, who also composed poems and stories while we waited for the billy to boil over the manuka fire.

On one of those early expeditions to the south coast, I told my story of the bird and the hawk and the bogie (pronounced by me 'birdie', 'hawt', 'bodie'), and although the telling of the story is a reinforced memory as Mother often recalled it, mimicking even my gesture of sympathy as I put my head on one side and said, 'Oh! poor little birdie', I do remember the occasion chiefly because I remember seeing in my mind the huge, dark shadow of the bogie as it came from behind the hill: 'Once upon a time there was a birdie. One day a hawt flew out of the sky and ate the birdie. (Oh poor little birdie.) The next day a bid bodie came out from behind the hill and ate up the hawt from eating up the little birdie.'

I remember, too, the fierce attempt to *make* my audience, Myrtle and Bruddie, sit absolutely still and my asking Mother for help. 'Mum, Myrtle and Bruddie's wiggling. Tell them to stop wiggling while I tell my 'tory.'

The poems that Mother recited to us on those picnics were prompted by the surroundings — the lighthouse at Waipapa, the Aurora Australis in the sky. 'Look, the Southern Lights, kiddies.'

> The lighthouse on the rocky shore
> the seagulls' lonely cry
> and day departing leaves behind
> God's pictures in the sky.

There were other poems that Mother had not composed herself — tales of shipwreck, of tidal waves: 'High Tide on the Coast of Lincolnshire', 'Come up, Whitefoot, come up, Lightfoot, Jetty to the milking shed . . .' Well, we knew about cows, and we knew about floods. 'When Myrtle and Bruddie were little, before you were born, Nini.' We'd had to 'give up' Betty when we shifted from Outram, and we now bought our milk from Mr Bennett on the hill opposite. We learned to love those beaches and rivers and the long shadows of a Southland twilight and the golden roads lit on each side by the gorse hedges and the ever-present hawks circling in the sky.

Myrtle and Bruddie started school at Glenham, and sometimes I went with them to the one-teacher school on top of yet another hill, and I sat in a corner, watching and listening to the 'big people'. I learned a special word at Glenham — *gored* — following a time of drama when Mr Bennett was *gored* by his dark brown Jersey bull and rushed to Invercargill Hospital, and everyone said the dark brown Jersey bulls were the fiercest.

I spent much time, too, at 'my place', enjoying its being there. Then one night Dad came home with his news: 'I've got a shift, Mum. To Edendale.' The arrangement was that we were to shift in the early summer, and in the meantime (it was now autumn) our railway house was to be pulled down and rebuilt at Edendale while we spent the winter in railway huts in the paddock overlooked by the school and the Bennetts' and our house: a paddock with a swamp in the corner and bulrushes and snowberries and penny oranges growing in the silken snowgrass.

Swamp red, beastie gold, sky grey, railway red, railway yellow, macrocarpa green, tussock gold, snowgrass gold, penny-orange orange, milk white, snowberry white, all lit by the sky of snow light reflected from Antarctica or, as we knew it, from Mother's constant reference, 'the South Pole, kiddies'. These colours filled my seeing and our excitement at the prospect of living *Outside*.

There were three railway huts (possibly a fourth, with a copper, to be used as a washhouse): a kitchen-living hut, a bedroom hut with bunks for Myrtle, Bruddie, and me, a bedroom hut for Mum and Dad and the baby Isabel, each hut being about six feet by eight feet, except for the slightly larger kitchen-living hut, which had a stove with a tin chimney poking through the roof. Each hut was painted railway red and had its own door. The lavatory, or 'dumpy', as we called it, was the usual enclosure about a deep hole, with a railway-red seat. Our lighting was by candle and kerosene, and only the kitchen hut had a stove. The anticipated delights, intensified by Mother's ability to pluck poetic references from those many rooted in her mind, began to die with the first touch of the Southland blizzard. Tales of gypsy camps, or Arabs folding their tents, of Babes in the Wood, could scarcely defeat the bitter cold. It seemed to be always snowing, with the snow lying deep around the huts and in the central courtyard.

I think I knew unhappiness for the first time. I was miserable, locked away each night from Mum and Dad and unable to reach them except by going through the snow. I was at an age to be teased, and because I had let it be known that I was afraid of rats in the wall, I was teased with cries of 'rats in the wall, rats in the wall'. We were all sick, with colds, and I began to suffer the pains in my legs that became part of my childhood. I was feverish and delirious, seeing insects crawling up and down the wall. The 'growing pains' and the fever were rheumatic fever. Everywhere was damp and cold, and the world was full of damp washing and nappies covered with green mess as if the baby, like a calf, had been eating grass. Mum was still breast-feeding Isabel. I had stopped feeding when I was two and had started biting, although Mother's titties were always there, like the cow's teats for an occasional squirt into our mouths. Yet, while Mother 'believed' in breast-feeding her children for as long as possible, she also took pride in our early use of cups and knives, forks and spoons. She would say proudly of me that I was 'drinking from a cup at six weeks'. When she finally wanted us to know that her titties were not for us but for the newest baby, she smeared a bitter substance over her breasts.

In spite of the misery of Inside, the times around the kitchen stove were cosy, and bathing in the round, tin bath in front of the stove — rub a dub dub, three men in a tub — was always pleasant. And Mother, as was to become her habit, helped to lighten our (and no doubt her) misery by pointing out the beauty of the snow and telling us stories of the snow and the rain and Jack Frost, who was 'after our fingers and toes'. She'd look out into the country-black dark through the small, chill uncurtained window of the hut and murmur, 'I wonder, is Jack Frost coming tonight . . .' She knew and we knew that he came every night, but I was fascinated by the reference to him as a person with a name, and I think I believed in his existence more surely than I ever believed in that other night traveller, Santa Claus. Also, in the warm of the kitchen hut Mother would play her accordion and sing while Dad, sometimes striding up and down in the snow (he insisted that you had to stride up and down while you played the bagpipes), played his bagpipe tunes — 'The Cock o' the North' or 'The Flowers of the Forest' or others from his book of bagpipe music.

It was late summer when we shifted into our rebuilt house at Edendale, into the heart of our railway country — beside the railway line and the goods shed and the engine shed and the turntable and the points and the watertank painted railway hut red on its railway-hut-red stand beside the railway line and the spindly red-painted little house high up where the signalman lived and hung out his signals and the resting or retired railway carriages and trucks and trolleys. Among our games was 'trolley works', where we pretended to be trolleys on the railway line. I spent much time playing around the railway territory among the railway weeds and flowers — dock and wild sweet peas — and in the goods shed, where the sacks of grain were piled high and I, suddenly powerful as a 'jackdaw', climbed to the top of the sacks, or 'climbers' as we knew them, and swooped down upon Myrtle and Bruddie, flapping my wings and making a hawklike cry. 'Nini's the jackdaw,' they said at meals when Mum or Dad asked what we'd been doing. 'Nini's the jackdaw, and we've been climbing up the climbers.' I'd not seen jackdaws, but I'd heard stories of the way they swooped upon bright objects to carry them to their nest.

It seemed that we had scarcely settled in our new-old house when word came that we were to shift once again — to Wyndham.

5 Ferry Street, Wyndham

Wyndham, the Southland town of rivers, with our house the usual kind of railway house by the railway line but this time in a street with a name — Ferry Street — which I interpreted as *Fairy* Street. From a pixie-inhabited Outram to a fairy-filled Wyndham did not seem like a misuse of logic and experience. In Wyndham I discovered that the world held more people that I had dreamed of — I'd thought of the world as all sky, green paddocks, swamps, bulrushes, tussocks, snowgrass, sheep, cattle; and the wind in the telegraph wires along deserted roads; and the railway coming from and going to; and one or two neighbours who gave us milk and apples in exchange for some of Dad's fish — rainbow and brown trout, whitebait, oysters — or our kinds of plums and apples; and people, especially in Outram, as relations, coming and going and talking of Up Central and Middlemarch and Inchclutha; and then, as in Glenham and Edendale, the world as a place where we lived alone with the weather; with our mother and father working all day and singing and playing the accordion and the bagpipes in the evening while we children played from waking till sleeping.

Our Wyndham house was one of a row of houses with gardens at the back adjoining the gardens of the houses in the next parallel street, and the railway line at one end and the paddock by the railway line where our new cow, a golden Jersey named Beauty, was to graze with her new black and white heifer calf, which we called Pansy. We had a fowlhouse, too, with White Leghorns with bright, floppy combs and a rooster with a tall, arched tail with the end feathers arranged like a hand of playing cards.

In my memory Ferry Street and the street at the end with the shops and the office of the newspaper, the *Wyndham Farmer*, were the only streets in Wyndham. Other landmarks were the railway line and the railway station, the school, the racecourse, the golf course, and the rivers, some near, some more distant, which became as familiar to us as the rivers and paddocks and plants and trees of the other places where we had lived: the Outram Lee Stream and the Outram Glen, the brown Mimihau, the swift Mataura.

And because, in a tally of people I had known, those of fiction (and of the past and distance that transformed them into a kind of fiction — ancestors, relatives, rulers, Eliza, Simon Legree, Jack Frost, the Gypsies, Wee Willie Winkie, the Babes in the Wood, bogies and pixies and fairies) and the people in songs and in fantasy exceeded those of flesh and blood, I thought of Ferry Street as a place of mysterious people who might appear in the flesh or just as readily in poems and songs. For instance, the

Murphys' house several doors away on the opposite shady side of the road with its high macrocarpa hedge, neat lawn, and moss-covered stone doorstep was the house in the song Dad sang in the evening: 'The Stone Outside Dan Murphy's Door'. I knew he was singing of that house and the moss-covered stone, and I'd peep through the hand hole in the gate or a gap in the macrocarpa hedge and stare and stare at the 'stone outside Dan Murphy's door', materialised from a *song*. I was filled with sadness and a peaceful feeling of belonging, for I felt that our family, too, was gathered into the song, and when Dad sang with such certainty:

> *Those friends and companions of childhood,*
> *contented although we were poor;*
> *and the songs that we sung*
> *in the days we were young*
> *on the stone outside Dan Murphy's door.*

I knew he was singing about us. I believed that most or all of the songs our mother and father sang referred to our life and places they had known.

> *East Side West Side all around the town,*
> *the girls play ring-a-rosie,*
> *London Bridge is falling down.*
> *Girls and boys together,*
> *me and Mamie O'Rourke*
> *trip the light fantastic*
> *on the sidewalks of New York.*

That was our place, too. I felt that I had been there, that it was another way of having a place without having to leave it.

And there were the sad songs about hanging men and women and the wearing of the green and the mournful bagpipe melodies that spiralled and shirrgled and moaned up into the sky; and the war songs that Dad began to sing — Tipperary, Blightie, Mademoiselle from Armentières — and the one which wrung our hearts with pity for him and the other soldiers, 'Oh, my, I don't want to die / I want to go home'.

There were the 'new' songs, too, which suddenly everyone was singing, sometimes as if with a touch of daring, 'Moonlight and Roses', 'It ain't no sense sitting on the fence all by yourself in the moonlight', which even then we children knew as 'It ain't no fun sitting on your bum all by yourself in the moonlight'. There was 'Tiptoe Through the Tulips', 'Hello Hello Who's Your Lady Friend', which was now Isabel's or, as we called her, Dot's song

— 'Hello, hello, who's your lady friend / who's that little girlie by nor tide,' she sang. And the forbidden song 'Hallelulia I'm a bum, Hallelulia bum again . . .'

And there was Dad's special song, which he sang to Mum. They'd kiss and laugh together, and Mum would blush and smile and say, 'Oh, Curly' or 'Oh, Sammy':

> Come for a trip in my airship
> come for a sail midst the stars
> come for a trip around Venus,
> come for a trip around Mars.
> No one to watch while we're kissing,
> no one to see while we spoon,
> come for a trip in my airship
> and we'll visit the man in the moon.

And from that song, Dad would start the one which began, 'Underneath the gaslight's glitter / stands a little orphan girl', and our hearts would swell with the sadness of knowing about the little orphan girl and with the warmth of having a mother and father and a house to live in and cows and hens and the baby rabbit found in the paddock.

Those Wyndham days were full of activity for our mother and father. Dad began painting pictures in oil on canvas and on velvet; he played us to sleep each evening with his bagpipes; he played football, breaking his ankle, which meant more time for painting the pictures. He played golf and dressed in plus fours, and one of our absorbing occupations became the unravelling of old (and sometimes new) golf balls to find what lay at the end of the crinkled thread of twangy, smelly rubber. (Theseus days indeed!) Dad went to the races, too, with Johnny Walker, the railway ganger from Australia who lived over the road and who taught us to play cards. And still there were the picnics to remote beaches and rivers, travelling in the grey Lizzie Ford, stopping on the hot, dusty roads while Dad fed water to the bubbling engine; while we looked up at the sky at what appeared to be the only other living creatures in the world — the skylarks and the circling and swooping hawks.

It was then, too, that Mother began publishing her poems each week in the *Wyndham Farmer* and soon became known, with pride, as 'Lottie C. Frame, the local poet'. There was also the exciting day when Dad brought home from the local auction a chiming clock, a set of Oscar Wilde with gold dust on the edges of the pages, a gramophone with records of 'The Wee McGregor' and 'Building a Chicken House Part One'. We played the gramophone, fascinated by the way the neck containing the needle could be swivelled and 'wrung' like a dead hen's neck, and we seized the Oscar Wilde Fairy Tales but did not read them until later, in Oamaru.

When I was two months from my fourth birthday, our youngest sister, June (Phyllis Mary Eveline), was born. That winter, like the winter in the railway huts, is remembered as miserable yet with the misery shared and banished by the way in which, instead of acting as my teasing enemies, Myrtle and Bruddie became allies against the terrible Miss Low — Miss Low, the sister of one of Dad's fishing mates, who came to look after us while the baby was born and during the first few weeks. I remember her as a tall, thin woman wearing a brown costume and spectacles with thin gold rims. Her face was unfriendly, her manner bossy: she disapproved of us. 'Lottie is too soft with them,' she said, speaking of Mother, beginning a refrain that was to continue throughout our childhood.

An evident believer in 'inner cleanliness', she gave us regular doses of castor oil from the hated slim, blue glass bottle. And although we stayed in the house, we were forbidden to go near the front room where the baby was born and where Mother and the baby were now sleeping. Therefore we turned our misery to delight by huddling together, telling 'Miss Low' stories, lurid tales of 'the time Miss Low fell over the cliff and was killed', 'the time Miss Low was struck by lightning', or drowned in a tidal wave, lost in the bush, starved in the desert, killed falling down a disused mine shaft (the English children in the comic cuts, which we were beginning to read, had many injuries falling down disused mine shafts). We rivalled each other in imagining a doom for Miss Low. 'Let's have a Miss Low story,' we'd say, snuggling together, deliciously yet miserably aware of our role as outcasts in our own home with a stranger trying to take the place of our mother.

Long after Miss Low had gone and Mum, looking after the new baby, Phyllis Mary Eveline (after Miss Low) June, whom we called Chicks, was in her ordinary place again, we continued to tell our Miss Low stories until one day, suddenly, we looked at one another, almost in embarrassment, with a sense of falseness, for we knew our need had ceased, we were happy again, and our Miss Low stories were past. We separated then, each to ourselves, focusing our attention on the new baby and on the White Leghorns in the fowl house. We became preoccupied with the hens, wrapping them in pieces of blanket, carrying them around in our arms, giving them 'make-a-betters' (our word for *enema*, the peculiar orange-red bulbous rubber with the pokey end that Mother stuck up our behinds when we wanted to go and couldn't or hadn't 'been'). For the hens we used lengths of straw. Then we'd tuck them into boxes while they, extraordinarily compliant when I think of the liberties we took with them, simply lay there, all blanketed, looking at us with their nearest eye, now and again shuttering down its white, crinkled lid over the bright steady gaze and letting out a muffled squawk.

Wyndham was the time of cabbages in the garden, of pump water, of candles and kerosene lamps at night with 'real' darkness and night shadows, the people in the twilight seen as if striding across the surface of the world, and at noon, standing in small people-clumps. I learned to think of everything as sharing its life and its place with a shadow; and when the candles were lit at night, Mother used to say, 'I have a little shadow that goes in and out with me.' Wyndham was also the time of other people, of neighbours whose back garden faced ours, the Bedfords with their children, Joy, Marjorie, Ronnie, each memorable for different reasons — Joy had tuberculosis, or TB, and was a patient in a sanitorium, *Waipiata*, a dreaded word in our lives. 'She's in Waipiata.' Marjorie had a 'thin little chest'. (Mother's judgment was spoken with contempt and sorrow. Every milking time she delivered a billy of milk to the Bedfords in the hope that the children would grow as 'sturdy' as we were.) Ronnie, the youngest, became famous for having stuck a bead up his nose . . .

Opposite us were the Mileses, Tommy Miles and his wife and family, whom we did not know for long, for Tommy Miles, a railway ganger, was run over by the express train on the railway line outside our place. His legs were severed, and he later died in Invercargill Hospital where, in the awful language of emergency, remembered from the time the Jersey bull 'gored' Mr Bennett, he was 'rushed'. In that accident people tore up sheets to use as bandages, and Mother used what we learned to call her 'earthquake-and-tidal-wave-voice', announcing with high-pitched urgency, 'It's Tommy Miles, it's Tommy Miles.'

And Wyndham was the time of the dentist and starting school and Grandma Frame's dying: all three memorably unhappy, although Grandma Frame's death was different in being world-sad with everyone sharing — the cows, the hens, the pet rabbit, even the stinky ferret as well as the family and relations — while going to the dentist and starting school were miseries that belonged only to me.

The visit to the dentist marked the end of my infancy and my introduction to a threatening world of contradictions where spoken and written words assumed a special power.

One night, after Dad had 'bagpiped' us to sleep, I woke crying with a painful tooth. Dad came to where I lay in the cot, which was getting too small for me, as my feet touched the bars at the end. 'I'll tan your backside,' Dad said. His hand stung, hitting again and again on my bare bottom, and I cried again and at last fell asleep, and in the morning, faced with the inevitable teasing of Myrtle and Bruddie — 'You had a hiding last night!' — I said calmly, 'Well, I was cold anyway, and it warmed my bottom.'

I was taken to the dentist, where I kicked and struggled, thinking that something dire was about to happen to me, while the dentist, in the midst of my struggles, beckoned to the nurse, who came forward holding a pretty pink towel. 'Smell the pretty pink towel,' she said gently, and, unsuspecting, I leaned forward to smell, realising too late as I felt myself going to sleep that I'd been deceived. I have never forgotten that deception and my amazed disbelief that I could have been so betrayed, that the words 'Smell the pretty pink towel', without any hint of anything fearful happening, had been used to lure me into a kind of trap, that they had not *really* meant 'Smell the pretty pink towel', but 'I'm going to put you to sleep while I take your tooth out'. How could that have been? How could a few kind words mean so much harm?

Grandma's death and burial contained none of the fury and resulting distrust of the visit to the dentist. For some time now Grandma had been in a wheelchair, and there was talk of having to amputate her other leg. I have a memory of my father coming in the door and announcing in a voice full of grief, 'The other leg's going, Mum.'

Not long after then, Grandma died, and when she was lying in the front room, Mother came to Myrtle and Bruddie and me, saying, 'Would you like to see Grandma?' The others said yes and went solemnly to look at the dead, while I hung back, afraid and always to regret that I did not see Grandma dead. When Myrtle came out of the room, I could see in her face the power of having looked at the dead.

'What was Grandma like?' I asked her, unhappily aware of the low status of second-hand experience and of my weakness at not being able to 'look'. Myrtle shrugged. 'She looked all right, just like being asleep.' For many years after that Myrtle was able to win many arguments with her triumphant 'I saw Grandma dead'. And some years later when Myrtle herself was lying dead in her coffin in the front room at Oamaru and Mother asked me, 'Do you want to see Myrtle?' I, never learning, still fearful, refused to look on the face of the dead.

Persuaded by one or two indiscretions, I was learning a measure of deceit. One day, after I'd been to the dumpy and looked down at it, at my big lots, comparing them with the baby's mess in her nappies, I saw little white things wriggling in the brown.

'Mum,' I said, 'there are little white things wriggling in it.' The alarm in Mother's face was frightening.

'Worms!' she exclaimed in horror. 'That child has worms.' That night at tea she told Dad, 'Nini has worms.'

I felt the disgrace of it. I resolved to keep my mouth shut in future.

Then, on one of our picnics, I again made a false judgment of what I should or should not say. Playing by myself in the paddock, I saw a sheep staring at me, in a special way, with its head on one side and its face full of meaning. I ran excitedly to where Mum and Dad were drinking their billy tea.

'A sheep looked at me,' I said, feeling the occasion had been momentous. I was aware that they were 'humouring' me.

'How did the sheep look at you?' Dad asked.

'With its head on one side.'

'Show us.'

Suddenly shy, with everyone staring, and sensing the ridicule, I refused; then, in a wave of (unconscious) generosity, unaware that I was creating an occasion that would be used for years to come, I said, 'I'll show only Dad.' I went to Dad, and shielding my face with my hand, I imitated the sheep's expression. Throughout my childhood Dad would say, 'Show us how the sheep looked at you', and while the others giggled, I performed my 'routine'.

A certain wariness, a cynicism about the ways of people and of my family, and an ability to deceive, flowered fully a few months later, when on my fifth birthday I began attending Wyndham District High School, where Myrtle and Bruddie were already pupils.

6   Hark, Hark, the Dogs Do Bark

One morning, during my first week at school, I sneaked into Mum and Dad's bedroom, opened the top drawer of the duchesse, where the coins 'brought back from the war' were kept, and helped myself to a handful. I then went to Dad's best trousers hanging behind the door, put my hand in the pocket (how cold and slippery the lining!), and took out two coins. Hearing someone coming, I hastily thrust the money under the duchesse and left the room, and later, when the coast was clear, I retrieved my hoard and on my way to school stopped at Heath's store to buy some chewing gum.

Mr Heath looked sternly at me. 'This money won't buy anything,' he said. 'It's Egyptian.'

'I know,' I lied. Then, handing him the money from Dad's pocket, I asked, 'Will this buy me some chewing gum?'

'That's better,' he said, returning yet another of the coins, a farthing.

Armed with a supply of chewing gum, I waited at the door of the Infant Room, a large room with a platform or stage at one end and double doors opening on to Standard One, and as the children went into the room, I gave each a 'pillow' of chewing gum, Later, Miss Botting, a woman in a blue costume the same colour as the castor-oil bottle, suddenly stopped her teaching and asked, 'Billy Delamare, what are you eating?'

'Chewing gum, Miss Botting.'

'Where did you get it?'

'From Jean Frame, Miss Botting.' (I was known at school as Jean and at home as Nini.)

'Dids McIvor, where did you get your chewing gum?'

'From Jean Frame, Miss.'

'Jean Frame, where did you get the chewing gum?'

'From Heath's, Miss Botting.'

'Where did you get the money?'

'My father gave it to me.'

Evidently Miss Botting did not believe me. Suddenly she was determined to get 'the truth' out of me. She repeated her question. 'Where did you get the money? I want the *truth*.'

I repeated my answer, substituting *Dad* for *father*.

'Come out here.'

I came out in front of the class.

'Go up on the platform.'

I went up on to the platform.

'Now tell me where you got the money.'

Determinedly I repeated my answer.

Playtime came. The rest of the class went out to play while Miss Botting and I grimly faced each other.

'Tell me the truth,' she said.

I replied, 'Dad gave me the money.'

She sent for Myrtle and Bruddie, who informed her with piping innocence that Dad did not give me the money.

'Yes, he did,' I insisted. 'He called me back when you had both gone to school.'

'He didn't.'

'He did.'

All morning I stayed on the platform. The class continued their reading lessons. I stayed on the platform through lunchtime and into the afternoon, still refusing to confess. I was beginning to feel afraid, instead of defiant, as if I hadn't a friend in the world, and because I knew that Myrtle and Bruddie would 'tell' as soon as they got home, I felt that I never wanted to go home. All the places I had found — the birch log in Glenham, the top of the climbers in Edendale, the places in the songs and poems — seemed to have vanished, leaving me with no place. I held out obstinately until mid-afternoon, when the light was growing thin with masses of dark tiredness showing behind it, and the schoolroom was filled with a nowhere dust, and a small voice answered from the scared me in answer to Miss Botting's repeated question. 'I took the money out of my father's pocket.'

While I'd been lying, I had somehow protected myself; I knew now that I had no protection. I'd been found out as a thief. I was so appalled by my future prospects that I don't remember if Miss Botting strapped me. I know she gave the news to the class, and it spread quickly around the school that I was a thief. Loitering at the school gate, wondering where to go and what to do, I saw Myrtle and Bruddie, carefree as ever, on their way home, I walked slowly along the cocksfoot-bordered road. I don't know when I had learned to read, but I had read and knew the stories in the primer books, and I thought of the story of the fox that sprang out from the side of the road and swallowed the child. No one knew what had happened or where the child had gone, until one day when the fox was walking by, a kind person heard 'Let me out, let me out!' coming from the fox's belly, where-upon the kind person killed the fox, slit the belly open, and lo, the child emerged whole, unharmed, and was taken by the kind person to live in a wood in a cottage made of coconut ice with a licorice chimney . . .

I finally arrived at our place. Myrtle was leaning over the gate. 'Dad knows,' she said, in a matter-of-fact voice. I went up the path. The front door was open and Dad was waiting with the strap in his hand. 'Come into the bedroom,' he said sternly. He administered his usual 'hiding', not exces-sive, as some children had, but sharp and full of anger that one of his children was a *thief. Thief, thief.* At home and at school I was now called *Thief.*

Another event that followed swiftly upon my stealing of fourpence and a handful of Egyptian coins and a farthing stays in my mind because even then I knew it to be a rich comment on the ways of the world. I was learning fast.

Margaret Cushen, the headmaster's daughter, with all the prestige attached to such a position, had a birthday. Miss Botting (still wearing the colour of the castor-oil bottle and linked in my mind with the bluebottle blowflies), announcing Margaret's birthday, asked her to stand on the plat-form while we sang 'Happy Birthday to You'.

Then Miss Botting gave Margaret an envelope. 'It's a present from your father. Open it, Margaret.'

Margaret, flushed and proud, opened the envelope and withdrew a piece of paper that she held up for all to see. 'It's a pound note,' she said with astonished joy.

The class echoed, 'A pound note.'

'Now isn't Margaret a lucky girl to get a pound note from her father for her birthday?' Miss Botting appeared to be as excited and pleased as Margaret who, still waving her pound note, returned to her seat, stared at with awe, envy and admiration by the rest of the class.

This sudden introduction to variations of treasure was more than I could comprehend; it is doubtful whether I had any clear thoughts about it; I had only confused feelings, wondering how money brought home from the war and clearly treasured could buy nothing, how a threepence and a penny were looked on by everyone as a fortune, and I as the thief of the fortune; yet people, especially fathers, gave their daughters pound notes for their birthdays, as if pound notes were both more and less valuable than fourpence. I wondered, too, about Miss Botting and why she had needed to keep me nearly all day on the stage, waiting for me to confess.

It happened that my new place as a school pupil who was also known thief coincided in its inklings of the unfairness, the injustice of the world, with a changed mood of the outside world, even of our Ferry Street Wyndham. There were now more swaggers passing down Ferry Street and more coming to ask for food, they being confused in my mind with the rhyme,

> Hark, hark, the dogs do bark,
> the beggars are coming to town.
> Some in rags, some in bags,
> and some in velvet gown.

The rhyme haunted me. I thought of the fate of the beggars and swaggers, most of whom were said to be thieves, and at night when the candles and lamps were burning I'd look out into dark Ferry Street, which was disturbed at night only by the night man with his night cart going his rounds, and I'd think of the beggars and swaggers in rags and bags and 'beastie dress' velvet, pursued by the barking dogs. I had been impressed, too, by the tales Mother told us in our Sunday Bible reading when we sat around the big kitchen table and pored over the red-letter Bible while she explained that a poor man might come to the door and be refused food or even have the dogs 'sooled' on to him, and lo! he would turn out to be an angel in disguise or even Christ himself. Mother warned us to be careful and not to laugh at people who we thought were strange or 'funny' because they, too, might be angels in disguise. One never knew; the world was full of people in disguise, and only God knew whether or not there was an angel inside a beggar or swagger, and even if an angel were not there, God still loved each one, no matter how poor or peculiar he might be.

Nevertheless, the increasing number of swaggers passing through Wyndham, and the horror and fear in people's voices when they talked of them brought a feeling of doom, of loneliness, as if something were happening or about to happen that would belong not only to us, the Frames of Ferry Street, Wyndham, but also would be part of the street and the neighbours and the other towns. Yet, literal as ever, I puzzled over the reference to some of the beggars in 'velvet gown', for I knew that velvet was the cloth of kings and queens as well as, in my experience, the coat of beasties in the paddocks. So what secret riches did the beggars and swaggers possess?

Mother, as usual, knew the answer; they were the riches of the kingdom. 'The kingdom?' 'The kingdom of the Lord, Nini.'

It may have been heavenly intervention; it was at least blessed for me and my reputation as a thief, that we, the railway family, were now transferred from Wyndham to a town called Oamaru in the north of Otago.

7 Fifty-six Eden Street, Oamaru

The long train journey is remembered as a dream of strangeness and strange landscapes: a rocketing over countless railway bridges, past swamps of flax with their tall black-beaked flax flowers, clumps of willows, the towns, their names borne along within the rhythm and the sound of the train — Clinton, Kaitangata, Milton, Balclutha — each a cluster of houses around its railway-coloured railway station. I had reason indeed to believe that the world belonged to my railway father, that he was in charge of it, directing it through its miles and miles of railway lines.

I was very sick on the train, and in my half-delirious train-sick sleep, when the train changed direction, emerging from Southland toward the coast, I felt we were returning to Wyndham, and throughout the remainder of the journey I could not determine the 'right' direction, and my head whirled as I tried to work out our place in north, south, east, and west. I lay covered with a coat, on a double seat in the carriage, listening to the sound of the wheels on the rails and the voice of the guard as we approached each station and the sound of the name of the station and the clang clang of the crossing bells — ting ting, Clinton Clinton, Inchclutha, Balclutha, Kaitangata Kaitangata. Kaitangata pursuing us when we had left it miles away, returning to us. Clinton Clinton. We passed over turbulent rivers, hodda-hodda on the wooden bridges; a desolate landscape of more swamps, flax, rushes, willows, all the kin of water.

We came to Lake Waihola. Someone said that Lake Waihola reached as far as the centre of the earth, it was fathomless, and I looked out of the carriage window while Mother in her indelible voice of mystery and wonder said, 'Lake Waihola, kiddies, Lake Waihola.'

We arrived at Caversham, where I was brought abruptly into my immediate past, for although Aunty Han (whom I thought of as Aunty *Ham*) and Uncle Bob, the baker, lived at Caversham, the chief landmark for me was the industrial school, which had been mentioned when I was 'found out' as a thief. 'We'll have you sent to the industrial school at Caversham.' It was Dad's favourite threat to Myrtle, too, when she was disobedient. I could not see the industrial school from the train. I did not know precisely what it was, but I had a picture of a school covered with dust in colours of punishment brown.

On our first night in Oamaru, we stayed with Aunty Mima (whom we thought of as Aunty *Miner*) and Uncle Alex, the taxi driver, on Wharf Street on the South Hill, and the next morning we went to where we were to live for the next fourteen years: Fifty-six Eden Street, Oamaru.

Seeing the long street and the rows of houses, especially the houses overlooking and surrounding us, Mother panicked, speaking in her earthquake-and-lightning voice. 'We've never been surrounded by houses before,' she said, as if the fact were a national and world disaster that caused us, too, to sense the enormity of Oamaru, where houses and people and streets replaced our familiar landscape of wild spaces, Southland skies with their shimmerings of Antarctic ice, paddocks of cattle and sheep, dark swamps, brown rivers, where each day and night could be felt in its existence, and the grass and the insects in the grass could speak and be heard.

We'd had to say goodbye to our cows, Beauty and Pansy, who'd gone to the sale yards. And Dad had 'given up' the Lizzie Ford. The Great Depression had begun.

We were to be real town dwellers with electric lights and a pull-the-chain lavatory instead of a dumpy hole, and at first the rush of water frightened us, and the brightly lit rooms with the furniture deprived of its big enveloping shadows seemed harsh and too public. We were to have town milk, delivered each morning, and Dad was to ride a bicycle to work. And stricken though we children were at such change, once we had recovered from the train journey, we were overjoyed at the house and the land and the hill of pine plantations at the back, a town reserve, separated from us by the inevitable 'bull paddock', with a creek from the reservoir flowing through it. There were new streets and street names, new trees, new people. And the sea. And a new school.

And coinciding dramatically with our life's upheaval, some months later there was the Napier earthquake with the news and the description being given full disaster treatment by Mother's voice as she stood in the light of our new dining-room window, in front of the silver-scrolled, brown-polished Singer sewing machine (daring the lightning to strike) and talked of the Napier earthquake. The dining room was the large middle room with the big, rectangular sash window (with its heavy pulleys and cords that we children soon snapped in our energetic climbing in and out), the only source of light in the room. In moments of family importance, Mother formed the habit of standing by that window, placing her feelings, like trophies, to be revealed and illuminated. That dining room held the King's sofa and the King's chairs and one or two items bought at the Wyndham auction rooms. It was used only on special occasions, for visitors and for feasts like Christmas and the New Year with its first-footing and for the announcement of family and national and world triumphs and disasters.

At the back of the house, next to the dining room, there was a kitchen with a coal range and a coal bin, which was used as a seat beside the fire. Beyond the kitchen was the back bedroom, its wallpaper patterned with small, pink roses, where Grandad Frame, who was now to live with us, was to sleep. The other door from the kitchen led to the scullery with the sink (and the cockroaches beneath it), while the scullery door led down five or six wooden steps to the backyard, with the washhouse at the right, with the copper and the copper fire, the tubs and the cracked window. Toward the coal house, at one end of the washhouse, was the lavatory with a shelf for a candle, as there was no electric light in the washhouse; with the lavatory door opening toward a dark spider-haunted 'under the house'.

The other door from the dining room led to the front passage with a bathroom at one end, with a real bath and shower and hot and cold water running from taps, and a front door at the other end; with three bedrooms leading from the passage — one nearest the bathroom, where Myrtle, Isabel, June and I were to sleep in the big double bed with the brass ends; one bedroom at the front where Bruddie was to sleep; and the room opposite, with the other double bed and the duchesse and the mirrored wardrobe, which was for Mum and Dad.

At the back of the house, outside, there was another opening to 'under the house', which we learned to call the cellar, where we played on wet days and from where we explored 'under the house'. There were fruit trees in the back garden — a winter pear and a honey pear growing on one tree, a plum tree belonging to the neighbours but leaning into our place, an Irish Peach apple tree, a cooking apple tree, an apricot tree, and gooseberries and blackcurrants. In front there was a flower garden bordering the lawn with a rose arch in one corner of the lawn, behind the high African thorn hedge, and at the side, near our parents' bedroom and beside the macrocarpa hedge, separating us from the McMurtries next door, was a summerhouse, covered with small cream banksia roses (which we called bankshee roses), which we came to use as a playhouse and theatre. The hedge on the other side of the section was holly, while the back hedge between us and the bull paddock was African thorn.

As soon as we arrived at Fifty-six Eden Street, Oamaru, we children began crawling and climbing everywhere, over every inch of the red-painted iron roof, along every earthy space between the piles under the house. We noted the inhabitants with whom we were to share our life: the insects, bees, mason bees, night bees, butterflies, grandfather moths, spiders, red spiders, furry spiders, trapdoor spiders; the birds, flocks of goldfinches, wax-eyes, blackbirds, sparrows, starlings. We found cat skeletons under the house and sheep and cattle skeletons in the long grass of the bull paddock, where there was no longer a bull, only, from time to time, a group of young, skittering steers. We discovered every climbable place in the hedge and trees and on the summerhouse, accumulating our treasure of new experiences, which soon included the neighbours on each side and across the road, and beyond the bull paddock to the hill with its caves and fossilised shells, the zigzag with its native plants, and the seat at the top with the plaque 'Donated by the Oamaru Beautifying Society'; and the pine plantations, to be known as the 'plannies': the first one harmless, where you could look through to daylight beyond, the second frightening with the trees so densely packed that halfway through it you found yourself in a brown pine-needle darkness and knew there was no turning back, the third planny, small and full of daylight, the fourth, of stripling gums leading into pines extending down the hill at the end of Glen Street Gully, near the 'orchard', which, because it appeared to stand alone, independent of any house or person, we believed to be ownerless and therefore, in the 'finds keeps' tradition, belonging to us.

We soon learned to know the creek, too, in its every change of flow regulated by the water in the reservoir. We knew the plants on its banks and in the creek the rocks, cockabullies, eels and the old weighted shredded sacks of drowned kittens and cats. Each morning we set out foraging for experience and in the afternoon returned to share with one another, while our parents, apart from us now, went about their endless adult work, which might better have been known as 'toil' in all its meanings — trap or snare, battle, strife, a spell of severe, fatiguing labour — meanings of which we were unaware. Dad worked all day, and sometimes, on night shift, all night, sleeping during the day, while we, the railway children, vanished into the pine plannies or along Glen Street Gully to our orchard or crept stealthily about the summerhouse, 'Sh-sh, Dad's asleep . . .'

All except June (or Chicks) attended the Oamaru North School, where I was in Standard One, Miss Carroll's class. I remember little of her except that she strapped me once for talking and her face was curved with the teeth scarcely contained and her mouth seeming scarcely able to close over her teeth to prevent them from flying out. More important in my memory is the walk between home and school, the various streets and houses and gardens, the blossoming trees lining the streets, the animals I met, the the exciting sense of the structure of the new town with its town clock, chiming every quarter-hour, visible from that one spot on our way to school — the corner of Reed and Eden Streets by Hunt's red corrugated iron fence. Here, as nine o'clock in the morning approached, we checked our earliness or lateness, using as a second reference a small, lame woman, with one shortened leg encased in a thick, black boot who passed the corner at ten to nine sharp each morning and became known to us as the Late Lady, for seeing her meant that to avoid being late, we'd have to run the rest of the way to school. It was the tradition, however, to walk to and from school in the morning and afternoon but to run home for lunch, partly because the lunch-hour was short and home was halfway up Eden Street. Having just turned seven, I accepted this tradition without question, as I accepted all the traditions of the Oamaru North School. I ran home for lunch each day, stopping only at Mrs Feather's corner store to collect the freshly baked sandwich loaf, which I carefully picked at on the 'mounted' side to level it. The big boys of Eden Street, running faster than I and with still further to go, wheeled, leaning around Hunt's Corner, using their bodies like machines, and as they passed me, one would hiss in my ear, 'I'm after you', an announcement which, I soon learned, was to be accepted with a mixture of pride and fear and told to others in a voice that held a hint of 'skiting' — 'One of the big boys is after me.'

Life at Oamaru with all its variety of new experiences was a wonderful adventure. I was now vividly aware of myself as a person on earth, feeling a kinship with other creatures and full of joy at the sights and sounds about me and drunk with the anticipation of play, where playing seemed endless, on and on after school until dark, when even then there were games to play in bed — physical games like 'trolley works' and 'fitting in', where each body curled into the other and all turned on command, or guessing games or imagining games, interpreting the masses of shape and colour in the bed-room curtains, or codes, hiding messages in the brass bed knobs. There were arguments and fights and plans for the future and impossible dreams of fame as dancers, violinists, pianists, artists.

That year I discovered the word *Island*, which in spite of all teaching I insisted on calling Is-Land. In our silent reading class at school, when we chose one of the Whitcombes school readers, those thin, fawn-covered books with crude drawings on the cover and speckled pages, I found a story, *To the Island*, an adventure story that impressed me so much that I talked about it at home.

'I read a story, *To the Is-Land*, about some children going to an Is-Land.'

'It's I-Land,' Myrtle corrected.

'It's not,' I said. 'It's Is-Land. It says,' I spelled the letters, 'I-s-l-a-n-d. Is-land.'

'It's a silent letter,' Myrtle said. 'Like knee.'

In the end, reluctantly, I had to accept the ruling, although within myself I still thought of it as the Is-Land.

I began reading more 'adventure' books, realising that to have an adventure, I did not need to travel in the lost Lizzie Ford, getting sick on the way, to beaches and rivers — I could experience an adventure by reading a book. And, as usual, being eager to share my discovery, I told the family about my new way of having adventures, instantly regretting my indiscretion, for whenever Mum or Dad saw me curled up on the coal bin with a book, they'd say in that humiliatingly knowing way, 'Have you come to the adventure yet?'

This concentration on adventures that to me meant simply amazing escapes from physical danger, rescues, being lost and found, triumphing in disaster, was increased by the teacher's repeated order for the class to write a composition, 'My Adventure'. It never occurred to me that I was allowed to make up an adventure, like a story. I mourned my apparent lack of adventures as I heard those of other children being read out to the class — visits to remote towns, museums, zoos. My staple adventure was crossing the bull paddock, where there was not even a bull, only a bunch of steers, and finding my way through the second 'planny' beyond the point of dark-ness when my heart began to beat fast and the green world was lost in the dark trees and the deep drifts of fallen pine needles, some many feet deep over the entrances to old rabbit warrens; but I felt shy of disclosing that adventure because it was different from that of the others in the class where the insistence was on the escapes, broken limbs, runaway horses . . .

My reading was limited to schoolbooks, including the School Journal, and the new comic cuts, which we were sometimes allowed to buy from Mr Adams — My Favourite, Rainbow, Tiger Tim, Chick's Own, with the best, which Myrtle and I read, being My Favourite because the print was smaller and there were therefore more stories, and Rainbow. Bruddie's comic was Tiger Tim, and Dots and Chicks had Chick's Own. An attraction of My Favourite was 'Terry and Trixie of the Circus', who inspired our current ambition to be trapeze artists, particularly as the song 'The Daring Young Man on the Flying Trapeze' was also in vogue.

Much of the School Journal dealt with celebrations of the British Empire, with articles and photographs of the royal family, chiefly the two little princesses, Elizabeth and Margaret Rose. There was a description, too, of their life-size dolls' house, with photographs. In contrast to the factual prose of the School Journal and the praise of the Empire, the King, the Governor-General, the Anzacs at Gallipoli, Robert Falcon Scott at the South Pole, the poems were full of mystery and wonder, with Walter de la Mare and John Drinkwater, Christina Rossetti, as the editor's first choices, followed by Alfred Noyes and John Masefield to give the rollicking touch. One poem that I liked at once was 'Meg Merrilees'. Gypsies, beggars, robbers, swaggers, slaves, thieves, all the outcast victims of misfortune who yet might be angels in disguise, had become part of my dreams and comprehension of the Outside World. I learned by heart 'Old Meg she was a gypsy . . .', and again, sharing my discovery at home by reciting it to the family, I was urged again and again to repeat it, and when I'd oblige and each time came to the line 'And 'stead of supper she would stare / Full hard against the moon', everyone would laugh, apparently at my earnestness, or perhaps because there was seldom any question that I, with known 'hollow legs' and the habit of devouring slice after slice of 'bread 'n' golden syrup' would ever have to stare at the moon instead of enjoying my supper.

When I thought of Old Meg, I felt the sadness that came with the way the words went in the poem, the same way the words went in the songs about Glasgow and the sidewalks of New York and the streets of Dublin, 'Dublin's fair city . . .' I pictured Old Meg as like Ma Sparks — I thought Ma Sparks and Old Meg might have been the same person — who everyone said was a gypsy the way she squatted at the top of her path outside her front door in Glen Street and stared down at the street and the small unofficial rubbish dump the other side of the street, into the bull paddock, and across the hill where the pigeons, kept by several people in Glen Street, were out for their evening flight, circling the hill, the plantations and the town with a sudden rush of wings over our house.

Ma smoked a pipe. They said she wore no pants, and you could see if you walked along Glen Street and looked up at her squatting there.

Beside the word *adventure*, other words began to appear repeatedly in our learning and written expression, and although they were not, I felt, attractive words, they had a dramatic effect in their use. I remember learning to spell and use these three words: *decide*, *destination*, and *observation*, all of which worked closely with *adventure*. I was enthralled by their meaning and by the fact that all three seemed to be part of the construction of every story — everyone was *deciding*, having a *destination*, *observing* in order to decide and define the destination and know how to deal with the *adventures* along the way. Partly as a result of the constant coming and going of our relatives and of our own shifting from place to place, I had an exaggerated sense of movement and change, and when I found I could use this necessary movement to create or notice adventures, I was overjoyed. Our teacher introduced lessons in observation, where we were instructed to make a habit of 'observing' on our walk to and from school, and once again it was this walk that gave me a fund of instruction. I had several choices of route (I could *decide* for myself), which I learned to vary. The 'ordinary' journey took me down Eden Street, past Hunt's Corner (and the Kearns' Alsatian dogs) into Reed Street, the cherry blossom street, and along Reed Street to the North School. Reed Street was a 'doctors' street, with Dr Orbell, our doctor, a teasing old man who frightened us with his jokes, living in his two-storeyed house near the corner, while further along the street, occupying a whole block, the garden walled like Buckingham Palace, the Smith-Mortons lived and near them the Fitzgeralds, in their two-storeyed houses. The doctors'· daughters had names like *Adair* and *Geraldine*, and they did not go to our school, but to boarding schools in another town in the North Island (Is-Land). They had dolls' houses, too, and ponies, Shetland ponies, and they 'learned' things, such as dancing, music, elocution. (To 'learn' something was the dream of our lives.)

Or I could walk to school up Aln Street, a narrow earth street always in shade, with a formidable high clay bank on one side with water always running down the bank and across the road. The expanse of yellow clay was more like a creature than earth, the way it leaned up against the hill. It was excitingly unformed, and I used to stand looking up at it half with interest, half with fear, and one day, as I stood staring in Aln Street, a woman came by. 'Hello, little girl,' she said. 'Here's two shillings.' With much wonder I took the two shillings. I didn't go to school that day. Instead, I returned to Mrs Feather's store, where I bought a shilling's worth of acid drops and a shilling's worth of chlorydyne lollies (a cough lolly containing chloroform, although I did not know this) and walked around the streets, eating my lollies, until it was after-school time, when I came home and fell asleep for eighteen hours, and when I woke I was violently sick. 'What happened?' Mum asked. 'A lady gave me two shillings,' I said.

Sometimes my walk took me, daringly, the length of Eden Street, past the Church of Christ near the corner, with its wayside Pulpit Thought For the Week, which I read carefully, taking literally the shortened parables about shepherds, sheep and sinners. If I went a little out of my way, I could stare at Fraser's Bacon Factory. On my way down Eden Street I always crossed over to the garage of Dewar and McKenzies, which I thought of as *Jewel McKenzies*, to sniff the petrol smell and ask if they had a free ink blotter, for they were known to have a supply of these, and the wildfire word was about, *Jewel McKenzies have free blotters*.

Along Humber Street (which I thought of as Humble Street), I walked by the railway and the engine and goods sheds and stopped by another place that haunted me — an old stone house leaning against a deserted shop. The house was plain, the garden overgrown with dandelions and dock and daisies, with a gate in the low Oamaru stone wall opening onto a long path leading up to the front door. Yvonne Baker lived there, it was said. The house resembled her, for she was small, her skin was damp, her hair lank as if she, too, lived on the damp side of the street and had grown cold and damp like the house. There was never any sign of life, no curtains in the blank windows, but the stone house, like the clay bank in Aln Street, had the appearance of being alive in its stone and moss, and it was one of my cherished 'observations' and adventures.

My other route was along Thames Street, which had become the point of reference in light and sound in our family, with Dad saying, 'Keep your voice down. You can be heard down *Thames Street*.' Or, 'What do you think we are, all the lights in the house blazing; you can see them from *Thames Street*.' In Thames Street my chief place of call was the lolly shop with its notice *High Class Confectionery*, which I read as High *Glass* Confectionery, kept by Miss Bee and her sister, also a Miss Bee. How I puzzled over their names and their origins and the meaning and appearance of their *High Glass*!

8 Death and a Sickness

From being a horizontal thread or path that one followed or traversed, time in that year suddenly became vertical, to be ascended like a ladder into the sky with each step or happening following quickly on the other. I was not yet eight. The Depression was at its height. There were beginnings, endings, gains, losses, with a large share of misery where there was no place to lay the blame; there was no help in saying, 'You're the *blame*', or in calling anything or anyone *Thief*, for it was a world misery; it was not even God's doing, for Mother insisted that God was kind, and although everything had its purpose, God always acted to love, and not to hurt, the people in the world.

Grandad Frame was living with us. He was old and thin, and his baggy pants had a shiny behind, and he slept in the back room. His head rested, tilted, on his neck, like a bird's head, and he wore glasses with thin gold rims, which he kept in a dark blue case lined with rich blue velvet, which filled me with sadness whenever I saw it: it was a colour that·had no end, like the depths of the sky in the evening, and it was like the question that I had begun to ask myself, dizzying my head with the search for an answer, 'Why *was* the world, why *was* the world?', which immediately gave the thought of *no world* and a feeling of everlasting depths from which one had to struggle to escape.

In some way, Grandad's glasses case and the sound of it snipping open and shut and the fact that he left it behind when he died made it for me the essence of Grandad Frame and his life with us. As my youngest sister, June (or Chicks), had not yet started school, he was her special friend, calling her his Mickey Mouse, his Itey-mitie; she was so small.

Grandad was not ill, nor was he very old; he must have been tired, for he died one night in his sleep, and he was put in a coffin in the front room with the blinds pulled down so that everyone in the street knew that someone in the house had died; that was the custom: you could tell if people were dead by the pulled-down blinds, and you could tell if people were home by the smoke coming out of their chimney.

On the day of the funeral the Fletts next door looked after us, giving us scrambled eggs to eat and teaching us how to knit with big wooden knitting needles. We looked through their holly hedge at the funeral going from our place, with all the relations dressed up and speaking in their high-up voices, and it didn't seem to be our place. The aunts were there, still talking of Up Central and Middlemarch (Middlemarch, Lottie) and Inchclutha; and the uncles with their shy Frame look and the particular set of the lips that said, 'Everything should be perfect. Why isn't it?' And on Sunday, when we all went to the cemetery on the South Hill to put flowers on Grandad's grave, I was surprised to find that Grandma was buried there beside him, after dying in Wyndham, and I imagined her making that same twisty railway journey from Wyndham, past the rivers and the swamps and the small railway-coloured railway stations and Lake Waihola and Caversham with the industrial school and Dunedin and Seacliff, where the loonies lived, and Hampden with the black swans and the lagoon, all the way to the South Hill, Oamaru. Grandma travelling with her black dress and her Grandma smell and her song 'Carry Me Back to Ole Virginny' and that other song for sleep and night-time, 'Shoo shaggy o'er the glen, Mama's pet and Daddy's hen . . .'

We put the flowers in their jam jar on Grandad and Grandma's grave, and we looked curiously at the tall tombstone with its list of Frame dead. There was one, Janet Frame, my name. Died aged thirteen months.

Soon the back bedroom became known as Bruddie's room instead of Grandad's room. It had no curtains because it didn't look out at houses and the street, only toward the hill and the plannies and, nearer, at the back garden and the patch of bright green grass where the tap leaked, next to the clump of dock which we valued for its flaming leaves in autumn and its green seed changing to red, from which we brewed our pretend tea. 'Do have a cup of dock-seed tea, Mrs . . .'

Grandad's death was different from Grandma's in that I did not feel that it belonged to us; it was an event that belonged to the grown-ups, who performed their duties of dressing correctly and talking of Middlemarch and Up Central and the 'Outram days, Lottie and George', and burying Grandad, while we children observed from a distance, trying to distinguish between rumour and truth. Myrtle said Grandad had been nailed down so he could not escape. But how could he escape if he was dead? He could escape as a ghost, she said. But there were no ghosts. Who said? The Bible said. (We were learning to apportion prestige to the makers of rules. *The Bible said* was a convincing source, while on a more mundane level, *Dad said* usually won over *Mum said*.

It was not long after Grandad's death that we were awakened one night by a commotion in the house. I heard Mum crying out, 'Bruddie's having a convulsion; Bruddie's having a convulsion.' I ran with the others into the dining room. We sat together on the King's sofa, watching and listening while Mum and Dad went back and forth from Bruddie's room to the bathroom. 'A convulsion, a convulsion,' Mum kept saying in her earthquake-and-tidal-wave voice. She fetched the doctor's book from where it was (unsuccessfully) hidden on top of the wardrobe in their bedroom and looked up *Convulsions*, talking it over with Dad, who was just as afraid.

In the meantime Bruddie had wakened, sobbing. 'A bath,' Mother cried. 'Put him in a bath.' Dad carried the crying Bruddie into the bathroom. We four girls were sent back to our bedroom, where we cuddled up to one another, talking in frightened whispers and shivering with the cold Oamaru night, and when I woke the next morning, my eyes were stinging with sleep and I felt burdened with the weight of a new awful knowledge that something terrible had happened in the night to Bruddie.

Our lives were changed suddenly. Our brother had epilepsy, the doctor said, prescribing large doses of bromide which, combined with Bruddie's now frequent attacks, or fits, as everyone called them, only increased his confusion and fear until each day at home there were episodes of violent rage when he attacked us or threw whatever was at hand to throw. There had usually been somewhere within the family to find a 'place' however cramped; now there seemed to be no place; a cloud of unreality and disbelief filled our home, and some of the resulting penetrating rain had the composition of real tears. Bruddie became stupefied by drugs and fits; he was either half asleep, recovering, crying, from the last fit, or in a rage of confusion that no one could understand or help. He still went to school, where some of the bigger boys began to bully him, while we girls, perhaps prompted by the same feeling of fear, tried to avoid him, for although we knew what to do should he fall in a fit at school or outside at home, we could not cope with the horror of it. Mother, resisting fiercely the advice of the doctor to put Bruddie in an institution, nursed him while we girls tried to survive on our own with the occasional help of Dad, who now combed the tangles out of my frizzy hair each morning and supervised our cleaning of our bedroom. His insistence that we sweep the 'skirting boards' gave me a new, interesting word: *skirting boards*. Another new word of that time was *wainscot*: 'A mouse in the *wainscot* scratches, and scratches', from the poem 'Moonlit Apples', by John *Drinkwater*.

After the first panic and whirlwind of having a sickness in the family and knowing there was no cure, there was a period of dullness and calm, perhaps as the rain from the cloud soaked into our bones. Bruddie left school. Mother now devoted all her time to him. Anyone observing me during those days would have seen an anxious child full of twitches and tics, standing alone in the playground at school, wearing day after day the same hand-me-down tartan skirt that was almost stiff with constant wear, for it was all I had to wear: a freckle-faced, frizzy-haired little girl who was somehow 'dirty' because the lady doctor chose her with the other known 'dirty and poor' children for a special examination in that narrow room next to the teacher's room. I had tide marks of dirt behind my knees and on my inner arms, and when I saw them, I felt a wave of shock to know they were there when I had been sure I had washed thoroughly.

Strangely enough, my consuming longing, in the midst of the shock of sickness in the family, was to be invited to join in the wonderful skipping games played by the rest of the class with a brand-new, golden-knotted rope owned and controlled by one of the girls. How could a length of ordinary clothesline rope, so new it still had the hairs sticking to it, confer such power? I stood there day after day by the Oamaru stone wall, waiting and waiting for the signal to skip, 'All in together / this fine weather', or 'Two little girls in navy blue / these are the actions they must do. / Salute to the King / bow to the Queen . . .', which, however, was not so desirable as 'all in together', for there no one had to worry about being chosen or not chosen, for it was all in together when I and the other timid children waiting could sneak in under cover and care of the game itself. Most of the time, however, the skippers were carefully chosen by those in power — 'The farmer wants a wife, the wife wants a child, the child wants a toy . . .'

There was one other child known as 'dirty': Nora Bone, whom I despised because she, like myself, was seldom asked to join the skipping, but whose need was so strong that she always offered to 'core for ever', that is, turn and turn the skipping rope and never herself join in the skipping. She was known as 'the girl who cores for ever'. There were only two or three in the whole school, and everyone treated them contemptuously. Nora Bone, the girl who cores for ever. There was no more demeaning role. No matter how much I longed to join in the games, I never offered to core for ever.

So Bruddie was a sick boy. The world swept on with its morning, noon, night, and the Great Depression stalked the streets and the homes of Oamaru, bringing the 'sack' and the 'dole' for many and wage cuts for my father, whose voiced fear, communicating itself to us, was of the 'sack' and 'going bankrupt', and as the doctor and the hospital bills began to arrive, Dad would sit at the end of the table, leaning his head in his hands, and say, 'Mum, I'm going bankrupt. I'll go mad and shoot meself. I'll go down and jump over the wharf.' And Mum would reply quickly, 'None of that talk, Curly. God will help us.' 'He'd better be lively, then, and jump to it,' Dad would say, always irreverent in mentioning God and religion, which he dismissed as mumbo jumbo. Mother would say then, like a gramophone record, 'Consider the lilies of the field . . . Take no thought of the morrow.'

Something new, a silent time of deeper thinking, had entered my life, and I associate it with those afternoons of silent reading, the very name of the activity puzzling me, when the silence was so full of inner noise that I could not make myself interested in the Whitcombes Readers. We were 'on to' Pinocchio; I thought it was a stupid story. I thought Don Quixote was a fool. I sat doing nothing on those dreary afternoons, full of thinking yet not knowing what I was thinking, watching the beams of dust, whitened with chalk, floating around in the window light and knowing that I used to think they were sunbeams.

Then, one afternoon, when we had singing from the Dominion Song Book, a class I loved, we sang a haunting song, 'Like to the tide moaning in grief by the shore, / mourn I for friends captured and warriors slain . . .'

We sang the Maori words too: 'E pare ra . . .' As we were singing, I felt suddenly that I was crying because something terrible had happened, although I could not say what it was: it was inside the song, yet outside it, with me. When school was over, I ran home, even passing some of the big boys at Hunt's Corner, and when I reached the gate, I was out of breath. I came around the corner into the back yard. Myrtle was standing there. 'The Old Cat is dead,' she said abruptly.

We buried the Old Cat in the garden. She had been black and fluffy, and when she grew old, her fur grew brown as if it had been scorched. Since we had lived in Oamaru, cats and their kittens had arrived from nowhere to live with us and there was a special place in the washhouse near the copper where they always had their kittens. Although we were never allowed to have the cats inside, we sometimes sneaked them in when Dad was at work, and we were close to them in their births and deaths. We did not then each have an animal. Myrtle's Old Cat was shared with all, and it was now unthinkable that another animal would not arrive to take the place of Old Cat.

The sad afternoon of the singing of 'E pare ra' became part of my memories, like the wind in the telegraph wires and the discovery of My Place. I thought it was strange that we could be singing of 'friends captured and warriors slain' while I could be seeing in my mind the lonely beach with the tide 'moaning in grief by the shore' and people on the beach who were the people in the song, the warriors, and others who were Myrtle, Bruddie and me at Waipapa or Fortrose; yet at the same time I could be feeling a dread and unhappiness that I could not name, which had little relation to this song, and still at the same time be sitting in the brown classroom, watching the dust travelling in and out of the beams of light slanting through the windows that were so tall that the monitors had to struggle each morning to open them, using ropes and levers and a long pole with a hook on the end; all school windows were thus, constantly at war with being opened or shut. And when Myrtle said, 'Old Cat's dead', I knew it already; yet it was something else, too, as well as Old Cat.

About two weeks later Myrtle arrived home from school with Lassie, the spaniel dog, which had quite naturally followed her. Well, Lassie was a bitch because she was fat with rows of titties, but we were forbidden to say the word *bitch*. In spite of arguments and threats from Dad and talk of hydatids from Mum, we kept Lassie and two of the pups that were born the following week. The others were tied in a sugar bag with a stone to weight them down and drowned in the creek. Gradually over the years, the bed of the creek became the resting place of many cats, kittens, pups, not only from us but from neighbours, with now and then, when the sack rotted, a wet cat shape with teeth set in a skeleton snarl, rising to the surface.

9 *Poppy*

One day I found a friend, Poppy, whose real name was Marjorie. She had lank brown hair, an ugly face with a wide red mouth, and her father whipped her with a narrow machine belt, which made cuts in her skin. Everything she said and did was new to me, even the way she talked and the words she used, her ideas and games and the folklore that I didn't think of as folklore but as truth rumours passed from one person to another. Poppy taught me how to cure warts by squeezing the juice of the ice plant over them. We'd sit on the Glen Street clay bank that was covered with purple-flowering ice plant, and we'd wriggle as the stems of the ice plant dug into our bottoms, and we'd squeeze the juice of the stems over our warts, and, miraculously, within a few days our warts disappeared. Poppy taught me how to suck the acid from the stalks of a plant she called shamrock — later I learned it was oxalis — and we'd sit, enjoying the stinging taste of the acid; she taught me how to suck honey from the periwinkle flower and to eat and enjoy the sweet floury berries of the hawthorn. She explained that if we were walking to school and separate with a lamp post between us, then we 'had the pip' with each other and were not allowed to speak until we linked little fingers, a gesture that was also necessary when we both said the same word at the same time.

These new rituals delighted me. Poppy taught me how to 'cadge' flowers, too. She explained that any flower which grew through the fence onto the road could be 'cadged' and belong to us, and it wasn't stealing, for they belonged to us *by right*. Each day we'd arrive at school and home with armsful of flowers, the names of all of which Poppy knew and taught me. We were studying grasses and weeds at school, and we were both drunk with the glory of the new names — shepherd's purse, fat hen (what a giggle!), ragwort, where the black and white caterpillars lived, though we preferred the woolly ones that turned into *Red Admirals*.

After school I used to go to Poppy's place to play school in her wash-house, where we lined up her father's empty beer bottles and made them breathe in and out, and do dry land swim with chest elevator, arms bend upward stretch, running on the spot with high knee raising. We also gave them tables and asked them to name and draw the clouds, cirrus, numbus, stratus, cumulus, while we chanted the names, cirrus, nimbus, stratus, cumulus . . . We made them learn the mountains in the mountain chains, too — Rimutaka, Tararua, Ruahine, Kaimanawa . . . And we strapped them, saying sharply, 'Pay attention. Come out here.' The beer bottles stood in a row on the bench facing northwest, lit golden by the rays of the setting sun shining through the dusty little window. Sometimes, if we broke a bottle, we looked through a piece of glass at the golden world.

It seemed to me that Poppy knew everything. She knew the names and uses that were not the ordinary uses of everyday things. She also had a 'place' that she spoke of, where she used to go to stay with relatives at Moeraki. She pronounced the word as if she owned it, the way the aunts pronounced Up Central, Middlemarch, and Inchclutha.

Then one day Poppy asked me if I would like to borrow her special book that she kept in her washhouse among a clutter of treasures in an old beer barrel. 'It's Grimm's Fairy Tales,' she said. I had never heard of such a book, but I said I'd like to borrow it. And that night I took Grimm's Fairy Tales to bed and began to read, and suddenly the world of living and the world of reading became linked in a way I had not noticed before. 'Listen to this,' I said to Myrtle and Dots and Chicks. They listened while I read 'The Twelve Dancing Princesses', and as I read and they listened, I knew and they knew, gloriously, that we were the Dancing Princesses — not twelve but four; and as I read, I saw in my mind the place in the coat cupboard in the corner of the bedroom where we could vanish to the underground world and the orchard that was 'our' orchard along the gully where the boughs of the trees honked and cried out when they were broken, silver and gold trees; and in the end it was Myrtle who married the old soldier who, in my mind, looked like Vincent, the man of twenty-two, to us, shrivelled and old, who had fallen in love with Myrtle, who was barely twelve when she went for a holiday to the Wyndham Walkers.

And the shoes, danced each morning to shreds, we knew about those, with our own shoe soles flapping away from the uppers, and Dad sitting carefully marking and cutting the leather, and with the tacks in his mouth, bending over the bootlast while he half-soled and heeled our shoes, complaining, like the king in the story, 'Where have you been that your toes are scuffed and your soles are worn through?' Where indeed!

What a wonderful story it was — orchards hung with silver and golden apples, boughs that spoke and sang and cried out, underground seas and rivers and splash splash through the dark caverns, then suddenly the lit palace and the ballroom.

All the stories had a similar measure of delight and excitement — 'The Blue Light', 'The Juniper Tree', the old favourites from the primer reading books — 'Hansel and Gretel', 'Snow White', all the tales of Mother, Father, Sister, Brother, Aunt, Uncle, none of whom were more nor less than we were, for all the list of extraordinary gifts, miracles, transformations, cruelties, and the many long years of wandering and searching, full of hope and expectation. *Grimm's Fairy Tales* was everybody's story seen in a special way with something new added to the ordinary rules of observation. Even the insects and animals in the stories had speech; I'd always felt as if they had; I'd known when the sheep looked at me that it was talking to me. And when the flies from the sticky flypapers were caught in my frizzy hair and buzzed and zoomed in my ear, there was no mistaking their frantic speech.

Poppy's *Grimm's Fairy Tales* became a treasured book to be returned and borrowed, again and again.

Poppy had two brothers, Bob and Ted, and an elder sister, Florrie, who was soon to be married. Bob, who had left school and was working, was an aloof boy with a black patch over his forehead where he was hurt trying to ride a bicycle down the hospital hill. Rumour said that if he removed his black patch, he would die. With Florrie's approaching marriage there was much talk among us of weddings and what happened when you married, with our parents giving unsatisfactory answers to our questions.

'What did you do when you married, Mum?'

'Your father and I jumped over a broomstick.'

'And where did the babies come from?'

'From the stork who brings all babies.'

Those answers were as meaningless as the teasing answer people gave you when you asked them what they were making: 'A wigwam for a goose's bridle.' Fortunately, Poppy had all the information I wanted.

'You fuck,' she said.

'Fuck?'

'The man gets on top of the woman and puts his thing in her.' She explained to me about fucking and Frenchies, which a man wore on his tool to stop a woman having babies, and how the woman had a cunt, and how a man 'came' and shot spunk everywhere, and if the woman started a baby and didn't want it she drank gin to get rid of it. Poppy told me the rhyme:

> *Pounds shillings and pence,*
> *a man fell over the fence.*
> *He fell on a lady*
> *and squashed out a baby.*
> *Pounds shillings and pence.*

She knew some Mae West stories, too. Everyone was talking about Mae West and Mae West stories, and at school now, in Silent Reading, we giggled together, changing Whitcombe and Tombs to Tit, come, and wombs . . .

Florrie married. We tin-canned her and her new husband and had a feast of fizzy drinks and cakes, and a few days later Myrtle and I and Ted and Poppy went up by the second planny, where the Council men had been cutting down some of the trees, and there, where the trees were lying, among the branches and the pine needles, Myrtle and Ted tried to 'do it' while we watched with interest, seeing Ted jiggling up and down on top of Myrtle.

This new experience pleased me, and anxious as ever to share the day's events, I said casually at the tea table that evening, 'Myrtle and Ted did it in the plannies this afternoon.'

'Did what?' Dad asked.

'Fucked, of course,' I said, quite unaware that I had said anything startling; I was merely recounting the day's events.

There was a sudden sweep of horror that touched everyone at the table, and Dad crashed his fist down, making the tea things (and us) jump. 'I forbid you,' he said, 'ever to speak to Poppy and Ted and any of that family again. As for you,' he faced Myrtle, 'come into the bedroom.'

'Mum,' he called, 'where's the belt.' Mother, who never hit us and was always afraid when Dad asked for the belt, made her plea, 'Don't hit her, Curly.'

The matter was too serious, however. Dad used the belt on Myrtle while I, terrified, and in a way to 'blame', fled with the others outside to the summerhouse. I could not understand the sudden transformation of Mum and Dad on receiving my simple item of news. I thought it was an occasion for celebration. I genuinely thought everyone would be pleased.

While Myrtle was crying and screaming in the bedroom, Dad managed to have someone fetch a doctor, for Myrtle, although only twelve now, which was young in those days, already had her 'monthlies', which Mum had announced by the sewing machine one morning in her disaster voice, saying, 'Myrtle's come, Myrtle's come', which was confusing until I learned it was not 'spunk' come but 'monthlies'.

The doctor arrived and went to the bedroom to examine Myrtle. We could hear her crying. Dad's fury and fear were unforgettable. The doctor spoke sharply to Dad, saying, 'She's hysterical; she's terrified.'

That night, like the night of Bruddie's illness, effected a change in our lives.

The next morning, when I saw Poppy, I said, 'I'm not allowed to play with you or speak to you ever again.'

She replied, with a tone of equal importance, 'And I'm not allowed to speak to you either.' For Poppy also, unaware of the need for secrecy, had 'told'.

The warning from our parents was so strong, the threat of the consequences of disobedience so dire, that Poppy and I parted forever, and I spoke to her only briefly once, a few years later. I returned her *Grimm's Fairy Tales*, comforted by realising that although I had returned her book, I still had many of the stories in my head, that the Twelve Dancing Princesses had their permanent home at our place. They and the Blue Light and the Juniper Tree. And in every Christmas hazelnut I could still imagine a tiny dress of gold and silver folded tightly, unfolded to life-size for me to wear 'Shake shake hazel tree / gold and silver over me'. And down by the garden tap where the grass was greenest I could still play and drink dock-seed tea and imagine the little goat feeding on the long grass and my saying, 'Bleat goat bleat / arrive table neat', and having eaten the feast before me, bid, 'Bleat goat bleat / depart table neat'.

Once again I was alone at school. Skipping went in and out, marbles came and went, and hopscotch was in, and I spent my time searching for smooth, round 'hoppy' stones, and I'd lie in bed at night just thinking of the hoppy stones waiting to be picked up. Dots and Chicks and I played hoppy out on the footpath, pausing now and again to shout abuse at the dolled-up young women who passed by on their high heels. 'Put a little bit more powder on your face, put a little bit more powder on your face!'

And Myrtle and I became closer friends. She was in her Proficiency Year at school, and all the talk at home was of whether she'd get her Proficiency, and Dad warned her that if she didn't get it she would have to go to work at the woollen mills, where she'd have to go anyway, as he couldn't afford to let her go to senior high school. And that, of course, was if she hadn't already been sent to the industrial school at Caversham.

The next wave of alarm in the family was caused by the mounting of our grocery bill at Mrs Feather's to a hundred pounds, with us having no hope of paying it. Feeling proud of having such a big bill, I told my class at school, 'My father's going bankrupt. Our bill is a hundred pounds,' and once again I was not able to understand why I should not have told about the bill. I had, in the meantime, devised my own method of shopping, going to each of the shops I passed on the way to school, asking for something that I knew the shopkeeper had to fetch from the back of the shop, and while it was being fetched, helping myself to goods on the counter, slipping them quickly under my arm and holding my arm stiffly by my side, and when the shopkeeper returned, I'd say convincingly that I didn't think Mother wanted that item after all. My usual snatch was an apple or a pear, or 'lollies'. One day, greatly daring, I tried my trick in the same shop twice, and when I returned for my second steal, the woman asked, 'Did you touch anything in the shop this morning?' Terrified, I said, 'Oh, no!' 'I'll put the police after you,' she said, 'if you touch anything in this shop.' I didn't go to that shop again, and although I didn't again steal from a shop, I began to buy 'fancy biscuits' from Mrs Feather, putting them down on the bill. I'd hide them in the hedge and help myself when I wanted a chocolate biscuit, although I quickly changed my hiding place when I discovered, one damp morning, a paper bag of sodden biscuits crawling with earwigs.

Sometimes I saw Poppy going on her way to school. We'd glance at each other, ashamed and shy, and cross to the other side of the road. We both knew that obedience promised less in pain than disobedience, and we were quite resigned to our separation. We were no longer friends.

Instead of having the wonderful games and stories and rumours and cadged flowers every day, I began to collect silver paper from my stolen chocolate biscuits, smoothing out the crinkled colours and pressing the pieces into a flat yellow tobacco tin, and sometimes I'd open the tin and sit enjoying the shining colours of the silver paper.

Unfortunately, my 'fiddle' with the household accounts was discovered at the end of the month. I was punished. I gave up silver paper and my ambition of making pictures with it and acquired my own ranch and my own brand of cattle, Bar X, between the yellow japonica bush and the rose arch. And then one day I was sent to buy, honestly, both chocolate and fancy biscuits stuck together with icing, because Aunty Maggie was coming to stay.

10 O.K. Permanent Wave

Aunty Maggie, Dad's sister, had cancer of the throat. We were told that her throat was closing up, and when it finally closed, she would die. We were also told that Aunty Maggie (or *Mag*, as Mum and Dad called her) was very clever at knitting and fancy-work and that we were to behave while she was visiting us and not stare at her trying to eat. We sat at the table fascinated and horrified as she put more and more of her meals aside on her plate, with an apologetic glance at Mum, 'I'm sorry, Lottie. I can't manage that.'

We also watched her knit cable stitch, a supreme accomplishment that divided the world into those who could and those who could not knit cable stitch. I heard Mum talking to Mrs Walsh over the fence, 'Dad's sister, Mag, is staying with us. She can knit cable stitch.' Mum, not interested in sewing and knitting, and, in the shadow of Dad's accomplished sisters, not trying to compete, continued with her practice of her religion and her writing of songs and poetry and letters to the paper about the government. She no longer played her accordion, while Dad's bagpipes and bagpipe music now stayed untouched in the cupboard, and there was no more singing in the evenings. Once Dad took out his oil paints and added to the hunting scene that he had copied from a cigarette card, but he put the painting aside, unfinished, and never painted again, leaving one of the dogs forever without pupils in its eyes. Why? I wondered. It would have been such a small effort to make the two dots that would give the dog sight. Looking back, I think that my father's reluctance or inability to give sight to the dog was an indication both of the extent of his despair and his sense of the imperfection of everything. One could say (as he did again and again) when we children pestered him to finish the picture or to play the bagpipes in the evening, as he used to do, that he 'hadn't the heart any more'.

When Aunty Maggie came to visit us, although she was dying, she brought new life into our home, with news of the outside world, of motion pictures, and new words. The Depression was news everywhere. More interesting, however, was the permanent wave. We knew that Mrs Walker, our Wyndham neighbour who had shifted to Gore and kept in touch with us, had written to tell of her permanent wave, causing Mother to gasp with horror at her submission to something so 'unnatural'. And now Aunty Maggie was talking in an ordinary way about people who had permanent waves, and who'd had *second* permanent waves. I knew the meaning of *permanent*. I had supposed that a permanent wave meant just that, and the prospect of a word's lack of truth gave me a feeling of shock. If *permanent* was *everlasting*, like forever, like the stiffly petalled flowers in their bell jars upon the graves, then how could a permanent wave wear out? I was constantly preoccupied with the idea of 'truth' ever since Miss Botting had questioned me on the infant school platform, 'Tell the truth. Why don't you tell the truth?'; although I had learned that the consequences of telling the truth were as dire as those of lying. And now no one seemed to care that 'permanent wave' was not the 'truth'.

Day after day Aunty Maggie sat quietly knitting her cable stitch or sewing her fancy-work, using *crewel* (which I thought were *cruel*) needles and Clark's stranded cotton, holding the strands up to the light to count them. She and Mum used to laugh together about the Outram days and the visit of the Duke and Duchess of York. And one evening Mum and Aunty Maggie went to the pictures, the only time Mother ever went to the pictures, where they saw *Alf's Button Afloat* and *Viennese Nights*, and I'd never seen such a sparkle in Mum's eyes as she sang (for she still sang as she worked),

> *As the years roll on*
> *after you are gone,*
> *You will remember Vienna,*
> *you will recall*
> *evenings in May,*
> *sweethearts have gone*
> *and vanished away . . .*
> *Where did they come from,*
> *where did they go,*
> *Vienna will never let you know . . .*

Like all the songs, it was sad, and Mum and Aunty Maggie would look at each other in a homesick way, and Mum would say, 'Oh, Mag! Just think.' And Aunty Maggie would nod her head. And perhaps if Dad were home, he'd say boldly, 'Where's the *Happy Mag*?' The *Happy Mag* was a magazine of jokes that Dad and Mum liked to read, and we, on our first encounter with Aunty Maggie had thought she was some relation to the woman on the cover of the *Happy Mag*.

And then one day, when I came home from school, I found that Aunty Maggie had gone away; they had taken her to the hospital, where she died. She was buried beside Grandma and Grandad in the family grave, and her husband, Uncle Alex, a stern man who disliked the Frame family, put a bell jar of everlasting flowers on her grave and was reported to have said, 'That's got rid of the Frames!'

Mother, who met every death including the recent one of her father, whom we had never known, with a biblical quote, repeated, 'And God shall wipe away all tears from their eyes; and there shall be no more death, neither sorrow nor crying, for the *former things are passed away*.' The word *permanent*, then, had its own kind of revenge on those who misused it, for the Bible said that nothing was permanent, and everything came and went — the seasons and the animals (Old Cat), the people (Grandma, two Grandads, Aunty Maggie). And Poppy.

Aunty Maggie's visit and death coincided also with the latest expression, 'O.K., *chief*', which we children were forbidden to say, but when Dad was at work, we relentlessly pursued our mother, saying 'O.K., chief, O.K., chief', while Myrtle, who as the eldest was very grown up and rebellious, openly defied orders by saying, 'O.K., chief' to Dad. *Openly*. The *openly* seemed to be important, for Dad repeated it several times before he sent Myrtle to the bedroom and locked the door. 'You'll get the belt,' he said. They were now at war.

'O.K., chief' was best said while you were chewing *chutty* or chewing gum, drawing the chutty out of your mouth and stretching it as you watched the adult alarm at this apparent irresponsibility of speech and appetite. In the continuing arguments between Myrtle and Dad over every new phase of her life — the desire to wear slacks (forbidden), lipstick (forbidden), to go dancing, to go downtown on Friday nights, the chewing gum and the 'O.K., chief' were the culmination, those final chewing speaking blasphemies that became, ironically, a remembered part of Aunty Maggie's visit, Aunty Maggie, whom we watched struggling with food and word until she died, with her throat closed up.

Hurrah for the free spit-wheeling chutty and the joyous 'O.K., chief'! With a new exuberance, in spite of everything, our life continued.

11 *The Prince of Sleep*

It was a fact that most of the girls who left school early went to work at the woollen mills 'out the North Road'. We'd see the mill girls riding their bikes in the morning and hear the mill whistle at eight o'clock and at lunchtime and in the afternoon, a sound which shared the otherwise sleepy air of Oamaru, the white stone city, with that of the Oamaru town clock and the constant roaring of the sea on the foreshore. If we climbed the zigzag to the wooden seat of the Beautifying Society and looked out at the view, we'd see in the distance the tall chimneys of the woollen mills. A future spent working there or locked in the industrial school at Caversham which, like the breaking wave, would fall first on Myrtle before it reached me, too, in time, did not deter us from a range of suddenly acquired ambitions.

For all the enormity of our grocery bill and our apparent inability to pay it, Mrs Feather generously decided to give each of us children a threepence each week to go to the local pictures on Saturday afternoons, and now that we 'went to the pictures' every week, a new selection of ambitions in a completely new world was offered to us. Myrtle, who did resemble Ginger Rogers with her golden hair, planned to be a dancer or a film star or both, and to start her career, she sent for the free book on Professor Bolot's dancing course, which arrived as a pamphlet with details of the number of guineas to be paid and a large photo of Professor Bolot himself, dark-haired, with a moustache, and dressed in black, flared Spanish pants, dancing a Spanish dance. I had similar encouragement and setback from my 'free' book on ventriloquism. We gave up sending for instructions, although, some years later, I wrote to Scribe, Amorc, California, for the 'Secrets of the Universe'. Since a blind child violinist had performed at the Opera House, I had dreams of being a blind violinist, but, more practically, because I had curly hair and dimples, I also saw myself as perhaps another Shirley Temple.

Myrtle had some reason for wanting to be an actress, for she played Joan of Arc in the school play, dressed in silver cardboard armour. She played in *The Mikado*, too, and was the captain of the HMS *Pinafore*. She recited over the wireless, too, 4XD in Dunedin, where the sister of the sister-in-law of Aunty Isy was a real wireless aunt, Aunt Molly. We went next door to the Fletts' to listen through the static of their wireless to Myrtle's faraway voice reciting her favourite poem, 'The Prince of Sleep'. Or, as we knew it, 'I Met at Eve'.

I met at eve the Prince of Sleep,
His was a still and lovely face,
He wandered through a valley steep,
Lovely in a lonely place.

His garb was grey of lavender,
About his brow a poppy-wreath
Burned like dim coals and everywhere
The air was sweeter for his breath.

His twilight feet no sandals wore,
His eyes shone faint in their own flame,
Fair moths that gloomed his steps before
Seemed letters of his lovely name.

His house is in the mountain ways . . .

There were other verses, too. Myrtle recited them all, showing clearly that she was halfway to becoming a film star. She could run and jump, too, and swim and so would be strong enough to be at M.G.M. or R.K.O. studios sharp at six each morning and yet still be able to go to the Hollywood parties in her backless.

Then, toward the end of the year, when she was running in the school sports, she collapsed and was brought home, and the doctor who came to examine her said she had a heart defect and could die at any time. This was how Mum explained it to us, although she said 'go' instead of 'die', while we received the news with shocked disbelief, for Myrtle was so strong and alive, with only one scar on her body, where she had tried to walk on stilts in Wyndham, and with her curly golden hair like Ginger Rogers, and her plans all arranged for a film scout to notice her and ask her to sign a contract for millions . . .

For a time we watched and waited, curiously and fearfully, but Myrtle didn't stop breathing, and we soon forgot, for death was stillness, and Myrtle was full of movement and dancing and a wireless star, too, with her favourite poem, 'I Met at Eve the Prince of Sleep'.

With the discovery of Myrtle's 'bad heart', it was advised that she leave school, and of course she could not work at the mill. Instead, it was arranged that she help Mrs McGimpsey, a widow with two daughters, who lived down the road in a house with a balcony in front. And now that Myrtle had a few shillings each week to spend, she was able to buy lipstick and powder and Friday night milk shakes and the 'forbidden' magazines that we read under the bedclothes — *True Confessions*, *True Romance*, with their photographs of real people, beautiful women and handsome men kissing and cuddling. I had no doubt of the 'truth' of these stories simply because they were labelled 'true stories', for I had still not learned to accept the deceit of words and had only some weeks earlier rushed into a new shop that had opened downtown, *The Self Help*, expecting to be able to help myself to anything, free!

The 'Truth' was also revealed in the weekly newspaper of that name which Dad bought from Adams's in a bundle known as 'the books'. 'Go down and get the books,' he'd say. And one of us would go down to Adams's and watch fascinated while the one-armed Mr Adams, leaning his stump in its floppy sleeve upon the books arranged on the counter, rolled and tied and snipped the bundle — *Truth*, *The Humour* (the finest collection of the world's wit), *The Happy Mag*, *The Exporter*, for Mum to read the poem or paragraph she'd sent, and our comics.

Although we were forbidden to read the *Truth*, we did glimpse now and again the blurred photographs of old verandahed houses where the murder had been committed, the unshaven, wild-eyed faces of the criminals or the escaped mental patients, the swampy paddocks with the arrow showing where the body had been found; and although our parents tried to keep from us the news of unsavoury events, somehow the facts and rumours of chocolate poisoners and baby farmers managed to reach us. In our parents' view 'natural' disasters, such as earthquakes, tidal waves, even fires, were somehow 'clean' whereas murders, baby farming, shady chemists who did a side trade in abortions, these were too terrible to be discussed or even acknowledged. Even in the realm of the terrible, had our parents known about him, was the old man who sometimes followed us up to the Beautifying Society seat or into the gardens and, smiling in a funny way, opened his fly and showed us his tool. We thought him a joke, giving him the name of *Fizgig* and admitting him to our circle of peculiar people, like old maids and gypsy Ma and the town prostitute and the Catholics and the Germans and Chinese, anyone who was different, with rhymes chanted about them. 'Catholic dogs stink like frogs'. 'Ching-chong Chinaman born in a jar christened in a teapot ha ha ha', or the general rhyme that could refer to any race:

> In nineteen hundred and four
> the Germans went to war.
> They sat on the rocks
> and played with their cocks
> in nineteen hundred and four.

Sometimes we chanted, 'The Maoris went to war'. We had learned about the Maoris at school, but there were few in Oamaru. Mother had told us how she had been 'brought up among the Maoris' because her mother had step-sisters and brothers who were Maori. And Myrtle's friend was a Maori and yet not a Maori, for her father, Dad's work mate and fishing mate, was described as 'full-blooded', as if this were something better than his daughter, who was talked of as being 'only a half-caste', as if it were something to be ashamed of. I gave none of this much thought, only sensing the feeling behind people's words; I thought the word *half-caste* was related to Dad's fishing casts and cast sheep and the worm casts on the front lawn after the rain and the song Mother would suddenly begin to sing because it reminded her of her 'dear old headmaster, Mr Howard':

> *Old Tom is cast*
> *and the Christchurch bells ring one two three four.*
> *Our Christchurch?*
> *No, the Christchurch of old Dr John Godfrey . . .*

There were so many ways of talking about people, of admiring them or scorning them for the strangest reasons, sometimes just because they were dead or lived in another country; and then people were admired for what they could do, like Aunty Maggie with her cable stitch and the children who danced and sang in the competitions; or for what they had or who their parents were, and even if you didn't know people, you decided about them, and arranged your feelings for them and told everyone how you felt . . . in your lofty adult voice; while below, we children caught all the travelling opinions, like falling stars, keeping some and letting some slip through.

At this time in our lives, Mother (who always said of herself, 'I'm firm in my opinions, mind you', causing us to say as we drank our dock-seed tea or dahlia wine, 'I'm firm in my opinions, mind you, Mrs . . .') had suddenly found herself beset by opinions and advice from all sides. It was Bruddie's illness, you see. While Myrtle and I became best friends and Dots and Chicks became best friends, admitting to their play Molly Robson over the road, Bruddie was ill, day after day and night after night, while Mother looked after him and searched for a 'cure'.

12 Cures

The doctors, Mother said, were little help, prescribing medicine that made Bruddie more confused and angry and stupid, when he was a bright little boy who had walked and talked earlier than the others, except Myrtle. It was Dad's opinion that Bruddie could 'stop his fits if he wanted to', and for a time, Mother, influenced by Dad's certainty, joined the cry, 'Stop it, Bruddie, stop it at once', when the familiar signs of an attack began to show. Someone suggested the illness could be 'beaten out of him', and Dad did whip him once or twice to try to cure him. This failed of course, but Dad maintained that Bruddie could 'stop it if he wanted to'. The answer, he said, was discipline and willpower.

With the prospect of a cure unlikely, Mother began searching for the cause to correct it and once again found herself laden with opinions and advice. 'It could be his spine,' someone said, adding that they knew someone who'd been miraculously cured by a chiropractor who insisted that the answer was always in the spine. So Mother took Bruddie to the chiropractor near the foot of Eden Street, in the large house with the double driveway and the antirrhinums or snapdragons in velvet. The chiropractor was a tall, sallow-faced man in a grey suit. His eyes looked as if he were squeezing something behind them. 'Without a doubt,' he told Mother, 'it's the boy's spine.' For months then, Mother took Bruddie to the chiropractor at ten shillings a visit, although we didn't always pay that, as we had a garden full of vegetables and there was always a catch of salmon or whitebait or crayfish to give away.

For a while, then, the grown-ups talked to one another about the mysteries of 'the spine', and the way they talked there was no doubt in my mind that the spine was a great mystery and wonder, in fact, Bruddie's spine was something to be envied. Looking through the doctor's book, the *Ladies' Handbook of Home Treatment*, we children, in secret, stared fearfully at the coloured plates showing 'deformities of the spine', 'tuberculosis of the spine'. When, however, it became clear that the answer was not 'the spine', Mother accepted an opinion that said, 'It could be his eyes.' Then followed daylong journeys in the train to Timaru to see the 'eye doctor'. Next — perhaps it was the ears? Once again there were journeys to Timaru to visit the ear specialist.

Finally, it seemed that perhaps the mystery was solved: the answer was diet, a more inexpensive answer than spine, eyes, and ears. Someone gave Mother a book, *Hints on Healthy Living*, where the answer was said to lie in the brown bread and bran — in roughage. 'I knew it,' Mother said. 'Your grandmother with her diabetes was told to drink nothing but cabbage water. Whole wheat and vegetables . . .' Except for not always having brown bread and bran, we had always eaten well, even luxuriously, for there were always big tins of honey and raspberries from Up Central and sacks of oysters from down south and the salmon, whitebait, crayfish, trout that Dad caught.

While Mother's search or pilgrimage continued, we children became more 'wild' and unruly, passionately embracing every craze of town and school and neighbourhood; we became members of gangs (The Green Feather) and secret societies. We ripped the backs from the King's dining-room chairs and used them as sledges, first greasing the 'runners' with drippings from the kitchen. We rushed up and down Thames Street, trying to spot the organised mistakes in the shop windows and thus win a prize; we crowded into the newly opened bright-red McKenzies on hearing the news that Frenchies were for sale, only to discover that they were finger-stalls, after all. At home, when the Christadelphians were having their meeting in the dining room or when Mother was talking poetry, as she did with a group of young men who came to the house to read her their poems, we chanted abuse at them, mimicking them, and squashing their hats. The dogs, too (there was Myrtle's Lassie and Bruddie's Laddie and the one or two pups which were always around), joined in our expeditions, rushing here and there, barking their excitement.

It couldn't last. The neighbours, complaining of 'dogs jumping in and out of the Frames' windows', sent Mr Crump, the health inspector, who arrived without warning and, standing fiercely in the middle of our bedroom, next to the full chamber pot with its mixed shades of amber, and pointing to the unmade bed and the general untidiness, threatened Mother that if we did not get rid of the dogs and if 'those children' didn't do something to help around the house, he would send us to the *Welfare*.

So Lassie and Laddie and the two pups which we had watched having their tails cut off (we were told, but didn't believe it, that it didn't hurt) were put in sacks and drowned in the creek, and about two weeks later Myrtle brought home another black, fluffy kitten, which we kept and which was to become known as Big Puss, mother of generations. Also arrived, perhaps in response to a letter from Mother, was our Grandma Godfrey, whom we'd never met but about whom Mother talked often and lovingly so that, as far as we could judge, Grandma Godfrey was the perfect mother.

13 The Birds of the Air

I disliked Grandma Godfrey at once: she was a stranger, and she behaved toward Mum as if she owned her, when everyone knew that Mum belonged to us, and the saddest fact was that Mum appeared to agree with Grandma Godfrey's ownership, to accept it and enjoy it. How they talked! Grandma saying Lottie this and Lottie that, and Mum calling her *Mother*. Oh, the old times down Waikawa Road, Mr Howard, Mr Stocker, Old Caps, the Piranos, the Kennys, the Godfreys, the Joyces, Heberley, Dieffenbach, the Pebble Path, Wellington and Kirkaldies, on and on into the 'olden days' of the *pioneers* and the *surveyors* with their their *white feet* or their *white foot*, like a snail's foot, for Mother always talked of the surveyors as treading with their white foot . . . We knew the stories by heart, and we knew Grandma Godfrey's wonderful nature, of the walks we would have with her 'along the gully', of her skill in bush craft, her understanding and love. We knew how she would be 'like a sister' to us. 'Like a sister to you, you'll see.' And how the birds of the air, surely with much reason not to trust people, would fly down to feed from Grandma's hand, for all creatures trusted Grandma. We had listened, sometimes interested, sometimes bored, to the stories of Grandma Godfrey, and now that she had arrived, we resented her. She began at once to complain about our behaviour, how we 'walked all over' our mother, how we 'cheeked' her, how she waited 'hand and foot' on us when she was not preoccupied with our brother, and how our brother could get better if he 'put his mind to it'; and how our father was a heathen, and 'everything' was the result of Mother's marrying out of the Christadelphian religion; and the house was a pigsty with none of the children 'lifting a finger' to help or having 'any respect'.

We'd heard it all before, combined with the description, 'devils at home, angels abroad'. Mum, her fair-skinned face patched with red, tears in her eyes, her loyalty torn, said nothing. Perhaps she wished that the longed-for visit by Grandma Godfrey had never been. The dreamed-of walk along the gully was a failure. We were self-conscious. We did not respond to Grandma's jokes, for we disliked 'jolly' adults, like old Dr Orbell, cracking jokes we couldn't understand and pretending there was some secret understanding between us. We had our own fun in our own way; besides, we were sick to death of the silly 'pioneers'.

Grandma Godfrey cut short her visit, and her parting remark was that if we were her children, she would take the belt from the wheel of the sewing machine and give us all a sound whipping. Was that *really* Mother's mother?

we wondered. Mum's eyes were full of tears again. She knew that we knew now that her own mother had not been so perfect, after all, that she was just like all the mothers around, other mothers that we knew, those that whipped and shouted and wouldn't let anyone walk on their cleaned, polished floors; thin mothers with no lap and no titties; all the other mothers except our own, who was·soft and went on about nature and God but who would never be cruel to anything or anyone, and when she told us about the birds of the air, flying down to feed from Grandma Godfrey's hand, Mother was really talking about herself, for the little green birds, the wax-eyes, came always and planted their tiny feet in twig shapes in the palm of her hand. And we were sure the birds listened (as we did) when it was raining outside with Oamaru rain, mixed with sea, different from Wyndham rain mixed with river, and Mum looked out the window and sang that sad song,

> Come in, you naughty bird,
> the rain is pouring down,
> what will your mother say
> if you stay there and drown?
> You are a very naughty bird,
> you do not think of me.
> I'm sure I do not care,
> said the sparrow on the tree.
>
> The little bird was drowned . . .
> So never say you do not care
> for do not care, you see,
> is certain to be drowned
> like the sparrow on the tree . . .

We knew she was singing to the birds and to us, for it was the only way she could warn us that we were not always well behaved . . .

She could not reprimand her family. She was cruel to nothing: well, maybe to the fleas we had when the dogs were alive. Crack crack in the night, and we'd hear Dad saying, 'Got one, got one, you have to crack their backs.'

Grandma Godfrey did not visit us again. She died a few years later, and the relations sent Mum a small sum of money, about fifteen pounds (which she spent on us) and a dark painting of a storm at sea that was a companion to the other dark painting hanging over the mantelpiece in our bedroom — a mother dead in childbirth surrounded by her mourning family. The

Storm at Sea hung in the passage, where it was so dark that you could see only the white tops of the waves and the white stone of the lighthouse.

14   *Pastimes*

Myrtle found a friend to talk to, a Mrs P., widowed or divorced who lived down the road in a house with an untidy garden where straggly flowers grew through the wire fence. When Myrtle's friendship with Mrs P. became known, the word Dad used was *association*, and the instruction was 'I forbid you to associate with Mrs P.' Which meant that her reputation was 'unsavoury', as if it were the promised whirls of vapour arising from a meal cooking. I knew that 'unsavoury' could mean many things, from using bad language like 'bugger', 'O.K., chief', 'God Almighty', 'bitch', 'bastard', or wearing shocking clothes like slacks and dresses with only thin straps over the shoulders or bathing suits with the back cut too deep; or smoking and drinking and going out with boys or loitering downtown on Friday night or outside the pie cart after the pictures. I never discovered why Mrs P. was unsavoury, for when Myrtle took me on her forbidden visits to Mrs P.'s place, Mrs P. said hardly a word. She was usually busy rolling pastry (I think she cooked for people) with a cigarette dangling from her mouth. She'd give us something to eat and a cup of milk or tea and listen while Myrtle told her how awful it was at home, with Dad and everything. Sometimes she gave Myrtle a cigarette while I watched admiringly as Myrtle smoked and puffed out and blew smoke rings. I'd smoked pine-needle cigarettes in the plannies but never real ones, although I liked to watch Dad with his book of tissues, which he called *tishees*, and his tin of snuffly-smelling tobacco, as he carefully rolled a cigarette, twirling it between his first and second fingers, pulling the loose threads of tobacco from each end, tapping each end, then, starting at the left, lick along the licking-line of the tissue, then closing it, tap it, fatten it a little, then smoke it or stack it in a tin.

Mrs P. taught Myrtle songs that were also thought of as unsavoury:

> *And when I die (and when I die)*
> *don't bury me at all.*
> *Just pickle my bones*
> *in Alco Hall.*

I found out later that the word was *alcohol*, known in our family as 'drink', pronounced differently from ordinary 'drink', as in 'Would you like a drink of water, or Boston Cream, or lemon syrup?' but with a mixture of fear, horror, and judgment, 'He's fond of *drink*' or 'the drink'.

When our parents heard us singing, 'And when I die . . .', they forbade us to continue.

When I was not going to Mrs P.'s with Myrtle or downtown to look at the boys, I now spent my time with Dots and Chicks, preparing for our lives as actresses and concert performers. Each week the scene was set for the following week by the Saturday afternoon 'picture'. We went to every film, watching through the news, the cartoon, the Pete Smith Novelties, the James Fitzpatrick travel talks, the serial, and, after halftime or interval, the 'big picture'. Sometimes I went with Myrtle, who was keen on Jack Dixon, the projectionist at the Majestic, who lived up the road in a house with a high macrocarpa hedge in front. When the music and the funny pastel advertisements of Oamaru shops had finished and the programme was about to begin, we'd see him walk the length of the aisle, go through a small door down by the stage, 'to turn on the sound', Myrtle would explain, then, returning, walk past us again, along the aisle, to go upstairs to the projection room, and sometimes we'd look up and see his shadow, high up near the ceiling at the back, and Myrtle would nudge me again and say, 'There's Jack Dixon moving around upstairs. The pictures are starting.'

There'd be a funnel of light directed onto the screen, the whirring noise of the film, and Jack Dixon was at work in earnest. He was a neat young man, rather pale but handsome, and the coat of his striped suit was always buttoned in front, the way George Raft buttoned his coat, except that George Raft was a villain.

Each week the manager, Mr Williams, appeared on the stage to announce competitions and to remind the adults about the community sing that was held at the Majestic each week. Mr Williams took the promotion of his films very seriously, and every serial had its special competition. We loved the serials, although our belief in them changed to a cynical tolerance when we realised that the hero and heroine were immortal in spite of those episodes where they lay beneath the stone crusher or in the caves with the sea advancing. Three memorable serials were *The Lost Special*, about a train that disappeared; *The Invisible Man*, who needed only to press a contraption on his belly button to disappear; and *The Ghost City*, a Western. The Ghost City was lettered in our minds, for each week we were given cardboard letters, each a letter of the title, and the person first completing the title won the prize. There was furious searching, swapping, but what could be done with five Y's or three C's? I had a handful of H's. It was no use; we never won.

Then a chance came at the Opera House for someone in Oamaru to make 'the big time' in films. We knew what would happen. We'd seen it often enough in the films and read of it in the *Motion Picture Weekly*: the performance in the small-town theatre, (Oamaru), the presence in the audience of the Hollywood talent scout, then the contract, Hollywood, and the Big Time, with a house full of white telephones, dresses made of sparkly, scaly stuff like mermaids' dresses when you attended your premiere.

It happened that an Australian company wanted a young actor. Filled with the anticipation of being 'discovered', we flocked to the Opera House to find that when the Australian producer called for volunteers to go on stage and, leaning towards an imaginary mine, cup their hands and cry, 'Look out, there's dynamite down there', only a handful of children were bold or brave enough to offer. We watched, amused, scornful, envious, admiring, while each performed. Some were scared at the last minute. Some made fools of themselves. Not so Avril Luxon, whose glory shone a little on us, for he lived in the house on the other side of the bull paddock and his father was the butcher, going around with a horse and cart and wearing a striped apron with a worn leather bag like a bald sporran dangling in front, where he kept the money. Avril was a short, stocky boy with a red, freckled face and red hair, but his 'Look out, there's dynamite down there' echoed through the Opera House, and his performance is the only one I remember. He didn't win the part, though. Someone from Auckland, where people were more clever, won the film test and went off to Australia, on the way to Hollywood and the coveted Big Time, while our life in Oamaru settled again to the collection of letters for The Ghost City or playing the film we'd seen that week or writing our secret codes or trying to dance the Highland Fling, the Sword Dance, the Sailors' Hornpipe, the Highland *Chantreuse* (which we knew as the *Shottish*).

Living then changed from its vertical state to one resembling a simultaneous exhibition, with us hurrying here and there to catch up with all the displays; it was as this chapter has been, a selection of views of the Is-Land. There were many more occupations — how can I describe, for instance, the excitement merely of discovering a new shop, a new flower, a song, game, or name; a new fact — 'You can buy pork bones cheap from the bacon factory', 'You can buy specked fruit from the fruit shop'. Threepence worth the specs please . . .

Or the visiting of the parts of Oamaru that caused you to shiver with the sense of yesterdays — down by Tyne Street, the grain stores and the tall stone buildings, some untenanted with broken windows (The Ghost City!), down by the Oamaru Mail, near the gas works, which I thought existed only for the destruction of cats and dogs by the authorities and gas itself as something which people used when they wanted to commit suicide.

In that part of Oamaru the grass grew up between the stones of the street, and I believed I was in London in the chapter of our history books which began 'When grass grew in London streets', that it was also the home of the Press Gang, and the place of the Great Fire and the Great Plague, and I'd hear in my mind the cry, written beneath a vivid illustration in our history book, 'Bring out your dead, bring out your dead'.

In our endless games we were reluctant to let Bruddie play with us in case he fell in a fit, and he overcame this exclusion by accumulating power with goods salvaged from the Coquet Street rubbish dump, goods that we needed for our games and plays, and because he owned the furniture when we played house and the theatrical set when we staged plays, he was able to appoint himself as landlord and stage manager (we were happy to have him in the latter role because he was good at organising and at figures). Sometimes, as landlord, he threatened to turn us out of our house, making use of a situation that was always with us in 'real' life. Each month when the bills came in, Dad ranged through all the fears available to us: one was that we would be turned out onto the street for not being able to pay the rent; yet each month Mother dressed in her best clothes and went to the lawyer's office, Lee-Grave-and-Grave, to pay the rent.

One of Bruddie's welcome finds was dark red velvet curtains that we could use as stage curtains in the summerhouse. Bruddie also provided the 'gold' (a glittering brass chain) for use in *Honest Jacob*, which we adapted from a story found in an old schoolbook, of the man who found gold in the bread and took it back to the baker: an example of honesty. Another was *Hugh Idle and Mr Toil*, similarly adapted, a haunting tale of a small boy who decides to play the wag from school, and everyone he sees in the town is a twin of Mr Toil, the headmaster, in fact, the same man. We found it to be a nightmare tale, as it was for Hugh Idle.

Our plays were performed with song items between — 'Morning Has Broken', 'Deep in the Forest', 'Now You May Sail, Matangi', and another that haunted me, 'Tender Wood Dove Softly Cooing in Your Nest':

In the elm tree gently swaying, take your rest,
I long to watch your gentle flight,
your spreading wings' snowy white . . .
All the day at work I hear you,
tender dove,
take my little song to cheer you,
with my love.

The song haunted me, because as I sang it, I believed and felt that I myself was singing to the wood dove; then, when I sang the line 'All the day at work I hear you, tender dove, / take my little song to cheer you', I felt that because I did not think of myself as 'working' or being 'at work', then the song must belong to my mother, whom I thought of as being at work all day and able (unlike Dad, on the train) to listen now and again to the birds singing outside; and so, as I sang, I seemed to be my mother going about my work, feeling lonely and sad and depending on the song of the dove for comfort.

We recited our favourite poems, too — 'Old Meg She Was a Gypsy', 'I Met at Eve the Prince of Sleep', and Myrtle sang her special songs, including 'By the Light o' the Peat Fire Flame' and 'The Minstrel Boy to the war has gone / In the ranks of death you'll find him', singing it as if the Minstrel Boy were a boyfriend of hers, which I half believed him to be.

Our father, too, had found a pastime to while away his evening. He'd look at Dots and start to sing the song which, we all knew, terrified her:

> Don't go down in the mine, Dad,
> dreams very often come true.
> Daddy, you know it would break my heart
> if anything happened to you.

That one verse was enough to produce the expected result: Isabel began to cry and crept under the table, and we knew and Dad knew that it was because she loved him so much and couldn't bear to think of his dying in the mine. Dad would then take the gas mask he had brought home from the war and, putting it over his face, advance toward Chicks, to frighten her because everyone knew that was her special fear, and Chicks, seeing the monster and stranger approach, would also hide and cry. The game with me was to stand me in the middle of the room, where everyone could observe my twitches and tics and the funny faces I pulled, and the more I tried to stop, the harder it became. 'Just look at her, look at her, she's got St Vitus's Dance,' Dad would mock.

On happier evenings, although Dad did not sing as he used to sing in Wyndham, he sometimes entertained us with his 'hard-boiled egg' dance and song:

> I'd rather have a hard-boiled egg,
> I'd rather have a hard-boiled egg,
> I'd rather have a hard-boiled egg . . .

or his 'Ragtime Cowboy Joe' dance and song, which we loved:

> *Way out in Arizona where the bad men are*
> *the only thing to guide you is an evening star . . .*
> *roughest toughest man by far*
> *is Ragtime Cowboy Joe . . .*

Ragtime Cowboy Joe. That was Dad. How we roared with laughter to see his performance!

So that was that. I was almost nine years old now. In moments of family despair, when Mother dared to say, 'We should never have left Wyndham', and Dad agreed, one part of life untouched for me, still perfect, was the world outside, the seasons. The flowers still came out in their proper time, the dandelion seeds or one-o'clocks never failed to float away into the sky, the poplar trees at the corner where the two Miss Darlings lived changed colour and lost their leaves, Jack Frost was about (look out, look out!) after our fingers and toes, and always there was the sky and the clouds and my shadow, and in the evening the moon walked with me, and when I stopped, it stopped, too; and I thought of Old Meg:

> *Instead of supper she would stare*
> *full hard against the moon.*
> *Her brothers were the craggy hills,*
> *her sisters larchen trees.*
> *Alone with her great family*
> *she lived as she did please.*

And I thought of 'I Met at Eve the Prince of Sleep', Myrtle's poem.

15   Gussy and the Invercargill March

I felt desolate at school. I longed for impossible presents, a doll's house, a sleeping doll, birthday parties, pretty dresses, button-up shoes, patent leather, instead of the lace-up leather shoes with their heavy soles and heel and toe plates, hair that fell over my face so I could brush it away, saying,

'My hair's always getting in my eyes . . .', instead of frizzy red hair 'up like a bush' with everyone remarking on it.

I missed Poppy and the cadged flowers, although I'd collected in my mind many good stories since I read *Grimm's Fairy Tales*, and I especially treasured the story of Pandora and of Persephone and the Pomegranate seeds which were so vivid, bright red, split, with juice oozing from them, that anyone would have wanted to eat them. There were stories of the Australian desert, too, and Central Africa and South Africa, and the stories from the books each was now given as a prize at the end of the year. Isabel's *The Joyous Travellers*, a kind of Junior *Canterbury Tales*, became a loved part of our play with its *Hop-About Man*. We devised a Hop-About Dance, 'Ring a Ding Dill':

> *Ring a ding dill*
> *The Hop-About Man*
> *Comes over the hill.*
> *The Miraculous Pitcher,*
> *the Little Crippled Boy . . .*

Suddenly, in the midst of my discontent and longing, I was promoted to Standard Four, to Gussy (or Reuben) Dimmock's class where I became, inexplicably, the teacher's 'pet'. It had always been other children who were the teacher's pets — pretty little girls with clean hair ribbons — and hair that accepted a hair ribbon as natural — and nice clothes and well-mannered little boys with clean shirts who confidently played their role unperturbed by the certain number of envious and unkind remarks it attracted. You'd always see the 'teacher's pet' catching up to walk to school with the teacher, with a hop and a skip, keeping in step; and in school you'd see the teacher turn habitually to the 'pet', letting her or him fetch and carry things, smiling at her or giving him the job of special monitor to open the windows with the long, hooked pole or to return the exercise books with the corrected 'My Adventure' or 'My Holidays' compositions.

How proud I was of myself in Standard Four! Gussy used to sit me on his knee while he taught the class, and sometimes he would give me a small, special table in front of the class to share with his small son, who was known as a 'mongol' and whom I helped with his lessons. And one day Gussy asked us to write a poem beginning 'When the sun goes down and the night draws nigh . . .'

At home that evening, the writing of that first poem sparked my first argument over writing as an art, for when I read my poem to Myrtle, she insisted that the words 'touch the sky' should be 'tint the sky':

When the sun goes down and the night draws nigh
and the evening shadows touch the sky
when the birds fly homeward to their nest
then we know it is time to rest.

When rabbits to their burrows run
and children have finished their daily fun
when the tiny stars come out to peep,
then we know it is time to sleep.

I disagreed with Myrtle, who then insisted that there were words and phrases you had to use, and when you were writing about evening shadows, you always said 'tint', just as you said the stars 'shone' or 'twinkled' and waves 'lapped' and the wind 'roared'. In spite of Myrtle's insistence, I preferred 'touch' to 'tint' but in deference to her obvious wisdom and wider knowledge I changed the word to 'tint' when I took my poem to school. But later, when I wrote it in my notebook, I reverted to 'touch the sky', having my own way.

The poem, the usual kind of child's poem, was a success only in its predictability, for when Gussy sat me on his knee and began reading, the class was able to guess the last line of each verse and so join in with the words. I found that when I 'shared' my new triumph at home that evening, the family was proud of me, and my father promised to bring home a railway notebook from the loco foreman's office for me to write down more poems. The railway notebooks where Dad, who was union secretary of the Engine Drivers' Union, wrote the members' union contributions, had attractive marbled colours on the edges of the pages that set together formed a marbled pattern which fascinated me. Dad's other books were of equal fascination — the bagpipe music books with their peculiar heavy print and signs in code, which we 'played', reading or conducting from them until, as with almost every household item we touched, we 'wore' them out or, in adult words, 'ruined' them, leaving them torn, written on, with pages missing; the fly book with its leather cover salt-smelling and smeared with patches of fish scales, with the parchment pages, the bulk closed by an elastic band, each page filled with brilliantly coloured feather flies on hooks with beautiful names like Red-Tipped Governor, Greenwell's Glory . . . and at night Dad would sit at the table and 'read' his fly book, naming each fly as he turned the crackly pages. We were never allowed to touch his fly book, only to look over his shoulder as he 'read' it or to feel the fatness of the closed book. In our ritual of play we sometimes said, 'I think I'll get out m' fly book.' There were homemade books, too, which we laboriously sewed in place and covered with scraps of wallpaper from the wallpaper shop downtown.

The prospect of having a real notebook and being able to write poems, with numbered pages and an index, made us dizzy with delight, for the others would have notebooks too, under the rules of fair play. We were all hungry for words. Seeing a musical film, we were tortured by not knowing the exact words of the songs, and when one day Myrtle brought home a small booklet with the words of the popular songs of the day, our excitement was acute. In what I might call my 'cowboy and prisoner' period, a year or two earlier, I had written in the homemade notebooks the words of the sad cowboy songs — 'The wheel of the wagon is broken and it ain't gonna turn no more', 'There's a bridle hanging on the wall, there's a horseshoe in an empty stall . . .' and the 'Prisoners' song that Poppy taught me, telling it to me as if it were *her* song in the way that *Grimm's Fairy Tales* were *her* stories:

> *The pale moon is shining a shining so bright*
> *on the lovers a-wandering by my window tonight.*
> *Their laughter so merry brings tears to my eyes,*
> *as a prisoner I'm lonely for the moonlight and skies . . .*

Poppy told me the song one evening when we were playing in the house next door to hers, which was only half built, with the foundation and the framework exposed to the bright summer moon of Oamaru, and while we played, we were in danger of being cast into prison, for one day the owner had caught us playing there and astonished us (for we thought the house was *ours*) by calling out fiercely, 'Hop it, you. Hop it, you.' We then named him Hoppityou. 'I saw Hoppityou today.'

Under Gussy's care I blossomed then both as a scholar and as an athlete, for Gussy believed that because every child had a special talent he, as a teacher, had to give everyone a chance to discover the talent. Gussy was known as something of a fanatic in the classroom and on the sports field, and being in Gussy's class meant that when you were running in a race you were training to find out if you would qualify for the Olympic team. The slow, awkward children who couldn't read aloud in those excruciating reading lessons discovered they might be future Olympic champions or they might be 'good at' gardening or handwork, which, Gussy stressed, were of equal importance, and with such encouragement, some, their confidence returning, even learned to read aloud and recite their arithmetic tables. In spite of Gussy's teaching that all were equal and special, I did have the joy of being his pet, and as I lacked the customary qualifications for such a post, I never discovered the reason for his choice, unless it was that he thought it was the only way to deal with me and my tics and terrors. He inspired everyone. At home we practised his voice as he, first assistant to the headmaster, marched us into school each morning with his military cry, eeep-ite eeep-ite, eeep-ite, while Ernest Calcott beat upon the kettledrum strapped around his neck. We also practised Gussy's voice at the beginning of a race and the way he had explained each inflexion: 'On your marks.' To be spoken briskly but matter-of-factly. 'Get Ready.' The Get Ready given no more emphasis than usual, in contrast to our suspense-building Gee-e-e-et Re-e-e-ea-a-a-add-dyyyyyy. Then the final short, sharp Go. We also practised for that great day, School Sports Day, when the North School and the South School struggled for possession of the Primary School Sports Shield, and all the schools marched around the Show Ground Field with the Oamaru Brass Band playing 'Colonel Bogey' and 'The Invercargill March'. 'Now we're in front of the grandstand,' we'd say, feeling again in our stomachs the surge of excitement. 'Now we're coming around the Outside . . .' Then . . . de-de-de-de-de-dedede . . . *The Invercargill March*.

I ran in relays. I hopped, stepped and jumped. And in the flat race, as soon as the gun went off, I ran as fast as I could, not being able to understand why, if I was running as fast as I could, I didn't come in first instead of my usual third or fourth. I knew I could feel my legs trying their hardest, and I had been taught that if you tried your hardest to do something, you could do it. Everyone was always lecturing us about 'trying', pointing out the achievements of great men and women and suggesting that they attained their greatness because they tried their hardest, and in our competitive school world, if you tried your hardest to win, you won: everyone said so. I puzzled over this until I realised it was not the 'truth'. I knew truthfully that I ran my fastest in the race. I realised that I didn't win because I didn't have long legs like Audrey Nimmo or extra power like Madge Robertson, the champion dancer, or the other champion dancer from the South School, Beatrice Macfie.

Even Gussy was always telling us to do our best and more or less promising us whatever we wished to have. I was in a mood for homilies that year. Every morning we had long Scripture lessons taken by one of the local ministers. I always listened intently, but I learned more from the hymns, for as kinds of song they appealed to me. 'There Is a Green Hill Far Away'. 'All Things Bright and Beautiful' (thought of as strictly a junior school song). 'What a friend we have in Jesus. There's a friend for little children above the bright blue sky . . .' When I came home singing, 'There's a friend for little children', with its promise of heaven, I found that Mother disapproved because heaven on earth was the Christadelphian belief, not heaven in the sky. Mother explained that when you died, you died, staying in your grave until the Second Coming and the Resurrection and Judgment Day (which I imagined as a heavenly kind of Sports Day with the Oamaru Brass Band playing 'The Invercargill March' and the Pipe Band playing 'The Road to the Isles'). At the Resurrection, Mother said, all would be as they were just before they died and would then be judged as worthy or unworthy, and if they were found unworthy, they would be struck dead again for ever.

'And will everyone wake up on Resurrection Day?'

'Everyone.'

'Even Grandma?'

'Of course.'

'And what about the animals, Old Cat and Lassie and Laddie?'

'The animals have no place in the kingdom.'

Because I could not accept that there was no room for all creatures, I did not adopt Mother's religion. 'There must be room for Old Cat and Laddie and Lassie.' I could not understand why Mother, so liberal in her views of the world and such a lover of 'creatures', could have them so dismissed from glory.

As that year was ending, I was told that I was Dux of the School, equal with another girl from another Standard Four. Some said it was because I was Gussy's 'pet', and it may have been so in that he encouraged me in my lessons. On the last day I wore a white dress with a cape collar (sent by Aunty Polly), and as I walked from the stage, having received my gold medal, I suddenly panicked, not feeling the medal where it had been pinned. I hurried back onto the stage, searching the boards until I realised that my medal was still safe. My humiliation was acute when I realised I may have revealed to the world how proud I was to have a Dux medal!

I knew that in being Dux I had pleased my father, and this pleased me, for day by day as I brought home tales of life in Standard Four, Dad had begun to say, 'Well, are you going to be Dux, then?'

When all the excitement was over, I remembered that the envelope presented to me with the Dux medal contained a year's subscription to the Oamaru Public Library, known as the Oamaru Athenaeum and Mechanics' Institute. 'I can go to the Athenaeum free,' I said, not·quite sure what *Athenaeum* meant. And in the holidays, when one day I went to the loco foreman's office with a hot pie for Dad's lunch, I heard Dad say, 'My daughter goes to the Athenaeum.'

16 The Athenaeum

The Athenaeum was a two-storeyed building in Thames Street with the lower floor used as a museum for caged rocks, pieces of bone, greenstone and stuffed native birds, including a huia labelled extinct, while, guarded at the foot of the stair by a huge glass-eyed reconstructed moa also labelled extinct, the upper floor contained the library where the librarian, named, I supposed, from her own habitat, Miss Ironside, sat behind an iron grille, issuing and returning books. The Juvenile Section (Fourteen and under Twenty-One Silence Please Do Not Turn the Leaves Down) consisted of one wall of books by the windows overlooking Thames Street.

'Books' meant books mostly of the English language for reading, as opposed to those other books I knew — the bagpipe music; Dad's fly book; Dad's union books; God's Book — the big Christadelphian book with pictures of God in a swirl of cloud and thunder; the Bible; the Doctor's Book, with instructions on childhood sickness and a chapter on the lying-in woman who, the illustration showed, was 'bearing down' pulling hold of a sheet attached like a roller towel to the iron bed head; the autograph books with their pastel-coloured leaves; the birthday books (Mother's, the Whittier Birthday book); our numerous homemade books; the comic books; our schoolbooks; and lastly Aunty Maggie's 'needle books' with flannel pages pierced in formation by crewel (cruel) needles.

'What will I get from the library, Mum?' I asked, suddenly ignorant and feeling in awe of the world of books in a library, having no idea what to choose and clinging to Grimm's Fairy Tales and the School Journals, and the poems I knew, and having no desire to read the 'children's' books I was meant to have read — Alice in Wonderland, The Wind in the Willows, Peter Pan, the Just So stories . . . Mother, in a rapture, exclaimed, 'Oh, Mark Twain (Samuel Clemens), Innocents Abroad, oh, Uncle Tom's Cabin, oh, David Copperfield (Dickens, oh, the Christmas Books, kiddies, it's a cold night, said the King of the Goblins).'

My new library subscription was a family affair. I brought home for Bruddie a 'William' book, which we all read. I found Grimm's Fairy Tales, the same kind of red-covered book with the thin pages packed with black print that I'd borrowed from Poppy. I found a Western for Dad and a Dickens for Mum, who had no time to read it but who touched it and opened it and flipped the pages and read out striking descriptions, saying, 'How wonderful, kiddies, Charles Dickens, born in poverty, growing up to be a great writer.' Then, after a prolonged season with the Brothers Grimm

I became bold enough to read other books — The Bumper Books for Girls and Boys, Boarding School books, while I continued, on the side, as it were, with Myrtle's *True Confessions* and *True Romances*.

Summer holidays again. Endless play, make-believe, roaming the plannies, the hill, the gully. My days at the Oamaru North School over, I looked forward to the junior high school, learning French and algebra and geometry and singing and hearing new poems. The junior high school also held the junior and senior high property room, full of scenery and stage clothes and masks, all described to me by Myrtle; and there were the teachers, they, too, made famous by Myrtle's descriptions of them. And in particular there was the French family of the French book that I'd already tried to read — Marcel and Denise and their parents Monsieur and Madame Desgranges

Going to junior high school meant, however, wearing a special uniform that, unlike the uniform at the Oamaru North School, was compulsory and included the correctly pleated light grey flannel tunic, winter and summer hats (black beret or black felt and white panama, with regulation hatbands), blouses, summer and winter, white cotton and grey flannel, black stockings, black pants, black shoes, with gym shoes for sports. Fortunately, the Dux medal, which gave me the library subscription, had also reminded relations who might have forgotten that the Frame girls might need clothing if they were 'going on' to high school; and so there arrived a parcel of assorted clothes from Aunty Polly and from Aunty Isy — 'aunt-smelling' clothes in 'aunts' colours', brown, purple, maroon, dark blue, which we divided amongst ourselves but which did not help toward a school uniform. Mother bravely faced the man in Hodges to buy 'on tick' some grey flannel from which she tried to make a tunic, which turned out as a disastrously sewn and shaped hybrid garment, neither tunic nor dress, with a curiously cutaway yoke that exposed most of the front of my bunched white blouse (bunched because I was growing, and a larger size saved money in advance). Although I knew that my school tunic was 'funny', it did not worry me at that stage of my life, for I was too much engrossed in the prospect of new lessons, of Marcel and Denise, and 'Bright is the ring of words / When the right man rings them', another of Myrtle's poems learned at junior high.

17   Clothed in White Samite

Our teacher in the first year was Miss Romans, known to everyone as Iris Beatrice, who, in the language of the time, was rumoured to be 'fast', a sherry drinker, a bridge player, a party-goer — known qualifications for 'fastness'. Also, she was pretty, and she wore high heels.

Of that junior year I remember little apart from the fastness of Miss Romans (which I never observed in action) and the fact that she wore a black gown and moved her elbows as if she were flying, as she walked into the room; and I remember the delight of learning French words and songs and the names of science apparatus (Bunsen burner, litmus paper); the cooking lessons, lemon sago, puff pastry, cream crackers; how to scrub a wooden table; the sewing, embroidery with the eternal *crewel* needles and the Clarks stranded cotton, all of which had to be bought and therefore asked for at home and the reply endured, 'You'd be better off working at the mill,' and the final consent received under the weight of that Dux medal and the new parental dream, 'She's going to be a teacher like Cousin Peg, who emigrated to Canada.'

There might have been a time when the supply of crewel needles and stranded cotton, the pens, pencils, nibs, blotters, compasses, set squares, protractors, rulers, exercise books 'ruled feint with margin' (at which Dad made his joke, 'Faint all right, at the cost of all this'), journal covers, journal pins . . . all might have ceased had not that year, 1935, become the year of the first Labour Government with its promise of Social Security, free medical treatment, free hospital treatment for all. Our debts to the doctor and the hospitals were then so enormous that we had given up hope of paying them, and Dad, with his skill as a fisherman, was still making peace offerings of salmon, trout, whitebait and crayfish. The election of the Labour Government was almost like a Second Coming, so great was the joy in our household, and so revered the new prime minister, 'Micky' Savage, whose poster-size photograph was now pinned to our kitchen wall, where it stayed for the rest of the time we lived at Fifty-six Eden Street, and even when the Second World War was declared, Micky Savage was moved only slightly to make way for the map of the world with the tiny pinned flags, 'Flag the Movements of the Allied Forces from Day to Day'.

When the Social Security Act was finally passed, Dad, in a spontaneous dance of delight in which the family joined, removed the bills from behind the clock and, taking the poker from its hook by the stove, lifted the cover and thrust all the bills into the fire. Mother, a true Godfrey (all the

Godfreys were known as 'weepers'), wept, and we children made whooping cowboy shouts of joy. And from that day, as each political hero and heroine appeared on the scene, Micky Savage, John A. Lee (especially revered because he was a writer), Bob Semple, Mabel Howard, Paddy Webb, took pride of place beside Longfellow, Dickens, Mark Twain, John Greenleaf Whittier, Cousin Peg, the Godfrey, Joyce, Frazer and Nash ancestors. And when, a few years later, we bought a wireless on tick and Parliament was broadcast, Mother went about her everlasting work with the wireless switched to Parliament while she made her own interjections, and as each speaker finished, she praised the 'goodies' and criticised the 'baddies', using the first names of the members and talking of them and to them with an intimacy that not even our old friends and neighbours, the Walkers, John and Bessie, forever known as Mr and Mrs, could claim, although, unlike the M.P.s the Walkers came to us for holidays and sent their daughter to our place for her honeymoon.

It was in my second year at Waitaki Junior High School that, making up my mind to be a 'poet' when I 'grew up', I began to write poems regularly in my small railway notebook. This renewed interest was prompted no doubt by our teacher's interest in poetry: devoted to verse speaking, she gave us a number of haunting poems to learn and recite, and although I objected to the singsong way she expected us to speak, some of that singing trapped me, with my passion for songs, in a world that seemed to have no boundaries and was part of the world of Old Meg, the beggars and swaggers, angels, too, and Poppy and Hoppityou and the Twelve Dancing Princesses, and the playground songs, and like to the tide moaning in grief by the shore, E pare ra. Also, Miss Lindsay used to read for hours from Tennyson's *Idylls of the King*, as if it were her personal poem, and it was partly her absorption in it that compelled me to listen and wonder. I can still see her as she gazed toward the classroom door, as if toward a lake, saying, 'an arm rose up . . . clothed in white samite, mystic, wonderful . . .' as if she had experienced it, as if the jewelled sword Excalibur 'all the haft twinkled with diamond sparks, / Myriads of topaz-lights, the jacinth-work / Of subtlest jewellery . . .' had been a part of her life that she, like Sir Bedevere, was reluctant to give up. She mourned, too, the passing of Arthur, in a way quite unsuited to *our* Miss Lindsay with her ordinary brown clothes and patchy face:

> And call'd him by his name, complaining loud,
> And dropping bitter tears against a brow
> Striped with dark blood . . .

Miss Lindsay conjured up with equal vividness the Last Minstrel, 'The way was long, the wind was cold, / The Minstrel was infirm and old . . .', all in a world of cities and kingdoms new to me, a part of history not found in our history books, for whereas our history books encouraged unalterable opinions of characters, certain kings and leaders being irrevocably 'good' or 'bad' or 'weak' or 'strong', with their actions permanently described thus, in the world of King Arthur and the Last Minstrel and the Duke of Wellington ('Who is he that cometh like an honoured guest?'), we could think or feel as we wished toward the characters, or as the poet, discounting history, invited us to; we were the poet's guest, his world was his own kingdom, reached, as one of the poems told us, through the *Ring of Words*:

> Bright is the ring of words
> When the right man rings them,
> Fair the fall of songs
> When the singer sings them.

This other land revealed to me by Miss Lindsay, whom we laughed at because her face was like a cow's face, with a dewlap, and she wore funny shoes with pointy toes, could contain all the unspoken feeling that moved alive beneath the surface of each day and night and came above the surface only in the way earthworms came, when there was too much rain; and these feelings were secrets that this new land could receive without shock or horror or the need for revenge or punishment; it was yet a private place, even described by Miss Lindsay when she read the lines:

> A place
> where no one comes
> or hath come since the
> making of the world.

I brought home news of the poems, reciting them again and again, with Mother receiving them as an exile receives sight of a long-lost native land. 'We had "Ring out Wild Bells" today,' I said, whereupon Mum, with a gasp of recognition, repeated, 'Ring out wild bells to the wild sky, / The flying cloud, the frosty light . . .' to be joined by Myrtle, a most recent exile, saying in a homesick voice, ' "The year is dying, let him die . . ." We had that.' It was enough to remind Myrtle of The Minstrel Boy and 'I Met at Eve the Prince of Sleep' and Un-deux-trois-quatre-cinq . . . , the knowing of which gave her a power and satisfaction that she hadn't found in her new life of growing up and arguing with Dad and going to dances and seeing Jack

74

Dixon operate the projector at the Majestic. 'We had *The Lay of the Last Minstrel*, too,' I told the family, whereupon Mum exclaimed, 'Oh, oh. Sir Walter Scott. *The Lay of the Last Minstrel*.'

Her favourite poems were those of first and last, the newly discovered and the long lost, all of which seemed to fuse with her preoccupation with the 'latter days' creating opposite images of total darkness and loss with total light and revelation. This feeling, in its simplest form, prompted her pity for all that had been left behind or abandoned or neglected. In contradiction to her denial of the 'Kingdom' to animals, she wrote verses about stray cats and wounded birds and also about deserted gardens and houses and days that had been, and in her choice of subjects she influenced me. I wrote about 'days gone by':

> *The pine trees whisper as they sway*
> *caressed by some kind gentle breeze,*
> *sadly, lonely through the day*
> *bringing back sweet memories*

concluding after two more verses with,

> *A memory, half-forgotten day*
> *so full of spring sunshines*
> *told by trees that gently sway*
> *and whispered by the pines.*

I wrote poems about everything around me. I wrote a poem about the sand, the sky, the leaves, a rainbow (taking care to list the exact colours — 'orange, yellow, red, and heliotrope, a lovely green and blue'. I wrote about Marie Antoinette and the Palace of Fontainebleau:

> *Ah, Queen of Sorrows, I wish you were here*
> *to see the sunset, a beautiful pink,*
> *you might take a book and sit by the mere,*
> *or stoop to the crystal and drink.*
>
> *The times are hard, the smiles are few*
> *there is bloodshed and many men die,*
> *no time to look at the rainwashed blue*
> *or the sunset in the sky . . .*

I wrote, too, about a mystery ship, 'I gazed at it through seablue eyes, my old old mystery ship . . .'

Inevitably there was the poem about my mother, whose reverence of motherhood inspired her to write many such poems and who kept reminding us about other 'strays' of the world, 'Don't forget, she may be somebody's mother.'

I enjoyed writing my railway book. I kept an index of poems, and I remember part of the first index:

Captain Scott.
Sand.
A longing.
My Rainbow . . .

My poems were a mixture of conventional ideas about 'poetic' vocabulary and the cowboy and prison songs recorded in my other notebooks and the contents of the small popular song books brought home by Myrtle and the songs sung by my parents and grandparents. I continued writing my poems, sensing the approval of my parents — of Mother, who saw the birth of something she had mourned as lost from her life, whose overwhelming might-have-been was *publication* of a book. She once sent a collection of her poems to Stockwells, England, which advertised regularly in New Zealand newspapers and magazines, and her joy at having the poems accepted for publication was lessened only by the knowledge that she couldn't afford the sum of money they quoted for publication, and although she resigned herself to never having the money, she could say proudly now and again, 'I've had a book of poems accepted for publication by Stockwells, Ilfracombe, England.' Nor could she afford to copyright a song that won first prize in an Australasian competition, for when she sent to the copyright office for the necessary document ('I've put in for the copyright of my song'), she found there was a fee that she could not pay, and so the song remained uncopyrighted. She was left with knowledge of the procedure, however, and she often talked of it: 'I have an application for copyright of my song.' And over the years her recollection became more fruitful than disappointing, 'I've been in touch with the copyright office about my song.'

Mother talked of 'Fleet Street, London' also, making it part of her dreams, and it could have been that her tolerance of our reading of comics was the result of our discovery in the small print at the end of the comic 'Printed at Farringdon House, Fleet Street, London E.C.4'. Her response to this discovery was rapturous, 'Oh, kiddies, Farringdon House, Fleet Street, London E.C.4.'

We ourselves in our modest way communicated with Fleet Street, London, in unanswered letters requesting free badges, booklets, trinkets. Mother talked of publication and of Fleet Street, London, with the same longing as that with which she talked of Bruddie's recovery ('When you grow out of it, Bruddie . . .'), for the magic instrument was now thought to be natural growth, and of the Latter Days and the Second Coming and the Resurrection, and, on a more domestic level, of the icing set with which she would some day write (the ultimate domestic literacy) words and phrases on the Christmas and New Year cakes she baked each year. Words and phrases that could be eaten!

Dad, remembering Cousin Peg and my Duxhood, also showed delight, of a more restrained kind, in my writing of poems. Described by Mother, rather sadly, as 'like all the Frames, a dour Scot, your father's a dour Scot, kiddies', Dad was yet a glutton for jokes, listening eagerly to the comedy on our newly acquired wireless, and reading the jokes in the *Happy Mag* and *Humour* before he cut the paper into squares as wiping paper for the lavatory; yet he seemed to be unable to accept that funny events happened in real life, in his own home, and he listened glumly to Mother's laughter as she recounted the many humorous events that she still found in each day, both at home and over the wireless. Dad's interest in words was formal. Words were to be sought and explained and not used for 'airy-fairy' purposes, and although he was proud that I was writing poetry, his special interest was in letting others know and in hoping it might win prizes. He liked to sit in the evenings, working out puzzles in magazines and organising words in crossword puzzles. I, who disliked most puzzles, particularly jigsaws after the experience of being left always with a spare piece of sea or sky or grass beside an already completed sea, sky and lawn, used to feel a shock of pride when Dad asked me to help him with the crossword. I felt as if the King of the World were enlisting my help, but I'd conceal my feelings and work very calmly to find the word. I remember one evening, hour after hour, with one word to be found, and Dad refusing to give in, and I, infected with his determination, searching and searching, and although bedtime came, neither of us gave in and early next morning I heard a shout of triumph from the kitchen, where Dad was getting ready for work.

'*Rattan*. It's *rattan*.' And it was *rattan*, a word that was new to me, but that remains memorable in my life with *decide*, *destination*, *adventure*, *permanent wave*, *O.K.*, *skirting board*, *wainscot*, and others.

The fact that I was allowed to continue my library subscription (it was now unthinkable that the family should not have access to so many books) also strengthened the interest in writing. There were other influences, too. The year was 1936. There had been an epidemic of polio (known then as infantile paralysis) with cases of meningitis, and there were still isolated cases, with the number expected to increase over the next summer; and attention was focused on the 'crippled children' who had overcome their disability — notably, Gloria Rawlinson, the child poet. It was the time, too, of the Hollywood 'child stars': Shirley Temple, Jane Withers, Freddie Bartholomew. The surge of performing children, of their ambitions and the ambitions of the parents was at its height in Oamaru and elsewhere, and particularly in our home there was a continued association between disability and proven ability, as Mother repeatedly tried to console Bruddie with stories of Beethoven and his deafness, Milton and his blindness, Julius Caesar and his epilepsy, with the implication that surely Robert Frame of Fifty-six Eden Street, Oamaru, had a life to look forward to in the hope of either a miraculous recovery (for God performed miracles daily) or the development of a talent that could bring him fame and fortune, or, fame and fortune being of this world only, that would allow him to wander in the Garden of Beatitudes, living meekly, poor in spirit, a peacemaker, a mourner for all that was lost and missed, and, in the end, inherit the earth as a child of God.

Whatever the reasons, the children of the town and the province and the country began not only to perform and dream of performing their dances, songs, piano music, violin music, drama, but also to write their own poems and stories, encouraged locally by the children's pages in the newspapers — in Otago by Dot's Page for Dot's Little Folk, of the *Otago Daily Times*. Dutifully we children wrote our letter in its conventional form, 'Dear Dot, Please may I join your happy band of Little Folk. I am so many years old, etc.', ending with 'Love to all the Little Folk and your own Dear Self'.

In spite of the embarrassment of the effusiveness of 'your own Dear Self', I wrote my letter, asking to be known as 'Golden Butterfly', an unoriginal name that, already taken, Dot changed to *Amber Butterfly*. The others, except Chicks, who was given the name she asked for, Dancing Fairy, also had their chosen names changed — Bruddie's Sergeant Dan (after the Royal Mountie on the Creamota packet) became Sergeant Dick, Myrtle's Good Queen Bess was changed to Good Queen Charlotte, and Isabel's Apple Blossom to Apple Petal.

Continuing the emphasis on the disabled, sometimes a blind pianist or violinist or a 'crippled' singer performed over the wireless, with the announcer, aware, too, of the number of children being 'struck down' with infantile paralysis, stressing the performer's disability as if it were somehow a part of the ability, even necessary to it. I came to link the two. I perceived that in a world where it was admirable to be brave and noble, it was more brave and noble to be writing poems if you were crippled or blind than if you had no disability. I longed to be struck with paralysis so that I might lie in bed all day or sit all day in a wheelchair, writing stories and poems. That is, if I could not, as I also longed to do, learn music and dancing and singing, performing at the regular competitions, winning prizes that would enable me to go to Hollywood.

The year ended. I received two small leather-bound books for a prize and a bursary for five pounds to help me 'go on' to senior high school, where there were three courses — professional or academic, commercial, or domestic, with no mixture of subjects as in the junior high school. My parents, now taking it for granted that I would become a teacher, decided to allow me to continue at school, although Dad warned me that if times were hard, I might have to leave school or change to 'commercial' and work in an office. Most of the girls in our neighbourhood planned to leave school in their third or fourth year to work in shops or offices, and most were to take a commercial course. Poppy, whom I saw distantly now and again, exchanging formal greetings, was to take 'commercial'. I had already suffered the corruption of literature by taking to heart yet another of my favourite poems — 'Old Grey Squirrel', by Alfred Noyes, where a young boy dreams of a life at sea, and when he grows up, his dream unfulfilled, he works in an office, slowly 'dying inside'.

> He is perched upon a high stool in London.
> The Golden Gate is very far away.
> They caught him, and they caged him, like a squirrel.
> He is totting up accounts, and going grey.

In my mind that high stool could be found in Oamaru, in the lawyer's office where Mother paid the rent. A grey tired-looking man perched there on a high stool before a high, sloping desk, working at his accounts, and when he came to take the rent money, I could see his nose sharp like a pen-nib with a drop of nosey instead of ink on the end. Such was my trust in the 'truth' of literature that I believed the Alfred Noyes version of commercial life, looking on life in an office as a betrayal of anyone's dearest dreams. 'I'll never take commercial,' I said vehemently.

Acres of Christmas holidays lay before us. There was the celebration of Christmas which, with New Year's Eve and Guy Fawkes Day, were happy family times. On Christmas morning there were always presents in the stockings (Dad's grey work socks) lying on the macrocarpa branches in the dining-room fireplace, seldom the presents we asked for but welcome and exciting because they were presents and surprises; and on New Year's Eve, after the Scottish tradition, there was first-footing and a midnight feast with the laden table that promised plenty throughout the year. Then, on Guy Fawkes Night, year after year, we stood in the backyard while Dad lit the sparklers, Catherine Wheels and the one skyrocket, while we lit our penny crackers and threw our throwdowns.

At Christmas there was always the beach, Oamaru's Friendly Bay to go to, or sometimes an excursion to Timaru's Caroline Bay. And the Christmas holidays of this year had already been spent in swimming, for Miss Lindsay had unceremoniously taught me to swim by pushing me in the baths, as I had refused to submit to her usual method of teaching, which was to tie a belt around the learner's waist and haul her along by a pole attached to the belt. However great the shock of being pushed in, I was now a keen swimmer.

So we spent the days at the beach or the baths. Myrtle and Isabel were both good swimmers. Myrtle was also a good diver, and at the town baths we'd watch our favourite divers on the high or low springboards, and then Myrtle would have her turn at diving her special dives. We had discovered that the baths were a better place to watch the boys, because they were either in the water, easily observed, or stretched out on their towels at their end of the baths by the diving boards, or flexing their muscles and showing off because they knew they were being watched. When Jack Dixon started going to the baths, and we saw how pale his skin was, not at all like Errol Flynn's or Clark Gable's, Myrtle lost interest in him. 'He's weedy,' she said. Weediness was a boy's ultimate disgrace.

So, from our vantage point on the seats, we watched the boys arriving and leaving with their towels and trunks draped around their necks, and we heard their casual reference to their 'togs', whereas we arrived with our 'togs' carefully rolled in a parcel under our arm and left with them again rolled tightly, and as we went out into the street, we endured with a certain delight the way the boys flipped their towels at us in a gesture of challenge while we, our togs rolled more tightly than ever, walked haughtily on our way home.

Then, as the days moved from quiet blue January into February and another summer, they were long and hot and full of cloudy doom and weariness. I dreaded returning to school, for I needed yet another school uniform for the senior high, another tunic, dark grey serge, with a black felt hat and black beret for winter and a white panama hat for summer; grey flannel blouses and white cotton blouses as for the junior high, a white dress for the garden party at the end of the year and the school breakup in the Opera House; and a coloured girdle, the colour depending on which of the four Houses, named after the first four principals of Waitaki, we were balloted into. Fortunately, Aunty Polly had volunteered to sew my school tunic and, hoping that all would be well but dreading that it wouldn't, I waited for the parcel from Petone.

Everything that had been summer blooming was in the first stages of decay; the fluffy asters in every pastel shade were curling and browning at the ends of their petals; the cream banksia roses of the summerhouse were already shrivelled and fallen. We lay on the parched front lawn, looking up at the clouds, interpreting their shapes, asking, What do you see? What do you see?

18 Picnics

We found a friend that summer — Marguerite, who with her parents and her elder sister Noraleen and her young brother John had lately shifted to the house across the road. Marguerite overwhelmed us with her difference, her different mannerisms, speech, vocabulary, clothes, her parents, her house, even her religion, Roman Catholic, which meant that she attended a different school and was taught by nuns. A born actress, she took advantage of her *glamour*, insisting, truthfully or not, that she was really Spanish. Her beguiling certainty about everything left no room for us to doubt her. As soon as we met her, we began to replace what we now thought of as our tired unsuitable vocabulary with Marguerite's more interesting words — a writing table became an escritoire, a sofa a chesterfield, a costume an *ensemble*. Her mother had clothes, too, in contrast to our mother's wet sugar-bag aprons and torn singlet-dresses for ordinary days and the navy blue costume for paying the rent or taking Bruddie to find a cure — that costume having been bought mail order, to fit, from Glasson's Warehouse, Christchurch, and paid for at so much a week. This first venture into time payment wasn't made lightly; it was like a loss of financial virginity. With visits to the doctor and Bruddie's hospital treatment (for times when the fits would not stop) now free, we were able to buy blankets, too, on time payment and a quilt, also bedsheets for visitors. Mother subdued her uneasiness in using time payment for 'material goods' as opposed to the ordinary grocers' and butchers' bills, with the remark that we were valued customers, which indeed we must have been, for every six months a cyclostyled leaflet arrived from the firm, in the form of a letter which began, 'Dear Valued Customer . . .' And we did indeed pay our bills. We had almost paid Mrs Feather's long-standing bill.

We were relieved to find that Marguerite's mother and father also had bills. Her father had more than one suit, and in his work he didn't get covered with oil and coal on his blueys, nor did he carry a leather workbag with his lunch (salmon sandwiches or onion sandwiches), bringing home lumps of railway coal to feed the kitchen fire and railway notebooks to feed our craze for writing.

During the Easter of 1936, as a celebration of the election of a Labour Government and the possible arrival of the days described in Uncle Scrim's song,

> There's a new day in view,
> there is gold in the blue
> there is hope in the hearts of men . . .

we went for our first family holiday, on the train to Rakaia, travelling in a first-class 'bird cage' on our annual free ticket. Dad had arranged everything. A lorry carrying bales of straw met us at the station and brought us (all on the back of the lorry) along country roads and through paddocks until we came to the river bank where we pitched our bell tent. Dad put straw in one corner for our beds while Mum arranged the food, including the tin of water biscuits, near the entrance, and we fetched wood for the fire, and after the billy had been boiled, and Dad had warned us that if we touched the inside of the tent while it was raining, it would leak, Dad set out with his salmon-fishing gear — his rod and reel and new shining spoons and fishing bag — to find a salmon pool. My recollection is that we children spent all weekend exploring the gum trees, listening to the magpies, watching the hawks, avoiding the inevitable Jersey bull, eating the water biscuits, while Mum kept the fire going and made cups of tea, sitting with a wet hanky over her brow, her face glistening in the sun, her fat legs in their wide shoes stretched out, showing their sores, big red patches, blotched with Rexona ointment, green, medical-smelling, which she smeared on the sores in the hope they would vanish. She sat there reciting poetry, making up humorous rhymes about Dad and the salmon he would catch and the ones that would get away and about the time Dad and Jimmy Peneamene caught a salmon that vanished,

> One day when Jim and I went up
> to the house for a bite and sup,

*someone stole into the shed
where we were to lay our head.
Someone stole our salmon,
someone stole our salmon . . .*

Or she sat staring beyond the willows to the raging green (snow-fed, kiddies) Rakaia and talked of her 'girlhood' and its perfection.

Then, during the night, when the rain up-country made the river rise to within a few feet of our tent and we were forced to get up in the dark to move the tent to higher ground, we felt we had experienced the adventure of our lives, the kind of adventure that other children with their many holidays seemed to take for granted.

Now, having our new friend, Marguerite, we had a chance to tell again the story of our adventure, reliving the water rising, the escape, the magpies, the water biscuits (a whole tin of water biscuits!), the salmon eaten round the camp fire, crossing the bull paddock to Langley's farm for milk, all the grizzles, the laughs, and the nights lying on our bed of straw, playing games of pretend, listening to the river sound, daring each other to touch the canvas to see if what Dad had said was true and finding that it was, fighting and making up, planning, dreaming, comparing our past, our glories, our bodies; then, outside again, gathering manuka for the fire, trying to make flutes out of willow, trying to divine water, staring dreamily at the river and the swirling branches and the occasional dead sheep or cow flowing down to the sea. With Marguerite as our audience, our 'Last year we went camping to Rakaia' became 'Every year we go camping to Rakaia'.

And when Dad decided that we would go again to Rakaia these holidays and we asked Marguerite to come with us, she accepted, and once again we began our Rakaia stories, overjoyed that 'someone else', someone who lived in the usual kind of house with the usual kind of parents and family, with ordinary happenings that were not disasters or nightmares, would share the Rakaia glories. We began at once to behave like couriers, treating Marguerite as if she were about to become a tourist in a foreign land. There was some doubt at first about travelling, as the epidemic of infantile paralysis had worsened and the newspapers each day reported the mounting number of cases. There was talk of the schools being kept closed until the peak of the epidemic was over. On the other hand, Mother believed that in a tent under God's open sky, away from the crowded cities, we were out of reach of the epidemic. Also, she had faith in our health. Had she not breast-fed each of us until we were big enough to start biting her? Did we not have enough milk in our early years, with always plenty of fish to give us brains, tins of honey, vegetables from the garden, and fruit, and coarse oatmeal to keep our bowels open?

Once again at Rakaia we explored, played, ate, boasting to Marguerite, yet submitting to her foreign power, speaking her language, playing her games. Myrtle wore her grey slacks, which everyone, even Dad, accepted now, for many women had begun to wear slacks. Women smoked, too. Marguerite's mother smoked and wore make-up, this adding to Marguerite's glamour. And how we envied her mysterious life with priests and nuns and Confession and holy water.

At the end of our memorable sunburn-filled holiday Dad took our photographs with the box camera he'd bought at the auction in Wyndham, which he used when relations came and we had our photos taken at the gardens, standing on the Japanese bridge. When the photographs of Rakaia were developed, Mother gave a gasp of horror when she saw that in one of the photographs Myrtle appeared to be transparent: all except Myrtle had taken flesh and blood photographs. It made her feel afraid, Mother said, everything coming at once, the death of Grandma Godfrey, the beautiful Rakaia River, snow-fed, flashing green and blue, the Southern Alps with their autumn snow, the epidemic that filled the country with sadness and dread, and the sight of the victims who'd escaped severe paralysis, walking about with their leg irons to support them; all combined to bring to the surface the buried fear that Myrtle might die at any time.

19 A Death

The school year began. The schools were not to reopen. We were to have lessons by correspondence. My school tunic arrived from Aunty Polly. It fitted closely, with two instead of three pleats, but I was satisfied enough to let Dad take my photo to send to Aunty Polly.

As if school holidays and summer had been destined to go hand in hand, yet another summer came, with hot winds, nor'westers burning from the Canterbury Plains, copper sulphate or 'blue-stone' skies, and no place for comfort except the water, the sea, or the baths, with us going back and forth from both. And on the last Friday before the book lists and the first school lessons were to arrive, Myrtle suggested we go swimming first and then go downtown to look at the boys, but I refused, interested now in my lessons, how to get my new books without too much pleading and argument, wondering whether I'd like senior high, thinking, too, of the notebooks I would fill with poetry. Myrtle and I quarrelled about my refusal to go with her; only the quarrel was really about me as 'Dad's pet' because I'd been Dux, and I was now going to senior high, to be a teacher like Dad's Cousin Peg, who immigrated to Canada; I was entering the world that Myrtle had once shared with Joan of Arc and the Prince of Sleep, with the promise of many more wonderful characters lost; besides, Dad was cruellest to Myrtle, who was rebellious, daring, openly disobedient, always under the threat of being sent to the industrial school at Caversham, whereas I who wanted only to be 'good' and approved of, was timidly obedient except where I could deceive with a certainty of not being caught.

As a result of that afternoon quarrel, Myrtle went with Marguerite and Isabel to the baths while I stayed home, dutifully preparing myself for the new school year. It was late afternoon when someone knocked at the door, and Mother, thinking it was a salesman, opened the door, said quickly, 'Nothing today, thank you', and was about to shut the door in the man's face when he, like the stereotype of a salesman, wedged his foot in and forced his way into the kitchen, while Mother, who had told us tales of such actions, prepared herself to, in her usual phrase, 'floor him'. I was standing by the door into the dining room. The man glanced at me and said sharply, 'Send that child away.' I stayed and listened. 'I'm a doctor,' the man said, 'I've come to tell you about your daughter Myrtle. She's been drowned. They've taken her body to the morgue.'

I stared, able only to absorb the news, 'They've taken her body to the morgue.' We children had always fancied we knew which building was the morgue, a small, moss-covered stone hut down by the post office, near where the Oamaru creek rolled green and slimy over an artificial waterfall. We used to frighten one another by referring to the morgue as we passed it on our shortcut through Takaro Park toward Tyne Street and the beach, and sometimes we tried to look through the small barred window ('for air, so the bodies don't smell') to see within. The place was so small, sealed, inaccessible that we knew it must be the morgue, and when we spoke of it at home, Mother had always shown fear, which encouraged us, after the many examples from our teasing father, to repeat the word.

'Morgue, morgue.'

'Don't say that word, kiddies.'

Now, when the doctor had delivered his news and gone, Mum herself spoke the word, for it had convinced her, too, that Myrtle was dead, drowned. At first I was glad, thinking there'd be no more quarrels, crying, thrashings, with Dad trying to control her and angry with her and us listening frightened, pitying, and crying, too. Then the sad fact came home to me that there might be a prospect of peace, but the cost was the entire removal of Myrtle, not just for a holiday or next door or downtown or any-where in the world, but off the face of the earth and out of the world, a complete disappearance and not even a trial, just to see how it worked. And where would be the fun-loving, optimistic, confiding, teasing Myrtle with the scar on her knee and her grown-up monthlies, and the ambition to go to Hollywood to be a film star, to tap-dance with Fred Astaire, singing and dancing her way to fame and fortune? Where would be the Joan of Arc with her painted silver armour and helmet, the wireless performer who recited 'over the air':

> I met at eve the Prince of Sleep,
> His was a still and lovely face.

Myrtle's entire removal was stressed when she didn't come home that night to do the things she ordinarily did, to finish what she had begun in the morning, bring in the shoes cleaned with white cleaner and left to dry on the washhouse windowsill in the sun. Dad came home early and put his arms around Mum and cried, and we'd never seen him cry before. And everyone seemed to forget about Isabel, and it was quite late, almost dark, when Isabel came in, her fair hair still wet and bedraggled from swimming in the baths, her small, scared face telling everyone where she had been and what she had seen.

That night we cuddled in bed together, and as the next day passed and the next, with the grown-ups talking about inquests and coroners and undertakers and Mother naming each with a sharpness of tone that allowed them to take a share of the 'blame'; and the talk of the funeral and the mechanics of burial, I gradually acquired a new knowledge that hadn't reached me through the other deaths in the family; but this was Myrtle, her death by drowning, her funeral notice, her funeral, her flowers, her coffin, her grave; she had never had so many possessions all at once.

After the inquest, when they brought her home in her coffin into the sturmer-smelling front room and Mum asked, 'Do you want to see Myrtle?' I said no. 'We'll see her on Resurrection Day,' Mum said, conjuring once again in my mind the turmoil of Resurrection Day, the crowds, the wild scanning of faces, the panic as centuries of people confront each other and only a miracle provides room for all.

Myrtle was buried, her grave covered with wreaths from many people in Oamaru, including the swimming club where she had been a member, and some of the boys that we'd watched showing off with their muscles and their togs. And soon the rain rained on the flowers, and the ink on the cards was smudged, and the coloured ribbons frayed and rotted, and the grave itself sank until it was level with the earth. 'It always sinks, you know,' they said.

And one afternoon, when I was putting fresh flowers on Myrtle's grave and crumbling Aspros into the water in the jam jar because 'they' had said Aspros made the flowers last, I saw Miss Lindsay nearby visiting her mother's grave, Miss Lindsay of the 'jewelled sword Excalibur and the hand clothed in white samite mystic, wonderful'.

'Is Myrtle there?' Miss Lindsay asked.

I nodded.

'What are you putting in the water?'

'Aspros,' I said. Miss Lindsay's suddenly gentle tone and her ooze of understanding infuriated me.

'They won't bring her back,' she said gently.

'I know,' I said coldly, explaining the reason for the Aspros.

I had lately learned many techniques of making flowers and other things 'last', for there had suddenly been much discussion at home and amongst people who came to the house to offer their sympathy in our 'sad loss'. They were obsessed with means of preventing the decay of their 'floral tributes', of preserving the cards and ribbons. They spoke of Myrtle, too, of keeping her memory 'green'.

'And you'll have photos of her, too, Lottie,' they said to Mother (as they sat patting and arranging their 'permanent' waves). And that was so, for when we finally realised that Myrtle had really collapsed in the water and been drowned, that she was never coming home again to wear her clothes and sleep in the bed and just be there, everyone searched for recent photos and found only the 'ghost' photo taken at Rakaia and one other, with us all in our bathing suits, I with a beginning titty showing where my shoulder strap had slipped; but it was Myrtle's photo that was needed. The photographer downtown was unable to extract Myrtle entirely from that family group, although he was forced to leave behind one of Myrtle's arms that had been around Marguerite. Undaunted, the photographer fashioned for Myrtle a new photographic arm and at last presented us with a complete enlarged photo of Myrtle. Everyone said how lucky we were to have a recent photo, and only those who knew could discern the grafted arm.

20 Once Paumanok

The epidemic continued. The school sent its list of required texts and exercise books and a questionnaire about our choice of subjects. I found I could 'take' either Latin or geography, but the decision was made for me by Dad, who compared the prices of the two textbooks. 'You'll take geography,' he said.

Somehow, allowing for the goodwill of the two stationers, W. E. Adams and Jeffrey and Smith, I was able to buy on credit all the books I needed as well as an expensive item like a geometrical set. My excitement was tremendous — the new books, their colour, their smell, the algebra and geometry and arithmetic books all with *answers* at the back. To be trusted with answers to all the problems! From the secretive way the teachers always dealt with and revealed answers, I had concluded, naively, that we were taught mathematical calculations at school to collect answers, like prizes, at the end, like a quiz show; I realised now knowing how to arrive at the answer, even if the answer were wrong, was more important; also knowing how to state the question or problem. My heart swelled with a feeling of adulthood at the thought that I'd not have to ask the teacher for the correct answer to each problem. There were books of French fairy tales, too, the first of the series; *Contes et Légendes*, which touched me with its extraordinary rightness and timeliness, with the stories from *Grimm's Fairy Tales* and others revealed in another language, presenting a richness that I felt to be like receiving a fortune. There were the Shakespeare plays for study, *A Midsummer Night's Dream* with a companion volume, *Approach to Shakespeare*, a book of ancient history, and a book of poems, *Mount Helicon*.

I completed my first set of lessons, writing the inevitable 'My Adventure' composition. I began to explore the poetry book, and to my amazement I discovered that many of the poets knew about Myrtle's death and how strange it was without her. After the funeral was over the visitors had gone and my new lessons arrived, the everydayness of life had returned; yet in each day there was blankness, a Myrtle-missing part, and it was upon this blankness that the poets in Mount Helicon were writing the story of my feelings. I could scarcely believe their depth of understanding. Mother, who revered all poets, was right, as usual, and her habit of murmuring from time to time 'Only the poets know, only the poets know' was now explicable to me; I understood also why she wrote so many of her verses about poets: there was the one I had recited at school,

> He was a poet, he loved the wild thunder
> as it crashed in the Universe. Now he sleeps under,
> under the grass he loved. Stilled now his hand
> only a poet's heart could understand.
>
> He heard the whispering of the pine trees.
> Always within his heart, sweet melodies.
> Glories of morning awoke in his heart.
> He was himself of nature apart.
> Softly he slumbers. Does someone care?
> Nature showers o'er him leaves from her hair.

Mother sought the poets not necessarily for their poems but for the romantic idea of them, as if they might be a more tangible Second Coming, and when she began her familiar praise of them, Dad became jealous, as he became jealous of her references to Christ, and his jealousy always resulted in scorn.

A long poem in *Mount Helicon*, 'The Lost Mate' from *Sea Drift* by Walt Whitman told everything I was feeling — the two mocking birds, the disappearance of one, the long search by its mate, with all the false alarms and pondered might-have-beens, the anger and regret and the desperate reasoning that enlisted the help of magic, ending in the failure to find what was lost and the letting go of all hope of finding it. I understood all the deceptions of thought and feeling which tried to persuade the mourning bird that there'd been no loss, that its mate would soon be home, had simply 'gone away' for the day or had been delayed and would be home some time, 'you'll see'. I read the poem to my youngest sister, Chicks, who also understood it. She and I read the poem again and again. I was amazed that my book should contain other such poems about Myrtle — 'Annabel Lee' — 'It was many and many a year ago / In a kingdom by the sea . . .' A kingdom by the sea! Oamaru, without a doubt. Oamaru with its wild sea beyond the breakwater and the friendly bay safe within, with the sound of the sea in our ears day and night.

There was yet another poem, 'Evelyn Hope':

> Beautiful Evelyn Hope is dead!
> Sit and watch by her side an hour.
> That is her bookshelf, this her bed;

> She plucked that piece of geranium-flower,
> Beginning to die too, in the glass . . .

> Sixteen years old when she died!

What marvellous knowledge of the poets who could see through my own life, who could be appearing to write poems of people in Oamaru, which everyone knew was halfway between the equator and the South Pole, forty-five degrees south, and which yet was not nearly so well known as Auckland or Wellington or Sydney or London or Paris, any cities in the Northern Hemisphere where many of the poets (who were dead) had lived! Another poem, beginning, 'The pines were dark on Ramoth Hill', told how,

> my playmate left her home
> and took with her the laughing spring
> the music and the bloom . . .

Ramoth Hill? Surely that was the poet's way of writing of the Hill, our hill, and the pine plantations, the plannies?

> And still the pines of Ramoth Wood
> are moaning like the sea,
> the moaning of the sea of change . . .

I understood that the poets, of course, invented many details, changing names and so on, as Poppy and I had called Hoppityou by *our* name for him and not by his real name; I knew that the poets had *woods* where we had *bush* and their pine woods were our plannies. They were also inclined to exaggerate goodness and beauty, for Myrtle was not really beautiful nor was she 'my darling'; she had just been my teasing, pinching, thumping elder sister who knew more than I and who would some day have made music, boys, clothes, love, a mansion — all the fruits of the Hollywood Big Time.

The epidemic over, the schools reopened, and I set out to Waitaki Girls Senior High, wearing my new uniform but discarding for home use only the blazer that Aunty Polly had sewn the wrong colour. The schools were so particular about our having the correct uniform, and anything that made one's appearance different from the others was a cause for alarm and worry. We had to be in step always, just as in the early days of Miss Lindsay when she marched us into school with her intoned orders, 'Toes meet the floor first, toes meet the floor first . . .', when any girl's faltering or misplacement of foot brought her a sharp rebuke.

Our third-form class was small, with eighteen girls, and as we brought a reputation for verse speaking and for being a 'bright' class, the headmistress, Jessie Banks Wilson (known as J.B.) engaged a special elocution teacher to continue our verse speaking. Miss H. was young, pretty, with black hair and rosy cheeks; she was 'soft' and a target for mischief. The poems she taught us were, I felt, less distinguished than the elocutionary exercises accompanying them — 'Three tired toads trying to trot to Tilbury Towers . . . Round the rugged rocks the ragged rascal ran . . . Peter piper picked a peck . . .'

> Mumble and Mutter are muddlesome men
> making mistakes again and again.
> Three grey geese in the greenfield grazing,
> Grey were the geese and green was the grazing . . .

So we chanted our way through our 'set' pieces — The Pipes of Pan, Tarantella, The River (Clear and Cool), none as haunting as Miss Lindsay's 'hand clothed in white samite mystic, wonderful', 'Bright is the ring of words when the right man rings them . . . I met at eve the Prince of Sleep . . .' Myrtle's poem.

The poetry was memorable for the French fairy tales, for the poetry, for new music, and the study of ancient history, tales of people, cities, animals, birds, insects, that were now vanished 'from the face of the earth'. Once again I called to mind Mother's teaching of creatures extinct and civilisations buried beneath land and sea, and how when we brought home the fossilised shells from the caves on the hill, she had reminded us that Oamaru had once been beneath the sea. This change in civilisation and land and sea forms pointed for her toward the 'latter days' and the time when not only the past would be changed. I sat in the ancient history class, dreaming my dreams of the Sumerians, how they lived, what they wore, the Phoenicians, the Tyrian traders, half listening as Miss Hall, our form and history teacher, a fair, transparent person with a custard kind of personality and hair that was pale brown with the light showing through it, taught us from our book of ancient history.

I found solace in such learning of all those new worlds, of changes in the past; I felt able to observe more clearly the present changes in our home since Myrtle's death, the new fearfulness shown by my father, not in keeping with his usual forcefulness and dominance of the household. Although he did complain when we girls asked for clothes that we could not have, as our school tunics had to be worn in and out of school, he was no longer angry with our demands, even with our 'Other girls wear ordinary clothes at home', which he ignored or countered with 'Do you have to do everything the other girls do?' Instead, he began to concentrate his anger and disappointment upon our brother, who had somehow missed the mellowing, for Dad still believed that in some way Bruddie's epilepsy was Bruddie's 'fault', that he could stop it if he had more control over himself. Dad now turned to him, mocking and scorning him, criticising his every move while Mother, on Bruddie's 'side', tried to explain, but the explanation failing, reverted to biblical quotes, 'Blessed are the peacemakers for they shall be called the children of God.' 'Although I speak with the tongues of men and of angels and have not *charity . . .*'

Another world new to me was that of the kind of music I had not known before, introduced to me by the songs in our Dominion Song Books and by one of the girls in the class. Her name was Shirley Grave, and I first became aware of her through the teachers' complaints about her lack of order, her absentmindedness, which were apparently balanced by her imagination. 'Shirley has imagination. She writes poetry.' 'What a dreamer you are, Shirley! Always lost in your poetic world of imagination!'

I looked with interest and envy at this girl who had the poetic attributes I longed for. I wanted to be a poet, and I knew that poets must be imaginative, dream great dreams. No one had ever called me imaginative or poetic, for I was a practical person, even writing poems which were practical, with most never failing to mention some new fact I had learned or giving lists of people, places, colours. For example, my poem about Scott's expedition read,

> *Oats Evans Bowers Wilson and Scott*
> *by the word forgotten not . . .*

For all my ambition, no one could have called me a poet!

Also, I was clever at mathematics and enjoyed working out problems, whereas the 'Shirley has imagination . . . What a dreamer' comment was usually made when Shirley became confused over a mathematical problem.

Then, at the music festival, Shirley sang 'To Music', from our Dominion Song Book.

> *Thou holy art in many hours of sadness*
> *when life's hard toil my spirit hath oppressed . . .*

I felt that I had never heard such a beautiful song, both in the piano accompaniment and the words. I learned at the festival that Shirley also played the piano, that only three girls in the class did not study the piano. And then, to make perfect Shirley's enviable endowment, her father died, and while Shirley was absent, the teacher told us about the death and reminded us to be kind to Shirley because her father had died.

I was overcome with envy and longing. Shirley had everything a poet needed plus the tragedy of a dead father. How could I ever be a poet when I was practical, never absentminded, I liked mathematics, and my parents were alive? Well, I thought, if I can't be the necessary dreamer, I can at least pretend, and so I wrote a poem about dreams, believing that if I used the word *dream* repeatedly in some way I would be creating dreams.

> *I dream of misty hills at dawn*
> *I dream of skies when it is morn . . .*

How could anyone, reading those lines, deny I was a dreamer?

I sent my poem to Skipper of 3YA, who unexpectedly gave it a prize in a poetry competition. My poem was read over the wireless, and because I was genuinely surprised that it was judged to be good, I supposed that the word *dream* had had its effect; therefore in future poems I used the word *dream*, particularly as I now noticed that most of the poets were using it, perhaps engineering the same deception. 'Tread softly lest you tread on my dreams . . . We are the musicmakers, we are the dreamers of dreams . . . They have their dreams and do not think of us . . .'

I began to collect other words labelled 'poetic' — *stars, grey, soft, deep, shadowy, little, flowers* . . . some having begun as my words in my poem but being used, in the end, because they were the words of 'poetry', and because poetry emphasised what was romantic (dim, ineffable, little, old, grey) I felt that I was well on the way to becoming and being known as 'poetic and imaginative', although I was wretchedly conscious that I had none of the disability esteemed in poets: I had not even a parent dead. There had been Myrtle's death, of course, and in the poetry lessons her name was often mentioned, 'Yet once more ye laurels and once more ye Myrtles . . .', written of a drowning, too . . . and hearing the name in class sent such a piercing shock through me that I clenched my toes and gripped my hands on the lid of my desk to stop myself from bursting into tears. Somehow, Myrtle's death did not really 'qualify'; it was too much within me and a part of me, and I could not look at it and say *dreamily, poetically*, 'Ah, there's a tragedy. All poets have had tragic lives.'

My brother's illness did not 'qualify' either; it was too present. No one seemed to be able to accept it as possible. Mother still talked of 'when you grow out of it, Bruddie'. He educated himself with books that I brought home from the library and from the many books, originally from the library but now marked *Cancelled*, that he found in the town rubbish dump and brought home on his trolley. There was little hope of a job for him, for when he did find one, someone would disclose that he had epilepsy, and he'd be dismissed. 'They found out about me, Mum,' he'd say bitterly.

My father concentrated his attention more and more on the 'abilities' of his daughters. Each day, when I came home from school, he'd say, slightly in jest, mostly in earnest, 'Were you top of the class today? Who did you beat today?' He learned the names of our 'rivals' at school and would ask, 'Well, did you beat M. or S. or T. today?'

This attitude was not unusual; it prevailed in the classroom among the 'top' girls, who were forever comparing notes and answers and marks. The competitive spirit flourished throughout the school, and if you were near the 'top' as I, to my surprise, found myself, you lived in glory and privilege, whereas if you were among the 'rest', you suffered constant sarcasm from the teachers. A selection of four or five girls, who were not, however, among the top scholars, maintained a concentration of power and privilege through sheer personality and so were less likely to suffer the taunts directed at the slower pupils. This group was the core of the class, with their activities at home and at school the source of most of the class interest and news; the rest of us moved on the outside in more or less distant concentric circles, looking toward the group whose power, in effect, surpassed even the glory of the scholars who, after all, were sometimes known contemptuously as 'swots'.

On the rim of the farthest circle from the group which was my usual place, I found myself with a tall, asthmatic girl, Shirley's friend, who talked constantly of her brothers at university, quoting them incessantly, with their quotes being chiefly from Karl Marx. Karl Marx says this; Karl Marx says that . . . I sat with this girl for lunch while she explained communism and talked of Karl Marx while I looked with envy toward the place where the group sat, eagerly talking, shaking with laughter as they recounted what *Mummy* and *Daddy* had said and done during the weekend at the *crib* by the sea. The power and happiness flowing from them were almost visible as they talked. Their lives overshadowed the lives of the rest of the class; even Karl Marx was no match for them. Their families were happier, funnier, more exciting, than any others; and they all lived on the fabled *South Hill*. Even the teachers could not resist them, giving them regularly parts in class play-reading while we others watched and listened enviously. It was they who travelled on the Golden Road to Samarkand, who lived through *A Midsummer Night's Dream* and the *Merchant of Venice*; Portia, Titania, Puck, were among them while the rest of us had to be content with playing

Mary Frame (née Paterson), born on 7 September 1857 in Paisley, Scotland; and Alexander Frame, born on 4 November 1855 in Hamilton, Scotland. They were married on 11 May 1877.

Grandad and Grandma Frame.

Alfred Godfrey, Picton.

Mother at Picton before her marriage.

Above: *George Samuel Frame (Dad) aged about 18, before the First World War.*

Above left: *Dad (left) at Taumaranui where he was working to lay the railway in the early 1900s.*

Left: *Dad as a soldier, First World War.*

Aunty Isy and Aunty Polly, Dad's sisters, in the second row.

Ravensbourne Association Football Club, 1911 (Dad second from left in the back row).

Grandma Frame and Mother.

Dad as a young man returned from the war.

Granny Frame in her wheelchair, and Uncle Charlie.

Alex Frame's taxi at Uxbridge Railway Siding Station on the Kurow line in the 1920s.

Aunty Isy with Myrtle, early 1920s.

Grandad Frame with Myrtle and Bruddie in the early 1920s at Outram.

Dad and Uncle Charlie with the car, early 1920s.

Dad with Myrtle and Bruddie, at Outram in about 1923.

Aunty Isy with Myrtle and Bruddie at Outram in about 1923.

*Myself as babe-in-arms under the walnut tree with Mother,
Myrtle and Bruddie at Outram.*

Myself sitting on the grass.

Myself exploring in Outram.

Bruddie and Myrtle, with me as a baby, sheltering my eyes with my arm.

Myrtle, Bruddie, Isabel, June and myself (looking at Myrtle), Wyndham.

Mother at Wyndham with baby June and cows, about 1929.

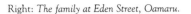

Right: *The family at Eden Street, Oamaru.*

Below: *Myrtle, myself, Isabel and June in our new dresses with puffed sleeves, at the Oamaru Gardens when Aunt Polly came to stay.*

Form 1B, Waitaki Girls Junior High School (myself second from left, second row).

Form 5B, Waitaki Girls High School (myself second from right, second row).

Myself in new school uniform, 1937.

Mother, June, Marguerite and Bruddie
at Rakaia in March 1937.

The family with Marguerite at Rakaia.

The family at Rakaia, just before Myrtle's death (1937). Myrtle,
Marguerite Miller, June, Isabel, myself (with titty showing), and
Bruddie in the back row.

Dad, the day of Myrtle's funeral.

Myrtle with her 'constructed' arm.

Myself and Isabel with Mac, Eden Street.

lone fairies or first, second or third voices offstage.

At the end of the year I was given a prize, *Boys and Girls Who Became Famous*, which I and my sisters and brother read eagerly during the holidays. We came to know and love the story of the Brontës — the bleak setting of the Yorkshire Moors, the parsonage, the churchyard. We felt close to the self-contained family with the 'wild' brother, the far-off parents going about their daily tasks, the Brontës with their moors, us with our hill and gully and pine plantations. They knew death in their family, as we had, and their lives were so much more tragic than our life which, in spite of everything, was predominantly joyful, that we could give them, thankfully, the sad feelings which sometimes overcame us, and giving our feelings to the Brontës was a much more satisfying exercise than offering them to Jeanette MacDonald and Nelson Eddy, the current 'stars' with their fulsome musical pleas of

> *Sweetheart sweetheart sweetheart*
> *will you love me ever . . .*

Even my cherished cowboy songs and sad poems ('The dog at his master's grave') could not receive what we gave to the Brontës and what I now gave to the newly discovered music ('Thou holy art in many hours of sadness').

I felt that I was no longer the mourning bird of 'Once Paumanok'. I felt that life was very serious now. I thought sometimes, with curiosity and apprehension, about the state known as the future.

21 The Hungry Generations

Some time during that year I had a brief meeting with Poppy, now also at senior high school, taking her commercial course. The word *commercial* aroused so much horror in me that I could scarcely believe in Poppy's survival. If I walked beneath the windows of the classroom where the 'commercial girls' did their work, I could hear the sound of their typewriters and imagine the doom waiting for them.

I met Poppy near the corner of Glen Street by the bank of ice plant where years ago we had squeezed the juice out of the ridged stalks to magic away the warts on our hands. The forbidding of our friendship, the absolute, even proud, acceptance of our parents' ruling, and our completely separate lives since then, gave us a special, distant interest in each other's life now, and when Poppy repeated in a matter-of-fact way, 'You know I'm taking commercial', I felt a snobbish sense of betrayal, for *everyone* knew that *commercial* girls were a little beneath *professional* girls, and I did not want Poppy to be despised.

'Yes, I'm doing shorthand, typing, double-entry bookkeeping.'

How could she!

'Do you like commercial?' I asked politely.

'So many grammalogues,' Poppy said.

I did not know of grammalogues.

'We're learning grammalogues all the time.'

'Oh. Are you?'

There was a resigned air, a seriousness about our meeting. We could have been two soldiers on a battlefield, exchanging notes about our possibility of survival. The seriousness was somehow accentuated by our dark grey serge tunics, the mark of *Seniors*. The woven girdle around Poppy's tunic was red, the colour for Burn House; mine was green, for Gibson. We stared at each other, noting these facts.

Then, suddenly, Poppy seemed to come to life, the same old Poppy who defiantly insisted that other people's flowers growing through the fence belonged to us, we had a right to 'cadge' them, the Poppy who showed me geraniums, their stain and smell, the Grimm's Fairy Tales Poppy.

'We're having "Ode to a Nightingale",' she said. 'It's in our *Mount Helicon*.'

I'd not read 'Ode to a Nightingale', my dislike having been aroused by a poet who could go into such boring detail about his feelings as to say, 'My heart aches, and a drowsy numbness pains / My sense . . .'

'We have to learn some verses,' Poppy said, beginning to recite,

> *Thou wast not born for death, Immortal Bird!*
> *No hungry generations tread thee down;*
> *The voice I hear this passing night was heard*
> *In ancient days by Emperor and clown:*
> *Perhaps the self-same song that found a path*
> *through the sad heart of Ruth, when, sick for home,*
> *She stood in tears amid the alien corn;*
> *The same that oft-times hath*
> *Charmed magic casements, opening on the foam*
> *Of perilous seas in faery lands forlorn.*

Poppy's recitation took me by surprise. She spoke with passionate intimacy as if the poem were directly related to her, as if it were a milestone in her own life. She'd given me so much all those years ago, and now, at Glen Street corner, near the bank of ice plant, she seemed to be making, reluctantly, her declaration of withdrawal from childhood, even in the way she appeared to accept Keats's description of all our lovely fairylands as 'forlorn'. The inner noise and desperation of 'No hungry generations tread thee down' haunted me, though I scarcely understood it; the words swept out of Poppy like a cry of panic. Why? The poem seemed to be so unrelated to her, the 'commercial girl' with the shorthand-typing and double-entry bookkeeping; yet she had proclaimed the poem and its contents to be her very own.

Her recitation had the reality of a precious parting gift that I did not know how to take because I could not understand it. In my ignorance, not even familiar with the biblical story of Ruth, I thought only of a girl at school, Ruth, who had left school early to have a baby; and having no experience of nightingales, my Eden Street having been filled night and morning with the moaning and cooing of the pigeons of Glen Street, and with the chattering of the flocks of goldfinches that haunted our garden, I felt the reality only of those 'hungry generations', the perilous seas, and the faery lands forlorn.

'We're learning it by heart,' Poppy said again, breaking the spell.

'We haven't had it yet,' I said, talking, as we did, of literary works as if they were a disease.

'I must go,' Poppy said.

We said goodbye. I never talked to her again. I heard that she left school at the end of that year and soon married and settled in one of the coastal towns of Otago.

22   The Kingdom by the Sea

The summer holidays convinced me that Myrtle had really vanished forever. Almost every Sunday during the year we had visited her grave, which was now just another grave among graves with dandelion, dock, chickweed, beginning to grow there. We stopped going to the cemetery. Myrtle was gone. The days of *Secret Confessions*, *True Story*, *True Romance*, the violent quarrels, had rushed by, and I, now the eldest girl who was going to be a schoolteacher like Cousin Peg, who emigrated from Scotland to Canada, did my best to smooth the surface of life, to be, in a sense, invisible, to conceal all in myself that might attract disapproval or anger. I had no close girlfriends at school and no boyfriends. I looked on Marguerite as I looked on Poppy — from a distance as part of the past and another life, and high school with its prospect of years of study, homework, examinations, gave me a new, serious life without play. I still belonged to the Athenaeum and Mechanics Institute, having read through all the books in the juvenile library but not yet eligible to begin on the adult section. Reminding the family that I would soon be in the fourth form with more study and homework, I was allowed to shift into the front room, where before only the dead and guests had slept, with the Sturmer apples in the corner, far enough from the kitchen to stifle my ears to the arguments beginning to centre now on my brother, who was about fifteen and had discovered the billiard room downtown, the equivalent in those days of a fun parlour, looked on as a den of vice.

We girls usually spent the evening doing homework, writing or listening to the wireless — Dad and Dave of Snake Gully, Fred and Maggie Everybody, The Japanese Houseboy, the quiz shows, Parliament in session, and the hour-long Inspector Scott of Scotland Yard with its ritual ending, 'All right, take him away', and titles such as 'The Case of the Hooting Owl', 'The Case of the Nabob of Blackmere'. We were also enthusiastic listeners to the children's sessions — Big Brother Bill of 4YA with his nature session and Skipper of 3YA with the serial, 'David and Dawn in Fairyland', introduced by a music which we always wished would last and which we thought of as 'David and Dawn' but which I learned a few years later was 'The Dance of the Flowers' from *The Nutcracker Suite*. We still had dreams of performing — singing, dancing, playing some musical instrument; we still haunted the local competitions, gaining admission to a cheap afternoon session and desperately trying to memorise the steps of the dances so that we might practise them at home. We wrote regularly also to *Dot's Little Folk*, with Monday morning full of excitement for me as I cycled down on Dad's bike to buy the meat and the paper (sixpence worth the skirt steak, twopence worth mince and the paper), and when I'd bought the paper, I'd sneak a glance inside the back page to see our letters or poems and Dot's remarks.

The school year began once again, and once again I had a small bursary of five pounds, which helped in the buying of books. There were the usual worries about money and an increasing worry for me about my school tunic, which was now too tight over my growing breasts but which had to last me until I left school. And there was a feeling of being nowhere, not being able to talk about life at home, and seeing the apparent confidence and happiness of the other girls in the class, particularly those in the Group, all of whom returned to school. One or two had left school, including Shirley, whose widowed mother, it was said, could not afford another year for her. When I heard that Shirley ('To Music Thou holy art in many hours of sadness, / When Life's hard toil my spirit hath oppressed . . .') was working at the Polytechnic or Bulleids or some place like that selling 'notions' — ribbons, laces, cotton (Clarks Stranded), crewel needles, I felt a dreariness and a sense of waste: Poppy taking 'commercial', Shirley working in a shop, like a repetition of 'Old Grey Squirrel':

> They caught him, and they caged him, like a squirrel.
> He is totting up accounts, and going grey.

What about the 'hungry generations'? And the practice of the 'holy art in many hours of sadness . . .'?

I realised that I *was* a dreamer simply because everywhere reality appeared to be so sordid and wasteful, exposing dreams year by year to relentless decay.

Once again my memory of the year, with Miss Gibson as our form teacher, is of the delights of French and English literature and the excitement and formality of the mathematical problems and the geometry theorems: Given to Prove. Construction. Proof. Conclusion. We were again a small class, with another larger professional fourth form separated from us by the double doors that were opened for English lessons and occasional mathematics and French. The room was the old assembly hall with the honours board and the lists of war dead. The large 4B class, most of whom, unlike us, with our years at junior high, came directly from country schools or — a crime in Miss Gibson's eyes — were 'bus' girls or boarders, became the target of Miss Gibson's (or Gibby's) sarcasm, while we, 4A, sat smugly nurturing our feelings of superiority.

Our class still contained the Group, now rulers of the Fourth, able to impose upon the rest of the class their taste in dress, manners, leisure activities, films, books, and their opinions on all topics. I used to observe them closely, fascinated by their power. All were neatly dressed with correct complete school uniform, even those items that were optional and that few of the others could afford. There was P., chubby, freckled, a natural comic who held the attention of all at lunchtime when she recounted those adventures at the weekend crib with Mummy and Daddy. Her father was an auctioneer. There was M., small, dark, an accomplished pianist (her mother was a music teacher), a writer of nobly patriotic essays, a generous, thoughtful girl invariably voted the most popular in the class. Her father was also an auctioneer and from time to time mayor of Oamaru. Then there was B. (her father, too, an auctioneer), an accomplished dancer who won many prizes at local and national competitions, a champion runner, too, and 'good-looking' in the accepted style of the time. The artist of the group was L., a pretty, dark-haired girl, whose father was a carpenter and who always won the art prize. The last member was J., another comic, thin, known affectionately as 'Skinny', awkward, intelligent, with a sharp imagination that was not always appreciated and of which the teachers were often unaware. She was, in the accepted sense, ugly.

Apart from the Group but at times moving within it in a kind of fourth-form dance, were J. and M., who was also an accomplished pianist with depth and stillness in her playing. She was small, and like most of the others, 'pretty'. Somewhere, at some time, I had been infected with a snobbishness that caused me to wonder why L., whose father was 'only a carpenter', became part of the Group. The occupation of one's father did matter, in the class and in the school, and it was possible to survive and flourish on an accumulation of the resulting prestige of having an illustrious father (mayor, councillor, doctor, dentist) or a relation who was such or (as in the case of one of the girls) having a double helping — W.'s father was manager of the woollen mills and her cousin was a teacher at Waitaki!

I remained part of the small group of 'scholars', who compared their answers to problems and often worked ahead of the others on extra mathematics. The brightest of our group was usually W. (her father, the manager of the woollen mills), who lived beside the school and had a large doll's house on her front lawn. W. was advanced in reading, too, having read all the children's classics — *Alice in Wonderland*, Kipling's *Jungle Books*, *Toad of Toad Hall*, and she knew the answers to questions that we thought obscure and unanswerable, such as quotes from poems we had not read or heard of. She was the girl to whom my father referred when he said to me, 'Well, did you beat W. today?'

I longed to be close to my father. Sometimes he still asked me, 'How did the sheep look at you?' and dutifully, after all those years, I'd hide my face and put on my 'sheep look' as a way of sharing painlessly with my father. I shared the crosswords, too, and the quiz sessions and the detective stories that he had begun to bring home — small square books, in appearance like the 'love' and the 'boarding school' and the 'Westerns' that we girls read now and again. These were the *Sexton Blake Library*. I despised the way they were written; yet I kept my criticism to myself, dutifully reading each new volume.

'I read the latest Sexton Blake,' I'd say to Dad. 'It's pretty good.'

Dad would answer (the gratitude in his eyes made me pity him), 'Well, it was so-so. I'll bring home some more in the weekend.' I felt, now, that I could see through my father's feelings, and the tragedy I thought I perceived filled me with sadness. When Mum happened to say, 'Both Jean and her father like reading those detective books', I felt an inordinate pride and gratitude.

And while I read 'Sexton Blakes' at home and study books and other books from the library, the Group was reading Rafael Sabatini, Nordhoff and Hall (*Mutiny on the Bounty* books), Georgette Heyer (*These Old Shades*), all of which I refused to read because my choice of reading was my area of rebellion against the dominance of the Group. When they read a book, they embraced it utterly, talked of it, analysed it, and soon the whole class was reading it. The themes of their current reading did not interest me, for the love of physical adventure that I'd so much cherished in my early reading, had vanished, and the duels and knights and costume books and films bored me: my swashbuckling days were over. I did condescend to read the Anne books of L. M. Montgomery and enjoyed them, especially the references to Anne's 'imagination'. So that was how one should be if one wished to be 'imaginative' — the Shirley Grave characteristics again — dreamy, poetic. In spite of my longing, I remained uncomfortably present within the word of fact, more literal than imaginative. I wanted an imagination that would inhabit a world of fact, descend like a shining light upon the ordinary life of Eden Street, and not force me to exist in an 'elsewhere'. I wanted the light to shine upon the pigeons of Glen Street, the plum trees in our garden, the two japonica bushes (one red, one yellow), our pine plantations and gully, our summer house, our lives, and our home, the world of Oamaru, the kingdom by the sea. I refused to accept that if I were to fulfil my secret ambition to be a poet, I should spend my imaginative life among the nightingales instead of among the wax-eyes and the fantails. I wanted my life to be the 'other world'. I thought often, gratefully, of the generous poets who had entered my world to write about Myrtle and our kingdom by the sea, mixing fact and fantasy in a poetic way that only made more vivid the events in Oamaru — 'sixteen years old when she died', 'this was her bookshelf, this her bed . . .' That was indeed Myrtle, 'in her sixteenth year' as the obituary notices said. As for her 'bookshelf and bed', that was indeed fantasy, for we girls slept all together top and tail in one bed, and the only bookshelf in the house was the one in the kitchen with Oscar Wilde, the dictionary, the Bible, God's Book, the Zane Grey Westerns, a book for children published by a tract society, *Stepping Heavenward*; *We are Seven*, which I always thought was meant to be our life story, for our family numbered seven; *The Last Days of Pompeii*; *The Vats of Tyre*; *To Pay the Price*;

From Jest to Earnest. John Halifax, Gentleman. Dr Chase's Book of Household Recipes . . .

And just as I was inclined to submit to the Group's judgment in matters that they had experience of and I didn't — clothes, social life, dancing — I felt I had to submit to the poets in their conventions, their choice of words, and so I continued to write my verses replete with their dreams, dawns, and little old men with grey faces.

That year, also, I discovered the Ancient Mariner. One morning Miss Gibson came into the classroom and without any preliminary discussion sat at her table, opened a book, said in her 'announcing' voice, '"The Rhyme of the Ancient Mariner" by Samuel Taylor Coleridge' and began to read. She read the entire poem and said, 'Write an essay on the Ancient Mariner for next week', then left the room. The lesson was over.

I had not known of the Ancient Mariner, and while Miss Gibson was reading, I listened, only half understanding, to the story of the grim journey; and all else vanishing, I, too, was alone on the sea, living the living death, feeling the nearness of a seascape that was part of Oamaru. The sighting of the albatross was at the same time a farewell to the nightingales, for although I had never seen an albatross, Mother had talked of them and in our days at Fortrose and Waipapa she had sometimes pointed to distant seabirds and murmured, 'They may be albatrosses, kiddies.'

I did not comprehend the curse and the blessing of the mariner, only the journey and the suffering, and when in the last stanza Miss Gibson adopted her familiar preaching tone to read, 'He prayeth best who loveth best', I resented her intrusion and the intrusion of the land and the land-scape and the reduction of the mariner, seen through land-focusing eyes, from a man of mysterious grandeur even in guilt to a 'grey-beard loon'.

All that day I lived within the dream of the Ancient Mariner, a massive, inescapable dream that Miss Gibson had thrust upon us without explanation or apology, a 'pure' dream of that time on the sea in the embrace of weather that existed of itself without reference to people or creatures and their everyday lives of church, wedding guests, long-drawn-out tales. And of school, studying, playing basketball, swimming, writing poetry. And of milking cows.

For it was partly with the halcyon memory of the 'perfect' days 'before we shifted to Oamaru' and partly for the practical reason of supplying a growing family of people and cats with milk that Dad bought a cow from Luxons.

23   Scrapers and Bluey

The cow, a Jersey with big bones that suggested she might be a Jersey-Ayrshire cross and long, inward-curving horns, was already named Scrapers after her habit of scraping her hooves on the concrete floor of the byre. I found myself recruited to milk her as Dad would be too busy at work, Mum also was too busy, Isabel and June were too small, Bruddie too often sick. Nevertheless, June and Bruddie had learned to milk in case they might be called on to help. Scrapers was to be grazed on the reserve for a small fee, the reserve including all the pine plantations and the hill as far as the north end of town, which meant a long walk to find her, and so I formed the habit of taking Winkles, my cat, on my walk. Myrtle's black, fluffy cat, Big Puss, whose fur, like Old Cat's before her, now had a brown tinge of age and wear and tear, had given each of us our pet cat, each of a different colour. Winkles was striped grey, named Winkles after her habit of blinking her eyes at me after one of those prolonged stares that cats like to direct at people.

Sometimes I'd milk Scrapers where she stood on the hill. Other times I'd bring her down to the small byre at the end of the garden, opening onto the bull paddock with a gate made from one end of Grandad's old iron bedstead. As I led Scrapers through from the reserve to the bull paddock, I'd put a rope over her horns and walk in front, and when we came to the creek, I'd jump across and, pulling at the rope, try to persuade Scrapers to jump the creek. To my surprise, she readily accepted the routine but once or twice Winkles, in her eagerness, leapt into the creek, whereupon, again to my surprise, she swam strongly to the bank and climbed out. Then, when I had milked Scrapers, I'd return her to the hill and walk with Winkles to the top of the hill and, Winkles having now jumped onto my shoulder, I'd stare down at the familiar kingdom by the sea, listening to the waves crashing over the breakwater, seeing again Cape Wanbrow with its dark mass of pines and the ramble of buildings that were the Victoria Old People's Home, the town clock, the flour mill, the creek, the morgue, Thames Street, Reed Street, the Railway Station, the Engine Sheds, and, far out the North Road by the Boys' High, the tall chimney of the woollen mills. As I looked out at Oamaru, I'd compose a poem to write in my notebook later.

Now, at home, there was once again the sound of the separator being turned in the kitchen with the milk and cream spurting from their separate funnels into their separate bowls, grinding of the wooden churn, the wood smooth and mellow with use, Mother singing as she patted the butter into shape with the ribbed butter pats and, as she 'scalded' the separator to clean it, intoning the word *scald* with an urgency, a hint of injury that she could not erase from its use in order to describe even a harmless act. There was milk to spare, a warmth of half-remembered infancy in the full, frothing-over bucket. This conscious attempt to recreate the 'old days' failed for me, because my 'old days' in Wyndham were of my being known as a thief, and I was thankful to escape, and because I was too much aware now of the present reality of my morning thorn-scratched school stockings, my milk-and-mud-splattered tunic and shoes, the sleepy dust in my morning eyes, the rush to get to school in time for assembly at nine o'clock, and the know-ledge that after school I must go again in search of Scrapers. Even so, I knew that my time spent fetching, milking and returning Scrapers and the pre-cious moments gazing down at the kingdom by the sea, with Winkles rocking on her uneasy claw hold, my shoulder, were happy times as I was alone with my thoughts and my poetic dreams.

There were some days, however, when I was humiliated by not being able to understand the actions of Scrapers. I had no knowledge of the sexual life of cows, only that cows and bulls 'did it' standing up. Also, I had long ago closed my mind and forgotten all I had learned years ago about the workings of sex. Therefore, when Scrapers on some days began to dance around the paddock, refusing to let the rope be thrown over her horns, sometimes turning on me with horns lowered as if in anger, I felt sad that I was failing in my role as a milkmaid, for normally Scrapers and I were friends, and I was proud of the way she allowed me to milk her without a leg rope, anywhere on the hill, without her moving or putting her foot in the bucket. There was no answer at home to my confusion, for when I men-tioned Scraper's strange behaviour, Mother said casually, 'Leave her. I'll get Mr Luxon to take her.'

Apparently Mr Luxon had a bull 'out Weston way', and so Scrapers would be taken to Weston, returning a few days later as her former placid self, and when eventually a calf was born, I was unable to understand the mutilation performed on the bull calves when they were a few months old and we, who had been feeding them, had grown fond of them. The operation was usually done at night, in secrecy, by a strange man who hur-ried away, leaving the bull calf hot-nosed and bleeding between its back legs. There was an element of ugliness, brutality, unhappiness, in the deed and in the casual way my parents answered my questions. I half knew and half didn't know. I knew that if Myrtle had been alive, she would have told me honestly with her mixture of fact and rumour, 'They've cut its things off so it won't be a wild bull.'

The scar was on its balls: I could see it. And, for the life of me, I didn't know what balls were for, except perhaps to hold 'spunk'. I knew that the bull calf now became a bullock, growing to a different shape from a bull standing heavy and deep in the grass, more resembling a cow but with shrivelled balls and a tiny, dangling thing.

The air of pretence about the matter infuriated me. I was usually left with the thought that a strange man had deliberately wounded our little bull calf, which we'd fed almost from the time it was born, putting our hand in its mouth and saying, 'Sook, sook, sook' to get it to start sucking, first in the bucket of yellow milk, then after a few weeks, of skim milk; that he'd deliberately wounded it and no one cared, not even our mother, only my sisters and I, because my brother already knew about the secret, and nobody was telling.

It was a different story with a heifer, an unexpected bonus because she could be sold. One, a pretty blue colour, we decided to keep; and because she was a family animal, we could not call her any of the fancy names we were beginning to call any kittens that were not drowned at birth: the new calf was to be known as Bluey. Scrapers and Bluey. Scrapers and Bluey grazing there in the heartlands of my poetic world.

24 *Faust and the Piano*

There were few occasions when I earned money. In my primary school days, when I won a prize for a composition on 'My Visit to the Flour Mill', I, influenced chiefly by the old schoolbooks and stories praising a mother's love, bought Mum a cup, saucer and plate, Royal Doulton, on the advice of Mr Burton in the hardware and china shop. I also won small prizes for handwriting in the annual Agricultural and Pastoral Show, but none, to my disappointment, for my exhibits in the flower-arrangement class where year after year I entered the section Gent's Buttonhole and once, daringly, the Miniature Garden. I had recently written a poem for the *Railway Magazine* for which I received one guinea. The poem, later included in Tom Mills's anthology of verse by New Zealand children, was my usual factual account of the natural world:

On wintry mornings such as these
when crystals decorate the trees
when mists hang low upon the hill
and frost is patterned on the sill . . .

After my introduction to the 'new' kind of music of the Schubert, Handel, and Mozart songs and the yearning to be able to play such music, I decided to use my guinea to pay for a term of piano lessons from Jessie C., who lived further up Eden Street with her mother and a white parrot in a spacious house, and who had offered to teach me music at a reduced rate, letting me practise on her piano, as we had none. Aunty Mima, the wife of Uncle Alex, the taxi driver, who lived on the South Hill and who had a piano, offered also to let me practise there in the weekends.

I confess that part of my joy at the prospect of learning music came from knowing that during the term when the teacher made her usual list of those pupils who 'learned' such things as dancing, music, elocution, I would at last be able to include my name, which had always been one of the two or three that, to their shame, 'learned' nothing.

Jessie C. was a small fair fluffy kind of person, perhaps in her thirties, a quiet contrast to her mother, who was known as the town gossip, for she and her parrot were able to glean facts and rumours that no one else knew. We could hear her parrot screeching during the day, when we'd say to one another, 'There's Ma discussing the latest with her parrot.' No one had ever seen or heard of a Mr C., and it was impossible to imagine one.

On my first visit to the house, Jessie showed me the piano in a carpeted, upholstered room full of knick-knacks and patterns of roses, a cherished room as if a mother had lavished her love upon it as upon her children — well fed, face polished, warmly dressed with the black wood of the piano shining and the keys sparkling with darting graphs of light.

Jessie sat beside me on the padded 'duet' seat. 'Let me see your hands,' she said.

I showed her my cow-milking, fingernail-picked hands.

'You bite your fingernails, Jean.'

'I only pick them.'

'You'll never be able to play the piano unless you have nice fingernails.'

She held for my inspection her delicate hands with their beautifully curved and half-mooned nails. I had no half-moons. My shortcomings had been well catalogued in our comparing sessions at home: I had webbed fingers, I was not double-jointed, and I had no half-moons.

'You know of Middle C of course? Here's Middle C.'

I hadn't known of Middle C. At the end of the first lesson, when I'd been taught how to sit and how to place my hands and how the notes were named, Jessie gave me a small manuscript book and an instruction book for my homework. Dad had made it clear that there would be no money for examinations.

During the weeks that followed I learned to play 'Robin Adair', ('What's this old world to me, Robin Adair?') and a number of short pieces of the raindrop bird-hop tinkling variety. Then one day Jessie explained that it was important for me to have one first complete piece of music.

'A pianist always remembers her first piece of music,' she said dreamily, adding that she wanted me to have that special memory. She had already chosen the piece — 'Puck' — which I was to buy at Begg's, the music shop.

I went home. 'I have to buy a piece of music,' I said.

Mum looked apprehensive. 'I don't know whether your father . . .'

I milked the cow and waited for Dad to come home. I knew by heart the conversation that would follow. 'Dad, can I have some money to buy a piece of music?'

'What do you want a piece of music for? I told you learning the piano would cost more than you thought.'

'It's only a small piece. Ninepence.'

'I'm made of money, of course. Anyone would think I won Tatts every week.'

Here Mum would put in a word, saying how well I was doing on the piano, whereupon Dad, at the prospect of his daughter's future shining, would probably relent. It happened more or less according to the supposed script.

The next afternoon, on my way home from Beggs with the piece of music (which I'd already opened) in my hand, I met Jessie C. going downtown. I had no time to close the one new-smelling sheet of music that was 'Puck'. I felt ashamed and fearful that she had perceived my excitement. My embarrassment increased when at the next lesson she said slyly, knowingly, 'I saw you the other day with your first piece of music.'

I quickly learned to play 'Puck', a staccato piece in F Major, meant to depict, I supposed, the frolicking of Puck:

> *Over bush over briar*
> *thorough flood thorough fire*
> *I do wander everywhere*
> *swifter than the moone's sphere.*

Then, once again, there was more music to be bought, this time a collection that, Jessie assured me, would last for years: *Masterpieces of World Music*.

And once again Dad found the money for me to buy the music, a fat book packed with 'pieces' from all the great composers with few of whom I had any acquaintance, except those played in the school music festival — Schubert's 'Serenade', Brahms' 'Lullaby', Chopin's 'Minute Waltz'. I learned to play 'Londonderry Air', which I knew as 'O Danny Boy, the pipes the pipes are calling', and 'A Curious Story' by Stephen Heller. Then Jessie asked me if I knew of *Faust*. I didn't. She explained the story and introduced the 'Waltz' from the opera, which I learned to play. Next, Chopin's small 'Prelude in D', after which Jessie, who believed in milestones or keystones, said, 'My pupils usually give a recital to their parents when they have reached this stage.'

I knew of only one other pupil who had his lesson the same afternoon as I — a hairy, dark-eyed high school boy named Rex, whose father worked in the clothing store, he, too, a hairy, dark-eyed man with large, pale hands adept at flipping over the bolts of material as he measured the required length. Rex would be leaving as I arrived, and each time we'd glance at each other, I with a new, mysterious sense of excitement and adventure. His eyebrows were thick as woolly-bear caterpillars above his dark face.

One afternoon, then, Mum put on her costume, her straw hat and navy gloves, and came up to Jessie's to hear me play the piano. I played 'Londonderry Air', the waltz from the opera *Faust*, and the Chopin 'Prelude', and when I had finished, Jessie said to Mum, 'Jean's brilliant.'

This judgment pleased, confused and frightened me with an intrusion of opinion and expectation that would now deny me the world of making music as a place of private escape. The performance of music was so present and public. My only escape was within myself, to 'my place', within an imagination that I was not even sure I possessed, but where I hoped to avoid the praising, blaming scrutiny of others. Therefore, although I was proud of being thought 'brilliant', I wanted to hide, and, noting this, Jessie said to Mum, using that identity-destroying third person, 'She's shy.'

During the remainder of the term I learned several pieces from the collection, going faithfully twice a week to practise and fearful lest Jessie or her mother or the parrot were listening at the door, I was never comfortable trying to practise in that comfortable room, and I hadn't realised how much I enjoyed the bare wooden floor at home, where slaters and earwigs came up through the cracks and cockroaches scuttled away into the dark. On Saturdays I went with June to practise on Aunty Mima's piano, which was old, out of tune, with the keys refusing to move from their bed. There, knowing that no one was listening, I spent the time 'tinkering' and experimenting after I'd played my pieces once to impress June with my cleverness.

Somehow the intrusion of judgment into my playing had blighted my interest. I began to make more mistakes, learning the pieces too quickly and then not being able to find my place in the music. I became self-conscious, with Jessie beside me on the duet seat, watching my nail-bitten, un-half-mooned fingers searching the keys. At the end of the term I finished my music classes with my last two pieces, the 'Shepherd Boy' ('like some vision of far-off time lonely shepherd boy') and 'To the Evening Star' ('O star of Eve'). Sometimes I felt lonely for the beautiful black shining piano and the warm, sealed room and the music, and now and again I'd see Rex, a part of the nostalgia, his music case banging against his long, hairy legs, walking up Eden Street to his lesson. We'd glance at each other, close as skin and distant as horizons.

25 Marking Time

My life centred on my schoolwork and my walks on the hill and reading and trying to write poetry. I was beginning to find that when I answered a question in school, the reaction of the class and the teacher was one of surprise, often of amusement. 'Jean's so original,' the teacher said one day, causing me once again to feel trapped by the opinion of others. I did not think of myself as original: I merely said what I thought. Yet an acknowledgment of an apparent 'difference' in my thinking seemed to fit in with the 'difference', as I thought it to be, of my life at home with the dramatic terrifying continuing episodes of my brother's illness, the misunderstanding of it, the confusion of our parents trying to 'face' it, our brother's loneliness, my father's subdued withdrawal of 'control' over his daughters, our fervent promises not to 'stay out late, go with boys, drink, smoke', with the supposition that such an innocuous way of life would cure all; and when the idea of 'difference', given to me by others in a time when I did not know myself and was hesitant in finding out, for I was not an introspective person, was reinforced by Miss Gibson's remark to Isabel, 'You Frame girls think you're so different from everyone else', I came to accept the difference, although in our world of school, to be different was to be peculiar, a little 'mad'.

I believed always, however, in the politics of use, and now when I was asked about my reading and I (wearing the mantle of difference with pride) mentioned a novel few had heard of, the teacher would again say, 'Jean's so original.'

Therefore in an adolescent homelessness of self, in a time where I did not quite know my direction, I entered eagerly a nest of difference which others found for me but which I lined with my own furnishings; for, after all, during the past two years I had tried many aspects of 'being' — a giggling schoolgirl who made everyone laugh with comic recitations, mimicry, puzzles, mathematical tricks, such as 'Think of a number, double it', attempts at ventriloquism; and now I was at home, with some prestige and fairly comfortable.

And while I struggled, enjoying my ambitions and my supposed 'difference', out in the 'world', far from New Zealand, the Nazi Party was in power in Germany with speeches by Adolf Hitler being broadcast over the wireless. We mimicked his raving delivery, the Nazi salute and the goose-stepping armies. I had little historical or political awareness. I knew only that Micky Savage and John A. Lee were 'goodies', while Forbes and Coates were 'baddies'. From time to time our history teacher had talked of the concept of 'purity of race' which, she said, was desirable. Intermarriage of races, she said, produced an inferior 'type', citing the intermarriage of the Maoris and the Chinese. She spoke with pride of the 'purity' of the white race. Also at that time, by some subtle transmissions within the community, people who were Jewish were now identified as such and often spoken of in a slighting way. The word *nigger* was accepted as a description of African races and as a name for black cats, a colour for shoe polish and items of clothing. And those people who were known to be 'half-caste' were spoken of as unclean.

This increased attention to 'purity of race' had come to our town no doubt by way of Nazi Germany and the British Empire, and there was much talk at school of *eugenics* and the possibility of breeding a perfect race. Intelligence tests became fashionable, too, as people clamoured to find themselves qualified for the 'perfect race' and to find others who were not so qualified.

In our home, however, Mother, like the mother bird of the world, sprang always to defend all races and creeds (not quite; she condemned Roman Catholics) and colours as if they were her own 'youngkers' (our word for baby birds); while Dad, too, was without prejudice except toward the 'toffs' of the world and royalty.

And so, although at school we were often reminded of the distance of New Zealand from the rest of the world, the infection of Nazism did reach us in our town and we listened dutifully as our teacher painted some races evil, some good. One chapter in our history books, 'The Yellow Peril', told of Eastern races and their evil designs on the West. Although we children had once chanted rhymes after all strange people, I remembered an elderly Chinese man walking by one day and our chanting at him and the baffled expression on his face when he looked at us, and I felt uneasy, as if I had dome something I couldn't undo. Also, in the serials over the wireless and in Dad's Sexton Blake books, the villains were invariably described as 'yellow-skinned, slant-eyed, evil'.

Then, when during the year Dad was rushed to hospital with append-icitis and had for his neighbour a young Chinese man who, with his family, became family friends, we learned something of Chinese people. They came to visit us, and we visited them, and one day the young man brought us a beautiful plant, a narcissus growing, budding and blossoming in water. We kept the plant on the sewing machine near the dining-room window, in the light, and whenever I looked at it I was aware of a new kind of beauty, a delicacy, which I tried to take and keep, for, in a way, my awareness of it helped to efface my growing consciousness of my body, the now-too-tight tunic often dirtied with cow muck and byre mud, the cobble-mended stockings coarse and thick, my frizzy tangle of red hair, which seemed to alarm everyone the way it naturally grew up instead of down, causing people to keep asking, 'Why don't you straighten it? Why don't you comb it flat, *make* it *stay* flat, put oil on it or something; *no one* else has hair like yours.' And no one had, except Fijian and African people in faraway lands. At school I was now called *Fuzzy*.

I had my fourteenth birthday. I could now use the whole of the Town Library and write to Dot's Senior Page. At school the Group's topic of con-versation was new clothes — brassieres, corsets, corselets, each one being defined and the rules given for wearing each; the talk was of such urgency that I pleaded that evening, 'Mum, can I have a corset and brassiere?'

Mother, never having had either, said mildly, 'I'll not have you putting restrictions on your body.' O blind Mother, she did not even notice how tight my tunic had become across my developing breasts.

When Dad came home, I again brought up the subject, saying, 'All the girls at school are wearing them', whereupon Dad made his familiar response, 'If all girls hopped to school, I suppose you'd hop, too!'

'That's different,' I said sourly.

But he was right, of course. It was just that the Group was so powerful I found myself wanting things simply because they made them seem to be such an urgent necessity. It's this or death. They were now taking lessons in ballroom dancing, looking forward to a time when they would be 'coming out'. They talked of their dancing partners at the Boys' High dances, the Bible class socials, bike rides out 'The willows' with the Bible class boys, and of what they would wear for their First Communion and Confirmation. I was ignorant of such ceremonies, we did not belong to any established church, and when I heard one girl say to another, 'Are you being confirmed?' and the other girl reply, 'Yes, I'm being confirmed', I felt sick with envy of the mystery and its urgency. How closely I listened to and studied the Group! I had no need to read Rafael Sabatini or Georgette Heyer to find myself in another world of costume drama: the other world was here, on a stone seat by the ivy-covered wall of Waitaki Girls' Senior High.

That year the speech contests were begun. I found the idea satisfying, for in all my early reading of school stories there had been a Speech Day, and I had felt the constriction of language at Waitaki, which was also a boarding school, where I had hoped to be able to use other words I had learned from my reading — midnight feasts in the *dorm*, being *gated*, being a member of the *Fifth Remove*, having *Hols* at the *seaside* (this was a problem because Oamaru *was* the seaside). Our speech subject was 'An Inventor or Explorer'. My heroes of exploration having been for many years Burke and Wills and Mungo Park, I chose Mungo Park, inventing many details, which I learned by heart and which to my delight and the delight of my parents, won First Prize.

And suddenly once again it was summer. Myrtle had now disappeared almost without trace. Sometimes when I tried to picture her, I found that her image had faded; I remembered only the white centipede scar on her knee and her golden hair, her *coiffure* done in the style of Ginger Rogers; her punches, pinches, back thumps; and my worry over what would become of her. She had been so fearless, adventurous, rebellious, a rule-breaker, as my sister Isabel was growing up to be, defying the orders of adults, whereas I, still out of fear, obeyed them and even adapted myself to suit their opinion of me, my only place of rebellion being within, in an imagination that I was not even sure I possessed because, so far, no one had mentioned it.

That summer, perhaps not so inexplicably, we rediscovered Marguerite and her sister and brother and spent our time playing grown-up dolls who lived Hollywood-style lives with much loving, committing of adultery, divorcing, each of us propelling our tiny rose-pink kewpie doll with its stuck-together legs, dressed in its elaborately made rayon gown, from room to room to the rayon-cushioned cardboard-box mansions, and from bed to bed, with the appropriate gestures and dialogue.

They changed their clothes every few hours, with a glamorous gown for every occasion — their 'tea' gown, their 'sherry' gown. They danced, too, their bodies held close, after which they went out on the terrace to kiss and plan to 'go away together'. And the male characters, Nigel or Neil or Raymond, dressed always in evening dress, white front, cutaway coat, and a swath of black rayon for pants, as their legs, too, were stuck together, behaved always like 'wolves' who acted without ceremony when overcome by their desires. We graduated then, my sisters and I, from using kewpies to using ourselves and, embarrassed by our daring, referred to our play, usually in our bedroom, as 'one of those games'. 'Let's play one of those games,' we'd say.

They lasted the summer when, for whatever reason, simply because the time had passed, a barrier came between us and the games, and we no longer referred to them or played them. Instead, we returned to our long walks in the gully and over the hill. Scrapers was now 'dry' and Bluey, in calf for the first time, was also dry but would be calved by the beginning of the school year.

Isabel and June and I were now all writing poetry and prose. I thought of Isabel's as the 'best', for she covered a wide range of experience unknown to her, set in other countries, too, where she had never been. June's was, in my opinion, the most poetic, for she used the 'poetic' words, 'dream', 'misty', 'stars lost', and so on, although her poems were vague, with few facts. My own poems, which usually had a satisfying ending, were in strict form, usually with the expected rhymes, and lacking the vague otherworldliness which I admired in June's poems and which I equated with the elusive 'imagination'.

My life had been for many years in the power of words. It was driven now by a constant search and need for what was, after all, 'only a word' — imagination.

26 Early Spring Snow

Another year at school with our class, the Lower Fifth, even smaller than our Fourth Form, although we shared some classes with the 'country and bus' girls who came from 4B. Once again the Group had control, although with the prospect of future examinations and the emphasis on studies, our small scholar's group had its own glory. There was W. and M., who was Miss Gibson's cousin and who came from a farming estate in the High Country, and I, Fuzzy. In spite of my father's urging, my competitive spirit was not strong, at least not so consuming as that of W., who wrote our marks and answers in a small notebook. We three usually worked on our own in mathematics where I became addicted to the solving of problems and the joyful experience of their neat solution.

Our class teacher, Miss Farnie, was small, ugly in the accepted sense, with her nose and chin too big, her face a blotchy red, her hair dark and scraggy. Her voice was soft yet clear, her eyes a calm grey, and her manner of teaching generally thought of as inspired with her passion both for English literature and for mathematics, which, she explained to us, converting me entirely to the cause of mathematics, was a form of *poetry*. I believed her and therefore flourished in maths.

It was she, too, who 'converted' me to Shakespeare, who I'd previously thought was a bore. One day she walked into the room, opened our 'set' Shakespeare, *Macbeth*, and, with a witchlike voice that matched her appearance and swirling her black gown about her in a witchlike manner, began to read or drone,

> *When shall we three meet again?*
> *In thunder, lightning, or in rain?*
> *When the hurlyburly's done,*
> *When the battle's lost and won.*
> *That will be ere the set of sun.*

Miss Farnie then allotted parts to us (I was given First Witch) and asked us to read as witches would read, after which she announced that at the end of the term we would perform the Sleep-Walking Scene and I was to be Lady Macbeth. I could scarcely believe my good fortune. Year after year it had been the girls from the Group who performed the major parts.

At home I practised my role of Lady Macbeth. I read it in class, and I knew it was good. I dreamed of the coming performance. I began to take an interest in Shakespeare, in the wild Scottish moors and battles and battlements and the hauntings that were inseparable from the lives of the characters, and in the language used to describe the weather, the sky, the dark, to match the nightmare within the characters. My sisters and I read *Macbeth* at home, taking it to our hearts as we had taken the story of the Brontë sisters and using it as part of our conversation with one another, saying as Eden Street and the hill and the gully grew dark and the pigeons flew home to Glen Street:

> *Now o'er the one half-world*
> *Nature seems dead, and wicked dreams abuse*
> *The curtained sleep.*

As the weeks passed and I perfected my role of Lady Macbeth, gradually the demands of preparation for examinations invaded the class timetable, frivolities like acting were set aside, and no further mention was made of the performance of the Sleep-Walking Scene. It was hard for me to believe that something so memorable for me had been forgotten by the teacher and the class, and so I lost my chance to be Lady Macbeth. Even so I gained Shakespeare, whom I had longed to 'like' and to enjoy reading, as all the English teaching had given him unquestioned supremacy and I felt it would be impossible to think of being a writer if I didn't like reading Shakespeare; yet I'd found it impossible to pretend to admire him. Miss Farnie's approach had converted me.

It is strange to think of my life being lived as I then lived my 'real' life, so much within and influenced by English and French literature, with my daily adventures a discovery of a paragraph or a poem and my own attempts to write. It was not an escape in the sense of a removal from the unhappiness I felt over the sickness at home or from my own feeling of nowhereness in not having ordinary clothes to wear even to prove that I was a human being and there was a peopled world beyond home and school; there was no removal of myself and my life to another world; there was simply the other world's arrival into my world, the literature streaming through it like an array of beautiful ribbons through the branches of a green, growing tree, touching the leaves with unexpected light that was unlike the expected deserved habitual light of the sun and the seasons. It was the arrival, as of neighbours or relatives or anyone who belonged there and was at home, of the poets and the prose writers and their work at Fifty-six Eden Street, Oamaru, 'the kingdom by the sea', bringing their hosts of words and characters and their special vision.

Miss Farnie, in her praise for my weekly essays, so encouraged me that writing my essay became the highlight of my week, but as the reason for her praise was obscure to me, I tried to ensure its continuing with my emphasis on 'dreams, silver, mists, little old ladies, and little grey men'.

'Across the sea lies Shakespeare's isle, the land he loved and praised, the land that has seen happiness and sadness with her tired old eyes . . .' I recall that opening sentence of one of my essays. I was painfully aware that I had no originality, no imagination, and I could not understand this sudden praise for my essays.

Those first few months in the Lower Fifth Form were happy. I rejoiced in my studies, encouraged by Miss Farnie's insistence not only that mathematics was poetry but also that poetry existed where few searched for it. This statement challenged me: out of a desire to be myself, not to follow the ever-dominant personalities around me, I had formed the habit of focusing in places not glanced at by others, of deliberately turning away from the main view, and I recognised in Miss Farnie someone with a skill in looking elsewhere or, looking at the general view, seeing an uncommon sight.

My memory of myself contains now myself looking outward and myself looking within from without, developing the 'view' that others might have, and because I was my body and its functions and that body was clothed during most waking hours in a dark grey serge tunic that I hated increasingly because it was far too tight now in the yoke, it was rough, scratchy material; and in long, black stockings with their sealing effect; and in blouses, pure white in summer, grey flannel in winter, all with cuffs buttoned tightly over my wrists and pointed collars closing with pearl buttons high upon my neck, completing the seal; and in the black shoes laced in complete capture of my feet; in the regulation gloves, hat, or beret; and, as a final imprisonment, in the red and black tie knotted around my neck and the green Gibson House girdle also specially knotted around my waist, because of these clothes I saw myself as powerlessly in harness. Added to that view was my sisters' opinion of my 'figure' seen free and naked before the bedroom mirror, compared and contrasted with theirs and with the film stars and with the ideal, and although my opinion was important, I submitted readily to the general view. We concluded that we all had 'good' figures which, in our prancing before the mirror, we referred to in high-pitched American tones, 'Do you like my fig-ewer, Jebs?' (Jebs being short for Jebalus, who with May Cooney had been imaginary childhood friends.) My face, according to my sisters, was 'ordinary' except for my Shirley Temple dimples. We studied also the state of our skin and the number of blackheads or pimples on our face, the current influential advertisement being of a woman who could never wear 'off-the-face' hats because of her many hickies, which she successfully removed with a special soap or ointment.

There was also the question of 'personality'. One had to have 'personality'. I wasn't aware that I had any, although I had seized upon and embellished certain attributes that I may or may not have had. When Miss Farnie, having seen my poems in Dot's Page, said one day, 'You do write poetry, don't you, Jean?' and I blushed and looked embarrassed, and she said to the class, 'Jean's so shy', I seized this (already given by Jessie C., the music teacher) as a welcome, poetic attribute and made shyness a part of my 'personality'.

Looking out at the world, then, from my position of physical discomfort, I felt restricted to the point of being nastily bad-tempered at my task of milking Scrapers and Bluey, for Bluey and Scrapers had calved and both cows were 'in milk'. I began to write a diary, agreeing with the convention and aware that diarists began 'Dear Diary'; yet thinking such a form of address to be absurd, I compromised by writing 'Dear Mr Ardenue', Mr Ardenue being pictured as a kindly old man with a long, grey beard and 'smiling' eyes, who ruled over the Land of Ardenue, which I celebrated in a poem. Where before I had written most of my verse about the world around me, I now focused on the Land of Ardenue, which I could people as I wished. The important consistent characters were Mr Ardenue, the ruler of the kingdom; the Sea-Foam Youth Grown Old, who came to mind one day as I watched the waves breaking and the foam on the beach turn quickly brown; the Scholar-Gipsy, from Arnold's poem, the Scholar-Gipsy being perhaps my first 'love', my ideal man, reawakening my early feeling for gypsies and my kinship with Old Meg Merilees and my special feeling for all beggars and swaggers passing through town in the dark, glistening night and prisoners, again at night, in the moonlight, longing for freedom yet possessing a special freedom like that of the Scholar-Gipsy. Having read Arnold's poem for the first time that year, I was able to weave my dreams of the future about his life both as a scholar and a free wanderer, shy, seldom glimpsed, at home with the natural world of wood, weather, and sky and season.

There were a few unlikely characters in Ardenue, mostly invited there to satisfy my strong attraction to ordinary everyday objects that might in the end become extraordinary: *The Dishes I Washed*. That was how they were known and how they were greeted in each entry of my diary. There were also *The Little Golden Ladies of New Zealand*, installed in Ardenue under the continued influence of Mother's poetic interest and the fondness of her and her poetic friends (she corresponded with one or two people who wrote poetry) for writing of *Kowhai Blossoms*. Indeed, one of Mother's friends had lately published a book of poems entitled *Kowhai Blossoms*. I, impressed, read it, noting from the foreword that the author, true to the growing tradition, was blind, a fact that Mother cherished, using it once again to demonstrate that handicaps could be overcome and glory achieved. My own *Little Golden Ladies of New Zealand* were some fallen kowhai blossoms that I saw in an Oamaru garden. I seized also the much-loved poplar trees, and each pine plantation was transplanted in Ardenue, and the moon that I watched each evening as it rose over the sea. In the creation of Ardenue I gave a name and thus a certainty to a new inner 'My Place'.

So tightly encased were we girls in our senior high school tunics, that I am surprised at the ease with which in August of 1939 the first menstrual blood was able to find its way out of my body. I should have been prepared for the escape; I was not. I'd forgotten the faraway time of Myrtle and her 'monthlies'. I didn't even know what to call menstruation, for 'monthlies' was a word of the past, out of date, and the girls at school talked of being 'unwell'.

I was nearly fifteen when I woke that morning to find blood between my legs. Panic seized me. I ran from the bedroom into the dining room and stood in the place where Mother herself stood in time of crisis — that honoured place in the light of the dining-room window, by the sewing machine, where we had been warned not to stand should there be a storm and danger of lightning.

'There's blood between my legs,' I said tremulously.

'It's the monthlies,' Mother said.

Gradually my memory returned. I had forgotten, however, the reasons and the mechanics that I knew so well at eight years old: Mother cut an old bath towel into rectangular strips, giving me one to pin back and front to my singlet, for bought sanitary towels were unheard of in our household.

'It will show,' I said, looking unhappily at the bulk.

'No, it won't show,' Mother lied valiantly.

I knew it showed. For the remaining years at school I suffered those bulky strips of towelling with the blood seeping through so that by the end of the day, if I bent my head toward my desk, I caught the smell of stale menstrual blood, and realising that others would also smell it, I felt unceasing shame. The bulk and the stink and the washing of the towels became a haunting distaste. I did not even experience the coveted prestige of feeling 'unwell' and being sent to 'lie on the bed in the prefects' room', where L., the class artist, had often to go, her Lady of Shalott face deadly pale.

That month of August there was a late, unexpected snowstorm, the kind that kills the newborn lambs in the high country, and even Oamaru, the kingdom by the sea, had a few days of deep snow. The timing of the snowfall, following so closely my shock of being bathed in blood, had a literary perfection not thought of as being a part of the untidiness of living and a shape, drawing together the past of *Grimm's Fairy Tales* and the repeated incidence there of blood upon the snow as a catastrophic or miraculous moment deciding the direction of the character's future, touching, too, my present life as a chrysalis-bound schoolgirl. Because I could feel yet not express the pattern, I wrote two poems that I sent to Dot. 'Early Spring Snow' was in my usual style, beginning:

> A cloud of softly whirling flakes has o'er the hillside bent.
> The violets murmur drowsily steeped in their fragrant scent.
> A wintry wind has wailed all night a tale of lone lament.

We had been studying William Cowper's poem, 'To Mary':

> The twentieth year is well-nigh past,
> Since first my sky was overcast;
> Ah would that this might be the last!

The other poem, 'The Blackbird', read:

> Surely O surely the message is Spring
> with snowdrops in delicate white . . .

And so on. Concluding with:

> The whole world awakened and thrilled to the song
> no more was the bleak hillside cold,
> for nodding and whispering in garments of sheen,
> a crocus began to unfold.

To my delight, Dot praised both poems, using 'The Blackbird' as the Poem of the Week, a place normally reserved for poems by 'real' poets. I was annoyed that she changed 'gay' blackbird to 'blythe' blackbird, for I thought 'blythe' too clumsy. Over the years I remember my irritation over the change of my chosen word, just as I remember Myrtle's pressure to change 'touch' to 'tint'.

I had my fifteenth birthday. Birthday parties were unknown luxuries in our home and the day passed more or less as usual. At home I still practised my Lady Macbeth speech, more aware now of its meaning — 'Here's the smell of the blood still. All the perfumes of Arabia will not sweeten this little hand.'

My own hands were strong, from the exercise of milking the cows.

The land of Ardenue continued to absorb me, and I dreamed again and again of the Scholar-Gipsy, especially as Miss Farnie had recommended a book, *Towers in the Mist*, by Elizabeth Goudge — a tale of Oxford University that captured the whole class, including the Group, with its romantic descriptions of Oxford and the scholars: 'Seen by rare glimpses, pensive and tongue-tied, / In hat of antique shape, and cloak of grey, / The same the gipsies wore . . .' (I thought of Old Meg's 'chip hat'.) 'Have I not pass'd thee on the wooden bridge, / Wrapt in thy cloak and battling with the snow, . . . / Turn'd once to watch, while thick the snowflakes fall, / The line of festal light in Christ-Church Hall . . .'

Towers in the Mist made Oxford and the Scholar-Gipsy even more desirable, and yet I felt an uneasiness, almost a disappointment, that Miss Farnie, with all English literature to reveal to us, thought so highly of a book where the writing reminded me of L. M. Montgomery and the Anne books, lacking a solidity, a factual concreteness in the midst of the misty vagueness. Certainly it was gentle writing, with all the green and gold and little old men and women, the dreams, and most of the vocabulary that I still thought necessary to poetry.

But Miss Farnie was a teacher of her time, middle-aged, unmarried, as far we we knew, with the inevitable rumours of her 'boy' being killed in the Great War and her journey of a lifetime 'home' to England completed and the memories carefully preserved in the 'slides' that she showed the class as a special treat — the English lanes, the country cottages, the ruins, the castles, the universities, ah, the universities, Oxford and Cambridge . . . the towers in the mist . . . she passing on her dreams, which we made part of ours, for there was much preoccupation now with university examinations, with degrees and careers, and some of the girls with older brothers and sisters at university told of their experiences, while I, investigating the world of literature, discovered that many of the poets had been to university.

I have often wondered in which world I might have lived my 'real' life had not the world of literature been given to me by my mother and by the school syllabus, and even by the death of Myrtle. It was my insistence on bringing this world home, rather than vanishing within it, that increased my desire to write, for how else could I anchor that world within this everyday world where I hadn't the slightest doubt that it belonged? Oamaru, the kingdom by the sea. Did I not already know people in Oamaru who had been 'trodden down' by the 'hungry generations'? And did we not have the natural ingredients for literature — a moon, stars ('Pale star, would I were steadfast as thou art'), sea, people, animals, sheep and shepherds ('Go, for they call you, shepherd, from the hill'). We had skylarks dipping and rising above the hill ('Hail to thee, blithe spirit!') and pigeons and goldfinches and wax-eyes clamouring to have their say above the nightingales . . .

In early September of that year, in the midst of a concentration of characters from fiction and poetry, and inhabitants of the Land of Ardenue, in a setting of blood and snow, that storm and that lightning which I had defied by standing near the light of the dining-room window, with the sky beyond, struck not only our house but also all the houses in Eden Street, in Oamaru, New Zealand, the world, in the outbreak of the Second World War.

27 'That's Not You, Jasper.'

Had I been a city, the shock of war would have torn apart all buildings, entombing the population, or as after a volcanic eruption there might have been an overflow of numbness, like lava, preserving all in a stone mask of stillness and silence. I had never felt so shocked, so unreal. I knew that war happened in history and in places far away, in other nations; that my father had 'been to war'; that some of the stories I most loved featured young soldiers 'on their way to the wars' or wounded old soldiers coming 'home from the wars'. I had relished Miss Lindsay's reading of 'Ode on the Death of the Duke of Wellington' and the battles of the time of Arthur: 'So all day long the noise of battle rolled . . .' And year after year in the School Journal I had read:

> In Flanders field the poppies blow
> Between the crosses, row on row
> That mark our place; and in the sky
> The larks, still bravely singing, fly
> Scarce heard amid the guns below . . .

In the Anzac Commemoration at the Waitaki Boys' High School Hall of Memories I had heard Mr Milner proclaiming the British Empire's glorious deeds in battle and sung, feelingly, without translation of the scene into one of undue horror:

> O Valiant Hearts, who to your glory came
> Through dust of conflict and through the battle-flame;
> Tranquil you lie, your knightly virtue proved,
> Your memory hallowed in the Land you loved . . .

I knew of the pacifist belief of Mother's religion, that two of her brothers had been conscientious objectors in the First War and imprisoned for their refusal to kill. I tried to imagine the people I knew in Oamaru — the Walsh boys, the Easton boys, the Luxons, even Jack Dixon, becoming characters in this new story and with knapsack or kit bag setting out cheerfully for the war. I had honestly believed that the days of war were over.

Recovering a little from the shock and feeling an inconsolable sadness and disillusionment, I turned once again to the poets, who, I believed, were rightly described by Shelley as 'the unacknowledged legislators of the world'.

I felt, too, that 'poetry redeems from decay the visitations of the Divine in Man'. I felt that to know which way the winds of the world were blowing, to gain knowledge of human behaviour, of the working of the human mind, I had only to study the world's poetry and fiction. Just as the poets had taught me of death and included my own experiences in their writing, so they would teach me about war.

Oamaru and New Zealand appeared suddenly to be seized by a kind of madness as if the Declaration of War were an exciting gift. There was a flurry of anticipation in our home as both my father and my brother thought of being soldiers. Dad searched out the 'puttees' which he'd brought home from *his* war and which had lain untouched in an old suitcase. 'My puttees,' he said with a new affection, demonstrating how they were used by winding them over his trouser legs. 'Keep out the mud of the trenches,' he said knowledgeably. He'd seldom talked of the trenches before. The word was used only by Mum to explain why Dad was so often either sad or angry, 'Your father fought in the trenches, kiddies', and by us at primary school in scoring points of prestige, 'My father fought in the trenches'.

There was a kind of war fever in the town. Young men hurried to enlist with few questioning the duty to 'rally round to help the Mother Country'. Flags appeared on buildings. The wireless played 'Rule Britannia', and even Mother, the pacifist, clenched her fist and said, 'We'll show Hitler!' The newspaper issued a large map complete with flags with the markings of the Maginot Line and the Siegfried Line and other places and the instruction *Flag the Movement of the Allied Forces from Day to Day*, as if the affair were a game. And both Dad and Bruddie went downtown to join the army with Dad returning as a member of the newly formed National Reserve, complete with uniform, and Bruddie, who was unfit, as a member of the Home Guard with a porkpie hat gathered from somewhere. At school there were subtle shiftings of prestige as girls, previously ignored were found to have fathers with the rank of colonel or major or brothers in the First Echelon. Dad had been a corporal, a signaller and stretcher-bearer in the First World War, by which name it was now officially known, its greatness being finally in doubt.

I went about my daily tasks at home — milking the cows, often sharing the job with Bruddie, taking my 'turn' at riding Dad's bike downtown for the messages, trying to maintain my school tunic now scratched and torn by the wire fence of the hill and the bull paddock; arguing, comparing, contrasting with my sisters, helping as little as possible with the housework but occasionally cooking in an experimental way my 'discovery' of mock whitebait: for wartime was the time of 'mock' food, with the very notion causing a consternation of betrayal in our home similar to the news of permanent waves.

The poetry that I then explored was generally an easy kind of poetry made more attractive for me by the usual handsome photograph of the young poet in his soldier's uniform. Unable to face the City of Dreadful Night 'As I came through the desert thus it was . . .', which was the reality of war, I turned to the shallow acceptance of glorifying the war dead, with Rupert Brooke as my hero and 'If I should die think only this of me' setting the tone. And how quickly we learned the new language of war! Men suddenly became known as 'boys', 'our boys', returned to childhood with a licence to kill. Our boys, the brave. At school we talked familiarly of echelons, quislings, fifth column, the blitz, the names of planes and places; and in my poetry I wrote:

> Brown soft brown in the tall gold grass
> a skylark rested, and far away
> the song of pride in the men who pass
> dreaming of war in a boyish way,
> tumbled its notes to a quiet street.
> O surely, surely the day is sweet
> when the soldiers march!

The poem of several verses concluded with:

> When they, the brave, have gone have gone
> and flowers weep with the lovely dew,
> then, little bird, be glad, sing on,
> sing and the world shall list to you.
> And we shall laugh, yet creeps a tear
> and clutches the heart a silent fear
> When the soldiers march.

That poem and many others in a similar vein were printed in the local newspaper, and I was not ashamed of them as I am now. I was humanly naive and ungrown, using to describe a dire event the latest 'poetic' words in my vocabulary — *dreaming, boyish, sweet* — with the old standbys — *lovely, little, laugh* . . . I had good tutors, you see — Rupert Brooke — 'Laughed in the sun and kissed the lovely grass . . .' Flowers, dew, stars, skies . . . the words ruled, you see; they held the keys of the kingdom, and I did not realise until I had spent a few more years growing and observing that the kingdom which glorified those words was as much a prison as my grey serge tunic and knotted tie and lace-up black shoes.

The remainder of that year is memorable only as the continuing nightmare of war and certain nightmares at home, alleviated once again by the solace of the seasons, the weather, reading and writing poetry, learning passages by heart, and receiving a present. I gave my speech on Speech Day — 'A Character from Literature' Silas Marner (the little old man), making him a romantic character. I won the Speech Prize. At the end of the year I was asked to choose my class prize, and once again Mother's influence showed in my choice of Longfellow, a handsome book with illustrations shrouded in tissue paper and, uncovered, revealing a bronzed handsome Hiawatha, more handsome than Rupert Brooke, carrying Minnehaha in his arms:

> Over wide and rushing rivers
> In his arms he bore the maiden

Then there was the present, with Dad giving me five shillings to buy myself a book for Christmas, the first book I had ever bought.

I went to Jeffrey and Smith's and asked for my chosen book, *Lavengro*, by George Borrow, because it combined many of my interests? Old Meg the gypsy, the Scholar-Gipsy, it contained also the passage that I'd read often in our schoolbooks and that I longed to possess, to read again and again, especially now in 1939 in the midst of war: the passage beginning, 'That's not you, Jasper . . .', and ending, 'Life is sweet, Jasper. There's day and night, Jasper, both sweet things. There's sun, moon and stars, brother, all sweet things, there's likewise a wind on the heath. Who would wish to die?'

28   University Entrance

I think of the remaining years at school as part of the nightmare of the war, the daily casualty lists, the hymns and Bible readings in school assembly:

> Eternal Father strong to save
> whose arm hath bound the restless wave . . .
> O hear us when we cry to thee
> for those in peril on the sea . . .

and

> Fight the good fight with all thy might . . .
> Christ is thy strength and Christ thy right.

and

> Peace perfect peace in this dark world of sin
> the blood of Jesus whispers peace within.

I recall the seriousness and fervour of my singing, the (then innocently) sexual languor of the many hymns steeped in blood, such hymns being favourites with the girls, most of whom in the past year or two had acquired a new relationship to blood, made strange by the repeated reference to the spilling of blood in wartime, and the everlasting preoccupation with blood in a country that based its economy on the killing and eating of farm animals.

I began my year in the Upper Fifth Form with Miss Macaulay as my form teacher and Miss Farnie still my mathematics teacher, with another bursary to help to pay for books. This was the year of the University Entrance Examination. It was also the year of the country's centenary, with celebrations to be held in Wellington and a party from the school arranging to go for educational purposes, these being the chief point of the argument of my sisters and me when we pleaded to be able to go with the school party. Once again we were infected by the desire to belong in a school activity, when year after year we'd had to refuse the visit to Mount Cook (which I have still not visited), camping trips, and so on. Also, we pointed out to our parents that we'd have our free railway ticket, and with so many relatives in Wellington there'd be no need for us to be 'billeted'. The cost would be slightly more than an allowance of pocket money each, although we had never had pocket money. When the list was made, however, we tasted the rare glory of inclusion, partly because the prospect of another 'Exhibition' had prompted Mum and Dad to remember with nostalgia the South Seas Exhibition in Dunedin:

'When Myrtle and Bruddie were little and Aunty Grace and Uncle Andy lived at Balclutha. And Myrtle and Bruddie had candy floss . . .' The candy floss was always mentioned as if it were the sweetest kind of uncomplicated happiness known only then, in the days of the Dunedin Exhibition, after the Duke and Duchess of York and the Prince of Wales had toured the country (O the lovely Prince of Wales!) after the King's furniture had been paid for, and there was no longer danger of the King's representative coming to inspect the iron bed and the wooden kerb and the dining table with the four Morris chairs and the sofa and the oval hearth rug . . . Oh, they were heaven days 'when Myrtle and Bruddie were little . . .' 'So be sure to have some candy floss,' Mum said. 'You may never have another chance. They only have it at Exhibitions and such-like . . .'

The journey in the ferry was rough with all the girls seasick and Miss Lindsay, one of the chaperoning teachers, also sick. During the night she had held my head as I vomited again and again while she reminded everyone, 'Go with the motion of the boat, go with the motion of the boat', and when morning came with its awful sea-green light there was Miss Lindsay, her face grey green as she sat miserably on the stairs, pointing out the geographical features of the approaching Wellington Harbour, for 'after all, girls, this is an educational visit!'

The party, billeted at Newtown School, carried out its plans while we three girls, separated from the others, discovered new aunts and uncles and cousins 'on Mother's side', while we spent our two days at the Exhibition and our pocket money by enjoying the attractions of the Fun Fair and the Hall of Mirrors, riding the Ghost Train, and finally having our handwriting analysed by a *gypsy*, who warned me what I already knew, that my 'personality' was in trouble, that I was too shy, too self-conscious.

Returning from the Exhibition, we wrote the inevitable essay. I wrote about the pleasures of the educational and industrial courts. We had tasted candy floss (surreptitiously in case we were 'seen', as Waitaki girls were forbidden to eat in public), and partly sensing our parents' use of it as a memory of vanished happiness, we proclaimed ourselves unimpressed by it; we preferred, we said, to eat something more substantial. I know that Mother's expectations were disappointed when she realised that she could not re-create her old memories from our new ones, that the halcyon time of 'when Myrtle and Bruddie were little' was out of reach, had even been cancelled.

Nevertheless, June and Isabel and I had our own kind of candy floss: that educational visit was always remembered as a time of great freedom and fun when, for a time I even forgot the war — and the University Entrance Exam.

Once again in Oamaru we faced the casualty lists, the rumours, the morning hymns, the reference to the exam. I returned also to my life within the poetry and prose I was discovering. Reading a poem acknowledged to be 'great' (such as 'Ode on the Intimations of Immortality'), I was pleased to be 'moved to tears', as I felt that to be so affected helped to seal the greatness of the poem, and each evening when I wrote in my diary, I felt a certain pride if I were able to write to Mr Ardenue, 'Today I wept in class when we were reading . . .' naming the poem or prose. My weeping was not audible nor, as far as I knew, noticeable, although I did hope that the teacher might perhaps glance my way, see me wiping away a tear, and think, 'Ah, there's Jean, so moved by poetry, so poetic, so imaginative . . . a real poet herself . . .' I had no indication that the teacher thought such things . . . and still the longed-for imagination eluded me.

With the concentration on the coming exams and their very name — *University Entrance* — there was talk among the girls about their future university courses and of life at university, which some even dared (to my alarm at their familiar tone) to call *varsity*. *Towers in the Mist*, the Scholar-Gipsy, Wordsworth's 'Sonnet on Kings College Chapel, Cambridge', Jude the Obscure and the towers of Christminster, Shelley, Byron, Matthew Arnold, now combined as a dream to replace the dream of Hollywood, of dancing, singing and the Big Time among the stars, although these departing dreams did flare occasionally with the arrival of new adolescent singing stars — Judy Garland, Deanna Durbin, and the search through New Zealand for a *New Zealand Deanna Durbin*, with hundreds of girls trilling 'Il Bacio' ('Softly dawns upon me, dawns upon me morning's laughing rays . . . returning yes returning . . .') and the 'Pipes of Pan' ('Come follow follow follow the merry merry pipes of Pan . . .'), I experiencing and making use of the reflected glory of having my aunt's two nieces (aunt by marriage, alas!) reach the provincial final, only to give way to the heralded New Zealand's *own* Deanna Durbin, June Barson. From Auckland of course.

Gradually I was acquiring an image of myself as a person apart from myself as a poet, and in my reading I identified most easily with the stoical solitary heroine suffering in silence, the 'plain Jane' content to love the strong, inarticulate hero, who was easily beguiled by the flashily beautiful woman but who turned always in the end (regretfully too late) to the shadowy shy woman he had failed to notice. I saw myself as a 'background' person watching, listening. I was not Becky Sharp; I was Emma. Yet I was also Tess and Marty South, as I had once been Anne of Green Gables and Charlotte Brontë (Isabel being Emily, and June Ann). I was Maggie Tulliver and Jane Eyre and Cathy. And when I could find no heroine to become, I was myself simply adoring the heroes — Jude the Obscure, Raskolnikov, Brutus, rather than Mark Antony, whom *everyone* liked. There were the film heroes, too — Robert Donat, Laurence Olivier, Clark Gable. My lasting heroes were, naturally, the poets, French and English — Daudet, Victor Hugo, Keats, Shelley, Wordsworth, Rupert Brooke, Yeats (in his early phase of 'old men admiring themselves in the water' and 'the cloths of Heaven'), most of the poets from my fourth-form prize, *The Golden Book of Modern English Poetry*, and from our *Shakespeare to Hardy* — and the prose writers, Dostoevski, Hardy, the Brontës, George Eliot, Washington Irving, E. B. Lucas, Sir Thomas Browne.

And Shakespeare.

I knew of few New Zealand writers, only Katherine Mansfield, Eileen Duggan, William Pember Reeves, Thomas Bracken, all of whom I thought of as 'belonging' to my mother, and because I did not think of myself as belonging to her world, I had no desire to share 'her' writers. Her Long-fellows and Twains and Whittiers, yes, but not writers that she or her parents or grandparents might have known. For our speech that year, 'An Author', I chose Francis Thompson, whom I had 'discovered' for myself, and I felt curious when one member of the class, choosing Katherine Mansfield, was commended by the teacher for choosing a New Zealand writer when none of our English studies even supposed that a New Zealand writer or New Zealand existed.

My last years at school were also busily practical. I was a member of the B basketball team and eventually became captain. I gained my Elementary Certificate in Life Saving. I was a keen diver. Seized by a longing to play tennis, I used the pound note from my 'marks' for poems in the Children's Page of the *Truth* to pay for the frame of a tennis racquet, which someone Dad knew had offered to string for a reduced rate, but when the racquet was complete, my shame was overwhelming when I found the strings were black instead of cream. I pronounced the racquet 'funny'. I was not brave enough to parade my racquet in all its difference, and the one day I brought it to school, I was certain that 'everyone noticed it', and from then it remained unused, on top of the wardrobe beside the two big sleeping dolls, one dressed in pink, the other in blue, the clothes made by a friend of Aunty Isy and the dolls given to June and Isabel when they felt too grown up to play with them, which was just as well, for they were warned that the clothes were 'knitted specially by an old woman' and must be taken care of . . . The unused racquet and the unused dolls stayed there until my sister June had children who used them without fear of difference or of harming the 'specially knitted' dolls' clothes. By then, the friend of Aunty Isy, and Aunty Isy herself were dead.

That year our cats were stricken with what must have been feline enteritis, and one by one they died. I seized on Winkles' death to write an elegy, which I sent to the *Mail Minor* under my nom de plume, Amera. I was prepared to make use of everything in the interests of poetry, like a bird lining its nest, an apt comparison, for a new interest now occupied members of the Group, their influence still unbroken and powerful in the classroom — the preparation of their 'box', a term new to me. Instead of being given isolated birthday and Christmas presents, they were now collecting household items, such as linen, cutlery, china, with each addition discussed and described in detail. No matter how distant I felt myself to be from them, I could say that they and I were engaged in similar pursuits — all collecting materials for the future we hoped to have, they their household goods, I my experiences and fictional characters. When I say that I 'seized on' Winkles' death to write an elegy, I could say that I also felt an obligation to the poets who had written about Myrtle's death, to share the death of Winkles and my feelings about it, and that all experiences collected for the future were not for individual use only like household linen and cutlery, but for common use within a stream which, I was beginning to sense, might be called history.

When I wasn't able to plead the excuse of 'studying for exams', I still milked the cows, the duty now shared with Robert and June; walking the hills in search of Bluey and Scrapers, gazing out at the harbour and the sea, the cape, familiar sights, placing in my mind that tiny, windowless building that we still knew as the morgue; the park where Wirth's Circus and Six-penny Zoo camped each year and where we, desperate to see a circus and never seeing it, tried to peep under the tent; the tree-lined street; missing Winkles balanced on my shoulder, but consoling myself with thoughts of the Sea-Foam Youth Grown Old, the Scholar-Gipsy, Mr Ardenue, and all the characters from the fiction I was reading; wondering about and dreading the future, for in spite of my dreams of university, I knew that I would have to train as a teacher, for teachers, unlike university students, were paid.

Our parents had receded from our lives. We discussed school affairs with them, asked them for money for this and that, and either were given it or not. We were impatient with their ignorance of school subjects. Aware now that Mother had turned increasingly to poetry for shelter, as I was doing, I, with an unfeelingness based on misery of feeling, challenged the worth of some of her beloved poets, aware that my criticism left her flushed and unhappy while I felt a savage joy at her distress. I had begun to hate her habit of waiting hand and foot, martyrlike, upon her family. When I was eager to do things for myself, Mother was always there, anxious to serve. I now felt the guilt of it, and I hated her for being the instrument of that guilt. Her invisible life spent on her distant plane of religion and poetry, her complete peacefulness, angered me just as I knew it angered my father, who sometimes tried to taunt her to show anger or accepted selfishness or any unsaintly feeling that might bring disapproval from the Christ she tried so hard to please. At such times Mother would flush slightly and, pursing her lips, begin to sing softly:

When He cometh when He cometh
to make up His jewels,
all His jewels, precious jewels
His loved and His own.

or the chosen song of the Christadelphians, 'Mine eyes have seen the glory of the coming of the Lord', the 'Battle Hymn of the American Republic', or the other favourite, 'Zion's King shall reign victorious, / He shall set his people free . . .', which, sung to the tune of the German National Anthem prompted my father to taunt, 'There you are, singing the *German* National Anthem.'

Our home was seldom happy now. The festivals that we cherished had lost most of their joy with our growing up. Our brother, who had discovered alcohol and made a strong brew of beer in the washhouse copper, was in a turmoil of adolescent confusion and depression at his sickness, having to bear Dad's continued belief that 'he could stop the fits if he wanted to' and Mother's urging, 'Be strong, Bruddie, be strong. Many of the great men of the world had epilepsy', and unable to fit into this expected role of super-boy, sometimes he was brought home after being found lying in the gutter outside the billiard room. Isabel tried to make him sign a pledge, 'A pledge I make / no wine to take . . .' Various people of the town who had promised him help with work had failed to honour their promises. Garfield Todd of the Church of Christ was one who did help.

And so day by day we polished Dad's buttons on his National Reserve uniform, read the casualty lists, accepted the new words of war, listened to the B.B.C. news, flagged the movement of the Allied Forces. And at school the University Entrance exam came and went, and I passed, remembering the exam now chiefly for the two guineas which it cost to enter and which I struggled to get, with my father insisting that I should leave school. A few years later my first published story in the *Listener*, 'University Entrance', earned me that sum, confirming for me once again the closeness, the harmony, and not the separation of literature (well, a simple story!) and life.

29 Imagination

Where in my earlier years time had been horizontal, progressive, day after day, year after year, with memories being a true personal history known by dates and specific years, or vertical, with events stacked one upon the other, 'sacks on the mill and *more on still*', the adolescent time now became a whirlpool, and so the memories do not arrange themselves to be observed and written about, they whirl, propelled by a force beneath, with different memories rising to the surface at different times and thus denying the existence of a 'pure' autobiography and confirming, for each moment, a separate story accumulating to a million stories, all different and with some memories forever staying beneath the surface. I sit here at my desk, peering into the depths of the dance, for the movement is dance with its own pattern, neither good nor bad, but individual in its own right — a dance of dust or sunbeams or bacteria or notes of sound or colours or liquids, or ideas that the writer, trying to write an autobiography, clings to in one moment only. I think of the times we used to sit by the Rakaia River, watching the branches and trunks of trees, the dead cattle and sheep, swept suddenly from the main stream to the many whirlpools at the side, where, their force no less swift, they stayed a moment only before being drawn down down toward the centre of the earth.

I struggled with the events of those last years at school. I felt bewildered, imprisoned — where would I go? What if my parents died suddenly? What was the world like? How could the word be at war? I asked myself that old question which haunted me as a child, Why was the world, why *was* the world? And where was my place? I had those recurring dreams of being grown up and returning to school only to be told, What do you think you're doing here? You're grown up.

My sisters and I immersed ourselves in our reading and studying. To pass the long, hot summer, we began our 'novels': mine was *The Vision of the Dust* from Chesterton's poem 'The Praise of Dust':

> *Rich white and blood-red blossom; stones,*
> *Lichens like fire encrust;*
> *A gleam of blue, a glare of gold,*
> *The vision of the dust.*

Isabel's title was *Go Shepherd* from 'The Scholar-Gipsy'; June's, *There is Sweet Music* from 'The Lotos-Eaters'. We did not get beyond the first few

131

chapters of our novels. We continued to send our poems to the *Mail Minor*, the *Truth*, and *Dot's Little Folk*, and one week memorable for me saw another of my poems, 'Blossoms', made Poem of the Week, and the other, 'The Crocus', also praised by Dot, whose remarks were: 'Thank you for the poems, Amber Butterfly. They show poetic insight and imagination. I'm making 'Blossoms' a poem of the week. I just wonder, though, if flowers, even poetically, dream of moons. Write again soon and do not mind my friendly criticism.' She had been referring to a line in 'The Crocus', 'and dream no more of the love of a golden moon'.

My reply to Dot began, 'Of course I do not mind your criticism . . .' It is obvious that I did mind it. I was convinced that if I said in a poem that flowers dream of moons, then the fault lay with the inability of the poem to convince, not in the idea. But, oh, how sweet were the words, 'poetic insight and *imagination*'. This was the first time anyone had told me, directly, that I had *imagination*. The acknowledgment was an occasion for me, and, as often happens, this one affirmation led to others, and soon I was being told at school that I had *imagination*. My dream of being a poet, a real poet, was nearer to being realised. There was still the question of a disability — Coleridge and Francis Thompson and Edgar Allan Poe had their addiction to opium, Pope his lameness, Cowper his depression, John Clare, his insanity, the Brontës their tuberculosis as well as the disablement of their life about them . . . Well, my sister had died, and the cats had died, and my brother had epilepsy, but for all that and for all my newly acquired or acknowledged imagination, I and my life, I felt, were excessively ordinary. I worried about my clothes or lack of them and my 'fig-ewer', whether or not I had 'curves' and 'oomph' and 'hickies', and having read *Ariel*, the life of Shelley, I felt keenly Shelley's probable disapproval of me, for he had complained of Harriet that she was interested only in looking at *hats*. I resolved I would *never* be like Shelley's wife. (From time to time it did seem that my ambition to be a poet became confused with a fantasy of *marrying* one!)

I wrote in my diary, 'Dear Mr Ardenue, *They* think I'm going to be a schoolteacher, but I'm going to be a *poet*.'

30 A Country Full of Rivers

The year of the Upper Sixth was a cruel year, the cruellest I had known. My school tunic was now so tightly fitting that it pressed on all parts of my body; it was torn and patched and patched again, but obviously it was no use having a new one, for I was leaving school at the end of the year. Also, I knew that my homemade sanitary towels showed their bulk, and the blood leaked through, and when I stood up in class, I'd glance furtively at the desk seat to see whether it was bloody, and when I stood in morning assembly, I placed my hymn book in one hand and shielded either my back or front, whichever was bulkier, with my other hand. Because I was now a house captain, I stood in front of Gibson House, unable to hide but thankful that my years of standing almost always alone in assembly would soon be over. I could never understand why no one 'formed twos' with me in assembly or physical education, when the command was given, 'Form Twos'. My shame was extreme; I concluded that I stank.

There in the front of the hall, trying to hide that bulk, trying to remain calm and unconcerned when we sang, 'the blood of Jesus whispers Peace within', I felt a permanent blush on my freckled, fair-skinned face. I felt impossibly old to be at school. My impatience to finish school and my feeling of horror at the thought of how unfitted I felt myself to be to 'take my place in the world' and my passionate desire to be a poet produced a number of tearful outbursts at home and school. A teacher's suggestion, based on a lone history essay, where I wrote feelingly of Mazzini (our history book said he was idealistic, imaginative — enough to win my heart), that I sit a scholarship in English and history and her disappointment when the next essay, on no such exciting subject as Mazzini, failed to meet her expectations, led to my 'dropping' history, geography and science, and facing a bursary examination with English, French and mathematics.

Our class had four girls, the old 'scholar' group, with the members of the powerful group all left to be kindergarten teachers, nurses, Karitane, or general, or to prepare to marry. The girls of the scholar group talked more certainly now of their future university careers and where they would stay in Dunedin. 'St Mags, of course,' they said, alarming me once again with such a familiar abbreviation of the awesome St Margaret's. I was preparing to apply for training college but sitting a bursary as practice for taking university subjects 'part time'. We were like young birds on the edge of a cliff; wings were fluttering; the air was filled with rustlings and testings and chatterings. The girls going on to university appeared to be calm, smooth, assured, with no doubt of their ability to fly and to soar. Our teachers, meanwhile, trying to capture their own vanished years, talked nostalgically of what to expect and how university had been in 'their day'. We pored over the university calendar, and my dreams had no bound when I turned to the list of graduates and the prizes awarded. I noted particularly the prizes for the composition of poetry and prose and dreamed of winning them.

My last year at school was made more insecure by the arrangements of the class into 'groups'. I was unable to determine how I would manage my area in space, now that I was freed after spending most of my life sitting by command at a desk in an atmosphere that was usually formal, for I had been taught in the 'old' way, where the pupils sat fast while the teacher stood in front of the class teaching, which meant talking and writing on the blackboard and asking questions responded to by the pupils' waving hands in the air, whereupon the teacher chose one pupil to answer, pronounced it right or wrong, then resumed the talking and writing on the blackboard. I was disconcerted to find we were now to move freely around the class-room, sitting in circles, in discussion groups, each member contributing ideas. I retreated. I was afraid to voice my ideas. I had grown used to the whole class being astonished or entertained by my remarks, which I could not bring myself to make face to face.

I was able to conduct the house choir in the Music Festival, 'Go, lovely Rose, tell her that wastes her time and me', and 'It was a lover and his lass', and to lead the sixth-form jazz band in:

> Who's the prettiest child
> drives the little boys wild
> as a rule they will all declare,
> It's the girl, it's the girl
> with the pigtails in her hair.

only because there was no disconcerting close contact with the choir, the band, or the audience. I was 'shy', you see. Was not the Scholar-Gipsy also shy?

> Seen by rare glimpses, pensive and tongue-tied,
> In hat of antique shape, and cloak of grey,
> The same the gipsies wore . . .

Toward the end of the year Miss Crowe, our form teacher, gave a sixth-form party for those who were leaving. I wore my tunic. I had my first drink of coffee. I sat aloof in my 'poetic' way (I was now known as the class poet, and I usually had high marks for my essays), obviously dreaming of 'other things', and during the party Miss Crowe, 'mixing' with the girls, asked me, 'Which musical instrument do you prefer?'

In spite of our one music lesson a week at school and my term of learning the piano, I felt ignorant of 'real' music. The classes were singing classes where we sang arpeggio jingles,

> This is the colour I like
> What do you think of today,
> Da Ma Nay Porto la Bay . . .

As well as the loved songs from the Dominion Song Book, 'The Trout', 'To Music', the Shakespeare songs, 'I know a bank, Where the bee sucks . . .', songs that never failed to transport me to a place which, I discovered, had been described for me by J. C. Squire in his poem 'Rivers' (another from the *Golden Book of Modern English Poetry*):

> There is something still in the back of my mind
> From very far away;
> There is something I saw and see not,
> A country full of rivers
> that stirs in my heart and speaks to me . . .

Thus, when Miss Crowe asked which was my favourite musical instrument, I was reluctant to show that I knew so little of music (this dreamy, poetic, imaginative Jean Frame!). 'I prefer the violin,' I said, thinking suddenly of the blind violinist of long ago. 'Yes,' Miss Crowe said. 'It *is* more emotional, isn't it?' Her reply embarrassed me. Who was talking of emotion? I sat in my corner, drinking my coffee, my face burning with all the feelings and fears in the world.

I sat the Scholarship Examination. In the English paper I wrote my 'appreciation' of the poem 'Lark, skylark':

> spilling your rubbed and round pebbles of sound in air's still lake
> whose widening circles fill the noon
> while none
> is known so small beside the sun . . .

I answered 'comprehension' questions on Stephen Spender's poem 'Pylons' without knowing the word. I remember these questions only as a result of the intensity of the moment: my fingers were spattered with ink, the clock in front of the hall tick-tocked; my heart rolled against my ribs; my head felt hilltop clear: I enjoyed exams.

The next event was the interview conducted by Mr Partridge, the principal of Dunedin Training College, where I tried to appear bright and teacherly, making sure that he knew I was a house captain, captain of the B basketball team, conductor of the house choir, leader of the sixth-form jazz band, a good student . . . I think he was impressed, probably seeing the bouncy, sporting, uncomplicated schoolgirl which I was not (I the shy, poetic, timid, obedient).

'Has anyone in your family ever been to training college?' he asked. I could have told him about the ever-present Cousin Peg. I could have told him that, apart from Uncle Alec's family of older cousins and Australian cousins, I was the first to go to high school, that my Grandma Frame signed her marriage certificate with a cross . . . then I remembered the aunt's illustrious nieces who had shone in the Deanna Durbin contest, and didn't Iona learn elocution also?

'My aunt's niece, Iona Livingstone, has been to training college,' I said.

'One of our best students,' Mr Partridge replied, looking impressed. 'A born teacher.'

I glowed in Iona's light, and a few weeks later word came that I had been accepted for teachers' training college.

Speech Day arrived. I gloried again in winning, having chosen Aurore Dupin, George Sand, as my subject, making use of her novel *Consuelo*, which Bruddie found in the rubbish dump — yet another *cancelled* book from the Oamaru Athenaeum and Mechanics Institute. *Consuelo* with its red cover, small print and thousand pages enthralled us. We fell in love with Count Albert. My new-found imagination and my ignorance of the actual life of George Sand and the influence of the character of Albert combined to produce in my speech an invented passionate George Sand forever in love with dark, handsome composers and poets, inevitably male. In my ignorance I was not even suspicious of a certain coyness that overcame the teacher when she mentioned George Sand. I — we — assumed the teacher's attitude related to her coming marriage; indeed her marriage was also on our minds at school. I composed a John Brown parody, which we sang:

The teachers of Waitaki are teaching us at school.
Their hearts are full of algebra, their minds are keeping cool.
Some of them discover now that marriage is the rule

so they go marrying off
from English French and mathematics
to
Pots brooms electroluxes . . .

The end of the year was celebrated with the usual last assembly and the speech by the invited guest, usually an Old Girl who reminded us that our school days were the happiest of our lives. What else could we expect from the chosen Old Girl of a school modelled on a boys' public school, where we even sang, with identification and fervour: 'On the ball on the ball on the ball / through scrummage three quarters and all . . .', and 'Forty years on and afar and asunder / parted are they . . .', concluding with, 'And the fields ring again and again / to the shout of the twenty-two men . . .'

We sang our school song: 'Green the fields that lie around / Waitaki's stately walls . . .', then 'God be in my head', and the Hymn for the End of Term, 'Lord dismiss us with thy blessing'. And finally, because the world was still at war and we, too, had night blackouts and air-raid practice; and echelons and convoys still sailed away; and neighbours' sons were missing in the desert, and others were wounded or killed; and day by day still the casualty lists appeared in the newspapers — we sang, 'Peace perfect peace in this dark world of sin / the blood of Jesus whispers Peace within . . .'

There were many other end-of-term functions that I had no part in — dances, socials, afternoon teas, bike rides. I knew no boys except those next door (too old, and one dead in the war), over the road (too young or too old); my social recreation was the 'pictures' now and again and walks on the hill and along the gully. Although we girls often felt our life had a tragedy and difference compared with the apparent life of others of our age, toward the end of my years at school I emerged from a shocked concentration on the turmoil of being in Oamaru, the state which received so much blame for so much that had happened to us, to a realisation that many other girls had not even reached high school because their parents had not been able to afford it or made the sacrifices to afford it as our parents undoubtedly did. I thought of the family of seven children up Eden Street who went barefoot, not always by choice, and of how I'd seen them running to school on a frosty morning, their feet mottled blue with cold; and of the family in Chelmer Street who lived only on soup made from pork bones from the bacon factory. And nearer home, as I seemed to awaken from a long, troubled family sleep, I was suddenly aware of other girls with 'funny' uniforms that were flared without the regulation pleats. I was astonished to discover that apparently K., who was in the sixth form first year and had been accepted for training college, showed no embarrassment over her peculiar dress and that of her sister in a lower form. We became friends. They were a clever family with versatile talents of writing and drawing; they issued a family magazine to which they asked us to contribute. We obliged once or twice only, in awe of their initiative and talent and their apparent lack of concern over their 'funny' tunics. Once I visited their home and was impressed by the closeness, the almost island state of their family. They were 'poor', their father, a carpenter and lecturer in carpentry at Tech and appearing to be very old with a shock of white hair and a habitually teasing way with children: peeping through the hand hole of our red-painted gate, seeing him pass, wheeling his bike (there was a point in Eden Street when everyone had to dismount and wheel their bikes up the steep slope), we as children used to be afraid of his peculiar gruff joking. His voice was pleasant, however. The mother was a neat woman with contained brown plaits wound close to her head. I cherished the memory of the glimpse of their big dining room table with everyone sitting around it, all drawing, working things out, reading, writing, in a quiet harmony of brown and gold, with no sudden disastrous crevices of being, no epileptic fits, no alarm, confusion, crying, fear. Or so it seemed to us. They had a little brother, Nat, who built and tinkered with wirelesses and could never catch up and didn't see why he should.

Our brother was now separated from us in his confusion. He was alone with Mother faithfully attending to his needs and trying to solve his problems, even if it meant only removing the bones from the cooked fish to prevent him from choking. We girls grew close to one another. Long ago Myrtle and Bruddie and I had 'banded' together against Miss Low when June was being born, telling our Miss Low stories; later we all 'banded' against the threat of the health inspector who dared to criticise our home, our parents and our beloved cats and dogs. There had been various 'bandings' since, and although Myrtle's death had been met chiefly in solitude, June and I had helped each other in our reading of 'Once Paumanok when the lilac scent was in the air and the fifth-month grass was growing'.

Now we were aware that I was about to face 'the world', with the others facing it also in a year or two. Our strategy took two courses: first, we wrote to Mr Nordmeyer, the Member of Parliament (who had also been a church minister and lived near us), asking to borrow twenty-five pounds to buy clothes and other supplies for our 'future'. We had no reply to our begging letter. The next course was an acceleration of our writing of prose and poetry, which served the purpose of the old Miss Low stories, uniting us against the fear and anticipation of the 'future', which, like Miss Low and the health inspector and the visiting Death, was now in control of us.

31 Leaving the Is-Land, Greeting the Is-Land

It is significant that the last chapter of this volume should deal with clothes, for it was around clothes that my life was suddenly centred, even as it had been years ago when I wore my velvet beastie gown, and as it had been during my school years when I lived trapped within a grey serge tunic. Appearance had always been important, and the appearance of others, their particular clothes, had brought a sense of comfort or of loss. My father's change of suit colour as his change of his brand of tobacco (for he *wore* his tobacco like clothes) could bring panic to his children. During the Depression days my father's suit was grey, and I do remember a search lasting hours up and down Thames Street to find a shop that sold a reel of grey cotton to match the thread of Dad's suit. After the Depression, when he changed to navy blue, our shock and feeling of strangeness were similar to our feeling when Mother cut her hair or put in her false teeth. In a life where people had few clothes and a man one suit and one overcoat, the clothes were part of the skin, like an animal's fur.

When I stopped wearing my school tunic after six years of almost daily wear, I felt naked, like a skinned rabbit; and the letter written by the warden of the teachers' college, listing the essential clothing of a training college student, was the cause of our panic and approach to Mr Nordmeyer.

I had never dreamed that people in 'real life' wore so many clothes. As I studied the list, I was overcome by a hopeless feeling of unreality. Where, except in films, did people own so many dresses, costumes, shoes, coats? And a dressing gown! At home there was an old relic, a flannelette checked garment known as 'Grandad's dressing gown', so foreign to our life that we looked on it as a piece of history; it was almost as foreign as sleeping between sheets instead of our usual grey blankets.

From the blossoming wealth of detail on the alarming list I pruned most of the unattainable 'fruits', leaving the agreed essential costume that became 'jersey and skirt'. I still had my navy blue school coat, and a blouse. These would have to 'do' until I saved enough from my (monthly) paycheck of nine pounds three and nine, and as I was to stay in Dunedin with Aunty Isy and Uncle George of Four Garden Terrace, Carroll Street, giving them only ten shillings a week for my board and keep, I did hope to save money.

And so the future, which had been talked of and dreamed of for so long, toward which our teachers had directed their urging, threats, even their own long-lost ambitions, had begun as the present once again, the Is-Land from which there is no escape, and I was equipped to face it as a shy young woman most at home and experienced with 'creatures' such as cows, sheep, dogs, cats, insects, anything living that was not human; with the natural world of sea, earth, sky, and the plants, trees and flowers; and with written and printed language with its themes and thoughts and its alphabet with the bowers of A's and O's and U's and D's large enough to hide in.

That summer I burned all my diaries of the Land of Ardenue and my notebooks of poems, although many of them had been published in the children's pages. Only in the *Truth* had I printed my real name, Janet Frame, by which I was now known, the old Nini and Fuzzy and Jean being discarded. Most of the girls in my class at school had also effected their personal transformation as a preparation for their 'future'; some had discovered their 'real' name or changed letters in their old name; others had changed their handwriting deliberately to a new style, often with a new colour of ink (royal blue to black or green), with a new signature (practised carefully over the pages of exercise books). Others chose a new hair style or a new word to use more often than formerly. And yet others revealed that they were one of twins or had been adopted after all.

In our family, we rediscovered that Isabel had been born with a caul, which gave her the magic power of never being able to drown.

I, too, practised my signature. It was a habit my father had, too, for signing his time sheets in an impressive way. He was very proud of his handwriting. He would sit at the kitchen table, writing on the backs of old time sheets, G. S. Frame, George Samuel Frame, followed by two lines that seemed to haunt him, for he wrote them everywhere, on old time sheets, the backs of envelopes, old bills:

> *Just a song at twilight*
> *when the lights are low.*

Janet Paterson Frame, I wrote, looping carefully.

In early February, as a member of a Railway Family with a privilege or priv. ticket, I travelled south on the Sunday slow train to Dunedin and my Future.

VOLUME TWO

An Angel
at my Table

This second volume
is dedicated to the Scrivener family,
Frank Sargeson, Karl and Kay Stead,
and E. P. Dawson.

Reste tranquille, si soudain
L'Ange à ta table se décide;
Efface doucement les quelques rides
Que fait la nappe sous ton pain.

Rilke, 'Vergers'

CONTENTS

PART ONE

Tricks of Desperation

Prospero: *My brave spirit!*
Who was so firm, so constant, that this coil
Would not infect his reason?

Ariel: *Not a soul,*
But felt a fever of the mad; and play'd
Some tricks of desperation.

Shakespeare, *The Tempest*, Act 1, Scene (ii).

1   The Stone

The future accumulates like a weight upon the past. The weight upon the earliest years is easier to remove to let that time spring up like grass that has been crushed. The years following childhood become welded to their future, massed like stone, and often the time beneath cannot spring back into growth like new grass: it lies bled of its green in a new shape with those frail bloodless sprouts of another, unfamiliar time, entangled one with the other beneath the stone.

2   Number Four Garden Terrace, Dunedin

The Sunday slow train, a goods train with a passenger carriage at the end, took seven hours to travel the seventy-eight miles between Oamaru and Dunedin, stopping at every station, waiting for at least half an hour by the gum trees at Waianakarua until the midday Limited rushed by on its way north, crawling by the wild-sweet-pea-surrounded sheds — the 'flag-stations' which I still ignorantly supposed to be named after the flag-lilies or swamp lilies, dark blue with pale white-blue throats specked with yellow, growing in the many swamps along the line. We stopped at Hampden where year after year we had travelled for the Railway Picnic, climbing from the train just before the cattlestop by the lagoon and its shadowy mass of black swans, walking higgledy-piggledy carrying kits and rugs down to the picnic ground by the beach with its beach 'dunny', the dark-stained wooden seat split down the middle, the concrete floor puddled muddy and salt-smelling, with here and there a splash of seagull mess as if the seagulls also used the changing-shed as a dunny. Now I, with memories created from the past as a foraging bee creates its own sweet architecture, looked out at Hampden and the black swans and the lagoon, remembering the sea and the beach of shells and the wet-floored dunny; and the railway raspberry drink, free.

Then followed the train's curious encircling of Palmerston with the stone monument on the hill appearing, disappearing, reappearing, with the few people in the carriage suddenly changing position, opening their windows, looking interested, for Palmerston was 'for refreshments', and the Limited had come and gone with its passengers, like locusts, eating through the supplies of ham sandwiches and sugar buns and hot pies, leaving only the 'stalks' for those on the goods train who were now seized, as everyone used to be at Palmerston, with hunger, and thirst.

The hills around Palmerston were burned by the sun and by fires, with only an occasional dead tree in a gully or halfway up a slope, and now and again a cluster of trees, some long dead, others shimmy-naked with only a thin layer of shiny leaves. More trees appeared as the train approached Seacliff and once again there was a movement in the carriage as the passengers became aware of *Seacliff*, the station, and *Seacliff* the hospital, the asylum, glimpsed as a castle of dark stone between the hills.

The train drew into the station. Yes, the loonies were there; everyone looked out at the loonies, known in Oamaru as those who were sent 'down the line', and in Dunedin, 'up the line'. Often it was hard to tell who were the loonies. A few people left the train here — they'd be the relations, visiting. We had no loonies in our family, although we knew of people who had been sent 'down the line', but we did not know what they looked like, only that there was a funny look in their eye and they'd attack you with a bread knife or an axe.

I was too fearful of the prospect of living in a big city like Dunedin to pay much attention to Seacliff station. The train now followed the winding track around the steep cliffs, looking down on the holiday settlements at Waitati, Karitane, where the 'group' at school had their 'cribs' by the sea where the world's mummys and daddys and big and little brothers and sisters had a life of fun with their beach and boats and sun and holiday games.

The train creaked, groaned, crawled, rocking, and the sea lay far below, calm, and grey, slightly ruffled with a shine like a seal's fur. Then the tunnel, Mihiwaka, the passengers coughing, shutting and opening and shutting the windows, the carriage filled with smoke; out of the tunnel, the inescapable sense of arrival: Port Chalmers, Ravensbourne, Sawyers Bay; Dunedin Harbour and the Dunedin Railway Station, a huge, steaming, noisy place, not as crowded for the late afternoon arrival of the goods train as it would be for the Invercargill or Lyttelton Express, but still inspiring fear and awe: I was alone in my first city. My mind loomed with the fictions of the great cities of the world, and of Dunedin as such a city. I thought of the 'dark Satanic mills', of people 'caged like squirrels'; of fire, and plague and the press gang; and although I was willing to follow the example of the writers and eventually 'love' the new city, as Charles Dickens, Hazlitt, Lamb, loved their London, I could think first only of desolation, the poverty which I was sure I would find, and of how living in the city might destroy me —

> *We poets in our youth begin in gladness;*
> *But thereof comes in the end despondency and madness.*

I who had scarcely left childhood and who knew by heart Wordsworth's 'Intimations of Immortality' had taken to myself the threat of

> *Full soon thy soul shall have her earthly freight,*
> *And custom lie upon thee with a weight*
> *Heavy as frost, and deep almost as life!*

with the certainty that the threat would be realised in a big city: Dunedin. My consolation on that dreadful day of arrival lay in the prospect of my new home with Aunty Isy and Uncle George — Four Garden Terrace, a place of light with a terraced garden looking down over the bays of the peninsula, with my room, sharing the view, bright with cretonne curtains, a matching bedspread, and sheets on the bed as if for a princess. And I'd attend Training College, and University in my spare time, impressing people with my imagination; everyone would recognise me as a true poet. I'd not yet completed the practical details of a poet's life as I found it beyond even my imagination to make the transition from fantasy to fact — all the poets I'd studied were safely dead, and so long ago, in such distant countries, yet although I might not have determined my own way of life, it was the poets who kept me company on my first journey away from my home and family.

My knowledge of Aunty Isy and Uncle George was limited. I looked on them as I looked on most relatives and adults as 'formidable', living in a completely separate world where I could not imagine myself as belonging — the world of constant recitation of comings and goings of countless relatives and friends, of names of places, all spoken with the certainty of possession, of knowledge that each person was in a destined right place or if not there were questions and rumours as countless as the former affirmations. I knew Aunty Isy only as the former dancer in the old photographs of the two beautiful sisters Isabella and Polly dressed in their kilts, their waist-long black hair flowing behind them in strands of silk; as the aunt who held Myrtle, Dad's first-born, in all the photographs in which Mother didn't appear, causing us to ask, 'Mum was Myrtle Aunty Isy's baby? Why weren't you photographed with baby Myrtle?'; as the kind aunt who sent a

Christmas parcel each year, prompting the anxiety the week before Christmas, '*The parcel* hasn't arrived yet!'; and lately I thought of Aunty Isy as aunt-smelling of mothballs and cloth and wearing dark colours and working where she had worked all her life, now as supervisor in the Roslyn mill; and still saying in a high voice, 'Lottie, Lottie, Middlemarch, Middlemarch.' And I thought of her husband, Uncle George, as a pale man in a grey overcoat; I think he was a commercial traveller.

Dunedin was half hidden in misty rain. My taxi made a short journey from the railway station to halfway up a hill street, Carroll Street, and there was Garden Terrace, and Number Four, the fourth small brick cottage in an attached group of six, their back and front doors reached by two narrow lanes from Carroll Street. Everywhere there were brick and concrete buildings, tall chimneys layered across the sky, grey streets, a view that I had seen in my mind's image of a city. Somewhere to the east was the sea, which, ever faithful, had accompanied me from the kingdom of Oamaru.

Aunty Isy (aunt-smelling) hugged me at the door. She smelt of wardrobes full of clothing made of materials such as voile, jersey, silk, serge, crepe-de-chine.

'Oh Jean, we're looking forward to your stay. We're all so proud you're going to be a teacher. We always look for your name in the paper at prize-giving; and the other girls, too. What a clever family!'

I stood smiling my shy smile, which was more close-lipped than usual because my front teeth were now in the last stages of decay, as the Social Security Health Service did not allow for dentistry beyond primary school, and my family had no spare money to pay for dentists.

Aunty Isy's sisters-in-law, Molly and Elsie, who lived next door at Number Five and whom I knew as Aunty Molly (the radio aunt) and Aunty Elsie, came to say hello to me.

'So this is Jean, and you're going to be a teacher?'

'Yes.'

The cottage was like a large doll's house, with a tiny scullery with sink bench just inside the back door, a sitting-dining room, known as the 'wee' room, next to it along a narrow passageway, with another slightly larger room, the 'best' sitting room, just inside the front door. Upstairs there were two bedrooms, both small. The bathroom was downstairs in the wash-house leading from the scullery.

'Your room is up here,' Aunty Isy said, 'at the top of the stairs.'

As we walked up the stairs she turned to the right to the room where she and Uncle George slept.

'Uncle George is in bed,' she explained. 'Would you like to say hello to him?'

I knew that Uncle George had cancer. I stood at the end of the bed.

'George, Jean has come to say hello to you.'

'Hello, Uncle George.'

'So you're the one who's going to be a teacher?'

I noted the grey pallor of his face with its soft-looking skin, like dead skin, and I wondered what dreadful sight was concealed beneath the bedclothes. There was an oily smell of lanoline, and a row of blue and white empty lanoline tubes, some squashed and rolled up, on the dressing-table. Sexually curious as well as ignorant, I wondered if the lanoline had anything to do with 'it', and I wondered if Aunty Isy and Uncle George 'did it'.

Perhaps you couldn't, if you had cancer?

'He spends most of his time in bed now,' Aunty Isy said, as we went downstairs for our cup of tea.

Later, I sat on my bed in my tiny room that looked out over brick walls, miles of buildings with tall chimneys. If I leaned out the window I could see, just inside the front gate into the alley, the small garden blooming with geraniums, which I had not thought of before as city flowers; they were dusty with soot layered over their own flame-velvet. I felt a stirring of anticipation and excitement as I realised that I was alone in my first grey city; then gradually the excitement gave way to anxiety. So this was how it was, face to face with the Future — being alone, having no one to talk to, being afraid of the city and Training College and teaching, and having to pretend that I was not alone, that I had many people to talk to, that I felt at home in Dunedin, and that teaching was what I had longed to do all my life.

3   The Student

My first week at Dunedin Training College was less painful than I had expected, for I shared my newness with many others, all apprehensive, all anxious to learn quickly the assured student ways, while the lecturers, not as remote as the adults I had previously known, amazed me by their insight as they explained our feelings, trying to fit us comfortably into the role of students. They called us Mr and Miss, with an occasional Mrs, but because the war had not ended, there were few men, who were quickly claimed by the beautiful blonde women while the rest, myself among them, survived by daydreaming of what might be and by concentrating admiration on the most handsome lecturers.

I had my first adventure in assurance when I heard the new language which I would soon speak but which I now approached with awe and with the fear of intimate reference and abbreviation. While the other new students were saying casually, *Training Coll, Varsity, Party* (for Mr Partridge, the Principal), *Crit Lesson*, I still could not bring myself to utter the magical words. The gradual learning of the language, the attitudes, customs of behaviour and dress, produced in me a euphoria of belonging which was intensified and contradicted by my actual feeling of isolation. At the Thursday morning assembly, while we waited for the appearance of the staff and *Party*, the second-year students began singing 'their' song, which was soon to be 'ours'. My heart turned over with the momentous import of the occasion as the second-year students sang,

> *Oh the deacon went down*
> *Oh the deacon went down*
> *to the cellar to pray*
> *and he darn got drunk*
> *and he stayed all day (and he stayed all day).*
> *Oh the deacon went down*
> *to the cellar to pray*
> *and he darn got drunk*
> *and he stayed all day,*
> *Oh I ain't gonna grieve my Lord no more . . .*
>
> *Oh the devil he's got (Oh the devil he's got)*
> *a hypocrite shoe . . .*
> *If you want to go to hell and burn in fire*
> *just don't you do the Lord's desire . . .*

I found the joyous singing as moving as if it had been an extract from the *Messiah*, performed by every choral society every Christmas and so familiar to those not directly in touch with that kind of music. The idea that soon I, too, would be singing 'Oh the deacon went down' (there were even a few now among the first-years who had joined the chorus) seemed to me like a promise of heaven. Everyone was laughing and talking and excited and everywhere the new language was being spoken with such certainty and power!

Then, when Party and his staff appeared, the singing stopped, and everyone, even the staff, wore a look of self-satisfaction as if they shared a tremendous secret, as if student life were the happiest of all.

Later I saw two ex-Waitakians, Katherine Bradley and Rona Pinder.

'College is fun,' they said.

I agreed. 'Yes, isn't it?'

During that first week, making plans to study English and French at university with the Education Department paying my fees, I was interviewed by Mr Partridge, who also lectured in education. I remember him as a small neat dark man in a dark suit. His aura of power came from his role of Principal, who, I had heard, pinned notes on the message board, requesting an interview, and none knew, although some suspected, whether a 'note from Party' would result in praise of condemnation.

Mr Partridge asked about my accommodation.

'Do you live in one of the hostels?'

'I stay with an aunt and uncle.'

He frowned.

'It's not always good to stay with relatives.'

'Oh, I get on well with my aunt and uncle. And I pay only ten shillings board.'

'Where do you live?'

'Four Garden Terrace, Carroll Street.'

He frowned again.

'Carroll Street? That's not a very nice area.'

I knew that Carroll Street was two streets from the notorious McLaggan Street, where prostitutes were said to live and the Chinese to smoke opium in their opium 'dens', but Carroll Street seemed harmless to me: I had found that it was known as the 'Syrian quarter'.

'Not a savoury area at all,' Mr Partridge repeated disapprovingly, giving no explanation for his opinion.

'So you want to study English and French?'

He consulted some papers on his desk, and frowned again. 'I suppose you realise that doing well at school doesn't mean you'll do well at University. There are students from all over the country here, you know. And Training College is a full-time course.'

Subdued, I nodded. 'Yes.'

He persisted.

'In fact several students who did well at school have failed their University subjects.'

Reluctantly he gave me permission to study Stage One English and French, and with his disapproval tearing painfully at the perfect edge of my new-found world, I left his office and walked home down Union Street, through the museum grounds to Frederick Street, into George Street, past the Octagon, into Princes Street, and into Carroll Street to my newly unsavoury address. I still could not see, however, why Carroll Street was not 'nice'. The people were poorer, there were few who went to Training College or University, and sometimes, perhaps, there were a few more drunks outside the pub at six o'clock closing . . .

I found myself defeated in coping with the initial requisite of belonging to Training College: the building was new and I was afraid of its newness, its nakedness. I had never occupied such a clean place. Unlike at high school, where each class had its own room which was treated as 'home' for the day, the rooms at the Training College were distinguished by subjects — the Education Room, the Art Room — with the only 'home' for the students being their lockers in the locker room where possessions and not people could be housed. The 'home' for the students was the *Common Room*, diminished in security for me by the vast space of its floor and its very newness, though I was delighted to be able to say at last, with the old dreams of University, Oxford, Cambridge, 'The Scholar-Gipsy', *Jude the Obscure* still burning in my mind, *Common Room. I shall go to the Common Room. They are in the Common Room.* In reality, I rarely used the Common Room.

I was overawed, too, by the lavatories. Near the wash-basin was an incinerator with a sign, *Deposit Used Sanitary Towels Here*. One had to walk, with soiled sanitary towel in hand for all to see, from the lavatory, across the tiled echoing floor, to the incinerator at the far end of the room. In my two years at Training College I carried my soiled sanitary towels home to Number Four Garden Terrace to put in the washhouse dustbin when Aunty Isy was out, or to throw among the tombstones in the Southern Cemetery at the top of the street, which had become my place to 'be', to think, to compose poems, my Dunedin equivalent of the 'hill' at Oamaru. During the weekend when Aunty Isy lit the dining-room fire and asked discreetly if I had 'anything to burn', I'd say, 'No, thank you.'

'Yes please.' 'No thank you.'

My few clothes shared the dressing-table drawer with used sanitary towels waiting to be thrown in the cemetery and with the wrappers from the bars of Caramello chocolate which I ate in my room. In my anxiety to be thought the perfect boarder, from the beginning of my stay I had explained to Aunty Isy that I ate very little, that I was a vegetarian (I had been studying Buddhism), and would be content to have my small meal on the sink bench in the scullery, and when Aunty Isy reminded me that I was welcome to eat in the dining room, I, excessively timid, made the excuse that I liked to study while I ate. Now, when I was less afraid of the city and was even learning to ride the tramcars, I was unable to revise my impression as the girl with the tiny appetite, and so I was often hungry. I'd grab delicious scraps of boiled corned beef, set aside as being 'too stringy', from Aunty Isy's plate among the pile of dirty dishes. And I bought the Caramello chocolate, a shilling a bar, to eat in my room.

I took little part in College social life. I yearned for the time when I could buy a crumpled gaberdine raincoat (the student uniform). In complete ignorance of the ways of love and sex, I watched with envious wonder the lives of those women who, finding their 'man', fulfilled not only their own expectations but those of their family and friends and thus added a bloom of certainty to their being. My only romance was with poetry and literature, at Training College lectures, and those newly begun at University, where I spent my dreaming-time. At University I was not called on to behave like a teacher. I could sit in the lecture room listening, not even asked to speak, dreaming unhindered by criticism or comment about the subject of the lecture and, at times, the lecturer. My concentration was intense. I marvelled at all the new knowledge, the enthusiasm and talent of the lecturers both at Training College and University, at the new language, each distinct, of Training College students and University students, and, in the English classes taken by Professor Ramsay and Gregor Cameron, at the newly presented language of Shakespeare and Chaucer, with Professor Ramsay analysing each word of Shakespeare, transmitting to us his own sense of wonder at Shakespeare's language and its meaning. Like the sea from Oamaru, Shakespeare and his language travelled with me to Dunedin and were treasured for sharing my new life and the life of 'the girl that was gone'. We studied *Measure for Measure*, which I had never read but which now became one of my favourite Shakespeare plays, with every line stirring in me a host of ideas crowding avenues of dreaming, lines of poems, the end-of-term examination papers, but not, to my regret, the literary essays I had longed to write. It was not then the way of University lecturers to ask for written or spoken comment from Stage One or Stage Two students. In Training College English assignments I was able now and then to satisfy my desire to write prose.

Many of my student days and experiences are now sealed from me by that substance released with the life of each moment or each moment's capture of our life. I remember and can relive my feelings but there is now a thirst for reason in what had seemed to be so inevitable. I did not realise the extent of my loneliness. I clung to works of literature as a child clings to its mother. I remember how *Measure for Measure*, the deeply reasoned play crammed with violations of innocence, with sexual struggle and comment, with long discussions on life, death and immortality, won my heart and persisted in my memory, *accompanied* me in my daily life:

What's yet in this that bears the name of life? Yet in this
life lie hid more thousand deaths; yet death we fear.

It is a stark play of honest language, of comfort and remedy, analysis of revenge and payment and life and death set in the scales. Writing now, I am impatient with my student self that was so unformed, ungrownup, so cruelly innocent. Although I had no means of knowing if other students lived in such innocence, I have since learned that many, in timidity and shyness and ignorance, lived as bizarre a life as I. I have heard of others who made detours along the bush-covered Town Belt to dispose of sanitary towels; and of one woman who spent her first week in a student hostel in darkness because she was too timid to ask for a light bulb to be replaced, and she had no money to buy one. Our lives were frail, full of agonies of embarrassment and regret, of misunderstood communication and strong with the intense feeling of wonder at the torrent of ideas released by books, music, art, other people; it was a time of finding shelter among the mightily capitalled abstractions of Love, Life, Time, Age, Youth, Imagination.

The Southern Cemetery where I threw my embarrassing litter was my favourite place. I was too shy to sit with Aunty Isy in the small dining room by the fire, and when the view of brick walls and desolate backyards and their overflowing rubbish tins became too depressing I climbed the hill and sitting in the long grass or on one of the walled graves, I looked out over my new city — Caversham and the grey stone building like a workhouse which I first thought might be the *Industrial School* but later I found to be *Parkside*, a home for old people, the 'Railway' end of Carisbrook football ground, the Oval with its weekday rainwater puddles and seagulls; crowded, poor, flood-prone St Kilda where I had lived for the first six weeks of my life. I looked out over the peninsula too and the waters of the harbour, and beyond, to the open sea, the Pacific, my Pacific.

My Pacific, my city: in my own way, I was making friends. Sitting among the old dead of old Dunedin (for the new dead had a special place, a headland overlooking the sea at Anderson's Bay), I earned or stole a little of their peace, there in the softly blowing long grass among the onion flowers and the wild sweet peas and the deep-rooted dock that used to be part of cemeteries, the accessories of both the railway lines and the dead. I'd compose a poem to write later when I returned to Garden Terrace. And as I walked by the telephone box at the top of the street, suddenly it would seem that the company of the dead was not enough, and one evening I telephoned Miss Macaulay, who had retired from Waitaki and was living with her elderly mother at St Clair. When she answered I found I had nothing to say yet I clung to the phone, putting in penny after penny as each three minutes wore away. I telephoned several times during the early months of my stay in Dunedin. The habit was killed abruptly one evening when Miss Macaulay said, 'You've spent one shilling, Jean!'

I had not realised that she could hear the money being fed into the box. My shame was intense. I did not dare admit my feeling of isolation. I had said again and again how wonderful it was, Training College and University. And the French classes? (Miss Macaulay had taught English and French.) Oh, I so much enjoyed them! That was true — both the English and French classes sustained me in my new life of a student teacher. I did not phone St Clair again.

A few weeks after that Katherine Bradley, Rona Pinder, and I, three of Miss Macaulay's 'old girls', accepted her invitation to afternoon tea at her home. We drank tea and ate slices of chocolate cake with chocolate icing in a house padded with cushions and dark furniture: an ordinary house. We talked of our studies and exchanged greetings with old Mrs Macaulay, all in the presence of the 'shadow' falling between the 'ideal and the real'. I had thought that our teacher, retiring, would continue her study of French and English literature, would perhaps write essays. Our conversation was unenlightening. I was haunted by the idea that all our teaching at school had been a pretence, that the great literature had been *endured* rather than *enjoyed*, then cast aside for worldly matters. Could that have been? I felt betrayed. Yet I knew that my teachers at University would persist in their studies until they died. Professor Ramsay and Gregor Cameron could never be imagined apart from Shakespeare and Chaucer.

Might they have been separated from their literature if they had an elderly mother to care for, if they were women? I was saddened by the knowledge that Miss Macaulay had been extracted from her place by the same domesticity that had denied my mother a sight of hers.

'Come and visit me again,' Miss Macaulay said.

I did not go again.

My visits home became fewer. I'd buy a privilege ticket to travel on the Friday night train, arriving at Oamaru between one and two in the morning, returning to Dunedin by the Sunday slow train. On the way home I'd imagine that all would be peaceful, different, at Fifty-six Eden Street, but as soon as I arrived I wished I had not come. Isabel and June were busy with their own lives, the antagonism between my father and my brother had increased, while Mother, self-effacing, maintained her role of provider of food, peacemaker, poet, with a new dream to add to 'publication' and the Second Coming of Christ — a dream that set her among the characters in fairy tales — that each of her daughters, now grown, should have a white fox fur on her twenty-first birthday. Her dream for

Bruddie, for health or fame in spite of ill-health, was unchanged.

My dissatisfaction with my home and family was intense. The ignorance of my parents infuriated me. They knew nothing of Sigmund Freud, of *The Golden Bough*, of T. S. Eliot. (I forgot, conveniently, that at the beginning of the year my knowledge of Freud, *The Golden Bough*, T. S. Eliot, was limited.) Overwhelmed with the flood of new knowledge I was bursting with information about the Mind, the Soul, the Child, both the Normal Child and the Young Delinquent, where I had only recently learned that there was such a creature as *The Child*. All were described, measured, labelled, expounded in detail to my bewildered parents. I was equally enthusiastic about my new knowledge of agricultural science and geomorphology. I talked of compost and rock formations. I explained theories as if they were my own. I had accepted the opinions on the classification of people partly because I was dazzled by the new language and its powerful vocabulary. I could now say to members of my family, 'That's rationalisation, that's sublimation, you're really frustrated sexually, your super-ego tells you that but your id disagrees.'

Mother blushed when I said the word 'sexually'. Dad frowned, and said nothing except, 'So that's what you learn at University and Training College.'

I explained to my sisters the significance of their dreams, how 'everything was phallic'. I also talked with exaggerated wisdom of T. S. Eliot and *The Golden Bough* and 'The Waste Land'. 'I love teaching,' I said, explaining how we had a month in College, a month in schools, how there were crit lessons, days of control, when we had the class by ourselves for one day, how we had a report at the end of the month.

'Aunty Isy says you're a lovely girl,' Mother said proudly. 'She says you're no trouble at all, she scarcely knows you're in the house.'

'Oh well,' I said, pleased that both she and Dad were pleased.

'And it's a help to have you in the house, with Uncle George ill.'

Uncle George. Well that was a mystery. Sometimes he got out of bed and went for a walk, I didn't know where, but he wore a grey overcoat and went out into the grey night and when he came home his face was grey, too, and Aunty Isy would help him off with his coat, unwind his scarf and see him up to bed, perhaps calling down the stairs, 'Jean would you mind running down to Joe the Syrian's for a tube of lanoline?'

And once again I'd fetch the blue and white tube of lanoline.

'And how *is* Uncle George?' Mother asked. (I had begun to call Mum 'Mother' as a sign that I was grown up.)

'I don't really know,' I said. 'He goes for a walk sometimes. Nobody mentions his illness.'

I knew they were pretending he was not ill. I hated the pretence. I hated being home, for I felt that I had left home forever, and except for occasional visits, I would never return. I could see the family so clearly enveloped in doom that it frightened me. I felt that my mother lived in a world which in no way corresponded with the 'real' world, and it seemed that her every word was a concealment, a lie, a desperate refusal to acknowledge 'reality'. I was not even aware that I, in my turn, had joined the world of pretence which I so condemned in others.

I could see my father as a helpless character struggling against the buffeting winds of a cruel world. In my mind I could see him as he rode his bicycle up the slope of Eden Street, his body leaning forward, determined not to give in to the hill and the head wind blowing straight from the snow, from up country, 'out Hakataramea way' towards the Southern Alps; and my brother, fresh-faced with his brown hair sticking up like Uncle Bob's hair, and his mouth tremulous with all those tears he had shed in his helplessness against his attacker; and my sisters — Isabel growing so like Myrtle in her nature, defiant, daring, a rebel and everybody's darling; and June, in the blue Wilson House girdle that somehow suited her quietness, full of vague poetry and music and most likely to share my tastes in reading and to understand my musings on the Great Abstractions — all my family were part of the shared 'we' which I knew to be lost. I tried to use 'we' when I talked of my life as a student, but I knew it was futile, that I was describing what 'they', the students did, where they went, how they felt, what they said, and in order to survive I had to conceal my 'I', what I really felt, thought, and dreamed about. I had moved from the second person plural to a shadowy 'I', almost a nothingness, like a no-woman's land.

I was named a 'student', 'one of them', complained about by the public of Dunedin, referred to affectionately or reprovingly by the lecturers as 'oh, you students!', or proudly by my relatives as 'a student, you know.' Sensing the excitement and pleasure of my fellow students in all the activities — drama, sport, debating, dancing, 'going out' with the opposite sex, I found myself almost delirious with excitement at the contemplation of the life of a student. I must have spent a fortune of dazzlement and wonderment, simply in knowing that I was *there*; and few experiences could have equalled the joy given by being at a University, perceived by me almost entirely through English literature — surely Gregor Cameron was the Grammarian of 'A Grammarian's Funeral'?

> *Here — here's his place where meteors shoot, clouds form,*
> *Lightnings are loosened,*
> *Stars come and go! let joy break with the storm,*

> *Peace let the dew send!*
> *Lofty designs must close in like effects;*
> *Loftily lying,*
> *Leave him — still loftier than the world suspects,*
> *Living and dying.*

Little did Gregor Cameron know that in the midst of 'Beowulf' and 'Piers Plowman', he stood on the platform in Lower Oliver, the English room, as Browning's Grammarian — 'our master, famous calm and dead'.

Everything was furiously swift, relentless; even the venerable stone walls of the university swirled with secret life, but where human life was being lived openly, as in the common room and the canteen, I was always afraid to venture. The student weekly newspaper, *Critic*, was set just outside the door of the university Student Union building, with an invitation, 'Take One'. Only three or four times during my life as a student was I bold enough to take a copy of *Critic*. With so much freedom how could I have been so confined by myself? I longed to be brave enough to submit a poem to *Critic*. When I eagerly caught the crumb-pages discarded on a desk or chair in the corridor, I studied the stories and poems and dreamed of seeing my poems printed, myself *speaking out* boldly, brilliantly, in denial of my timidity, isolation, and fear of The World. I knew that inside the Student Union building there was a postbox inviting contributions: I was not brave enough to enter the Student Union building. Although I dreamed of writing poems that would startle and satisfy with their brilliance, I knew that I had not the talent, the assurance, the wonderful maturity that spoke so clearly in the poetry pages of *Critic*. Everyone was writing free verse, discarding capital letters and punctuation, often leaping into the poem with the object only, 'Dreamed . . . tall sky, lowering . . .', etc.

Also there were favourite words used with certainty — cornucopia, thighs, phallic, molls, deathless, wordless, breathless, the eye, the heart, the mind, the womb; tough poems full of experience, one moment laconic, the next profuse. Heavily under the influence of John Donne, the men wrote poems about women, tangled metaphorical exchanges of hearts, beds, souls, bodies, while the women wrote of flowers, forests, the sea. Influenced by the 'sprung rhythm' of Hopkins and the vocabulary of Dylan Thomas, I wrote mysterious poems full of images derived from my past and tributary pasts, and my present, all focused through my newly acquired Freudian lens with its tint of T. S. Eliot's geraniums growing in the Waste Land and at Number Four Garden Terrace, and dead, shaken by a madman.

Always, as my mother had done, I allied myself with the poets. I adopted extravagant beliefs. After learning Shelley,

> *True love in this differs from gold and clay*
> *That to divide is not to take away.*
> *Love is like understanding that grows bright*
> *Gazing on many truths, 'tis like thy light,*
> *Imagination! which from earth and sky,*
> *and from the depths of human fantasy . . .*

I announced to myself and to anyone who might be interested that I 'believed' in 'free love' and 'polygamy' — I, grasping the abundance when I was not even in sight of the pittance!

The most magical word to me was still *Imagination*, a glittering noble word, never failing to create its own inner light. I was learning much about its composition from the University studies of the 'set book', Coleridge's *Biographia Literaria*. I learned by heart the passage,

> The Imagination then I consider either as primary or secondary. The primary Imagination I hold to be the living Power and prime Agent of all human Perception, and as a repetition in the finite mind of the eternal act of creation in the infinite I Am. The Secondary Imagination I consider as an echo of the former, co-existing with the conscious will, yet still as identical with the primary in the *kind* of its agency, and differing only in *degree* and in the *mode* of its operation. It dissolves, diffuses, dissipates, in order to recreate; or where this process is rendered impossible, yet still at all events it struggles to idealise and to unify. It is essentially *vital*, even as all objects (*as* objects) are essentially fixed and dead . . . Fancy, on the contrary, has no other counters to play with, but fixities and definites. The Fancy is indeed no other than a mode of Memory emancipated from the order of time and space; while it is blended with and modified by that empirical phenomenon of the will, which we express by the word Choice. But equally with the ordinary memory the Fancy must receive all its materials ready made from the law of association. Good sense is the body of poetic genius, Fancy its drapery, Motion its life, and Imagination the soul that is everywhere and in each; and forms all into one graceful and intelligent whole.

I was fascinated by the implied gap, the darkness, the Waste Land between Fancy and Imagination, and the lonely journey when the point of Fancy had been passed and only Imagination lay ahead. It became my goal, a kind of religion. No one had ever forbidden association with or frowned on Imagination, and although I had few illusions about my own share, I held it in my secret poetic life, it flowed between the poetry and prose I read and myself, and even the probable mockery of others, or my own more likely self-mockery with 'frustration', 'sublimation', could not hurt or destroy it for it was, as Coleridge and all the poets had said, 'supreme', and at that time of my life when I was learning that life is a presentation of many feasts from which one is often fearful of being turned away, I found the feast of imagination spread almost in loving fashion, in great kindness and abundance.

The war continued. I worried about my decayed teeth, my clothes, money, teaching. On pay day, cashing my cheque for nine pounds three and ninepence at Arthur Barnetts, I went with other students to the *Silver Grille* for a 'mixed grill please'. Some of the students even drank *coffee*. They — we — the quieter ones — talked of the wild exploits of certain other students, enviously noting who 'went with' a medical student, for medical students were said to 'know everything' about sex. 'Let me show you your spare rib,' they'd say.

And the war continued, giving an air of unreality layered upon the ordinary air of unreality, forming an atmosphere of sadness, pity, helplessness. The everlasting question was Why.

At Number Four Garden Terrace, Uncle George's pallor changed to the grey of approaching death. He no longer went out walking or came downstairs to visit Aunty Isy in the sitting room, and talk to her and to Billy the Budgerigar, who could say, 'Pretty Boy, Pretty Boy, Billy. Up the stairs to bed, up the stairs to bed.' More and more tubes of lanoline were emptied and disposed of. Before I went to my room I'd say hello to Uncle George, standing at the foot of the bed, scanning his concealed shape for signs of the cancer which he and Aunty Isy guarded so closely and fed so lavishly on Sharlands Lanoline.

Then one Sunday when I returned from walking in the cemetery, Aunty Isy met me at the door.

'Uncle George has passed away, Jean.'

I had not known him. Uncle George the commercial traveller, who had once lived at Middlemarch. Middlemarch. Middlemarch. The way Aunty Isy used to say it, I thought she owned Middlemarch and the world, but it was Uncle George she owned. And although I did not even love him, confronted by his dying, I felt a wild grief and, bursting into tears, I ran upstairs to my room. I did not go to College the next day, and when Mr Partridge asked me to explain my absence I said, consciously adopting a sad voice fitting for grief, 'My uncle died in the weekend and I stayed home to help my aunt.'

Uncle George's sisters had taken him next door to Number Five for the funeral, and I had the feeling that a long-lasting dispute about the possession of Uncle George had been settled by his removal next door.

The big bed in the room next to mine was covered with a new spring-bright bedspread, while the dustbin where I sneaked to dispose of wrappers and sanitary towels was packed with the familiar blue and white empty tubes.

Aunty Isy was still silent about the illness and the death. She took little time off work, a day or two to tidy the house and wash or burn a bundle of bed linen. Sometimes her face and eyes had a dusky look, like that of grief when there are no tears being shed. But she still talked of *Middlemarch*, reinvesting it with the feeling that now had nowhere else to go.

4   Again 'A Country Full of Rivers'

I kept the continuing war within the boundaries of modern literature, and when a new student would arrive, slightly older, limping, with one leg or one arm, I viewed him from the safety of myth as 'the old soldier home from the wars'. I emerged blinking from the half-dark of Dostoyevsky, the star- and sky-filled grandeur of Thomas Hardy's world with the isolating, oppressing, indifferent hand of doom upon each character, that is, from the writers who were dead, to discover there were writers who were only recently dead or who were living and writing in the midst of the war. I read James Joyce, Virginia Woolf, the poetry of Auden, Barker, MacNeice, Laura Riding (noting that she had been the wife of Robert Graves) and — Dylan Thomas, the hero, then, I'm sure, of every student who read or wrote poetry. I bought the *Poems* of Sydney Keyes, and took much time to gaze at his photograph and mourn his early death. I treasured a small volume of T. S. Eliot, a large anthology, *Poetry London*, with drawings by Henry Moore and writing by Henry Miller, and my *Poetry in Wartime*, where, isolated from our own casualty lists and the deaths of young men we'd known in Oamaru, brothers or sons of neighbours, I lived within the air raids on London, the routine of the fire-watchers and the air-raid wardens — many of the poems had been written 'while fire-watching'. I knew by heart Auden's 'September 1, 1939', poems on the 'Four Seasons of War', Lynette Roberts' 'Lamentation':

> *Five hills rocked and four homes fell*
> *the day I remember the raid so well.*
> *Eyes shone like cups chipped and stiff,*

the living bled, the dead lay in their grief.
Dead as ice-bone breaking the hedge,
dead as soil failing of good heart.
Dead as trees quivering with shock
at the hot death from the plane.

There was a national activity known as the *War Effort* which touched my life, as all were expected to take part. During the summer of that year other students and I were 'manpowered' to pick raspberries on Whittakers' farm at Millers Flat, Central Otago. I was excited by the idea of going 'up Central' to the place that had haunted me since infancy when I thought of it as a tall ladder with narrow rungs where aunts and uncles climbed up one side into the clouds, stayed the weekend or longer, then came down, saying with great satisfaction, 'I've been up Central.'

The reality was a journey in an old bus along dusty roads set in a moonscape of burned bare hills rising almost perpendicularly from the valleys, to a fertile plain by the banks of a turbulent green churned-white river, there known as the Molyneux, but further downstream as the Clutha. From my first sight of the river I felt it to be a part of my life (how greedily I was claiming the features of the land as 'part of my life'), from its beginning in the snow of the high country (we were almost in the high country), through all its stages of fury and, reputedly now and then, peace, to its outfall in the sea, with its natural burden of water and motion and its display of colour, snow-green, blue, mud-brown, and borrowing rainbows from light; and its added burden rising from its power, of the dead — withered or uprooted vegetation, the bodies and bones of cattle, sheep and deer, and, from time to time, of people who drowned.

After spending a year confined in the city, studying, writing, conscious always of boundaries of behaviour and feeling, in my new role as an adult, I now came face to face with the Clutha, a being that persisted through all the pressures of rock, stone, earth and sun, living as an element of freedom but not isolated, linked to heaven and light by the slender rainbow that shimmered above its waters. I felt the river was an ally, that it would speak for me.

I fell in love with Central Otago and the river, with the naked hills covered only in their folds by their own shadow, with their changing shades of gold, and the sky born blue each morning with no trace of cloud, retiring in the evening to its depth of purple. Day and night we tried to endure the heat of the sun burning the air outside and stored in the corrugated iron walls and roof of the large shed where we lived and slept. Every day, all day, we picked raspberries as we'd been taught, crouched, milking them gently from their stalks, dropping the soft furry blobs into the tin bucket hanging by a cord around our neck. Our hands were stained with raspberry blood and scratched with raspberry thorns that, singly, were soft to the touch, but massed against the stem could pierce like pins. My face and arms and legs flamed with sunburn. I was a slow picker, earning barely enough to pay my fare home to Oamaru.

The pickers, coming from strange places like Whakatane, Matamata, Tuatapere, seemed to me like goddesses, fascinating in everything they said and did. The farmer's sons were like younger gods: I watched their faces, their eyes, studied their hands, arms, legs, glancing briefly but often at the bulge, the snowball bedded in snowgrass, between their legs. The world was a feast with nothing denied except by the marking of the invisible boundaries: we were not rivers. The other students, the one or two whom I knew, were overpowered by their surroundings, by the knowledge of the war, by their own uncertainties. We were now halfway through our training as teachers: would we succeed? How would it be, in our senior year? There was the social studies assignment rumoured to take all year to write and (some said) expected to be the length of a book. And how would we fare in the year of 'C' Certificate? And what of our love life? We talked about longing and love, told our love-lorn dreams of those unattainable too few male students — miners, medical men — of our clinging to chance kind words that, falling on too receptive ears, inspired the right to repeat the melting poetry of

> My true-love hath my heart, and I have his,
> By just exchange one for the other given.

In the evening I walked on the hill, among the matagouri, a desert thorn bush with ragged stunted growth and small grey leaves like tarnished flakes of snow. I fell in love with matagouri, for though it grew on the hills around Oamaru, its name was new to me, given by one of the gods or goddesses in answer to my question, What is this marvellous plant? Matagouri (tumatakuru) grew its marvel overnight into my newly awakened world. I found, too, on the hills, a grass I'd not seen since early childhood — snowgrass, golden silk like the strands of tussock which I used to think was named after 'tussore' silk, a dreamed-of material out of my past, where school blouses were rayon or cotton and only the privileged few wore 'tussore' silk, the colour of cream with coarse threads electric to the touch in the midst of the noisy softness. I remembered how Myrtle had maintained a fantasy that she had a 'tussore silk dress' hanging in the wardrobe, and how she would skite about it, 'I've got a dress of tussore silk.'

That summer was a time of the dominion of sun, of love to give everywhere in feeling that could not be matched by the past written word: the agony, the rapture, the still-innocent longing, the painful pleasure and pleasurable pain (we had 'studied' the 'pleasure-pain principle'); the memory remains, for me, in the bounty of the river and the landscape, the matagouri and snowgrass, the flawless blue of the sky, set beside the nightmare of the burning corrugated iron enclosing us with its fire.

I returned home, my summer love slowly cooling. I understood why relatives had voiced their rapture about 'up Central' and how as an infant I had seen 'up Central' as a ladder into heaven.

At Fifty-six Eden Street the parched front lawn was scattered with dry cocksfoot seeds and faded tinker-tailor grass. There was ergot, too, to be collected for the War Effort; and in the bull paddock, rambler rose bushes laden with rosehips about to ripen.

Isabel and I lay on the lawn while I, the big sister, explained how it was at Training College and Isabel listened with her usual scepticism. She was preparing for her first year. Both she and I would be staying with Aunty Isy at Number Four Garden Terrace. I felt a sense of panic at the idea of having to 'cope' with Isabel.

5   Isabel and the Growth of Cities

Although Isabel and I were good friends, we were almost opposite in our behaviour, outlook, experience and ambitions. It was Isabel who instructed June and me in the 'ways of the world', that is, how to get a boyfriend, what to do when you had him and how to get rid of him when he outlived his usefulness; how to be beautiful in complexion and figure to make certain you did get your boyfriend; and how to triumph over authority and its narrow-mindedness. Isabel was inclined to teach us by example: her social experiences were many; she always had a boyfriend; she described in detail what they did together and although she hadn't yet gone 'all the way', she explained vividly what happened, with a mixture of fiction and fact accompanied by the favourite song of the time, sung by Fats Waller in a throaty voice,

Please don't put your lips so close to my cheek
Don't smile or I'll be lost beyond recall
. . . all or nothing at all . . .

Isabel was imaginative, clever, topping her school class in English and French and winning the Speech Prize and a Physical Education Shield; she also collected a place in an earlier long jump championship. Even in our competitive world we did not overvalue these awards; they gave prestige, however, and often came with a handsome book or medal or a cheque.

I envied Isabel her power of written description, the supply of detail gathered entirely from her imagination which made her seem to me to have travelled the world and lived in many times and places; she simply *knew*. When her ambition to be a doctor was curbed by her impatience with study and the cost of training, she decided to try teaching, even without spending time in the Sixth Form.

I, self-conscious, restrained, obedient, thinking of myself as responsible and grown up, felt alarm at Isabel's very first move — coming to Training College 'straight from the Fifth Form' without a year or two years enduring the Sixth Form as a kind of 'discipline for life'. I saw my own world falling apart, all my carefully cemented behaviour crumbling under the force of Isabel's unexpected weather. It was hard work studying both at Training College and University, and with the social studies assignment (the subject already given — 'The Growth of Cities') supposed to be the length of a book, I could not see how I could 'fit in' Isabel and my apprehension about her survival. My habit of behaving as I was expected to behave — 'obedient, no trouble at all', and my absorption in the world of literature, enabled me to enjoy living a monastic life because no matter how I might desire to be distracted along the way, my pursuit was poetry. My view forward was narrow, and when I glanced aside at others going their different ways, my view remained narrow. I wanted Isabel to be as the dolls had been (clothes-pegs wrapped in cloth) when we pressed them into tiny boxes and kept them there, safely wrapped and snug, able to move only with our help. I wanted her to be a good student, to 'behave', to obey, to study and be approved of by the students and the lecturers, perhaps, though I did not voice this to myself, causing the principal to say, 'We made no mistake admitting those Frame girls to Training College, they're two of our best students and teachers.' Aunty Isy, expecting another meek Frame who would do her best to be invisible and accept, uncomplaining, the conditions which I myself had set, welcomed Isabel to stay, and when we arrived at Four Garden Terrace and Isabel and I were alone in the small room that we were to share, Isabel was angrily incredulous at the thought of sharing the two-foot-six-wide iron bed with me. It had been my fault: I had said timidly, 'Oh that will be quite all right,' when Aunty Isy asked if we could manage.

'But even her thinking of it,' Isabel said angrily.

'Oh don't say anything,' I said, pacifying Isabel. We both knew there was nowhere else to stay at ten shillings a week.

We had little sleep, we were constantly irritated, quarrelling with each other, fighting over our share of the bedclothes, as we used to do at home. Horrified at the uncomplaining way I accepted our tiny ration of food, eating it at the bench in the scullery, Isabel threatened to 'tell Mum' that Aunty Isy was starving us, that she made us eat in the scullery, and sleep in a tiny bed in a tiny room scarcely big enough to swing a cat in, that we were frozen night and day with that cold wind blowing fresh from the harbour or down North-East Valley from Flagstaff and the outlying hills, while Aunty Isy ate in her dining room and toasted her toes in front of a blazing fire.

I persuaded Isabel not to say anything.

'Not just now, wait till the end of term.'

In Isabel's first weeks at Training College she made friends, she found a boyfriend, who became her 'steady' while she was there, although from time to time she had others, and she behaved as I had dreaded she would; she went 'wild', with a wildness that was alarming only to my exaggerated sense of restraint. She discovered roller skating and became an expert skater. She spent every evening at the skating rink, while I saw my dream for her future fading and all her 'education' wasted — why did she not study, why did she not seize the opportunity to read, learn? I said little about this to her, for I realised the dreams were mine, and I remembered feeling the same way about Myrtle.

At night, however, when we tugged the bedclothes our way, the extra vicious tug I made towards my side said something of my disappointment in Isabel.

With Isabel at Number Four Garden Terrace, life had 'episodes'. There was the 'time of the chocolates'. I had peeped, once, into the small front sitting room, where the blinds were always drawn and seen, propped around the picture rail, an unbroken row of large chocolate boxes decorated with satin ribbon and printed with English and Highland scenes, and winsome photos of animals. When I told Isabel about the chocolate boxes, she said, one day when Aunty Isy was out, 'Let's explore the front room.'

Just inside the door stood a tall chest with drawers full of clothing and photos. In the bottom drawer we found a set of white knitted baby clothes wrapped in tissue paper; there were baby blankets, too, and nappies. We knew that Dad's sisters Polly and Isy had stillborn babies or those who did not survive beyond a few days or weeks, and we'd had a stillborn brother, and even as children we had sensed a kind of hunger in Aunty Polly's and Aunty Isy's feeling towards us, particularly Aunty Isy's interest in Myrtle, and Aunty Polly's voiced desire to 'adopt' Chicks, or June. We quickly shut the drawer and turned our attention to the chocolate boxes. We noted that the cellophane seal appeared to be unbroken.

'She can't have kept them all those years,' we said. We knew Aunty Isy had won the chocolates for her Highland dancing.

'Let's look inside them,' Isabel suggested.

'Oh no, we couldn't.'

'We'll open one and test it.'

As eager as Isabel to explore the chocolate boxes but aware of the responsibilities of an older sister, I was yet happy to use language to conceal the moral problem.

'Yes, let's test them.' After all, testing was different. If the boxes did contain chocolates, *testing* would not be *eating*.

We dislodged one box from the picture rail, and carefully untied the ribbon and slipped off the cellophane cover and wedged the upper half from the lower and looked inside at rows of chocolates in their brown pleated cases.

We sat on the sofa and began to taste.

'They're good, not musty at all.'

We continued to eat, and when we had finished the box, we scattered the paper cases inside, shut the box, returned it to its cellophane cover, and retied the satin ribbon in a bow across the front. We climbed up and set the box on the picture rail.

During our stay at Garden Terrace we ate gradually all the chocolates from all the boxes around the picture rail, returning the boxes when we had finished, and each time we sneaked into the darkened front room we remembered the new baby clothes but did not look at them again, and as we ate our fill, we wondered about Aunty Isy and how her life had been and I told Isabel about Uncle George in bed, and the lanoline, and when we scattered the empty paper cases into the empty box we both felt distaste at what we were doing, eating Aunty Isy's cherished souvenirs: eating, eating. The frill around the paper cases was like the frill, withered at the edges, of those small shells you prise open on the beach, to find a small dead heap with a black dead eye lying inside.

It was at the end of the second term that the explosion came. Isabel finally wrote home complaining that Aunty Isy had starved me for a whole year and that we were both starving and during that winter we were freezing in one bed in a tiny room. Isabel's letter prompted a swift reply from Mother to Aunty Isy who then wrote to Dad, her brother, expressing the opinion that 'Lottie has always been a bad manager'. Mother's indignant reply was followed by Aunty Isy's accusation that she had been mistaken in thinking Isabel and I were 'lovely girls'. We had eaten all her souvenir chocolates! Apparently on a rare visit to the front room she found a stray chocolate case on the carpet.

In the exchange of letters, Uncle George's sisters found disparaging things to say about the 'awful Frames', how the children had always been out of control, running wild on the Oamaru hills, how the Frame home was like a pigsty, Mother didn't know the first thing about housekeeping. The bitter correspondence continued between Dad and Aunty Isy (Mother refused to 'lower herself' by writing after her first two letters), with Dad now using Mum's formal name, Lottie.

The result was that Isabel and I moved from Number Four Garden Terrace, I with shame and embarrassment and a sense of loss in being no longer thought of as a 'lovely girl, no trouble at all', and Isabel with triumph because we had asserted our 'rights', Isabel happily, sociably going to live among friends in a boardinghouse whose landlady was well known and liked by a succession of students, I to the only other place available, Stuart House, a hostel where I rented a 'cubicle' for the rest of the year — a narrow space in a large room where each bed was screened by a fibreboard wall about six feet high; and I found little solitude or privacy for studying, reading and writing — and sleeping.

I knew during the first weeks of Isabel's stay in Dunedin that she was lost from me, and I felt sad to lose her: after all, she had been Emily,

> *No coward soul is mine,*
> *No trembler in the world's storm-troubled sphere.*

I think her separation from me was accomplished in those evenings when she skated spinning round and round the rink almost as if unwinding an anchoring thread from her body. She spent hours swimming, coming home to Garden Terrace with her blonde hair green-tinged from the chlorine in the water, and when she opened the door of our room I would always see, behind the face of the student who had been swimming, the face of the child coming home from the baths the day Myrtle was drowned.

The shift from Garden Terrace almost completed our separation. If we saw each other at Training College, we said hello in an embarrassed way. And when the letter came from home we met each other briefly to talk about the awful news: Fifty-six Eden Street, which we'd rented all those years of our growing up, had been sold and the new owner, soon to be married, had given us notice to move out at the end of the year.

Shortly after that the warden of the College sent for me, and when I wonderingly arrived for the interview, she began, 'I want to talk to you about your sister Isabel.'

Isabel, she said, was making a guy of herself both by her behaviour and by the clothes she wore, in particular a skirt printed with a giraffe.

'Fancy wearing a skirt with a giraffe printed on it!' the warden said.

I murmured something sympathetic towards Isabel. Her clothes never shocked us; they were interesting, original. Knowing how many hours we Frame girls had spent trying to sew our own clothes, fitting petersham, making hems even, matching that awkward scoop at the arm of a sleeve to ensure the right sleeve was in the right arm, I thought Isabel's appliquéd giraffe was a triumph of dressmaking. The truth was that no one else had a skirt with a giraffe on it, therefore Isabel was condemned for her difference. The force of 'no one else' was a familiar feature of our lives.

'You, as her elder sister, are responsible for her,' the warden said. 'Try to influence her not to be so . . . so . . . outlandish.'

I, demure in my ordinary print dress and cardigan, said, as one grown-up to another, 'She's very young,' adding, as if I knew the reason for Isabel's behaviour (why should not Isabel have suffered the misery of being in the Sixth Form?), 'she came to Training College too early.'

Then, alarmed, indignant, unhappy, I murmured something about 'conditions at home'. There was sickness, I said, bursting into tears. 'And we're being turned out of our house and we have to find somewhere before Christmas.'

'Well,' the warden said, 'see what you can do to influence your younger sister.'

I said nothing to Isabel about my interview with the warden. I was angry with the concern over a mere giraffe, and now, so many years later, the episode seems unbelievable and wryly amusing but it does show the degree of conformity expected of us. I was ashamed, too, of bursting into tears, although later I hoped the episode had enhanced my poetic role — 'illness in her family — perhaps drink? — turned out of her home . . . a fitting source for a poet . . . what a tragic life . . .'

A few weeks later the warden again 'sent for' me, this time to congratulate me on the children's story I had written and to ask me if I had thought of 'taking up' writing for children. My work showed promise and imagination, she said, while I listened calmly, inwardly disdainful of devoting my life to anything but writing poetry, cherishing the idea of myself as a poet. At the end of the interview the warden said, 'Our little talk seems to have had an effect on your sister; she's much more subdued now and no longer wears that skirt with the giraffe on it.' I didn't explain that the giraffe had become dislodged and Isabel was hoping to sew it when she had 'time'. I knew that her time was taken up with Steve, her boyfriend, tall, handsome, blond, who had a friend Morrie, tall, handsome, dark and very shy, and on one of our meetings to talk about the 'search for a house', Isabel suggested I 'leave all that study' and come dancing with her and Steve, with Morrie as my partner. I rashly agreed and spent an unfamiliar but vaguely exciting evening being partnered by Morrie, who divided his time between dancing (and saying very little) and standing with me watching the dancing while he shuffled and hopped, doing a kind of private jig, and sang under his breath,

> Missed the Saturday dance
> got as far as the door,
> couldn't bear it without you,
> don't get around much any more . . .

adding repeats of a chorus, 'Don't get around, don't get around, don't get around much any more,' in his Southland drawl. I enjoyed the otherness of his presence beside me but we were both too shy and when we glanced at each other his face was a dusky red and mine, I know, had its self-conscious blush.

The warden's remarks about my writing encouraged me to think of entering the college poetry competition at the end of the year, to show her and others that I was *really* a poet. In the meantime, I had so much to do and think about and worry about that my only places of peace were the university English lectures, where I lived within Shakespeare and Old English, and the reference room at the Dunedin Public Library, where I read modern poetry, James Frazer, Jung and Freud. I hadn't even begun to write my 'Growth of Cities', a subject which excited me by its possibilities and repelled me by the prospect that I might have to record boring geographical and historical detail. As a result of cultivating what I thought of as a 'poetic spirit' I had become impatient with everything I decided was 'boring detail', either because I gave it little value in my ideal poetic world or because it reminded me that I was not as clever as I wanted to be and I was growing aware of, and refusing to accept the limitations of my mind. I couldn't even write the kind of poetry that was printed in *Critic*. Who did I think I was, to imagine I'd be a poet?

Faced with 'The Growth of Cities', I felt myself to be a miserable failure. My only hope was to write (and illustrate) the long essay in my own way, that is to attach my own giraffe to the ordinary accepted garb of prose. In the end the text became a geographical and historical and social version of *The Waves*, with bizarre illustrations cut from magazines, as I had not a 'flair' for drawing. I learned later that the verdict on my 'Growth of Cities' was similar to the verdict on Isabel's clothing, although I also learned that someone suggested there might be 'more in me than they knew'.

There were two main delights for me in that final year of College: the discovery of art in the inspiring lectures given by Gordon Tovey, and the performance of the college choir, where all sang, even those without musical voices. We sang 'The Lady of Shalott', 'At Flores in the Azores (the Ballad of Richard Grenville)' and the 'Hymn to Joy' from Beethoven's Ninth Symphony, under the tuition of George Wilkinson, known as Wilkie. I remember rehearsing and rehearsing, and finally singing, full of tears at the momentous occasion, surrounded by singing voices, all in a sensation of being in an upper storey of the mind and heart, knowing a joy that I never wanted to end, and even now when I remember that evening in the Dunedin Town Hall, the massed choir and the massed audience, and people who one never dreamed would be singing, and I too, singing

> soft and sweet through ether ringing
> sounds and harmonies of joy.

I remember the happiness and recognise it as one of the rewards of alliance with any great work of art, as if ordinary people were suddenly called upon to see the point of view of angels.

The year was ending. I sent my poems to the College Magazine and won the ten-shilling first prize for 'Cat'.

> Deaf to the hammering window
> and the idiot boy's mewing
> I leave the torn mice to flow
> through his vacant eyes
> and sit propped up by a fat thinking.
> But the will of the beating boy
> burgles me ear, creeps
> like a curled cat in my brain, purrs and sleeps
> and pads me from the house
> to the scratched clouds and the clawed moon;
> and the winds like torn mice
> flow through my vacant eyes.

The other poem, also printed, was 'Tunnel Beach'.

> Perennial of seagull, rooted in sea,
> dug in green ache, the seagull bush
> draws pleading enough to feed
> the dead ears of the cliff with crying
> or stuff interminably the world's eyes with tears.

> Here in the tunnel, severed from aching, the seagull bush
> strangles our groping throat in a white rush or blossom,
> acknowledges no roots
> in the green guillotine and the seawoman crying hush.

> Only where light leaks, where stone people,
> slabbing the beach call, call dungeon for their heart's house,
> as butchers' bargains, secret Spartan boys,
> there the stone minds, the mad minds break
> rooting the sea and the white bird
> in one bush infinite and alone.

I quote the poems because they, being of the time, speak of my George Barker-Dylan Thomas influences, and of my struggle to accept and be responsible for myself as a whole being without having to conceal my inner dreams in order to preserve them, or without having to deceive by playing roles of teacher, smiling, happy, 'a lovely girl, no trouble at all'.

Some memories have been diluted, mostly by the storms that followed or were given; the colour of those memories has been washed away, their shape is gone. I knew the family was desperate to find somewhere to live. Dad, who handled all the money, took shares in a newly formed building society with the hope of getting a loan from the monthly ballot, while Mother, who never had personal money, contributed her faith, 'God knows what you have need of even before you ask,' and, miraculously, the following ballot produced a loan of three hundred pounds, just enough to buy a ramshackle rat-ridden old cottage set in three and a half acres of land on the outskirts of Oamaru, just beyond the Gardens and the motor camp. The shift and the search must have been so worrying to me that I don't remember it. When College ended for the year, I went with the Bradleys and Rona Pinder to Stewart Island, where we stayed in a cabin on the beach. My memory of that time is contained only in the few snapshots of us prancing on the beach in our home-made sunsuits, of food cooking over a fire tended by two young men, of the interior of our hut with myself in bed, the bedclothes up to my neck, while one of the young men washes the dishes of the night before, when we'd had our 'beer party', the symbol then of complete adulthood.

I returned to Oamaru to find that we had shifted house from Fifty-six Eden Street to the old cottage in the grounds known as Willowglen.

6 Willowglen

Willowglen had belonged in turn to derelict families, seldom talked of singly, only as the 'awful D's' or 'those X's', whose children at school were barefooted and ragged and sometimes sick and, growing up, became the makers of social mistakes, the outcasts. During the Depression they had been the real poor, existing on beef and pork bones and specked fruit, getting their clothes in sugarbags from the 'relief depôt'. If you needed to go to the depôt, you were at the end of the world; people said you were stupid and a waste of time and you'd never learn and you infected others. I used to be fascinated by the word *depôt*, with that tiny hat, like a duncecap, above the o, which I later learned was a circumflex, sign of a lost 's'; I imagined the ravines in the landscape of words where the lost letters had fallen. The house had been empty since the M's left town. The three acres had been planted early in the century by a landscape gardener with English trees — five oaks, species of pine including a huge northern pine with draped branches which we called the 'ghost tree'; yew and cypress; an orchard of apple, cherry, quince, plum trees; a big pear tree leaning over the roof at the back; masses of spring flowers — daffodils, matchheads, crocuses, along the banks of the creek that flowed through the property. Along the driveway, council property giving us a right of way, there was a plantation of young pine trees. Willowglen was surrounded on three sides by paddocks of matagouri, of swamp, and on one side there was the railway line leading south out of Oamaru.

I remembered my stranded feeling of desolation when I walked through the lean-to that was set against the hill at the back of the house and littered with tides of last year's flow of pear tree leaves, and saw the kitchen with its floor partly of earth, for most of the old wooden floor had collapsed. The kitchen had a coal range and in the larger scullery adjoining there was an old electric range. A tap leading from the rusted water tank outside jutted through the scullery wall. Surprisingly, beyond the scullery there was a small bathroom with a bath and handbasin but no hot water, and, until the tank could be repaired or town water laid on, there was no water. The house had four rooms and the kitchen, scullery and bathroom, and in two of the rooms there were back-to-back fireplaces, long disused, filled with crumbling debris from the chimney; and every room had its heap of borer gold dust constantly increased as each human footstep on the rotted floors sent its vibration to the borer-riddled ceiling.

Outside beside the huge magpie-filled macrocarpa tree there was a decayed washhouse with a copper in one corner for boiling clothes washed in the wooden wash-tubs. Along the path from the lean-to, the 'dunny' beside the cypress tree, and soon known as 'the cypress', was covered with the small fragrant white roses known to us as 'dunny roses', and was without a door, while the dunny seat, long and wide like a beach dunny, was set over a deep hole half filled with old 'kiki' (our word for faeces) in varying shades of brown, topped with faded pieces of newspaper, the *Oamaru Mail* and the *Otago Daily Times*.

The family told me how Isabel and June had scrubbed the house, how they'd helped carry some of the furniture up the steep path but how most of it had to be left 'down on the flat' in one of the two old stables and farm sheds. Bruddie and Dad, their differences temporarily forgotten, worked together planning a water supply, a septic tank and restoring the roof. Mother, overjoyed at her first use of an electric range, set about baking pikelets and scones and rock cakes and rissoles, or, using an electric iron for the first time, she ironed Dad's workshirts and handkerchiefs, and said wistfully, 'If only we'd had these when the kiddies were little!' We girls also enjoyed using the electric iron, after our years of heating the old flat irons on the stove and, sometimes forgetting to wipe the soot from underneath, branding our school uniforms and blouses with black marks that could not be rubbed out; and how swiftly we could now press hems and pleats!

In spite of our ramshackle place we were already at home, or *they* were, for I'd missed the process of moving, and my arrival was like joining the family when the death and the shock of death and the burial were over. Already Dad had begun his routine of heaving 'spare' coal from the engine as he drove the train slowly around the curve by the Gardens and up the steep grade towards Maheno, and the others had learned to scramble with a sack through the wire fence by the wattle tree, among the clumps of wild sweet pea, to collect the precious lumps of railway coal, either 'bright' coal — Kaitangata, or 'dull' coal — Southland lignite. And already the hastily repaired henhouse had been stocked with a dozen White Leghorns, partly to justify the rusty grinder found in the old shed and make it work at grinding oyster shells for the hens' grit. The decrepit cowshed, roofless, with a broken bail, stood waiting at the foot of the hill by the apple shed.

Seeing the earth floor and the 'nowhereness' of the interior of the house, I felt depressed and lonely and I knew the Willowglen house would never be my home; it was too small, everyone was too close to everyone else; in the front bedroom you could hear the wireless from the kitchen as if you were in the kitchen. You could hear the arguments, too, the raised voices, and the soft murmur of pleading that you knew to be, 'Don't raise your voices to each other,' from Mother. My sisters and brother and I were now of an age when our lives held an 'inner room' not revealed to one another, although we still talked cheerfully of our dreams, and saw, with much laughter, the 'funny side' of everything. Indeed, that summer we made of the new owner of Fifty-six Eden Street a fictional 'baddie', telling one another stories about him and his certain fate, adding him to our list of villains — Miss Low, the health inspector, the M.P. who didn't answer our request for money to buy clothes, all of whom had been carefully enclosed, rendered powerless by our web of spoken words.

We gave to the land at Willowglen the kind of love we had not given to Fifty-six Eden Street, although every leaf and plant and insect and the earth itself and the arrangement of buildings and trees had served us nobly. Willowglen was the first home we had owned. Of course the building society had to be paid back, and the Starr-Bowkett booklet with its stamped receipts had a place of pride on our new mantelpiece besides Dad's tin of sixpences — a cocoa tin with a slit in the lid where he dropped all his sixpences until the tin was full, after which he cut strips of time-sheets, marshalled the sixpences into a long roll, and wrapped them carefully before taking them downtown to be changed into 'real' money.

How we dreamed that summer! Perhaps if we had shifted to Willowglen during the winter we might not have been able to dream our dreams, but it was summer, Christmas just past and we had our own holly tree and for the first time in our lives, our own pine branches instead of macrocarpa — what did we care that we now had no usable fireplace? The mass of blossoms borne by the orchard, the daffodils in their withered tops just showing in the long grass, the luxury of so many trees and so much grass, of swamphens and ducks and eels and water lilies in the creek, of so much summer sky, and 'down on the flat' a plantation of young pines to listen to with the wind blowing, all gave such delight that we fell in love with the 'outside' at Willowglen. During those marvellous green and gold summer days I found a place by the creek, an old log, like the old birch log of years ago. I sat for hours watching the water, the ducks, the swamphens, and, through the broken-down wire fence, the sheep nibbling the grass in the paddock of half swamp and half matagouri, *my matagouri*. My sisters and I explored the roads into town and beyond, and the Old Mill Road, which had been part of our childhood and adolescent folklore, when to 'live away out past the Old Mill' meant to live as far away as, on the other side of town, 'past the Boys' High', and when to 'go 'round the Old Mill' with a boy meant what you'd expect it to mean.

And when the first autumn dews appeared on the grass, on the days of late January, we picked mushrooms by our own pine plantation and on the hill opposite where you could look down through the gum trees at the Robertson's farm. They had the town milk supply. They had a son Norman going to University with a scholarship. I'd spoken to him once or twice. I remember thinking wistfully that perhaps he and I might fall in love and marry.

When Dad was home he too had his place. His end of the table was that near the coal range, where he could see through the small window if there were visitors coming up the path, and where he had light to read by. The sofa against the wall just inside the kitchen door was Bruddie's place; his rifle for shooting rabbits hung on the wall above, and in moments of family tension Bruddie would reach for his rifle and begin to clean it, slowly, deliberately, while Mother watched anxiously, and Dad, his lips pressed angrily together, smoothed the time-sheets before him on the table or reached for his cocoa tin and began to count his sixpences. Or he'd say, 'Where's my chalk, Mum?'

For years Dad had had stomach pains and because he suspected he might have cancer, he refused to go to a doctor; instead, he drank a medicine suggested by Aunty Polly or Aunty Isy, and known as 'chalk'.

And Mum would find the chalk, prepare the dose, and give it to him. And the episode would be over until the next time.

Like each of us, Mother had her dreams of Willowglen. Within her prison of toil, self-imposed (for we felt ourselves to be grown up and were willing to help, partly to erase our now uncomfortable memories of Mother's role as an everlasting servant), Mother looked out at her dream-place, near in reality, but seemingly removed from her in her prison. She dreamed of when she would go 'down on the flat', 'in the cool of the evening' and just sit, perhaps picnic, under the pine trees and listen to the wind in the trees. Willowglen, we discovered, had a special share of sun. Unlike at Fifty-six Eden Street, where the land lay full under the sun and the sky, the house at Willowglen, set against a western hill and facing an eastern hill, with the north boundary of hawthorn hedge, may trees, willow trees, had only brief sun in the morning, making the house cool even in summer, but if you looked from the cool and often cold world of the house you'd see, down on the flat by the creek and beyond it, a world where the sun stayed late, in summer until the evening; and perhaps if you looked out, as Mother did, when the day and working energy were fast being spent, you might feel 'down on the flat' to be an unattainable world of sun.

When I pleaded for Mother to come down on the flat in the sun, she said in the tone she used for talking of publication, the Second Coming, and, now, the white fox fur as a twenty-first birthday present, 'One of these days.'

She added, inserting the biblical language that made the 'flat' seem more distant and dream-like, 'One of these days "in the cool of the evening" I'll come and sit under the pine trees in the sun.'

Word came in January that I was to teach standard two at Arthur Street School, Dunedin. I had applied for a class of that age living in what we had learned was 'the latent period', when children were thought to be malleable, responsible, untroubled, or if they were 'troubled', it was secret, unrealised — oh how thoroughly we thought we knew that mythical 'child'!

And in response to my advertisement in the *Otago Daily Times*, 'Quiet student seeks board near Arthur Street School', I heard from a Mrs T. in Drivers Road, Maori Hill, offering me 'full board'. And so once again Isabel and I travelled south by the familiar slow train to Dunedin, Isabel to her second year at Training College and to Mrs R. in Union Street, where she'd stayed since we left Aunty Isy's, and I to the house of Mrs T. in Maori Hill and my year as a probationary teacher at Arthur Street School.

7   1945 (One)

When as children we experimented with our identity and place by moving from ourselves to encircle the planets, in our repeated inscriptions — name, street, town — Oamaru, North Otago, Otago, South Island, New Zealand, the Southern Hemisphere, the World, the Universe, the Planets and Stars, we were making a simple journey in words and, perhaps, a prophecy of being; we were lyric poets forced to realise the possibility of epics, and in a matter-of-fact way we included these epic possibilities in our ordinary thinking. I mention this because 1945, a year that began for me as a personal lyric, ended through accident of circumstance, of national and world events, as an epic embracing the universe, the planets and the stars, this time expressed in deeds, not in words.

I arrived with my growing self in Dunedin. This was to be the year of my twenty-first birthday at the end of August. 'Twenty-firsts', as they were known, were part of the continuing ritual of growing up, when one became 'of age', a legal citizen able to vote, to make a will, or, as the song said,

> I'm twenty-one today.
> I've got the key of the door,
> I've never been twenty-one before.
> I'm twenty-one today.

At the end of the year, also, I hoped I would gain my certificate as a teacher, after my probationary year at Arthur Street School. I hoped also to add another unit to my arts degree course, and as I felt that English III would prove to be too engulfing of my interest, I decided upon Philosophy I, a first year of psychology.

My secret desire to be a poet, fed by the publication in the College Magazine of my two poems ('Now they'll find out that I'm really a poet!'), occupied much of my planning. I was as anxious to impress with my imagination as I had been during my years at school, only here there were so many more people each with so much more imagination, prose writers and poets everywhere, for I was learning to get copies of Critic by lingering with apparent casualness around the entrance to the university near the Critic 'bin' with its enticement, 'Take One'. Contributions still needed a visit to the office where the poem or story could be placed. I don't know why I didn't post a contribution. I suspect that I was ignorant and innocent in most human activities, including posting letters. I was still not aware of the number of everyday chores dealt with by ordinary people. Based on my life at home, my supposition was that letters were written only to other towns with news of events such as births, deaths, marriages, or past or future travel, while telegrams were mostly a swift form of communicating the fact of death or the time of arrival of a train 'passing through' or depositing relations; and parcels meant Christmas. I had scarcely begun to study the primer of adult living. I knew of joy and of love discovered at the point of loss, and I had accepted death. I felt that I could see the feelings of people beneath their faces, in their eyes, their imposed or swift unguarded expressions, and in the words they spoke. The war still haunted and confused me — 'the pity of war, the pity war distilled', and it was the poets who continued to illuminate for me the places no one else seemed to want to talk about or visit. I thought often, with longing, of the prophecy, 'Nation shall not lift up sword against nation, neither shall they learn war any more.'

I boarded with Mrs T., a widow with a married daughter, Kathleen, living in the new government housing estate at Waikari, where Mrs T. spent most of her days, taking the bus after breakfast — 'I'm going over to Kathleen's' — and coming home at about the same time I came home from school. Mrs T.'s only topic of conversation was 'Kathleen, Bob and the children', what they did, what they said, how they felt, with much of her thoughts occupied by what she would give them for presents. 'I saw something in Arthur Barnetts and I said to myself, "That will be just right for Kathleen's youngest. Kathleen has been looking everywhere for something like that."' Bob worked in the Electricity Department, the showroom in Princes Street, and could get heaters at a discount.

For the sake of appearances, I sometimes had meals with Mrs T. instead of taking them to my room 'as I have study to catch up with and lessons to mark and prepare . . .' and then I would sit opposite her and listen, fascinated, while she described the day 'over at Kathleen's' — how they'd done the washing together and tidied the house, how Kathleen and Bob were hoping some day to get carpet 'edge to edge' in every room. 'There are quite a few carpeted now edge to edge.' I, the 'quiet shy teacher, no trouble, no trouble at all', spent most of my free time in my room, marking, preparing lessons and cutting out paper stars in different colours to reward the children's efforts; and studying my textbook of psychology; and writing and reading poems.

Mrs T.'s house was like Jessie C.'s house in Oamaru — a place where 'other people' lived; with carpets and wallpaper printed with roses, with plenty of furniture and knick-knacks, and upholstered sofas without a tear; and throughout the house, no sign of furniture stuffing or wooden floor or scrim behind the wallpaper. There was comfort with an air of concealment. Brought up in a house where we always knew and in many cases could see what happened behind the walls and beneath the floor, I never felt quite at home in the houses of 'other people'. Even at Willowglen, the desolation of having an earth floor gave a sense of reality (so strong it became unreality) that felt more a part of living than the padded secrecy of houses like Mrs T.'s.

I delighted in the children at school and in teaching. I was full of ideas for encouraging individual development. I revelled in the children's art and in their poetry, for they wrote poetry and stories almost every day, and these, with the paintings, I pinned around the walls for everyone to enjoy. I took pains, too, in teaching other subjects. My failure was as a member of the staff, for my timidity among people, especially among those who might be asked to judge and comment on my performance as a teacher, led to my spending my free time alone. Too timid to go to morning and afternoon tea with a room full of other teachers, I made excuses about 'having work to do in the classroom', aware that I was going against all the instructions about the need to 'mix in adult company, take part in social events and discussions with other teachers and parents', and that 'morning tea in the teachers' room' was an almost sacred ritual. My fear of being 'inspected' by the headmaster or inspector inspired me to devise a means of postponing the day of reckoning, by inventing a serial story which I could continue whenever I heard the steps of authority approaching along the corridor, so that a visit by the headmaster to a class sitting rapt with attention (the content of the story ensured a rapt audience), might 'prove' my ability as a teacher with the result that I could 'pass' my 'C' Certificate at the end of the year.

My escape from teaching was the psychology class and the psychology laboratory, where we performed a range of interesting experiments and tests supervised by two fresh young lecturers, Peter Prince and John Forrest, whom we called Mr Prince and Mr Forrest, but whom I nicknamed H.R.H. and Ash (after Ashley, the fair young man in *Gone with the Wind*, played by Leslie Howard). As these two young men — recent graduates, in a world where young men were few — were in a sense for public and student consumption, they became the object of rumour, speculation and fantasy. I preferred H.R.H. because, unlike Ash, he appeared to be an 'introvert', and according to the magical fixed classification of people, 'introverts' were the artists, the poets. I'd see H.R.H., his face turned towards the sky, his pipe in his mouth, striding with his long-legged springing gait, down Frederick Street towards the University, and I'd think, 'He's in another world.' He blushed easily, too, and like my admired G. M. Cameron, he had an endearing awkwardness of speech and gesture. Ash, not so tall, was handsome, fairhaired with a lock of hair draped over his forehead, and unlike H.R.H., who wore dark suits, Ash wore a rust-coloured sports coat and tomato-red socks, which he actually referred to one day in the laboratory, saying, 'How do you like my tomayto socks?' pronouncing tomato the *American way*.

Some of the women swooned over Ash.

It was Ash — Mr Forrest — who arranged for gramophone recitals to be held regularly in the gramophone room of the Music Department.

'All those records and few people hearing them,' he said in his forthright way. (He was becoming known for his 'forthrightness' and for his unconventional clothing.)

One day when I decided to go to the recital and I was standing outside the door of the gramophone room, trying to pluck up courage to go in, I heard the piano being played. I opened the door and peeped in and there was Mr Forrest playing the piano. He stopped at once and prepared the records for the recital. But I had heard him playing the piano, up and down the keys in a flourish and swoop like a concert pianist, marshalling the notes together in a travelling force going somewhere, and not simply picking out notes into a 'tune', separating them and giving them no say in the whole music. Apart from the loved Schubert songs and the 'tunes' of Walt Disney's *Fantasia*, and the new songs we had learned at Training College, including old carols

> *I think this child will come to be*
> *Some sort of workman such as we*
> *So he shall have my goods and chattels,*
> *My planks of wood, my plane, my drill,*
> *My hammer that so merry rattles . . .*

and

> *Little Jesus sweetly sleep do not stir*
> *We will lend a coat of fur . . .*

I still had little knowledge of classical music, and I had never listened to a long piece of music — a symphony or concerto. That day, Mr Forrest played a record of Tchaikovsky's *Symphony Pathétique*, and among the handful of students, I listened to the unaccustomed sounds dragging, dragging their awful burden of gloom, on and on, and when the music arrived at the 'tune' I knew as

> *This is the story of a starry night*
> *The faded glory of a starry night . . .*

I experienced the delight of recognition. I listened to the end, in love with the music and its churning sadness, and Tchaikovsky became (after Schubert) my favourite composer.

'I suppose you all know César Franck,' Mr Forrest said.

The audience looked as if they knew César Franck.

'We'll play César Franck next time,' Mr Forrest said, pronouncing the name with such assurance and familiarity.

The music room became another place where I felt at home and where I learned to listen to music that lasted more than three or five minutes. Why had I not known before that listening to a symphony was like reading a book in all its progressions, with its special shape, and silent and noisy moments? I learned to say, carelessly, 'Adagio — did you like the *Adagio*? That *Andante* passage . . .' I began to go to lunch-hour piano recitals in the town hall and although at first I clapped in the wrong places, thinking the music was ended, I soon learned the pattern. I talked, too, as people talked who regularly went to music recitals and symphony concerts, 'Oh, smell the mothballs in the fur coats! And all that coughing, right in the middle of that slow movement, they didn't even cough in the places where they thought it was fair to sneak in a cough or a cleared throat!'

And one day John Forrest startled me into a new perception of him by saying suddenly, in the music room, 'But Schubert is my favourite composer.'

Schubert! *To Music. Thou holy art in many hours of sadness.*

In spite of the worries about teaching and my future, I found the year mostly pleasurable. At school and University I gave little thought to my home and family, and when I spent one of my few weekends at home, I tried to detach myself from the place and the people. My family appeared like tired ghosts trying to come to life for the occasion, both Mother and Dad were still pursued by *toil*, and the extra weariness now lay in the long walk up the hill, Dad with his home-made leather work-bag crammed with railway coal, Mother, during the day when no one was home, carrying the groceries which the boy from the Self Help or the Star Stores had delivered to the shed. Coming home for the weekend, I'd always find that Mother had bought a jar of coffee, that dark sweet liquid with the splurp taste, known as Gregg's Coffee and Chicory, where the outside of the bottle became sticky with the spilled syrup. Drinking coffee was a sign of being grown up; therefore I drank coffee. Also, one of the lecturers at University had spoken to me using the name, *Janet*, when I had always been known as *Jean*; therefore I was now officially *Janet*. During the weekend, Dad would bring a pile of Sexton Blake library books for me to read, and I'd race through the exploits of Sexton Blake and Tinker so that I could talk about them with him. The attentive habits of my parents saddened, pleased and infuriated me, leaving me with a feeling of helplessness — what could I do for them? I could see the pattern of their past lives slowly emerging, like a script written with invisible ink and now being made visible to me, warmed by the fire kindled simply by my growing up. I could see, too, an illumination produced by that same fire, the shadows emerging as recognised shapes of a language full of meaning for me: the language of the love and loss and joy and torture of having a place fast within a family when all my awakening longing was directed towards being uprooted, quickly, without leaving behind a cluster of nerve endings, broken threads in danger of being renewed.

The year was half gone. My personal lyric began its silent terrifying progression towards the planets and the stars. At the beginning of the month when I was to celebrate my twenty-first birthday, my coming of age, the war was suddenly over, having pursued me through all the years of my official adolescence, as part of the development of my body and mind, almost as an ingredient of my blood, leaving its trace everywhere, even in my hair and my (picked or bitten) fingernails. There was the usual spring snowfall that year, killing the newborn lambs but letting the early crocuses survive. Everyone rejoiced that the war had ended, and it was enough to rejoice and not notice or think about the fact that the atom bomb had been born, it also given its own life and responsibility. My coming of age was lit by the mushroom fire that made shadows of all those caught in its brightness; a spectacular illumination of the ceremonies of death, 'ashes to ashes, dust to dust'.

On 28 August I 'came of age' without a party but with some special presents given to me by my family — 'things' showing that I was a part of the world, after all: I had a new wristlet watch, and a new pair of plaid pompommed slippers with fleecy lining.

That month, as a kind of surface skimming of all the feeling set to boil away until old age, I wrote and published my first story, 'University Entrance' for which the *Listener* paid two guineas.

And now the year was passing quickly with the school inspector's crucial final visit soon to be faced. Inevitably, one bright morning of daffodils and flowering currant and a shine on the leaves of the bush along Queen's Drive, where I walked to school each morning, of a hint of warm gold in the sharp lemon-coloured sunlight, I arrived at school to find that it was the Day of Inspection, and at midmorning the inspector and the headmaster came to my classroom. I greeted them amiably in my practised teacherly fashion, standing at the side of the room near the display of paintings while the inspector talked to the class before he settled down to watch my performance as a teacher. I waited. Then I said to the inspector, 'Will you excuse me a moment please?'

'Certainly, Miss Frame.'

I walked out of the room and out of the school, knowing I would never return.

8   1945 (Two)

At first, drunk with the sense of freedom, all worry gone, I simply enjoyed the sparkle of the morning. Then, reality, taking over, directed my route down London Street, the street of doctors, and I chose a doctor's rooms near the foot of the hill, and walked in to consult a Dr William Brown, as harmless and anonymous a name as I could find. I explained to Dr Brown that I was very tired and felt I needed a rest of a few weeks. 'I'm in my first year teaching,' I said, bursting into tears.

Dr Brown obligingly gave me a certificate for the headmaster, to explain my temporary absence.

After posting the certificate in the box at the corner, I began three weeks of pure freedom. I went to University classes, to music recitals. I read and wrote. 'I have three weeks' leave,' I told my landlady, who, absorbed in her family, at once began to talk of when Bob would be given his annual holiday. Kathleen and the children so much wanted to go to Queenstown.

'I have so much work to do,' I said, 'that you probably won't see much of me, for meals and so on, and I'll leave a note in plenty of time if I'm not going to be in to dinner.'

'You're so thoughtful,' Mrs T. said. 'I'm lucky to have such a quiet student. You wouldn't even know you were in the house, you're so quiet!'

(A lovely girl, no trouble at all.)

At the end of my third week when school again loomed before me I was forced to realise that suicide was my only escape. I had woven so carefully, with such close texture, my visible layer of 'no trouble at all, a quiet student, always ready with a smile (if the decayed teeth could be hidden), always happy', that even I could not break the thread of the material of my deceit. I felt completely isolated. I knew no one to confide in, to get advice from; and there was nowhere I could go. What, *in all the world*, could I do to earn my living and still live as myself, as I knew myself to be. Temporary masks, I knew, had their place; everyone was wearing them, they were the human rage; but not masks cemented in place until the wearer could not breathe and was eventually suffocated.

On Saturday evening I tidied my room, arranged my possessions, and swallowing a packet of Aspros, I lay down in bed to die, certain that I would die. My desperation was extreme.

The next morning, near noon, I woke with a roaring in my ears and my nose bleeding. My first thought was not even a thought, it was a feeling of wonder and delight and thankfulness that I was alive. I staggered from my bed and looked at myself in the mirror; my face was a dusky red. I began to vomit, again and again. At last my nose stopped bleeding but the roaring in my ears continued. I returned to bed and slept, waking at about ten o'clock that evening. My head still throbbed, my ears rang. I hurried to the bathroom, turned on the tap, and vomited again. Mrs T., who had spent the weekend at Kathleen's and had been home about two hours, came to the door of her bedroom.

'Is everything all right?' she asked.

'Oh yes,' I called. 'Everything's fine. I've had a busy day.' (No trouble, no trouble at all.)

'Kathleen and Bob are in the midst of it all,' Mrs T. said, not explaining but evidently pleased. 'In the midst of it all.' We said goodnight and I went to my room and slept.

The next morning, the dreaded Monday, I woke with only a slight headache.

'My leave has been extended,' I told Mrs T. 'I have research to do.' I was now so overjoyed that I was alive when my intention had been to die, that school seemed a minor problem. I explained to the headmaster, possibly over the telephone and later by writing, that I had been advised to give up teaching. I did not say that it was I who was giving myself this advice.

I found a job washing dishes in the student canteen. I tried to turn hopefully towards my future. I felt that I would never again choose to kill myself.

It happened that part of our psychology course was the writing of a condensed autobiography. When I finished writing mine I wondered whether I should mention my attempt at suicide. I had now recovered; in a way, I was now rather proud for I could not understand how I had been so daring. I wrote at the end of my autobiography, 'Perhaps I should mention a recent attempt at suicide . . .', describing what I had done but, to make the attempt more impressive, using the chemical term for asprin — *acetylsalicylic acid*.

At the end of the class that week, John Forrest said to me, 'I enjoyed your autobiography. All the others were so formal and serious but yours was so natural. You have a talent for writing.'

I smiled within myself in a superior fashion. Talent for writing, indeed. Writing was going to be my profession!

'Oh I do write,' I said. 'I had a story in the *Listener* . . .'

He was impressed. Everyone had been impressed, saying, 'The *Listener*'s hard to get into.'

John Forrest looked at me closely. 'You must have had trouble swallowing all those Aspros?'

'Oh, I drank them with water,' I said calmly.

That evening as I was preparing to go to bed, Mrs T., answering a knock on the door, called to me, 'There are three men to see you. From the University.'

I went to the door and there were Mr Forrest, Mr Prince and the Head of the Department, who spoke first.

Mr Forrest tells me you haven't been feeling very well. We thought you might like to have a little rest.'

'I'm fine, thank you.' (No trouble, no trouble at all.)

'We thought you might like to come with us down to the hospital — the Dunedin hospital — just for a few days' rest.'

I felt suddenly free of all worry, cared for. I could think of nothing more desirable than lying in bed sheltered and warm, away from teaching and trying to earn money, and even away from Mrs T. and her comfortable home; and away from my family and my worry over them; and from my increasing sense of isolation in a brave bright world of brave bright people; away from the war and being twenty-one and responsible; only not away from my decaying teeth.

'John will come to visit you,' the Head of the Department said.

John! The use of first names, common among the young lecturers and their students but still a novelty to me, pleased and alarmed me. 'That's kind of you, Mr Forrest,' I said primly.

And so I was admitted to the Dunedin hospital, to Colquhoun Ward which, I was soon shocked to find, was a *psychiatric ward*. The doctors, Marples and Woodhouse, two young house surgeons, were questioning and kind. The nurse, Maitland Brown, a member of the Evangelical Union training to be a church missionary, talked to me of her hopes and dreams. I remember only one other patient in the bed next to mine, a strange woman who'd had an operation and kept denying it. I, brought up in a film star world of instant judgment on the looks of people, thought her repulsive and ugly with her red face, coarse skin, her small eyes with their ginger lashes and her thinning ginger hair. The dislike of her was general. I wonder now about the treatment of psychiatric and other patients who release, as if it were a chemical, an invitation to be disliked and who therefore have to fight (inducing further dislike and antagonism) for sympathy and fairness. When one day two ambulance men arrived to take the ugly patient to 'another hospital', I learned that the 'other hospital' was *Seacliff*. Seacliff, up the main trunk line, the hospital of grey stone, built like a castle. Seacliff, where the loonies went. 'You won't be going there, of course,' Maitland said. 'There's nothing wrong with you.'

And after my three weeks in hospital for observation, that was indeed the verdict. Mother was asked to travel to Dunedin to take me home, and after a holiday at home I'd be as good as new, they said.

Faced suddenly with the prospect of going home, I felt all the worries of the world returning, all the sadness of home and the everlasting toil of my parents and the weekly payments on the blankets and the new eiderdown from Calder Mackays, and the payments to the Starr-Bowkett Building Society or we'd be turned out of our house again; and the arguments at home, and Mother's eternal peacemaker intervention; and my decaying teeth; and my inability to find a place in the Is-Land that existed by absorbing, faster and faster, each tomorrow. If only I had the world of poetry, openly, unashamedly, without having to hide it in secrecy within myself!

In my state of alarm about my future, when I saw Mother standing there at the entrance to the ward, in her pitifully 'best' clothes, her navy costume and her navy straw hat with the bunch of artificial flowers at the brim; with a hint of fear in her eyes (for, after all, I had been in a 'mental' ward) and her face transparently trying to adopt the expression *All is well*, I knew that home was the last place I wanted to be. I screamed at Mother to go away. She left, murmuring her bewilderment, 'But she's such a happy person, she's always been such a happy person.'

I supposed, then, that I'd stay in hospital a few more days then be discharged, find a job in Dunedin, continue my university studies, renouncing teaching for ever. I did not realise that the alternative to going home was committal to Seacliff. No one thought to ask me why I had screamed at my mother, no one asked me what my plans were for the future. I became an instant third person, or even personless, as in the official note made about my mother's visit (reported to me many years later), 'Refused to leave hospital.'

I was taken (third-person people are also thrust into the passive mood) to Seacliff in a car that held two girls from borstal and the police matron, Miss Churchill. Miss Churchill! How curiously events and people and places and names moved between fiction and fact!

9 *1945 (Three)*

Writing an autobiography, usually thought of as a looking back, can just as well be a looking *across* or *through*, with the passing of time giving an X-ray quality to the eye. Also, time past is not time gone, it is time accumulated, with the host resembling the character in the fairytale who was joined along the route by more and more characters, none of whom could be separated from one another or from the host, with some stuck so fast that their presence caused physical pain. Add to the characters all the events, thoughts, feelings, and there is a mass of time, now a sticky mess, now a jewel bigger than the planets and the stars.

If I look through 1945 I see the skeleton of the year and shadowing it with both the shadow of death and of life, the atom bomb, the homely crocuses surviving in the late spring snow, birthdays and deathdays, and two or three other events bringing those dreamed-of planets and stars within the personal world of myself and many others in New Zealand. The events were the publication of *Beyond the Palisade*, poems by a young student at the University, James K. Baxter, *A Book of New Zealand Verse*, edited by Allen Curnow, and a collection of stories edited by Frank Sargeson, *Speaking for Ourselves*. As a child I had looked on New Zealand literature as the province of my mother, and when I longed for my surroundings — the hill, the pine plantations, Fifty-six Eden Street, Oamaru, the foreshore and the sea to waken to imaginative life, all I could do was populate them with characters and dreams from the poetic world of another hemisphere and with my own imaginings. There was such a creation as New Zealand literature; I chose to ignore it, and indeed was scarcely aware of it. Few people spoke of it, as if it were a shameful disease. Only in the Modern Bookshop in Moray Place were there shelves of slim New Zealand books from small presses, and I had even bought some, and tried and failed to write poems like those in the books. James Baxter's poems with their worldwide assurance also intimidated me. The anthologies, however, were different: their force and variety gave me hope for my own writing while wakening in me an awareness of New Zealand as a place of writers who understood how I had felt when I imported J. C. Squire to describe my beloved South Island rivers, and though I read the poem again and again I had to be content with the Congo, Nile, Colorado, Niger, Indus, Zambesi: beautiful names but those of another world.

But here, in the anthology of New Zealand verse (they were still not brave enough to call it *poetry*), I could read in Allen Curnow's poems about Canterbury and the plains, about 'dust and distance', about our land having its share of time and not having to borrow from a northern Shakespearian wallet. I could read, too, about the past, and absences, and objects which only we could experience, and substances haunting in their unique influence on our lives: the poem 'Wild Iron' reads to me like part of a history of New Zealand and its people.

And there was Denis Glover using the names of our own rivers and places, and even writing about the magpies, perfectly recording their cries on a misty autumn morning. Each poet spoke in his and her own way and place, and there was Charles Brasch confiding in the sea as I had confided, without words, in the Clutha, 'Speak for us, great sea.'

The stories, too, overwhelmed me by the fact of their belonging. It was almost a feeling of having been an orphan who discovers that her parents are alive and living in the most desirable home — pages of prose and poetry.

Time confers privileges of arrangement and rearrangement undreamed of until it becomes Time Past. I have been writing of the memory of publication of stories and poems. In actual memory I am sitting talking to two borstal girls, on the way to Seacliff hospital, where I shall be a committed patient.

10   1945 (Four)

The six weeks I spent at Seacliff hospital in a world I'd never known among people whose existences I never thought possible, became for me a concentrated course in the horrors of insanity and the dwelling-place of those judged insane, separating me for ever from the former acceptable realities and assurances of everyday life. From my first moment there I knew that I could not turn back to my usual life or forget what I saw at Seacliff. I felt as if my life were overturned by this sudden division of people into 'ordinary' people in the street, and these 'secret' people whom few had seen or talked to but whom many spoke of with derision, laughter, fear. I saw people with their eyes staring like the eyes of hurricanes surrounded here by whirling unseen and unheard commotion contrasting strangely with the stillness. I grew to know and like my fellow patients. I was impressed and saddened by their — our — capacity to learn and adhere to and often relish the spoken and unspoken rules of institutional life, by the pride in the daily routine, shown by patients who had been in hospital for many years. There was a personal geographical, even linguistic exclusiveness in this community of the insane, who yet had no legal or personal external identity — no clothes of their own to wear, no handbags, purses, no possessions but a temporary bed to sleep in with a locker beside it, and a room to sit in and stare, called the *dayroom*. Many patients confined in other wards of Seacliff had no name, only a nickname, no past, no future, only an imprisoned Now, an eternal Is-Land without its accompanying horizons, foot or handhold, and even without its everchanging sky.

In my book *Faces in the Water* I have described in detail the surroundings and events in the several mental hospitals I experienced during the eight following years. I have also written factually of my own treatment and my thoughts about it. The fiction of the book lies in the portrayal of the central character, based on my life but given largely fictional thoughts and feelings, to create a picture of the sickness I saw around me. When one day a fellow patient, seeing workmen outside digging drains, said to me, 'Look, they are digging our graves,' I knew she believed this. Her words are an example of the words and behaviour I used to portray Istina Mavet. Even in my six weeks' stay I learned, as if I had entered a foreign land, much of the language and behaviour of the inhabitants of the land. Others also learned fast — the girls from borstal were adept at livening their day by a 'performance' based on example.

My previous community had been my family. In *To the Is-Land* I constantly use the first person plural — we, not I. My time as a student was an I-time. Now, as a Seacliff patient, I was again part of a group, yet more deeply alone, not even a creviced 'I'. I became 'she', one of 'them'.

When I left Seacliff in December 1945, for a six-month probationary period, to return to a Willowglen summer, the shiningest time at Willowglen, I felt that I carried within me a momentous change brought about by my experience of being in a mental hospital. I looked at my family and I knew that they did not know what I had seen, that in different places throughout the country there were men and women and children locked, hidden away with nothing left but a nickname, with even the word *nick*name hinting at the presence of devils. I noticed that the behaviour of my family had changed in subtle ways related to my having been a patient in Seacliff where the loonies lived. Why do I use once again the metaphor with a spider? It seemed as if, having been in hospital, I had, like a spider, woven about me numerous threads which invisibly reached all those who 'knew' and bound them to a paralysis of fixed poses and expressions and feelings that made me unhappy and lonely but gave me also a recognition of the power of having spun the web and the powerlessness of those trapped within it.

When I'd been home a week or two my family grew less apprehensive in my presence — the change showed in the lessening of fear in their eyes; who knew what I might do; I was a loony, wasn't I? Mother, characteristically, began to deny everything. I was a happy person, she said. There must have been some mistake. I found that everyone was pleased when I treated the matter as a joke, talking of amusing incidents at the 'country estate', likening it to a hotel. I described the surroundings. 'It's like a whole village,' I said. 'They have their own farm, their own cattle and pigs, and all the waste from the foods goes into the pig tin. They have their vegetable garden, and their flowers, too. And the grounds are full of trees, and there's a magnolia tree near where the superintendent lives.'

It was easier to talk as if I were a child describing what I had seen and what adventures I'd had on my holiday.

I didn't tell them how I had peeped through the fence of a building called *Simla*, away upon the hill, where there were strange men in striped shirts and trousers and some without trousers, walking round and round in a paddock with the grass worn away; and how I'd seen a paddock of women, too, wearing the dark blue striped clothes; and how there was a cart, like a rickshaw, that passed every day by the ward, how it was full of coal and two men harnessed to the cart carried the coal, driven by one of the attendants; how, curious as ever, I had peered into a room that stank of urine and was full of children lying in cots, strange children, some of them babies, making strange noises; their faces wet with tears and snot; and I didn't say how there was a special section for the patients with tuberculosis, and how their dishes were boiled in a kerosene tin on the dining-room fire, and the nurses spent some time in the small linen cupboard folding the cardboard to make the daily supply of boxes, like strawberry boxes, for the TB patients to spit in.

After Christmas it was suggested that perhaps a holiday would be 'good' for me, and so June and I set out for two weeks in Picton, Mother's old home town, where we spent the usual summer sandfly-bitten time travelling around the Sounds in launches, meeting relatives, hearing new details of family history, while I, strongly under the influence of my past year of listening to music, composed in my mind what I called my 'Picton Symphony in Green and Blue'. My memory of the holiday is scattered — like seeds, I imagine, a handful eaten by summer-visiting birds migrating from winter memories, or by native birds that feed time-long on the memory, others not surviving, others grown into plants that cannot be recognised or named. I know that I took home the memory of those steep green oppressive hills, their bushclad slopes rising as inescapably close as neighbours.

Asked to describe the holiday, June and I told the family what we knew they wanted to hear, to try to make everyone happy. We had grown up, you see, in a thorough school, in this with our mother as teacher. And once again I began to prepare for another year in Dunedin.

I planned to find a 'live-in' job, and to 'take' Philosophy II, Logic and

Ethics, but sit no examinations. I had been assured that although I sat no end-of-year psychology examinations, I would be granted a pass based on my year's work. Perhaps I neglected to fill in the correct forms: I discovered that I had been marked *Failed*. Failed!

In the meantime, at home, there was the problem of having my life savings of twenty pounds returned from the Public Trust Office, who had taken charge of my affairs as I was officially insane. Once again my sisters and my brother and I 'banded together' to try to assert our rights, with Isabel composing an earnest letter to the Public Trust officer, who replied that his confiscation of my 'property' was in my own interests as I was officially insane and would not have legal rights until my 'probation' period of six months had ended, and then only if the doctor declared my sanity.

Perhaps, then, I could be given a sickness benefit until I began working again?

My visit to the Seacliff doctor at the Oamaru hospital brought its own bewilderment, for the medical certificate stated: Nature of Illness; *Schizophrenia*.

At home I announced, half with pride, half with fear, 'I've got *Shizzofreenier*.

I searched through my psychology book, the chapter on Abnormal Psychology, where I found no reference to *Schizophrenia*, only to a mental illness apparently afflicting only young people like myself — *dementia praecox*, described as a gradual deterioration of mind, with no cure. In the notes at the end of the chapter there was an explanation that *dementia praecox* was now known as *schizophrenia*. *Shizzophreenier*. A gradual deterioration of mind. Of mind and behaviour. I suffered from *shizzophreenier*. It seemed to spell my doom, as if I had emerged from a chrysalis, the natural human state, into another kind of creature, and even if there were parts of me that were familiar to human beings, my gradual deterioration would lead me further and further away, and in the end not even my family would know me.

In the last of the shining Willowglen summer these feelings of doom came only briefly as passing clouds block the sun. I knew that I was shy, inclined to be fearful, and even more so after my six weeks of being in hospital and seeing what I had seen around me, that I was absorbed in the world of imagination, but I also knew that I was totally present in the 'real' world and whatever shadow lay over me, lay only in the writing on the medical certificate.

Towards the opening of the University year, when I advertised for a live-in job in Dunedin, describing myself as a 'research student', I received a reply from Mrs B., of Playfair Street, Caversham, who kept a boarding house and cared for elderly women. I was to be a housemaid-waitress-nurse, with three pounds a week 'all found', and afternoons free. Afternoons free. Time to write my stories and poems.

11   *The Boardinghouse and the New World*

Once again I travelled south by the slow Sunday train to Dunedin, stopping at every station, looking out from the old-fashioned carriage, tacked on for the few passengers, at the spiralling links of tarpaulin-covered trucks. As usual there were unloadings, loadings, jolts as the trucks were removed, long periods when the carriage at the end seemed to stand alone in the midst of paddocks of gum trees, tussock, manuka scrub, *matagouri*, swamp, sheep, derelict houses, as if it made an excursion into a nowhere that was also a yesterday, filled with peace and sadness. I looked out of the old-fashioned push-up window (as opposed to the newer wind-up windows of the express trains) and I felt a force that could only have been the force of love drawing me towards the land, where no one appeared to be home. I felt a new sense of responsibility to everything and everyone because every moment I carried the memory of the people I had seen in Seacliff, and this knowing even changed the landscape and my feeling towards it.

When the train stopped at Seacliff station I saw the few *parole* patients waiting on the platform to watch the train go by. I *knew*, you see. Inwardly I kept describing myself in the words that I knew relatives and friends now used, 'She's been in Seacliff. They had to take her to Seacliff.' And I thought of the horror in Mother's voice when, years ago, the doctor had suggested that Bruddie should go there, and Mother had replied, 'Never. Never. No child of mine will ever go to that place.' But I was a child of hers, wasn't I? Wasn't I? And she had signed papers to send me there. I felt uneasy, trying to divide out portions of family love to discover how much was mine.

I looked around the carriage at the 'ordinary people'. Did they know where I had been? If they knew, would they look at me and then turn away quickly to hide the fear and fascinated curiosity as if they were tasting an experience which — thank God, they thought — they would never know but about which they wondered furiously, fearfully? If they knew about me, would they try to find a sign, as I had done when I, too, used to stare at the 'loonies' on Seacliff station.

Well, I thought, the signs were often secret but I knew them now, I was an experienced observer, I had visited the foreign land.

Also, I remembered with dread, they say I have *shizzofreenier*. A disease without hope.

The wheels of the train, however, which all my railway life had said, Kaitangata, Kaitangata, Kaitangata, remained uninfluenced by my strange disease: their iron on iron said, obstinately, *Kaitangata, Kaitangata, Kaitangata*.

The train arrived at Dunedin station. I felt quite alone, as if I belonged nowhere. All those marvellously belonging days at Training College when we sang 'The Deacon went Down', and talked knowledgeably of Party, and crit lessons, and days of control; the English and French lectures, the year of teaching children I had grown to love, had vanished as if they had never been, an impression deepened by the fact that since my disappearance to Seacliff there'd been no word from College or school or University, except a letter from my friend Sheila and a note from John Forrest to invite me to have 'little talks' with him during the coming year. I clung to the idea of having someone to talk to, and relished the bonus that the someone was an interesting young man.

I was taking my new status seriously. If the world of the mad were the world where I now officially belonged (lifelong disease, no cure, no hope), then I would use it to survive, I would excel in it. I sensed that it did not exclude my being a poet. It was therefore with a feeling of loneliness but with a new self-possession, unlike my first fearful arrival in the big city of Dunedin, that I took a taxi to Playfair Street, Caversham, in the heart of the country of the Industrial School.

South Dunedin — Kensington, Caversham, St Kilda — was a poor community where lives were spent in the eternal 'toil' with the low-lying landscape reflecting the lives, as if effort and hope were here washed away in the recurring floods while the dwellers on the hill suburbs prospered. I had taught in Caversham school and at Kensington in the school 'under the railway bridge', and I had seen the poverty, the rows of decaying houses washed biscuit-colour by time and the rain and the floods; and the pale children lank haired, damp looking, as if they emerged each day from the tide.

My memory of the boarders and the landlord and landlady and their child is momentary, like a hastily sketched scene in black and white giving only the outline of each person with the hair growing like grass out of their skull. They still hold, however, an invisible bowl brimful of feeling, and it is their feeling unspoken and spoken, that I remember most vividly. They were unhappy anxious people trying desperately to pretend they were happy, and seizing occasions of joy to recount, each to the others, at meal-times, as a way of contributing to the possibility of happiness. The men usually were employed at the railway workshops, the women in the factories — the chocolate or jam factory — or a branch of the woollen mill. One young man lost his job every few weeks, found another, lost that, and at night, at dinner, the others talked about his success or failure, explaining, excusing, condemning. They criticised each other, poked fun, pounced swiftly on the unconforming. I remember the landlady's husband only as a tall pale stooped man who carried firewood from the shed into the sitting room, where everyone gathered in the evening, the women with their knitting, the men with playing cards or their sporting newspapers; and sometimes one of the boarders who was acknowledged to have 'failed' in life (as opposed to the others who still had valid excuses and reasons), a thin woman in her middle thirties, without a husband or lover (the basis for her being judged a failure) played the yellowing keys of the piano while the middle-aged bachelor, a salesman, plump, popular ('He's always the same, you know where you are with him') sang the current favourite song,

> Beyond the sunset
> to blissful morning . . .

From the moment of my arrival I explained that I'd be very busy out of working hours and so would prefer at times to have my meals in my room. I was a student, engaged in private research, I said — I with my ready smile (hoping that I concealed my badly decayed teeth), sympathetic voice, no obvious physical deformities; and my upstanding mass of frizzy ginger hair. My duties were to prepare and serve breakfast, to clean the house, and to attend to the four elderly women who lived, bedridden, each in a corner bed, in the large front room. I washed them, helped to turn them or arrange the rubber ring beneath their gaunt bodies where the skin hung in folds like chicken skin with bumps where feathers might once have been. I rubbed methylated spirits on their bedsores, and powdered their bodies. I fed them, sometimes with the aid of a white china feeding-cup. I helped them use the wooden commode or arranged a bedpan beneath their drooping buttocks.

I was surprised to find that one of the women was old Mrs K., Aunty Han's sister, Aunty Han being the wife of Uncle Bob, who, retired from his bakery in Mosgiel, now sat in a tobacconist's 'possie', an enclosure the size of a telephone booth, where he sold cigarettes, tobacco, *Best Bets* and

Sporting News and Art Union tickets. Old Mrs K., who was also the mother of the student whose name I had 'dropped' as being my 'aunt's niece' when I was accepted for Training College, was a tall woman with large defined bones and an imperious face with pointed nose and chin. The family came from 'up Central', and even Mrs K. had absorbed some of the Central Otago hill formation into her own body. Like her sister, Aunty Han, she had a mouth and lips prepared to register instant disapproval. Dad used to say that Aunty Han's mouth was like the behind of an egg-bound hen.

Here at Mrs B.'s, I became friends with Aunty Han's sister. I found that I had gentleness and everlasting patience with the sick and the old. I enjoyed waiting on people, attending to their comfort, doing as they asked, bringing the food they ordered. I had no impatience, irritation, anger, to subdue: I seemed to be a 'born' servant. The knowledge frightened me: I was behaving as my mother had done all the years I had known her, and I was enjoying my new role: I could erase myself completely and live only through the feelings of others.

My bedroom, once a linen cupboard, was small, with shelves along one wall and a narrow bed against the other wall. The view from the one small window was 'pure Caversham' — dreary grey stone buildings with a glimpse of the tall chimneys of *Parkside*, the home for the aged, resembling my idea of a nineteenth-century English workhouse. When I finished my morning's work I'd go to my room and sit on my bed and write my stories and poems, for just as when I had been a child there was a time for writing and the knowledge that other children were writing their poems, now I was aware of writers in my own country. My inspiration for my stories came partly from my reading of Willliam Saroyan, and my unthinking delight, 'I can do that too.' And besides the excitement of being in a land that was coming alive with its own writing, *speaking for itself*, with many of the writers returning from the war, bringing their urgency of experience, I felt the inspiration of my own newly acquired treasure — my stay of six weeks in a mental hospital, what I had felt and seen, and what I had become, my official status of schizophrenia. And while I fed the guests at the boarding-house, they fed me from that invisible bowl of their feelings.

My life away from the boardinghouse consisted of evening lectures on logic and ethics, and weekly 'talks' with John Forrest in a small room on the top storey of the University building known as the Professors' House. I also spent time in the Dunedin Public Library, where I read case histories of patients suffering from schizophrenia, with my alarm and sense of doom increasing as I tried to imagine what would happen to me. That the idea of my suffering from schizophrenia seemed to me so unreal, only increased my confusion when I learned that one of the symptoms was 'things seeming unreal'. There was no escape.

My consolation was my 'talks' with John Forrest, as he was my link with the world I had known, and because I wanted these 'talks' to continue, I built up a formidable schizophrenic repertoire: I'd lie on the couch, while the young handsome John Forrest, glistening with newly applied Freud, took note of what I said and did, and suddenly I'd put a glazed look in my eye, as if I were in a dream, and begin to relate a fantasy as if I experienced it as a reality. I'd describe it in detail while John Forrest listened, impressed, serious. Usually I incorporated in the fantasy details of my reading on schizophrenia.

'You are suffering from a loneliness of the inner soul,' John said one day. For all his newness and eagerness to practise psychology and his apparent willingness to believe everything I said, his depth of perception about 'inner loneliness' was a mark of his special ability. He next made the remark which was to direct my behaviour and reason for many years.

'When I think of you,' he said, 'I think of Van Gogh, of Hugo Wolf . . .'

I, in my ignorance, knowing little of either Van Gogh or Hugo Wolf, and once again turning to books for my information, discovered that Hugo Wolf 'd. insane', and that Van Gogh 'shot himself in despair at his condition'. I read that Schumann, too, 'suffered serious deterioration in mental health'. All three were named as *schizophrenic*, with their artistic ability apparently the pearl of their schizophrenia. Great artists, visionaries . . .

My place was set, then, at the terrible feast. I had no illusions about 'greatness' but at least I could endow my work and — when necessary — my life with the mark of my schizophrenia.

When John Forrest learned that I was writing poems and stories, he was delighted. He suggested that as I wrote each I should give it to him to keep, and I, therefore, began to bring him my stories and poems. I kept 'pure schizophrenia' for the poems where it was most at home, and I looked forward to John Forrest's praise of my efforts; and when I had saved enough money to buy a second-hand Barlock 20 typewriter and type my work using, at first, one or two fingers, I felt that I possessed all in the world that I desired — a place to write, time to write, enough money to live on, someone to talk to or at least someone to try to impress, for most of my thoughts I kept to myself, and a disease interesting enough to be my ally in my artistic efforts and to ensure, provided I maintained the correct symptoms, that I had the continued audience of John Forrest. I was playing a game, half in earnest, to win the attention of a likeable young man whose interest was psychology and art; yet in spite of my pretence at hallucinations and visions I was growing increasingly fearful of the likeness between some of my true feelings and those thought of as belonging to sufferers from schizophrenia. I was very shy, within myself. I preferred to write, to explore the world of imagination, rather than to mix with others. I was never withdrawn from the 'real' world, however, although I was convincingly able to 'use' this symptom when the occasion required.

I was not yet aware of sexual feelings, although I no doubt experienced them, innocently not recognising them. Then one day when I was exploring a case history of schizophrenia, I read of a woman who was afraid (as I was, although I also was deterred by lack of money) to visit the dentist, and on exploration in the Freudian manner, it was discovered that *fear of the dentist* was common in those suffering from schizophrenia, *fear of the dentist* being interpreted as *guilt over masturbation*, which was said to be one of the causes and a continued symptom of schizophrenia!

I pondered this: I was certainly afraid of visiting the dentist as I knew that my teeth were now beyond repair (the general opinion in New Zealand then was that natural teeth were best removed anyway, it was a kind of colonial squandering, like the needless uprooting of forests). As for masturbation, it was a word of which I was ignorant and an act of which I was innocent. This new fact, however, made me curious enough to investigate both meaning and deed, for surely I must know if it were to be thought one of the causes of my disease! It happened that both my sisters and I, feeling we needed further sex education and having no one to give it to us in its theory, sent for a widely advertised book which arrived in its plain wrapper: *Meeting and Mating*. Everyone who was *educated*, with a wholesome attitude to sex and marriage, was reading *Meeting and Mating* and recommending it. We found in it details we had searched for in vain in Mother's *Ladies Handbook of Home Treatment*, with its chapter 'God's Great Out-of-Doors' intended to be read by women about to marry. It referred also to masturbation, describing it in detail, explaining how it was acceptable in both men and women with no need for guilt.

And of course I tried it. And childhood was suddenly long long ago, for I *knew*, and I couldn't return to the state of not knowing, and the remaining curiosity was, How might it be if one never knew? A few weeks later I said to John Forrest, 'It's awful, I can't tell you, for years I've been guilty about it. It's . . . it's . . .'

He waited expectantly.

'It's masturbation, worry over masturbation . . .'

'It usually is,' he said, and began to explain, as our book had explained, how it was 'perfectly all right, everyone did it.'

The pattern of that 'little talk' was so perfect that I imagine (now) a fleeting triumph passing over John Forrest's Freud-intensive face: here was a textbook schizophrenic.

I continued to fear that I might once again be left with no one to talk to, that is, in a 'normal' state of nearness to mental breakdown, for I was on the usual adolescent path of worry and wondering how to 'cope' with everyday living; yet, strangely, in order to lessen my anxiety, I found myself forced to choose a more distinctly signposted path, where my journey drew attention and so, I found, drew more practical help. I don't think it occurred to me that people might be willing to help me if I maintained my ordinary timid smiling self. My life so far had trained me to perform, to gain approval by answering questions in examinations, solving problems, exhibiting flashes of 'cleverness' and 'difference'. I was usually ashamed of my clothing. I was baffled by my fuzzy hair and the attention it drew, and the urgency with which people advised that I have it 'straightened', as if it posed a threat. I was not fluent in conversation, nor witty, nor brilliant. I was an ordinary grey-feathered bird that spent its life flashing one or two crimson feathers at the world, adapting the feathers to suit the time in life. In my childhood I had displayed number riddles, memorising long passages of verse and prose, mathematical answers; now, to *suit* the occasion, I wore my schizophrenic fancy dress.

During 1946, when my 'probationary' period was over, I was declared sane; I felt a twinge of loss, very slight, for I had written a collection of stories and poems, which John Forrest had shown to Denis Glover of the Caxton Press, who was interested in publishing the stories in a book, with the poems perhaps following. I felt I had begun my career as a writer.

Then, towards the end of the year, John Forrest announced that he had applied for work as a psychologist in the U.S.A., where he hoped to get his Ph.D. He would be leaving New Zealand early in 1947. He suggested that if I needed someone to talk to, he could recommend his friend in Christchurch, Mrs R., with whom he had spoken about me, he said, adding that she, being of an artistic nature, was interested in my 'case'.

'I'll find a job in Christchurch and perhaps take a course at Canterbury University,' I said, very calmly as I saw my secure schizophrenic world of 'little talks' beginning to fall apart, leaving me alone in an alien city. I wondered why I had ever thought that I belonged in Dunedin or how I would ever belong in Christchurch. The Caxton Press was in Christchurch, and the book they were planning some time to publish — perhaps the book would be like a relation, living nearby, and I'd not be so isolated?

I wondered where I would go. I knew I could not stay beyond one or two months at home without being overtaken by unhappiness at the everlasting struggle of everyone there — for money, or love or power or an ocean of peace. There was always a hotel or boardinghouse to give me work, room and board, but why did 1946 need to end?

I stood on the cliff, trying to catch at the wings of 1946 as they beat at the salt-strewn earth and grass in preparation for their flight forward into

yesterday. In reality, I said goodbye to all at Playfair Street, Caversham —
the four old ladies and the boarders with their secret failures and shames
and small shared happinesses, and my landlord and landlady and their
small child of four, who still didn't speak although everyone pretended not
to notice; and I left with my brand-new reference should I look for work
in Christchurch, 'Polite to the guests at all times, industrious, a pleasure . . .'
and a tiny black kitten, supposedly male but actually female, which I named
affectionately, Sigmund, changed later to Sigmunde, known as Siggy; and
once again, a railway person bound forever to the dock and the wild sweet
peas and 'the rust on the railway lines', I travelled north on the Express and
as the train approached Oamaru, before the Gardens, I caught a quick
glimpse, looking left, of Willowglen putting on its gloss for the summer.

12   Willowglen Summer

I had not known a complete winter at Willowglen: only June and Bruddie
and Mother and Dad had suffered the misery when the creek flooded and
the driveway, churned by the cows (how could we have a ready-made cowbyre and three acres of land without cows to share it?), made the track to
the gate impassable; I had spent only weekends huddled under blankets,
clutching a stone hot-water bottle, in the freezing front bedroom, or,
dressed in farm clothing, gumboots and Dad's fishing raincoat, wandering
the hills to keep warm.

Dad and Bruddie had worked hard to make improvements to the house.
There was no longer an earth floor in the kitchen. The roof was watertight.
Pipes (which froze in winter) had been laid, connecting us to town water,
and a hot-water cylinder installed in the scullery. We now had a telephone
in the passage, a party line, with a long horn-like earpiece, and when the
telephone rang it was usually Mother who answered it. Dad refused, his fear
transparent, while Mother, equally fearful, prepared for the shock of what
the message might be, for a telephone, like a telegram, was used in urgency,
and could mean life or death. The telephone book was always on the 'fernstand', which, like some of the pieces of furniture small enough to fit into
the house, had always been part of the family, with names that spoke of
another age: the 'fernstand' — that never held ferns; Grandad's chess table,
with its dark burned engravings of a long-dead king and queen; the
chiffonier . . .

It was a paradisal summer. I had my place to sit, on the fallen birch log by the creek, where I could watch the pukeko, the ducks and the eels, and look through the sheltering willows to the paddock where the sheep and cattle owned by the stock and station agent were held each week before being driven up the road to the Waiareka saleyards to be trucked out to the Pukeuri freezing works, which I knew to be the *Abattoir*, although for many years I confined the word to a kind of porch of consciousness where words linger and come and go without an investigation of their meaning or an invitation to that lightning room of realisation. Sometimes, futilely, I was able to rescue a sheep from the swamp, and for this service, the stock and station agent, a tall man with a square face and horn-rimmed glasses and an appearance that I might have associated with a player of the cello or piano, paid me a fee of five pounds.

From behind the willows I could see, unseen myself, the road and the postman cycling to our letterbox, the last on the street before the farms and their paddocks and the Old Mill Road. I wondered would the postman bring me a letter? From where? From whom? Dad had made a letterbox in the shape of a house, with a chimney and painted doors and windows, red walls and a green roof with eaves, and when the postman had cycled past I'd search the letterbox house. At Christmas, John Forrest sent me a card. I treasured it, trying to work out the degree of affection expressed by 'Yours very sincerely'. Was it more or less than 'Yours sincerely'? With my destructive sense of realism I recognised that there wasn't much hope in 'Yours very sincerely', not even if it were examined letter by letter or repeated softly in a romantic voice. I was not in love with John Forrest, yet I needed his interest and attention and it was satisfying to notice the eagerness in Mother's eyes when she asked, 'Have you heard from Mr Forrest?' and to make sure I quelled any hopes she might have by replying, 'It's not like that, Mother, I am temporarily transferred to him. It's a known phenomenon. Freudian. You wouldn't understand.'

It was also a summer of foreboding and change. Isabel, swimming in the baths, had collapsed and just managed to pull herself from the water. The doctor who was called to her said, 'Her heart.' The repetition being too appalling to consider, we put the incident aside; I'm not sure whether we told our parents. Isabel had finished an energetic first year of teaching and she and her devoted boyfriend were considering engagement and marriage.

Isabel and June and I, summer-close after our inevitable grown-up separation, discovering in ourselves a new feeling for our parents and the sacrifices they had made for us, decided that now was the time to share what money we had to give Mother the holiday she had dreamed of, a visit to Picton, her home town. Dad showed no interest in going, for he had annual holidays at Aunty Polly's, usually in the football season, for test matches. Now Mother was to have *her* holiday.

'Oh no,' she said. 'You kiddies use the money.'

We insisted. Mother was naturally fearful after an absence of nearly thirty years.

We persuaded her to go, taking Isabel with her, and all — Dad, Bruddie, June, Isabel and I — contributed to her funds, and in early February, carrying her first-class free railway ticket in her new purse, and wearing her best — her only — costume and a new straw hat, Mother set off with Isabel for her dreamed-of holiday.

We saw them onto the Express train. In our newly found sensitivity to what we called with sadness, regret and guilt, 'the kind of life Mother must have had', we tried to calm her observed apprehension at the thought of leaving home. We gave instructions that either Mother or Isabel should telephone within the first few days of their arrival.

'Just to let us know.'

'And you *are* pleased you're going, aren't you, Mum?'

We knew she was pleased. We could see in her face the surfacing of former pleasure — Oh Waikawa Road, Oh Old Caps and down the pa, Oh the Sounds, and Port Underwood, Dieffenbach and the Pebble Path, remember the Pebble Path, kiddies, the storms and the shipwrecks. Oh the Pioneers . . .

We waved the train out of honest sight, that is, it disappeared past the engine sheds into pure flat distance, where the two railway lines merged as we'd been taught to draw them in our lessons on perspective, and soon the train and the people in it were a narrow line, an I, with a wisp of smoke, an S, above it, out past the Boys' High and Pukeuri on the way across the Canterbury Plains to Christchurch and Picton.

13   Another Death by Water

Mother's absence was like a death. Dad sat morosely at his end of the table by the coal range reading the latest *Humour*, with no one to sugar and stir his tea and share his excitement when the bubbles, portents of *parcels*, rose to the surface — Look, two parcels! . . . and no one to scratch his back and share his bed and complain to — 'Your feet are like lumps of dripping.'

June and I were to prepare the meals and help Bruddie with the cows, but after one day when the household was running smoothly and we'd surrendered to Dad's wishes not to 'cook anything fancy', Mother's absence was like black frost in the sunless house. We missed Isabel too, in a different way; we missed her endless preparations for this and that, seeing to clothes, lengthening or shortening hems, trying to mend her shoes, giving her frank opinions on everything and everyone; and imagining what her 'future' would be. She had felt that one year of teaching was enough. She would get married, but apart from that, she might be a journalist on a big newspaper, or — something, surely *something*. When the world overtook her in Dunedin she used to go skating; here in Oamaru she went swimming at the baths.

On the second afternoon of the Picton holiday, the phone rang, and June answered it, and heard through the static and crackle, that it was 'Picton calling'. Dad was at work, and Bruddie was out. Aunty Grace was calling from Picton. Then there was an invisible commotion in the kitchen, like static leaked from the telephone: Isabel, swimming in Picton Harbour, had collapsed and was drowned. There was to be an inquest, after which Mother would bring Isabel home by train.

There was no use even supposing that there had been a mistake: Isabel drowned. It was almost ten years since Myrtle's death, and this new blow, like a double lightning strike, burned away our thinking and feeling — what was there to think about, to feel?

The phone rang again. It was Dad: he'd heard the news and was coming home. Bruddie was coming home too. The news was everywhere: Family tragedy of ten years ago repeated. Oamaru girl drowned.

Some called her 'girl', some called her 'woman'. Isabel May Frame in her twenty-first year.

June and I were still alone in the house consoling each other when someone knocked at the back porch door. It was J.B.! The headmistress of Waitaki, Miss Wilson, known to Isabel, June and me as 'the magnificent Titanic, the mighty modern ship, fifteen thousand tons of steel . . .' I think the amazement of receiving a visit from the headmistress of Waitaki, after all those years at school in a vital separation of home life and school life, almost overlaid our shock. Miss Wilson actually sat on *our sofa*, our sofa with all its exposed springs and stuffing and the dark patch near the armrest, still mapping the place where, years ago, Bruddie's tomcat had peed, and where we'd tried to remove the stain and the smell with our Christmas bottle of carnation scent.

And suddenly Miss Wilson was putting her arms around us and we were all crying, and we thought, If only Isabel could see us, with J.B.!

My momentary feelings about Isabel's death, as with Myrtle's, that a problem may have been solved but at too great a cost, were overtaken by the dreamlike reality of the first death by water, and the fact that I chose to identify both in a quote from T. S. Eliot, reminding me that I still inhabited a literary world. I had lived through The Waste Land; I had met Phlebas the Phoenician, who,

> a fortnight dead,
> forgot the cry of gulls.

I had known and experienced the rhythm and feeling of Virginia Woolf's Waves, the tragedy of Tess and Jude and the blow after blow struck at the Brontë family. This new death came as an epilogue to the old stories and a prologue to the new, in our own land where the 'great sea' and the rivers would speak for us and we would 'speak for ourselves', where even now, Time had at last taken up residence, on the Canterbury Plains — not too far from Picton — as

> . . . the nor'-west air nosing among the pines
> . . . the water-race and the rust on railway lines

even those railway lines merging in the distance to a thin perspective that became the dark shaft of absence.

Once again our grief and tears fitted into the familiar pattern, as the ordinary objects became the most poignant: the unfinished sewing, the undone hems of summer dresses, Isabel's new 'jiffy' coat, a short coat with wide sleeves in fashion at the time, the white summer shoes lying in the middle of the bedroom, where they'd been dropped the day she left for her holiday. There was the added tragedy of Mother's holiday and the fictional perfection of the events with no account taken of fairness or unfairness. Mother's burden was unthinkable: the drowning, the inquest (her second inquest), and the long train journey home with what was now officially 'the body'.

We waited on the platform of the Oamaru station for the train from Picton. Everyone knew, and looked at Dad, Bruddie, June and me, with sympathy. Towards the end of the platform at the goods entrance by the men's lavatories, the funeral director waited with his hearse backed to the platform. The bookstall and tearooms were open for the Express, and the waitresses were standing behind the counter in a line, ready for the rush of passengers for their hot pies, sandwiches, cakes and soft drinks. Perhaps everyone didn't know — there were tides of knowing and not knowing surging back and forth as new passengers, strangers, arrived, and waited; and beyond the platform, past the rows of old red carriages and trucks, the calm summer sea, stony grey-green, gently floated fringes of waves among the rocks along the foreshore. I could not see the water but I knew it and even in my mind I could touch the bubbles of foam and feel the water like a grey-green stone suddenly transparent and flowing.

We heard the telephone ring in the loco foreman's office, and I thought, That's Pukeuri ringing, the train's on its way. I didn't know if my surmise was correct, I knew only that just before the arrival of every train, the telephone rang in the loco foreman's office: that was railway *lore*.

There was a rush of smoke and steam and the sound of brakes and everyone stepped back from the platform to avoid being 'sucked under' — another response to railway tradition. And then there was the funeral director with his hearse as near to the train as he could back it, and they were lifting out of the goods van a coffin coloured dull silver, only it was lead.

'To stop her from smelling,' someone whispered, but I can't remember who said it, for such a remark, inconsiderate then, could have been made only by Isabel herself!

And there was Mother coming down the steps of the carriage; hugging and tears, and few words, Dad's, 'the arrangements have been made', and our 'Miss Wilson from Waitaki came to see us', said with a kind of glee as if death had prompted us to begin a long accounting: loss and profit, the first bonus.

Mother was bewildered, her eyes were frightened and her hair beneath the 'picture hat' of straw had turned from brown-grey to white.

Willowglen, unlike Fifty-six Eden Street, Oamaru, with its big, dark, apple-smelling front room, had no place to accommodate the dead; besides the hill was too far and too steep for a coffin to be carried, and so Isabel remained at the undertaker's chapel and was buried from there, and only Bruddie and Dad and Mother attended the funeral. Perhaps some of my memories of that time were there, too, and were buried with Isabel.

The letters and telegrams of sympathy came and were answered. The undertaker's itemised bill came and was paid. There was a doctor's bill, addressed to Isabel, 'for attendance at swimming baths', for the time she collapsed. And among the letters of sympathy was one from John Forrest: beginning, 'I am deeply grieved to learn of the shocking bereavement you and your family have sustained' and ending, 'Yours very sincerely, John Forrest.' I remember the complete letter for the shock of its language and my inability to accept the formal conventional expressions of sympathy and to accept that John Forrest was so lacking in imaginative understanding that he could write such a letter. I felt betrayed by my own adopted world of language. What reached me was not a message of sympathy but language which I, harshly critical and making no allowance for the difficulty of writing such letters, condemned as the worst example of prose. Where were the personal, friendly words of the young man who said I suffered from a 'loneliness of the inner soul'?

I was not to know that John Forrest was putting language to good use: he was trying to escape from the several women students who had formed romantic attachments to him!

Death is a dramatic accomplishment of absence; language may be almost as effective. I felt that both Isabel and John Forrest had vanished.

We each bore our grief alone, for Isabel had shared with each, different aspects of her growing up. For many years it was 'Dots and Chicks' — Isabel and June — the inseparable companions as it had once been 'Myrtle and Bruddie', while I, the middle child, moved from group to group according to my age and interests, and when Bruddie became ill, and Myrtle died, I was alone until Isabel and I composed our group, after which June, growing up, again joined Isabel, while I became alone again. Bruddie, except in his earliest days, was always alone. Yet Isabel had been so full of life that her presence and her opinions were hard to dismiss, and when we began to deal with her 'things' we knew she would be furiously angry to see her best shoes and Jiffy coat and her fitting 'Shazaam' jersey being worn by others. She had once said, 'When I die and you take my clothes and wear them, I'm going to come down and haunt you.' Down? Perhaps she believed in Heaven?

When my eldest sister Myrtle died in her sixteenth year she did not leave parts of herself, her presence, at Fifty-six Eden Street, perhaps because the house never belonged to us and there was always the danger that we could be 'turned out on the street', whereas Isabel, who had loved Willowglen, did not really leave it, and although the house was small there was room for the memory of Isabel both inside and outside among the orchard trees and the pine trees, the silver poplars, the cypress and the five oaks; by the creek and the may tree, the elderberry and the hawthorn hedge; beneath the huge macrocarpa where the magpies lived, and the moreporks and the little owl, known during the war as the 'German owl' because it was said to attack smaller birds; and in the calm golden sunlit grass, 'down on the flat'.

The now familiar ritual of death and burial having been completed, I decided to keep to my plan of living and working in Christchurch. I needed to leave Willowglen. There was an undercurrent of 'I hope it doesn't affect Janet too much. You know . . . she's been in Seacliff.' Since my six weeks in Seacliff there was an unwillingness to discuss 'serious' matters with me, a special protectiveness which I disliked. Also, I was timid about meeting people, and when visitors came as they did often during the time of Isabel's funeral, I hurried to my room pursued by mother who stood in the doorway, bewilderment and reproof in her eyes, 'Why don't you come out?'

Or, if visitors were expected, Mother or Dad would say, 'Mrs W. is coming over this afternoon. Is Janet going to come out?'

I was in hiding. I was grieving. I didn't want anyone to 'see', for since I had been in hospital, I had found that people didn't only 'see', they *searched* carefully.

I scanned the Situations Vacant columns of the Christchurch *Press*. The only vacancies with accommodation were in children's homes, the School for the Deaf at Sumner, and the usual hotels and boardinghouses. Studying a map of Christchurch and its suburbs, I grew increasingly alarmed by the length of the streets and the unfamiliar names that were yet familiar — Linwood, Burwood (wasn't there a home for wayward girls, like the Industrial School at Caversham?), Burnham, with the miles of huts of the military camp; Rolleston, Templeton, Hornby (*Hornby* sharp in the memory because every year at Christmas, Bruddie had asked for a *Hornby train*). I thought of the Christchurch railway station echoing with people and train sounds and the whoosh of the steam; trains from everywhere, on different tracks, people asleep leaning on white pillows against the carriage window with the beads of water running down the pane; people wiping the steam with their sleeve, to look out, sleepily, at the yellow lights of the refreshment rooms and the ledge along the outside with the litter of other trains — the empty blue-ringed railway cups and saucers with their dregs of railway tea and soggy crusts of ham sandwiches and ends of cigarettes, De Reszke or Ardath . . .

I found on the map the street where the Caxton Press had my stories to publish. They were printing one in the new magazine, *Landfall*, under the name *Jan Godfrey*, the name being chosen to honour my parents — Jan because Dad called me Jan, and Godfrey, because Godfrey was Mother's maiden name. I found also the suburb where Mrs R., John Forrest's friend, lived. And there was the university — dare I go near it? I found it impossible to equate all my dreams with what appeared to be a formidable unyielding reality.

After receiving an application form from the School for the Deaf, and feeling that they wanted to know 'too much about me', I answered an advertisement for a housemaid-waitress at a small hotel in the city, quoting my reference, 'well spoken, polite to the guests at all times. Honest, industrious . . .' and found myself hired by the proprietor of the 'racing' hotel, the Occidental.

My early acquaintance with words and their significance comes to mind now. I *decided*. I had a *destination*.

Once again I set out on a train journey, north across the Canterbury Plains to Christchurch.

14 *Dear Educated*

Loss, death, I was philosophical about everything: I still had my writing, didn't I, and if necessary I could use my schizophrenia to survive. I enjoyed working at the hotel, learning the language of horse racing, of trainers, breeders, buyers, owners, who were the main clientele, and I found the routine satisfying — serving meals on time and bar lunch at five in the evening, and seizing the opportunity to speak French to the French buyers, and feeling slightly superior when they asked why I, with 'my education', worked as a waitress, and giving the usual reply because I was not yet able or ready to call myself a 'writer', 'I'm engaged in private research.'

After work, alone in my room, I saw my tiny triumphs of self-esteem fading as I angled the duchesse mirror, to contemplate the horror of my decayed teeth. There was no escape from them; they ached; my entire face throbbed. I snuggled under the bedclothes with a hot-water bottle pressed upon my jaw. I knew I'd be forced to act very soon. I knew that the public hospital would fill or extract teeth free, but how could I ever think of being brave enough to make an appointment? And all the time I was aware of a dreadful feeling of nothingness, which was somehow intensified by the city itself — the endless flat straight streets, the sky without a horizon of hills, the distant horizon without sea. I felt as if I and the city were at the bottom of a huge well walled with sky, and who could climb the sky? When people came to their front or back doors to look out, where did they gaze? I felt so lonely without even the hills close by, like human bodies, for comfort.

After a few weeks in Christchurch I arranged an appointment with Mrs R., John Forrest's friend, with the intention of asking her to help me with arrangements for having my teeth extracted and come with me to the dental department of the public hospital, but when I presented myself at her house in an exclusive suburb and she, a tall angular woman dressed in fawn and brown, opened the door, I, sensing the impossibility of being able to explain my plight, I, standing there (mouth closed), a blooming young woman of twenty-two with no obvious disabilities, again turned on my 'schizophrenia' at full flow: it had become my only way of arousing interest in those whose help I believed that I needed. Nevertheless, it was several weeks before I could say that my urgent problem was my decaying teeth. Mrs R. kindly arranged for me to have my top teeth extracted at the hospital; she would come with me, she said, and might it not be a good idea for me to admit myself as a voluntary boarder to Sunnyside Mental Hospital, where there was a new electric treatment, which, in her opinion, would help me. I therefore signed the necessary papers.

I woke toothless and was admitted to Sunnyside Hospital and I was given the new electric treatment, and suddenly my life was thrown out of focus. I could not remember. I was terrified. I behaved as others around me behaved. I who had learned the language, spoke and acted that language. I felt utterly alone. There was no one to talk to. As in other mental hospitals, you were locked up, you did as you were told or else, and that was that. My shame at my toothlessness, my burning sense of loss and grief, my aloneness, and now, with another sister, June, soon to be lost in a marriage, I felt as if there were no place on earth for me. I wanted to leave Sunnyside, but where could I go? I grieved for everything lost — my career as a teacher, my past, my home, where I knew I could never stay more than a few weeks, my sisters, my friends, my teeth, that is, myself as a person. All I had left was my desire to be a writer, to explore thoughts and images which were frowned on as being bizarre, and my ambition, thought to be suspect, perhaps a delusion. My only writing was in letters to my sister and parents and brother, and these were always censored, and sometimes not mailed: I remember one instance of a letter written to my sister June where I was actually quoting from Virginia Woolf, in describing the gorse as having a 'peanut-buttery smell'. This description was questioned by the doctor who read the letters, and judged to be an example of my 'schizophrenia'. For I was now officially suffering from schizophrenia, although I had had no conversation with the doctors, or tests. I had woven myself into a trap, remembering that a trap is also a refuge.

And when I had been in hospital several months beyond the voluntary period and was declared a committed patient, that was the beginning of the years in hospital which I have already described, setting out only, as I have said, the actual events and people and places, but not myself, except for my feeling of panic simply at being locked up by those who reminded me constantly that I was 'there for life', and as the years passed and the diagnosis remained, with no one apparently questioning it even by formal interviewing or tests, I felt hopelessness at my plight. I inhabited a territory of loneliness which I think resembles that place where the dying spend their time before death, and from where those who do return living to the world bring inevitably a unique point of view that is a nightmare, a treasure, and a lifelong possession; at times I think it must be the best view in the world, ranging even farther than the view from the mountains of love, equal in its rapture and chilling exposure, there in the neighbourhood of the ancient gods and goddesses. The very act of returning to the world, however, tends to remove that view to the storeroom of the mind described by Thomas Beecham as 'the room two inches behind the eyes'. One remembers the treasure and the Midas effect of it upon each moment, and sometimes one can see the glitter among the ordinary waste of each day.

The years that followed, until 1954, when I was finally discharged from hospital, were full of fear and unhappiness, mostly caused by my confinement and treatment in hospital. Early in my stay there were two or three periods of several weeks when I was allowed to leave hospital and each time I needed to return as there was nowhere else for me to live; I was fearful always, like a condemned person returning to the executioner.

During my first return to Oamaru I advertised in the Situations Wanted column of the *Oamaru Mail*, signing myself, 'Educated', and from the three replies, all of which began, 'Dear Educated', I selected one from Mr O., whose wife was bedridden, suffering from what used to be called 'creeping paralysis'. For a month I cleaned their house, washed and ironed, attended to Mrs O., who lay quietly immersed in the squalor of illness while her husband, even in his health and his absence all day at his work, bore the traces of his wife's immersion: he sweated into his white neatly ironed shirts, and there was always sweat on his forehead. They did not speak much to me except to note their physical conditions.

'My husband sweats a lot,' Mrs O. said.

'The doctor says her condition is gradual,' Mr O. said.

After waking with delight in the Willowglen surroundings, and walking in the crisp air through the wet grass, as if in a bath of sun and green and blue, taking the short cut through the Oamaru Gardens by the glittering pond noisy with ducks, up across the railway line to the lower part of the South Hill, and stopping briefly to look out over the town and the sea, all drenched with morning; and going up the O.'s path past the granny's bonnets to the front door, I'd enter this house of grey people washed with sweat and tears, and I'd feel the gentle flow of sunlight and morning drained away. There was not even a view from Mrs O.'s bedroom. A great dark wardrobe, placed half in front of the window, cast a steep shadow shaped like a warrior with arm raised to destroy.

I left the O.s'. My wages gave me enough money to buy a set of upper teeth. I decided to accept the invitation of my sister and her husband to stay a while at their Auckland home.

In Auckland I was in a state of sensitivity to everything around me — the strangeness and heat, the everlasting sound of the cicadas and crickets, the bite of the mosquitoes, my first experience of the subtropical light alternating between harsh brilliance and paradisal cloud softness, like a storm oppressively, perpetually brewing. It was nearing summer, and the world was filled with blue flowers that attracted the blue of the sky, almost drinking it in until at evening their colour darkened with the excess of blue. I experienced a feeling of nowhereness and nothingness as if I had never existed, or, if I had, I was now erased from the earth. I had somehow fallen into a crevice in time; and many of these feelings were a result of my being 'in touch' with no one, and of having no one to talk to from within. I was my usual smiling self, smiling, flashing my bulky new false teeth, and talking about this and that and daily matters. I wrote my poems, showing them to no one. A member of my family had found and read a story I wrote and voiced the strong opinion that I would never be a writer. Sometimes when I began to say what I *really* felt, using a simile or metaphor, an image, I saw the embarrassment in my listener's eyes — here was the mad person speaking.

During the early weeks of my stay in Sunnyside I had corresponded with John Forrest but his carboned letters, intended for family and friends, with their hearty *Dear Everyone*, chilled me, and when during my stay in Oamaru I learned that he had married, I, with a natural sense of being excluded, no longer wrote the freely confessional letters in my style of being 'kin' to Van Gogh and Hugo Wolf, where I voiced my fantasies and described my behaviour.

My stay with my sister and her husband was not successful. They and their infant son enclosed one another while I stood awkwardly in the background, and if anyone called and looked my way, my shyness and self-consciousness, arising from my feeling of being nowhere, increased when my sister's friends asked, 'How is she?' 'Does she like being in Auckland?' I had become a third person, at home at Willowglen and now here in Auckland. Sometimes, as if I were my own obituary, people asked, 'What was she?' As if an archaeological find stood before them and they were applying with eyes, heart and mind, a 'carbon' test to name, date and *place* me — and if only I had a place! It seemed to be and it was years since the Caxton Press had accepted my stories for publication. I had forgotten about them.

I could no longer bear the nothingness. I retreated to an inward state, that is, I put on such a mask, while at the same time totally aware of everything. I, in my nothingness and nowhereness was asserting the nothingness and nowhereness of everything and everyone around me. Such a condition, of course, led to my removal to the Auckland mental hospital at Avondale;

at least it was a 'place' for me where I was believed to be 'at home'. I quickly fitted into my adopted country, again speaking the language fluently. The squalor and inhumanity were almost indescribable. I retain many many scenes of the crowded dayroom and exercise yard, and were I to rewrite *Faces in the Water*, I would include much that I omitted because I did not want a record by a former patient to appear to be over-dramatic. The admission ward, Ward Seven (?), is remembered as an oasis with its park and willow tree and its friendly ward sister, and no one would ever have dreamed that beyond it stood the buildings known as *Park House*, where human beings became or were quickly transformed into living as animals.

The years spent there were compressed with tragedy and often with humour, although the prevailing mood was one of a doomed eternity, all hope abandoned.

During my stay in Avondale my book of stories, *The Lagoon*, was published. I had been transferred to the admission ward. I was thin, with sores, and a discharging ear; everyone in Park House had sores or infected limbs and, in spite of the weekly combing with kerosene, some had lice. I was in bed in the admission ward when my sister and her husband brought me my six free copies of *The Lagoon*. I spread them on the white government counterpane embroidered with the New Zealand coat of arms: Ake Ake, Onward, Onward. I thought the appearance of the book was beautiful, with its pale blue design like links of stalks of wild grass. I turned the pages, feeling the tiny grains within the paper.

'What shall I do with them?' I asked.

Knowing more about such things than I, they explained that if you were an author you signed your name beneath the printing of your name.

'Really?' I was impressed.

I signed my name in each copy, giving them away to those who, they suggested, 'ought to have a copy', keeping one for myself. My book. *The Lagoon and Other Stories*. The Caxton Press, not I, had decided the title.

It was then arranged that as my sister and her husband were about to visit the South Island, I should go with them home to Oamaru. My sister would fly with me and her two young sons, while her husband would drive from Auckland, arriving in Oamaru about ten days later.

During the flight to Oamaru there was a change of plane at Christchurch and while we waited, I, with my book still large in my mind, scanned a copy of the Christchurch *Press*, the book pages, to see what 'they' were saying about my new book. Towards the foot of the page, compressed into five or six lines, the review dismissed *The Lagoon and Other Stories* with phrases like, 'This kind of thing has been done before, too often . . . no originality . . . a waste of time to publish such a book.' The literary critics of the time, having been persuaded that our literature had 'come of age', found themselves embarrassed by so many writers writing of childhood: they supposed, How could a nation be adult if it wrote of its childhood? The longing for 'maturity' was desperate partly because, among other terms for stages of growth, maturity was a fashionable word.

Reading the *Press* review, I felt painful humiliation and rejection, an increased torment of not knowing where to *be* — if I could not live within the world of writing books, then where could I survive?

My sister's visit to Willowglen, with her two small sons, was an illuminating disaster. With apparently nostalgic greed for power over the young, my father pounced upon the boys, watching their every move, indeed, refusing to allow them to make a move without his uttering a sharp, 'Now, now,' and reverting to long disused phrases like, 'You'll feel the back of my hand in a moment,' 'You do that once more and I'll skin you alive.' The boys were about three and one and a half years and they were passionate rivals for possession of everything, from toys to attention. They became the focus of powerful feeling in all the adults. They were watched as if they were on exhibit; talked about, criticised, warned, reprimanded, described, and their future planned. My father watched them as he used to watch our cats when rarely he would allow them inside to play in the kitchen, while we grouped about them to share the enjoyment of their play, until suddenly, Dad, the commander, would shout, like a king overseeing his jesters — Enough! Out!

And the cats would be thrust, meowing and bewildered, into the cold night, while our enjoyment turned to disappointment and sadness.

I, as the acknowledged misfit in the family, felt the humiliation of seeing my mother talking intimately with my sister about marriage and bed and birth, where she had never dared to discuss these with me, and in later years when from time to time my sister would say, talking of a part of Mother which I never knew, 'When Myrtle was being born . . . before Bruddie came . . .', I would feel like a child excluded from her mother's attention. Always in our family there was the struggle between powerlessness and power where closeness to people and the ability to prove that closeness became a symbol of most power, as if each member of the family struggled constantly to move through a wilderness of deprivation, slowly planting tiny cherished blossoms in the waste, and needing to point to them, describe them, rejoice in them, to the other members of the family, who might not be so advanced in their journey through the desert. And an insight comes at last where each understands why the others must at times behave or speak with apparent glee at misfortune, or carefully set out the distances accomplished, naming the winners and the losers.

No letters came for me that summer. Who would be writing letters to me? My sister and her husband and the two wailing children flew north to their home. I was once again the mad Frame girl wandering the hills around the Old Mill with my cat Siggy, who enjoyed long walks.

I slept in the front room overlooking the flat.

'I don't want you ever to leave home again,' Dad said. He built shelves for my books: my *Speaking for Ourselves*, *A Book of New Zealand Verse*, *Poetry London*, *Poetry in Wartime*, *Deaths and Entrances*, *The Waste Land*, Rilke's *Sonnets to Orpheus* (bought in Christchurch), Shakespeare (given to me in Christchurch by June and Wilson); and others, including my copy of *The Lagoon*. Dad gave me money to buy cretonne from Hodges, to make bright curtains for my room, while Mother bought from Calder Mackays ('we are valued customers') a new rose-coloured eiderdown for my bed.

All setting the family scene.

If I talked of my time in hospital, I described only the amusing incidents and the stereotypes of patients — the Jesus Christ, the Queen, the Empress.

Dad built up his supply of Sexton Blake library books. ('Janet likes detective stories.')

Mother and I composed recipes to send to *Truth*, where we won first prize with a *Salmon Mousse*.

And although Dad treasured his flowers — the asters and dahlias and carnations staked in the small garden outside my window — he restrained his anger each time Siggy scratched among the dahlias or leapt from my bedroom window upon the frail stalks of the carnations. She would climb in the window at night and snuggle purring, at the foot of my bed, while I leaned down to stroke her black fur; whispering, 'Oh Siggy, Siggy, what will I do?'

15   Threading Needles

The answer was decided for me. I found work as a laundry assistant at the Oamaru Public Hospital, where I spent each day enclosed in the mangle room, drawing out the hot wet sheets as they appeared between the rollers, folding them and passing them to another assistant. Our faces in the steamy heat were flushed and sweating, and the conversation above the roar of the machinery was usually a shouted question and answer ('Are you going to the Scottish this Saturday?' 'Are you coming to Mary's shower?') enlarged upon during the tea breaks, when the desirability of the 'Scottish' (a hall used for weekly dances) was debated, and Mary's or Vivian's or Noeline's engagement 'shower' prepared for. I had no answers to the simplest questions: where had I been working before I came to the laundry? Was I 'going out' with anyone? Why didn't I get my hair straightened? I could discuss the radio serial *My Husband's Love*, which we listened to at ten o'clock each morning. I knew one or two racehorses, including *Plunder Bar*. I knew songs — 'Give Me Five Minutes More',

> *Only five minutes more,*
> *Let me stay*
> *Let me stay in your arms.*
> *All the week I've dreamed about our Saturday date . . .*

an outworn song even then, but I knew it. And I knew the names of Otago and Southland rugby favourites — the Trevathans, and the commentator *Whang McKenzie*. I felt out of place, however. (Siggy, Siggy, what will I do?)

Then one night, in the middle of the night, Mother had a heart attack. Waking, hearing the commotion, I was reminded of the night when Bruddie first became ill and we all woke and stood white-faced, shivering.

Now Bruddie came to my door where I stood in alarm. He spoke in the new tone used now by Dad and Bruddie when they spoke to me, as if I had to be 'managed' in some way, for fear I should break or respond in an unusual way which they could not deal with.

'It's all right. There's nothing to worry about. Mum has had a heart attack. The doctor has given her morphine and they're taking her to the hospital.'

I looked out to see Mother, seeming asleep, her face white as china, her long grey-white hair spread anyhow on the white pillow, being carried out on a stretcher. She opened her eyes and started to apologise for having fallen ill; then she closed them again. Dad and Bruddie went with her to the hospital, and I went back to bed. There was a dent at the foot of the bed where Siggy had been, and had leapt with fright out of the window. I looked out of the window into the tree-filled night. I heard the three o'clock morepork calling. And already the night was fading around the edges. I knew it was a night of the kind of violent change that always happens, and had appeared as a milestone in the landscape of our family.

In the morning, as it had been years ago on the first morning after Bruddie's illness began, I woke remembering the complex fearful change in our lives. I longed for everything to be as it had been, with Mother quiet, self-effacing, providing; but it was not so; Mother had spoken at last, in pain. What if she died? No, they had said, with plenty of rest she would recover, although *in future* she would need to rest more, care more for herself, be cared for.

And while she rested warm and safe in the hospital, I could see the desolation in my father's face — Dad, who always showed panic whenever he entered the kitchen and said, 'Where's Mum?' and she was not there, even for the moment not there, perhaps in another room or out at the clothes-line; but now she was gone from the house, and my father's face showed his complete loss and bewilderment.

I made the breakfast. I brewed the everlasting pot of tea for Dad, crouched in his chair at his end of the table, but I did not extend my attention to the refinements he sought, demanded, from Mother — the tea sugared, stirred, shoes cleaned, back scratched. I heated the electric iron to iron his handkerchiefs and his shirt. He set his own blueys to soak in the wash-house tub, poking them with the copper-stick. He also set and lit the fire and fetched the shovels of railway coal from the heap in the lean-to by the back door.

Mother had spoken at last; in pain. The magic of fires in the coal range, hot meals, batches of pikelets cooked on the polished black girdle, the continued attendance of the servant upon the household, was over.

How dare she fall ill! We were desperate to have her returned to us, returned whole without pain.

I saw Mother in hospital. For the first time, as a result of her complete, dramatic removal from her family, I saw her as a person, and I was afraid and resentful. Why, she was a person such as you meet in the street. She could laugh and talk and express opinions without being ridiculed; and there she was, writing poems in a small notebook and reading them to the other patients, who were impressed with her talent.

'Your mother writes lovely poems.'

What had we done to her, each of us, day after day, year after year, that we had washed away her evidence of self, all her own furniture from her own room, and crowded it with our selves and our lives; or perhaps it was not a room but a garden that we cleared to plant ourselves deeply there, and now that we were removed, all her own blossoms had sprung up . . . was it like that? And what of the blows she had, the search for cures, the two inquests, the daughter declared mad, the frail husband made strong only by his intermittent potions of cruelty?

Faced with the family anguish, I made my usual escape, the route now perfected, and once again I was in Seacliff Hospital. I knew as soon as I arrived there that the days of practising that form of escape were over. I would go away somewhere, live on my own, earn enough money to live on, write my books: it was no use: I now had what was known as a 'history', and ways of dealing with those with a 'history' were stereotyped, without investigation. Very quickly, in my panic, I was removed to the back ward, the Brick Building, where I became one of the forgotten people. When Mother recovered her health, she and Bruddie and Dad would visit me for Christmas and my birthday and on one or two other occasions during the year. It was recognised that I was now in hospital 'for life'. What I have described in Istina Mavet is my sense of hopelessness as the months passed, my fear of having to endure that constant state of physical capture where I was indeed at the mercy of those who made judgments and decisions without even talking at length to me or trying to know me or even submitting me to the standard tests which are available to psychiatrists. The state could be defined as forced submission to custodial capture.

In the back ward I became part of a memorable family that I have described individually in *Faces in the Water*. It was their sadness and courage and my desire to 'speak' for them that enabled me to survive, helped by the insight of such fine junior and staff nurses as Cassidy, Doherty (both Maori women), 'Taffy', the Welsh nurse now living in Cardiff, Noreen Ramsay (who gave me extra food when I was hungry) and others. The attitude of those in charge who unfortunately wrote the reports and influenced the treatment was that of reprimand and punishment, with certain forms of medical treatment being threatened as punishment for failure to 'co-operate' where 'not co-operate' might mean a refusal to obey an order, say, to go to the doorless lavatories with six others and urinate in public while suffering verbal abuse by the nurse for being unwilling. 'Too fussy are we? Well, Miss Educated, you'll learn a thing or two here.'

Dear Educated, Miss Educated: sadly, the fact of my having been to high school, training college and university struck a vein of vindictiveness among some of the staff.

It was now my writing that at last came to my rescue. It is little wonder that I value writing as a way of life when it actually saved my life. My mother had been persuaded to sign permission for me to undergo a leucotomy; I know that she would not have done so had not the experts wielded heavily weighted arguments — the experts, who over the years as my 'history' was accumulating, had not spoken to me at one time for longer than ten or fifteen minutes, and in total time over eight years, for about eighty minutes; who had administered no tests, not even the physical tests of E.E.G. or X-rays (apart from the chest X-ray whenever there was a new case of tuberculosis, a disease prevalent in the mental hospitals then); the experts whose judgment was based on daily reports by overworked irritable nursing sisters. I listened, trying to avoid the swamping wave of horror, when Dr Burt, a likeable overworked young doctor who had scarcely spoken to me except to say 'good morning, how are you' and not wait for a reply as he was whisked through the ward, *found time* to explain that I would be having a leucotomy operation, that it would be good for me, that, following it, I would be 'out of hospital in no time'. I listened also with a feeling that my erasure was being completed when the ward sister, suddenly interested that something was about to be 'done' with and to me, painted her picture of how I would be when it was 'all over'.

'We had one patient who was here for years until she had a leucotomy. And now she's selling hats in a hat shop. I saw her just the other day, selling hats, as normal as anyone. Wouldn't you like to be normal?'

Everyone felt that it was better for me to be 'normal' and not have fancy intellectual notions about being a writer, that it was better for me to be out of hospital, working at an ordinary occupation, mixing with others . . .

The scene was carefully set. A young woman of my age who had become a friend but who had remained in the admission ward, the 'good' ward, was also spoken of as about to have a leucotomy.

'Nola's having one,' they told me.

Nola's having her hair straightened, Nola's having a party dress, Nola's having a party — why not you too?

Nola suffered from asthma and the complication of being in a family of brilliant beautiful people. I can make no judgment on her 'case' except to say that in a period before the use of drugs, leucotomy was becoming a 'convenience' treatment.

I repeat that my writing saved me. I had seen in the ward office the list of those 'down for a leucotomy', with my name on the list, and other names being crossed off as the operation was performed. My 'turn' must have been very close when one evening the superintendent of the hospital, Dr Blake Palmer, made an unusual visit to the ward. He spoke to me — to the amazement of everyone.

As it was my first chance to discuss with anyone, apart from those who had persuaded me, the prospect of my operation, I said urgently, 'Dr Blake Palmer, what do you think?'

He pointed to the newspaper in his hand.

'About the prize?'

I was bewildered. What prize? 'No,' I said, 'about the leucotomy.'

He looked stern, 'I've decided that you should stay as you are. I don't want you changed.' He unfolded his newspaper. 'Have you seen the Stop Press in tonight's *Star*?'

A ridiculous question to ask in a back ward where there was no reading matter; surely he knew?

'You've won the Hubert Church Award for the best prose. Your book, *The Lagoon*.'

I knew nothing about the Hubert Church Award. Winning it was obviously something to be pleased about.

I smiled. 'Have I?'

'Yes. And we're moving you out of this ward. And no leucotomy.'

The winning of the prize and the attention of a new doctor from Scotland who accepted me as I appeared to him and not as he learned about me from my 'history' or reports of me, and the move by Dr Blake Palmer to have me spend less time in the hospital ward by using me as 'tea lady' in the front office and allowing me to have occupational therapy, where I learned to make baskets, to fill toothpaste tubes with toothpaste, and, from a book written in French, to weave French lace, and to weave on large and small looms, all enabled me to be prepared for discharge from hospital. Instead of being treated by leucotomy, I was treated as a person of some worth, a human being, in spite of the misgivings and unwillingness of some members of the staff, who, like certain relatives when a child is given attention, warn the mother that the child is being 'spoiled', spoke pessimistically and perhaps enviously of my being 'made a fuss of'. 'It will spoil her. Dr Blake Palmer will "drop her" and she'll be back in the Brick Building in no time.'

My friend Nola, who unfortunately had not won a prize, whose name did not appear in the newspaper, had her leucotomy and was returned to the hospital, where, among the group known as 'the leucotomies', some attempt was made to continue, with personal attention, the process of 'being made normal, or at least being changed'. The 'leucotomies' were talked to, taken for walks, prettied with make-up and floral scarves covering their shaven heads. They were silent, docile; their eyes were large and dark and their faces pale, with damp skin. They were being 'retrained', to 'fit in' to the everyday world, always described as 'outside'; 'the world outside'. In the whirlwind of work and the shortage of staff and the too-slow process of retraining, the leucotomies one by one became the casualties of withdrawn attention and interest; the false spring turned once again to winter.

When I was eventually discharged from hospital, Nola remained, and although she did spend time out of hospital, she was often re-admitted; over the years I kept in touch with her, and it was like living in a fairytale where conscience, and what might have been, and what was, not only speak but spring to life and become a living companion, a reminder.

Nola died a few years ago in her sleep. The legacy of her dehumanising change remains no doubt with all those who knew her; I have it with me always.

I was discharged from hospital 'on probation'. After having received over two hundred applications of unmodified E.C.T., each the equivalent, in degree of fear, to an execution, and in the process having my memory shredded and in some aspects weakened permanently or destroyed, and after having been subjected to proposals to have myself changed, by a physical operation, into a more acceptable, amenable, normal person, I arrived home at Willowglen, outwardly smiling and calm, but inwardly with all confidence gone, with the conviction at last that I was officially a non-person. I had seen enough of schizophrenia to know that I had never suffered from it, and I had long discarded the prospect of inevitable mental doom. Against this opinion, however, I now had the weight of the 'experts' and the 'world' and I was in no state to assert myself. There was the added fear of what might happen to me should I ever return to hospital. And there was still the fact, the problem that, had it been solved eight or nine years ago, I might have been left free to pursue the kind of life I felt I wanted to lead. A problem with such a simple solution! A place to live and write, with enough money to support myself.

There was also the frightening knowledge that the desire to write, the enjoyment of writing, has little correlation with talent. Might I, not, after all, be deluding myself like other patients I had seen in hospital, one in particular, a harmless young woman who quietly sat in the admission ward day after day writing her 'book' because she wanted to be a writer, and her book, on examination, revealing pages and pages of pencilled 0-0-0-0-0-0-0-0. Or was that the new form of communication?

In spite of all, I felt joyful returning to Willowglen, where I could at last go out under the sky, where I could perform even the simplest of human functions without either being ordered to do so or observed while I performed. I could *decide* for myself what I wished to do, where I should be, how I should feel, how I should think of my *future*. The words *decide* and *future*, which had loomed so large in my childhood, had a new intensity of meaning.

After being and feeling a nothing and nobody, and forced into a continued state of physical and emotional submission, I felt as if the world would sweep over and engulf me, while I would meekly accept and act upon suggestions and orders from others, out of the habitual fear that had grown within me, in hospital.

Ah, but it was a delight to roam the hills again with my now many-kittened Siggy, to sit near the matagouri among the sheep, and try to forget everything but the sky swept with its arrows of cirrus clouds, which I used to try so hard to draw with my double B pencil. I borrowed a small tent from Bruddie, who had been having his own adventures in New Zealand and Australia while I was in hospital. I pitched the tent under the pine trees, so great was my need to be among the trees and under the sky, and at night I slept in the tent and during the day I sat writing in the railway notebook given to me by my father in his sad haste to make all as it used to be, everyone small again and he the king of the world. He had retired from the railway and was now working as an engine driver at the lime works, coming home each day clouded with white dust as if he had been in a snow storm.

My time sleeping in a tent was cut short. Wasn't it rather . . . strange . . . for me to want to sleep in a tent . . . people were talking . . . I gave up the tent for my old bedroom up at the house.

'It's nice to have Janet home again,' people said, in my presence. 'How is she? Would she like some shortbread?'

I joined the new town library and discovered William Faulkner and Franz Kafka, and I rediscovered the few books left on my own bookshelf. I began to write stories and poems and to think of a future without being overcome by fear that I would be seized and 'treated' without being able to escape. Even so, the nightmares of my time in hospital persist in sleep and often I wake in dread, having dreamed that the nurses are coming to 'take me for treatment'.

Mother's health had improved under the care of Professor Smirk of Dunedin. Periodically she visited his clinic and was admitted for short stays in hospital, where once again she became a 'person' in the company of those who were not members of the family. Although scarcely sixty years old, and still dreaming of buying her daughters a white fox fur, she was worn out by her living (I thought) for her husband and children, as if without her own life, like a stake cut from a grand tree, stripped of its own shoots and set beside flourishing plants, bound to them, taking the force of the prevailing wind, moving only as the wind moved while the sheltered plants trembled lightly with only a rumour of storm. My vision of my mother combined strangely with her presence — her white thinning hair, her toothless mouth, for she had never been fitted with comfortable false teeth, her hawk-like Godfrey nose pointed towards her Godfrey chin, or, as we used to say, her 'Archbishop of Canterbury' chin, her used body in its Glassons Warehouse costume (it was her delight that Mabel Howard also bought clothes from Glassons) and McDiarmids 'on tick' wide-bodied shoes, her face serene as ever and her eyes always waiting to sparkle with humour about political or personal events. She had given up the Christadelphian meetings, disillusioned by too much quarrelling among the pacifists, but she was still a Christadelphian, *lover of Christ*. During the years of her married life Christ had been her one close friend. She still talked, however, and listed her childhood friends, 'Hetty Peake, Ruby Blake, Kate Rodley, Lucy Martella, Dorcas Dryden.' She remembered her boyfriends, too. And when Dad's friend from the Wyndham days, Johnny and his wife retired to live near us in Oamaru, Mother's diffidence made her unable to address Mrs Walker as *Bessie*. The strong feeling haunted me that Mother had never lived in her real 'place', that her real world had been her life within.

Her eyesight was now failing. Sewing buttons on the shirts and pyjamas, and stitching the frayed cuffs of the 'menfolk', she had to ask for help in threading her needle. I sat sewing, too, and my thread through my needle was keen and swift as a tiny spear. 'Janet, can you thread the needle for me?' and with an inside fury at this sign of her helplessness, I took the needle, not gently, and threaded it with the lightning accuracy of my twenty-ninth year. She had never aspired, against the glories of her sisters-in-law, to be a needlewoman, nor had she time during the years to sit and sew, while we girls had long ago been makers for better or worse of our own clothes; and to see Mother helpless in a role which had scarcely claimed her once-keen eyesight, reserved for matters of the heart and spirit, for poetry, for the making of fires and the preparation of food, for looking at the beloved 'nature', I felt the terrible reduction in her life, a final subtraction which I could not bear to face. I knew, also, that I would never be close to her, for my past and my future life were barriers against the intimacy that grows between mother and daughter.

I could postpone my future no longer. I answered an advertisement for a housemaid at the Grand Hotel, Dunedin, my references being an old letter from the mayor of Oamaru, and the reference from Playfair Street, Caversham, 'polite to the guests at all times . . . honest . . . industrious . . .' and once again, moving towards my Future, I travelled south on the slow train to Dunedin.

PART TWO

Finding the Silk

Separated from time as a silkworm from the silk.

16   Grand Hotel

I was about to live in Dunedin for the third time since I had left school, and each time, first with the months and now with the intervening years and experience, a difference had been wrought in my relation with the city that was now one of my oldest acquaintances, perhaps my only acquaintance. A curious process of scouring had occurred — the removal of the surface wonder of being a student; then, from the second visit, the days of anguish, of discovering schizophrenia, and music, and handsome young men, and writing my stories and trying to appear mad in poetic fashion, still clinging to the wreckage of my teaching career, wandering by the Leith, imposing upon myself an exaggerated sense of the tragedy of *me* — these too had gone, taking the spirit of Jude and Christminster, of the Scholar-Gipsy and Oxford,

> Have I not pass'd thee on the wooden bridge,
> Wrapt in thy cloak and battling with the snow,
> Thy face towards Hinksey and its wintry ridge?
> And thou hast climb'd the hill,
> And gain'd the white brow of the Cumner range;
> Turn'd once to watch while thick the snowflakes fall,
> The line of festal light in Christ-Church hall —

of all who ever dreamed by university rivers and old buildings of grey stone.

Now, on my third visit to live in Dunedin, the University and Training College were no longer my world: I had no world. Union Street, Frederick Street, Dundas Street, all the former surroundings were like toy streets with toy buildings where the toy people had been replaced by new toy people, still talking and laughing about the old topics.

I took a taxi from the railway station to the Grand Hotel, standing tall on the corner, with its varnished wood and polished brass, like a handsome ship. The manageress, dignified but slightly drunk, met me in the foyer, explaining that there'd been a mistake, it was a *waitress* they needed, not a housemaid.

'You may wish to go elsewhere, then, Miss Frame,' she said, while I, already uncurling my dormant bruised roots, said quickly, trying not to feel too frightened and dismayed, 'Oh, I have experience of waitressing. I'll be a waitress.'

'The pay is six pounds a week clear, all found.'

All found.

Like a child's refrain: All gone, all found.

My room was an attic room on the top floor looking out through the small window beyond the battlement kind of facade, to Princes Street and across to dental rooms and insurance offices. All the staff had rooms on the top floor.

I wore a starched white smock, white shoes and a starched cap. I was given a 'station', or set of tables, to wait upon and I quickly learned the language and the behaviour that was expected of me. I learned the routine as well, from the attitude to adopt towards the head waitress, the manager and his wife (who startled me by their resemblance to those I had known in Christchurch until I realised that such jobs were taken by persons of similar appearance and nature), to the kitchen routine and the setting of tables, the special way to fold the serviettes into their rosette. I learned also to sense the excitement among my fellow waitresses when guests were leaving and there was the hope that a tip would be left under the plate. The regular guests, the good tippers, were known, and there was rivalry to have them seated at one's station, but Doreen, the head waitress, a small fair woman in black with a white lace collar and cuffs, arranged the seating for important guests and then often took over the station, collecting the final trophies of service. There were sharp glances between waitresses, moments of anxiety as the guests set aside their plates, and a planned carelessness about the approach to the table and the discreet lifting of the plate and pocketing of the tip. I felt ashamed of my rising excitement on the day a guest was to leave, and of my concealed eager greed as I eased the tip into my hand, holding it there until I could sneak it, unobserved, into my pocket.

The Grand Hotel was a congenial place to work. I enjoyed walking about the dining room in my uniform with the table napkin draped over my arm. I took pride in remembering the orders and stacking the plates to be carried. The staff had freedom to make their own arrangements about holidays and working hours and often I'd be able to exchange with another waitress, to have two or three days free, when I'd go home to Willowglen or stay at the hotel, relishing the security of a place to sleep, good meals and earnings of six pounds a week *clear*. I bought a second-hand typewriter and began to write stories and poems. I wrote 'The Waitresses', 'The Liftman', poems that were published in the *Listener*. I wrote about Kafka and about a concert by the Alma Trio, and a poem, 'On Paying the First Instalment', a result of a rash move into the world of time payment, when I bought a radiogram and one record, Beethoven's Seventh Symphony, which I'd heard on the radio concert programme, and which I now could play softly in my attic refuge. The Dance. For me, it *was* the dance, filled with a special joy and freedom, with the strong beat in the last movement seeming like the wielding of a crystal hammer fit for the construction of a palace of crystal, without walls, the air and light flowing through it from all corners of earth and heaven.

Away from my refuge I gradually lost my honeymoon delight in the world of waitressing. To protect myself from questions about my 'past', I made it known that I was 'really a student' and 'hoping to be a writer'. I was unhappily aware that, not feeling myself to have a 'place' in the world, and being unwilling to accept that I existed in any place, I was inclined to adopt, when questioned, the air of a secret princess among the scullions; but not in public, only if one of the staff came to my room to talk over boyfriend problems, and should she, if he was married, and what else was there to do, a life of waitressing and ending up like T. or M.

Then I'd be asked, 'And what about you? What are you doing here?'

And I'd say that I'd written a book, but as I had no copy of *The Lagoon*, many of my books having vanished when I was looked on as being in hospital for life, that is, dead, my fellow waitresses were sceptical. I showed them my poem 'The Waitresses', printed in the *Listener* under my initials.

Their chief desire, however, was to make me one of them, to join with them in their activities.

'Your hair, your clothes, they're awful. And your lipstick's the wrong colour. You have to be careful what colour you wear, with your red hair. Never red — it clashes. Greens and browns. Or blue to go with your blue eyes. Why don't you come with us to the Saturday night dance at the town hall? And why don't you get your hair straightened? It would be much better, straightened.'

After years of being in the command of others, with threat of punishment by solitary confinement or 'treatment' if I disobeyed or, to use the official term, 'became unco-operative', I was willing to accept any suggestions. Green and brown became *my* colours. I daringly went to the cosmetic counter at the D.I.C., where the assistant testing lipsticks on the back of my hand chose 'my' shade of 'Tangee'. I bought rose milk for my skin, and Evening in Paris perfume in its deep blue bottle. And seeing my efforts to 'make something of myself', as they expressed it, the other waitresses were pleased. 'Now you're one of us,' they said.

After work we sat talking about our clothes, our hair, our boss and his wife, and each other, and how Mabel was dotty, and Laura was a bit 'funny' — who'd believe that tale of her engagement to the taxi driver when he never came near her? Who indeed, I thought, for Mabel and Laura were only two of the mental misfits who drift without much sympathy or help, from hotel to hostel and boardinghouse, finding a temporary home and work for 'so much a week and all found'. I felt myself to be one of them: where else could they live?

My honeymoon delight finally ended in the hotel kitchen. The servings of dinner were different for men and women, with men given a larger portion, and, of chicken, the *leg*, or *wing*, while women were served a smaller portion, and always *breast* of chicken, and thus when I came through the swing doors to call out my order I had to shout swiftly, *Chicken, a gent* or *Chicken, a lady. Beef, a gent. Beef, a lady*. My voice was soft, I was reluctant to shout, and I found the word *gent* distasteful. I therefore made my order, *Chicken, a man, beef, a man*; overturning all the tradition of the kitchen of the Grand Hotel. Chicken, a man, indeed!

The second cook, a brusque bully, launched a teasing, angry attack on my language and refused to fill my orders unless I gave them in the traditional way, and, sensing my reluctance, she insisted that I repeat my order again and again. The giving of meal orders became a torment. One day I ran in tears from the servery, up to my attic room, and when Pat, the waitress, came to my room, I said I wasn't well.

I wondered what I could do, where I could go. There was nowhere. I tried to be calm. I was free, wasn't I, no longer locked up? Was I free?

That evening I returned to the dining room.

'Don't take any notice of Molly, she's like that,' Pat whispered as we stood by the sideboard waiting for the guests to come in. 'They're late this evening. We'll be ages getting away. But don't take any notice of Molly.'

Pat was tall with dark curly hair. Her ambition was to go up north to manage a cake shop, and perhaps buy it.

'Are you coming to the Town Hall dance tomorrow night?' she asked. 'We're all going.'

I had bought some of the latest material, *everglaze*, which was all the rage, and a pattern from the D.I.C., and I was sewing by hand a dress to wear some night to the dance. That evening Pat inspected my dress and helped me with the hem of the circular skirt.

'Circular skirts are hard to turn up.'

'Are you really going to be a writer?' Pat asked.

'I hope so.'

'Don't take any notice of Molly in the kitchen. Second cooks are always like that. The first cook lords it over everyone, the second cook throws her weight around and the third cook does all the work. I felt awful when I first came here to work. I'd had a nervous breakdown, you see.'

'I've been in a mental hospital,' I said, bursting into tears.

The next evening Pat and I and two of the others all dressed up to kill, I in my new everglaze dress with the circular skirt and the leg-of-mutton sleeves, set out for the Town Hall, two blocks away.

'Isn't it great, living in a hotel, you can just walk anywhere?'

The Town Hall dance had begun, the band was playing, there was the shuffling sound of the dancers on the powdered floor, but so far the dancers were few. A line of men stood against one wall; a line of women against the opposite wall self-consciously waited for the men to ask them to dance, while the men looked them over, making jumping and jerking movements, half pawing the floor with their feet, like prize bulls at the show.

I sat with the other girls from the hotel. One by one they were invited to dance. I remained seated, still full of pleasurable anticipation, nodding my head to the music, tapping my feet as a way of showing anyone who might be looking my way that I was eager to dance; but not too eager, not so as to forget I had pride, though how much pride can you have when you must wait to be asked?

I had a secret: this was my first dance, apart from the hospital dances, where I had learned many steps and where I'd had two faithful partners — the bald middle-aged man, old enough to be my father, and the sad young ex-soldier, dark and handsome, who still believed he was in Italy fighting the Second World War. When I was a child, I was always excited by the adventure of a *first time*, and eager to share it with others. Now, I had missed so many experiences in ordinary living that my 'firsts', out of step with the 'firsts' of others, were felt to be a cause for shame. Also, I had read eagerly in the literature of first dances, including the story by Katherine Mansfield; but even her title, 'Her First Ball', had been given a crude interpretation by my sisters and me, as the young farmers who partnered Isabel to the woolshed 'hops' out in the country were apt to make remarks, picked up quickly by Isabel, about Farmers' Balls, Shearers' Balls, and so on, and the word 'ball' no longer applied to mother's dreamed-of Viennese Nights.

It *was* an occasion — my first dance, the sweaty smell, the chatter, the music; the shiny noses being blotted with a powder puff. I had sewn rubber shields in the armpits of my dress, and I could feel the sticky rubber against my arms. I still sat, patiently waiting, watching the dancers and trying to appear as if this were the reason for my being in the town hall — to watch the dancers. Ah, there was the Maxina, the Military Two-step, and — oh — the Destiny. I knew those. Ask me, ask me. An older woman sat beside me and began to talk.

'We could go upstairs and watch them. You get a good view from upstairs.'

I moved away to another seat. How dare she, how dare she assume that I was just like her, frumpy and not dancing! Even dotty Laura was dancing. And there was a row of men who still hadn't asked anyone. My pleasurable feeling began to fade, exposing its original surface of pain, a dull disappointment and hurt. I fiddled with my new evening bag, which was black with sparkles — sequins — oh for a dress, oh for a bag with sequins! I snipped open the bag and looked at my Max Factor compact and my Evening in Paris perfume. Then I shut the bag and trying to look calm, I walked from the Town Hall into the Octagon and down into Princes Street and home to the Grand. So much for my attempt and failure at living in the world, I thought, as I played my record of the Seventh Symphony. The Dance. I heard the others coming in late, making a cup of coffee or tea, laughing, talking. They'd had fun. And when, the next morning, they asked me, 'How'd you like the dance?' I answered, 'It was great, wasn't it?'

They agreed. 'It was a great dance.'

17 Mr Brasch and Landfall

Sometimes I browsed in Modern Books (the old Co-operative Book Society), where I hoped to glimpse one of the literary figures of Dunedin or one visiting from up north. I now knew by heart most of the stories from *Speaking for Ourselves*, as well as the biographical notes on the writers and the introductory chapter, which, like the introduction to the *Book of New Zealand Verse*, became my primer of New Zealand literature. I accepted every judgment without question: if a poem or story was said to be the 'best', then I believed it to be so, and searching it for proof, I always found proof. These two books were among my few links with 1945.

I bought a copy of *Landfall* and read it with awe — there was *avante garde* Maurice Duggan writing sentences without verbs, even one-noun sentences; and using italics; and painting New Zealand scenes unfamiliar to me, mostly from up north, with the subtropical heat crackling on the pages and the old jetties rotting and the mangroves deep in grey mud; he seemed to relish writing about the mangroves; and about long-haired women in bedrooms; and everything that glistened — leaves and skin and water: that was up north.

The poems of *Landfall* were obscure, scholarly, very carefully written, with formal stanzas and intricate rhyme and rhythm; occasionally there was a rogue free verse of half a dozen lines. I sensed that if you didn't appear in *Landfall* then you could scarcely call yourself a writer.

Then one day I saw Charles Brasch standing behind the counter selling books. Charles Brasch, the poet! I thought,

> *Speak for us, great sea.*
> *Speak in the night, compelling*
> *The frozen heart to hear*
> *The memoried to forget.*
> *O speak, until your voice*
> *Possess the night, and bless*
> *The separate and fearful.*

I bought a book of Allen Curnow's poems. I noted that Mr Brasch looked approvingly as he wrapped it for me. Then he said, as if startled, 'Oh. You're Janet Frame? Do you live in Dunedin now?'

'I've been here a few months. I live and work at the Grand Hotel.'

He looked uneasy, and said again, 'Oh.'

He then asked if I would like to come to his place for tea one afternoon. I looked shy.

'Yes.'

'What about this Thursday? At half-past three?'

'Yes, that will be all right.'

He gave me his address in Royal Terrace. He had a poet's eyes, a soft voice and thick black hair. I remember his poems in the *Book of New Zealand Verse*: they were mysterious poems, questions addressed to the mountains, the sea, and the dead, with the sad certainty that there would be no answer.

'I'll see you on Thursday, then. And remember, if you have anything to contribute to *Landfall* you can always leave it at the bookshop.'

'Yes,' I said, smiling shyly.

That evening I told Pat and Doreen that I was going to afternoon tea on Thursday at the house of a poet.

'He's one of our best poets,' I said.

'What will you wear?' they asked.

I was saving to buy a green coat I'd seen in the window of Mademoiselle Modes but I hadn't yet saved its price of ten pounds.

'I haven't a coat,' I said.

'Wear your jersey and skirt. And something to take away that bare look from your neck. Beads? Pearls would be better. You need pearls.'

'Where do you think I would get pearls?'

'Is the poet rich?' they asked.

'I've heard he is.'

'Well, you have nothing to worry about. Wear a brassiere though.'

The next day I went to the Fashion Centre in Moray Place, where a heavily built woman in black with a black strip of velvet around her throat and pearl earrings like Aunty Isy's ushered me into the fitting room.

'Will you have plunging neckline or petal cups?'

The attention of the others and their interest in the afternoon tea embarrassed me. Soon everyone knew I was going. Even the liftman mentioned it. He too was one of the sad misfits for whom a working and living place like a hotel became a shelter, and who, in the hotel surroundings, appeared strong and confident, yet who glimpsed in the street displayed like a banner the frailty and difference.

Thursday arrived, promising rain.

'Perhaps he will give you a coat,' someone said, 'if he knows you don't have one.'

I walked up the hill towards Royal Terrace. I was far too early. I loitered, looking down over the harbour and peninsula, picking out the landmarks of university, the museum, half glimpsed through trees, the Normal School and, scarcely visible at the foot of Union Street, the training college. I looked towards the Oval with its puddles and seagulls, and I thought of Number Four Garden Terrace and Aunty Isy, who no longer lived there. Separated at last from the chocolate trophies of her dancing, she had turned to the source of her skill, her former dancing master, and after a brief courtship they were married, and I had seen her with him, both laughing and happy, 'passing through' on the Limited on their way to live in Mangakino, in a house without trees in the garden.

I looked towards Caversham. I thought of the house in Playfair Street, blocked from view by the grim shape of Parkside Home for the Aged. And I thought of the Carisbrook football ground and Whang McKenzie announcing the teams at the 'Railway end' or the 'Cargill Road end' and *Whang*, it's a goal!

At last I found courage to knock on the door in Royal Terrace. Mr Brasch greeted me, then showed me to a large book-lined room where he served tea and seed cake while a white cat known as Whizz-Bang looked on. I told Mr Brasch that my mother had worked for old Mrs Beauchamp, Katherine Mansfield's grandmother, and for 'old Mr Fels', his own grandfather.

'She remembers you and your sister,' I said.

Mr Brasch looked stern. I felt that he disliked personal reminiscences and references, but what else could I say? I knew so little. He began to talk of New Zealand literature. I remained silent. I thought, he must know where I have been for the past eight years. I suddenly felt like crying. I was awkward and there were crumbs of seed cake all over my plate and on the white carpet at my feet. Then, remembering the introduction to *Speaking for Ourselves*, I murmured one or two opinions on the stories, quoting directly from the text.

'I agree with you,' Mr Brasch said.

Our conversation died away. Mr Brasch poured more tea from an attractive pot with a wicker handle arched above it.

'I'm fond of this teapot,' he said, noticing my glance at it.

'I'd better be going,' I said.

'Don't forget that if you have any stories or poems you can leave them at Modern Books.'

'Yes,' I said in a shy whisper.

When Mr Brasch opened the door, he said in a startled voice, 'Oh, it's raining, and you haven't a coat. Would you like a coat?'

'No thank you, I haven't far to go.'

When I returned to the Grand Hotel and my fellow workers asked about my visit, I said slyly, 'He offered me a coat.'

They were impressed.

'You should have worn pearls, though,' they said.

That week I typed a story and two poems for *Landfall*. The story, 'Gorse is Not People', dealt with a visit to Dunedin by another patient and myself in the company of a nurse. After many years in hospital I had almost no clothes, possibly because my family's image of people in hospital was that of patients in bed wearing nightgowns; and in any case, my family could not afford to give me clothes and I was reluctant to ask them; therefore the hospital authorities were sending me to Dunedin with a nurse who would buy me some underclothing and deal with the affairs of the other patient, a woman celebrating her twenty-first birthday, known as her 'majority'. She was Linda, a small wizened person who had been in hospital since her early childhood and whose explanation for her dwarf-like size was that she was 'illegitimate' and her mother had not wanted her to grow. Only the staff knew the reason for her being in hospital. The patients, myself among them, saw her as a small person, shrewd, tenacious of will, who was able to control many of the patients in the dayroom, either in the 'clean' dayroom or what was known as the 'dirty' dayroom. Linda also controlled the wireless with her choice of programme. For months she had been looking forward to her 'twenty-first', seeing in it the fulfilment of all her dreams, certain that when she became twenty-one she would be engaged, perhaps married, and allowed to 'get out of this dump'. In preparation for her engagement she had bought a pretty blue ring from the hospital store where we made our weekly visit to spend the five shillings personal allowance from the government. Linda was sure that her day in Dunedin was related to her coming engagement and freedom.

Her excitement was infectious. It was to be a wonderful day. Cakes, ice cream, perhaps the pictures, with us sitting in a 'real audience'. And Linda, also with no one to provide her with clothes, was to be fitted with a skirt and underwear.

My story tried to convey the reality of the visit. The nurse had explained to me that Linda was unaware of the reason for her being in Dunedin — she was to see a magistrate who would formally, now that she was twenty-one and adult, commit her to hospital 'for life'.

Even after our return from the city, Linda talked of the 'nice man' who had spoken to her 'specially' and who might have been her 'future husband, 'cept that he was too old. He knew I was grown up, though, that I'd had my twenty-first. I showed him my 'gagement ring, *saffirs*.'

The two poems I offered *Landfall* are best not remembered, their hand was so heavy. 'The Slaughter-House' began:

> *The mind entering the slaughter-house must remain*
> *calm, never calmer,*
> *must be washed clean, showered on where the corned hide*
> *holds fast to bits of bacterial thought, must await the*
> *stunning hammer*
> *in silence, knowing nothing of any future load.*

Electric shock treatment may turn many grim memories out of house and home; what is certain is that it invites as permanent tenants the grim memories of itself, of receiving shock treatment.

I left the story and poems at the Modern Book shop, in an envelope addressed to Charles Brasch, and I returned to the Grand Hotel to await the response. I sat in my room inventing all possible judgments, imagining Charles Brasch in his book-lined room, opening the envelope, taking out the pages, unfolding them, reading them and thinking, 'At last! Here's another writer of stories. We are indeed *Speaking for Ourselves*. What sensitivity! What subtle hints, never outright statements. The reference to the gorse is good — that chance remark of the nurse as the car leaves the *Kilmog* . . . What experiences this woman must have had (what tragic experiences!) to write in this way. A born writer.'

But — suppose he didn't think the work was good? Perhaps, like a school report, he would say, 'Can be improved. Not up to standard.'

I had made no copy of my story to re-read it. What had I done?

Before the end of the week I received at the Grand Hotel a long bulky envelope containing my story and two poems. Mr Brasch's comments were that the work was interesting, but the poems were not quite suitable, while the story, 'Gorse is Not People', was 'too painful to print'.

When I had read the note on its official *Landfall* paper, I began to realise how much I had invested in my *Landfall* contributions and their acceptance for publication. I seemed to have included my whole life and future in that envelope. I felt myself sinking into empty despair. What could I do if I couldn't write? Writing was to be my rescue. I felt as if my hands had been uncurled from their clinging place on the rim of the lifeboat. My unhappiness was eased, however, by the knowledge that at least the *Listener* had printed my poems. I comforted myself by remembering that in my years in hospital, when I clung to my copy of Shakespeare, hiding it under straw mattresses, having it seized and scheming for its return, not often reading it but turning the tissue-paper-thin pages, which somehow conveyed the words to me, I had absorbed the spirit of *The Tempest*. Even Prospero in his book-lined cell had suffered shipwreck and selfwreck; his island was unreachable except through storm.

That year I was declared officially 'sane', and in a burst of freedom following my newly acquired sanity, I accepted the invitation to stay with my sister and her husband in Northcote, Auckland. I left the Grand Hotel ('pleasant to the guests at all times') and returned to Willowglen to prepare for my Auckland journey.

18   *The Photograph and the Electric Blanket*

My adult life so far appeared to be a series of journeys, a dance north and south, back and forth across the country. Why did I now leave Dunedin?

Official labels carried weight: I was now officially, legally, a citizen, able to vote and make a will. Also I had decided that waitressing was not my kind of work. Up north (that magical 'up north') I would surely be able to work as a housemaid only, where I could spend my time on my own with my own thoughts, moving from room to room, making beds, dusting, polishing, without the daily conflict with the cooks in the kitchen. Also, in spite of my recurring hopes, I felt that my failure to be published in *Landfall* demanded that I take a clear view of my writing to find if my ambition were not simply an expression of 'ideas of grandeur'. Until Dr Blake Palmer had shown interest in my writing, the opinion had been that it was 'the last thing' I should do, that I should 'go out and mix and forget about writing'. The doubts came easily to the surface, and because I did not want to think about them, I planned my Auckland journey.

I brought home to Willowglen enough money to buy an electric blanket for Mother and Dad to help them through the awful winter, enough to pay for my fare and a few weeks' existence in Auckland, and to have my photograph taken at Clark's Studio in Thames Street. The photograph was urgent, a kind of reinstating of myself as a person, a proof that I did exist. In my ignorance of book publication I had supposed that all books carried photographs of their authors and I remembered my feeling, when copies of *The Lagoon* were brought to me in hospital, that I had no claim to the book, that there was not even a photograph to help stake a claim.

This, combined with my erasure in hospital, seemed to set me too readily among the dead who are no longer photographed; my years between twenty and nearing thirty having passed unrecorded as if I had never been.

I remembered how, as a child, I always stopped outside Clark's Studio to look at the photographs behind their column of glass: they were celebrations of events in the lives of people of Oamaru who could afford to have studio photographs — there were newborn babies, infants taking their first steps, church confirmations, rows of debutantes in evening dress, club reunions, family reunions, twenty-first birthday photos, engagement and wedding photos: the complete cycle, except for the dead. There were also no photographs of resurrections.

Within the first week of my returning to Willowglen I had my hair 'washed and set', with the hairdresser assuring me that my hair would never be attractive unless it was *professionally straightened*. I looked in the top duchesse drawer where the family 'treasures' were kept for the amber beads that Grandma gave me, but they were gone, as if I had died. Dad's medal from the war was there, and his identity disc and his soldier's paybook, and Isabel's tissue-thin *caul*, which had meant, we supposed, that she would never drown.

I wore my old costume, a blouse, and no beads. The finished portrait showed a healthy young woman with obvious false teeth, a smirking smile and a Godfrey chin. It was a fresh photo, of substance. Well, I was alive again.

I knew that the electric blanket was an attempt to give my parents more than physical warmth. I knew they wanted me to stay home and I felt guilty about leaving, as it was the tradition for the single woman to remain with her ageing parents. They were doubtful also of my ability to 'cope' in the world and, because they respected the expert opinion of the doctors, they feared that I might 'tax my brain' with writing. The electric blanket was also an attempt to bring the sunlit other world of 'down on the flat' into a house embraced most of the day by frost. I was haunted by the way Mother looked out with such yearning upon the 'flat', and by her ability to weave that sun on that grass among those trees into an almost biblical dream with fulfilment promised: some day, some day. The reminder that she was ill, that her death might not be far away, gave for me a piercing vividness to the words and gestures of those around her — my father, my brother and I — who had felt she was a gift to be cherished for ever and who could not imagine her death. Our excessive solicitude gave way at times to exasper- ation at her 'other-worldliness'. I felt hostile towards her because she was preparing to leave us, she was clearly tired, and her deep faith in the Second Coming of Christ and the Resurrection of the Dead gave her an inner sense of anticipation that made her 'going down on the flat in the cool of the evening' almost a superfluous exercise. It was she who was happy merely to dream of it; I wanted its reality, just to see her relax under the pine trees in the late sun. I could see too clearly, also, the fear in my father's face when he glanced at Mother: he could not bear her to leave him.

I booked my seat to Auckland. My family could not understand why I wanted to leave Willowglen, and I did not try to explain. With hopes that I might be able to have a sickness benefit while I worked at my writing, I wrote to Dr Blake Palmer, whose reply shattered my hopes by its suggestion that I might 'lose the habit of working' if I were granted a benefit. The shal- lowness of official thinking depressed me. More depressing was the reminder that terrible treatments had been forced on me, decisions made about me, without anyone getting to know me personally; and here was just another such decision being made. My reply was to send him two poems, 'The Kite' and 'Within the Glass Mountain', where I deliberately chose imagery known to be 'schizophrenic' — glass, mirrors, reflections, the sense of being separated from the world by panels of glass — in the hope that he would get my message. I felt that there should have been some attempt by the hospital to help with resettling patients into their new lives.

I set out for Auckland, Bruddie driving me in his truck to the station. We said goodbye. Soon, I'd come home for a visit, I said. And make sure

Mother takes her pills.

My lugggage held two copies of my new studio photograph in its mottled fawn frame.

19   Up North

Another journey. Across the Canterbury Plains and the rivers, Waitaki, peering out to find distant gum trees at Rakaia, the Rangitata; on to Lyttelton and the ferry; a calm night; then Petone, and Aunty Polly and Uncle Vere.

Aunty Polly's frog-green new car; driving around the district, pointing out General Motors, where Uncle Vere worked, the Hutt River; and, proudly, the house where Bob Scott, the All Black, lived.

'He lives not far from us. A local man.'

Aunty Polly was a slighter, female version of Dad — bright-eyed, quick of brain and speech, with an eye for detail and a passion for perfection. Aunty Polly was known to be 'fussy' — about her and other people's clothes, manners, ideas. She was known in our family as the aunt who had 'etiquette', and on her rare visits to our place in Oamaru her most-used sentence was 'You must have *etiquette*.' She would then list those of her family, friends and acquaintances who did and did not have etiquette, with highest praise given to her husband's twin sister, Gypsy. When Aunty Polly's visit to us was over, we children spent the rest of that week mimicking her in our play, 'Do you have *etiquette*, Mrs? . . . Oh, you must have *etiquette*. I've got *etiquette*!'

Mother was generous and slightly humorous in talking of Aunty Polly, 'Of course, Poll has etiquette.'

That evening I caught the train to Auckland and the next morning, shaken in all my bones, I felt the train arriving at Auckland station, and suddenly there was 'up north' again, the blue paradisal air and light.

And there were June, Wilson and their three children to meet me and drive me to their newly built house in Northcote.

Within a few days of my arrival in Auckland I found a live-in job as housemaid at the TransTasman Hotel, where, unlike at the Grand Hotel, Dunedin, with its family atmosphere, there were many rooms, many floors, a large staff and a sense of urgency about every activity. The staff dining room was always crowded. People, unsmiling, spoke briskly, abruptly. I was given a floor to myself and the usual duties of bedmaking, room dusting and cleaning, cleaning of the corridors and bathrooms, with my own quarters a tiny room upstairs in what was called the Gods, and there should have been no problems. I soon discovered that many of the guests on my floor were pilots and passengers (from the early morning Pan American flights) who stayed in bed until late afternoon, and it was on one of these afternoons when I was still struggling with unmade beds and uncleaned rooms when I should long ago have finished, that the housekeeper discovered me and threatened to sack me if I could not work faster. I burst into tears and that evening I left the TransTasman. I had survived only one week. Auckland was a real city, a harsh city like those I had read about. I made my escape in the ferry across the harbour to gentle bushclad Northcote to stay once again with the Gordons.

I spent the next week getting to know my sister and her husband and the three children. June told me that Frank Sargeson, the writer, had visited her one day, as he had heard that I was her sister. He had said that he would like to meet me if I ever came to Auckland.

'Would you like to see him?' they asked.

'Oh no. I don't know him.'

'We can take you. He lives in an old bach at Takapuna.'

Why should I visit Frank Sargeson? I knew *Speaking for Ourselves*, and I had read some of his stories in New Zealand and English *New Writing*. I hesitated about meeting him.

Then one afternoon, while they were showing me the sights of the North Shore, Wilson said suddenly, 'Frank Sargeson lives somewhere around here. Let's call on him.'

Our visit was short. What could I say? I was self-conscious, the 'funny' sister being taken for a drive. Mr Sargeson, a bearded old man in a shabby grey shirt and grey pants tied with string, smiled kindly and asked how I was, and I said nothing. He had an army hut vacant in his garden, he said. I was welcome to live and work there. I neither accepted nor refused, I was so overcome by my 'mental' status, and by seeing in person the famous writer whose anthology of New Zealand writing, *Speaking for Ourselves*, was a treasured book; the famous writer for whose fiftieth birthday I had signed a letter of good wishes, not knowing him and knowing nothing of the other signatories of the letter. Frank Sargeson. Mr Sargeson.

He suggested that I come to see him one day, by myself.

'How about this Friday?'

'Yes,' I said shyly.

And so on Friday I set out from Northcote towards Mr Sargeson's place in Takapuna, walking along the largely unformed road with paddocks of scrub and toetoe on either side, past swamps of mangroves — mangroves! — and stands of native bush. It was late spring of 1954, and I'd had my thirtieth birthday, an occasion for a photograph and, in poetic tradition, for a poem. I remembered Dylan Thomas's 'It was my thirtieth year to heaven', and I thought about his death and tried to picture my twenties as if I had lived in the world. People were talking of watersiders, of the waterfront strike, of escaped murderers, of McCarthyism; I knew little of these. I knew only of Prospero, Caliban, King Lear, and Rilke in translation, these, for me, being occasions of the past decade.

I skirted the native bush and emerged on the road to Mr Sargeson's house, past the streets named after English poets — Tennyson Street — and was that Milton Avenue?

I arrived at Number Fourteen Esmonde Road, walked through the gap in the high hedge and around to the back door, brushing past washing hung between the lemon tree and the house. I knocked on the door.

Mr Sargeson was home. He opened the door and said, smiling nervously and speaking as if to a child, 'Come in, come in.'

I walked into the main room while Mr Sargeson went behind the wooden counter and leaned on it.

'You've walked a long way?'

'About three miles.'

'Would you like to lie down on the bed?'

Already apprehensive, I moved nearer the door and said primly, poised for flight, 'No, thank you.'

'Robin Hyde always used to lie down. She would come limping in here and fling herself down on the bed.'

'Oh?'

'Have you read her books?'

'I've heard of them,' I said. 'I know some of her poems.'

I didn't say that I had read an essay which described her last novel as 'fantasy without ballast', the phrase staying in my mind as an example of what to expect from critics if one wrote a novel. What did it mean? Did fantasy need ballast? I felt interest in such territory because although I'd not had personal experience of inhabiting unrelieved fantasy, I had known those for whom fantasy was its own ballast. They were then free, but nowhere.

Mr Sargeson then began to talk of *The Lagoon and Other Stories* while I listened uneasily. I had not approved his choice of 'The Day of the Sheep' for the Oxford anthology.

'Do you have a copy of the Oxford anthology?' he asked. I had not. He promptly found his copy and gave it to me, signing it.

He then asked about future work.

'I don't know,' I said guardedly.

'Have you thought about coming to live and work in the hut? You'd be free to write. It's no good your living in suburbia among the nappies and bourgeois life.'

I hadn't heard anyone say the word 'bourgeois' since history lessons on the French Revolution, and I wasn't sure if I knew its modern meaning.

'I have to find a job, though,' I said.

'Why? You're a writer.'

I smiled with wonder. 'Am I? They've refused to give me sickness benefit.'

Mr Sargeson looked angry, 'After all those years in hospital? Look, I've a good friend, a doctor who's understanding and who will probably arrange a benefit for you while you work at your writing.'

'Really?'

I felt overwhelmed and shy, and protected. I accepted his offer of living and working in the hut, if he would allow me to pay him each week for my board. Although he objected at first, he finally agreed to take one pound a week. His own income was low. The first flush of publication and attention given to his work was over and he had reached the stage when he most needed money, for his books were out of print.

Both he and I were nervous that afternoon. I left saying that June and Wilson would bring me over in the weekend with my 'things' — two suitcases of clothing and books and my Remington typewriter from my days at the Grand Hotel. I felt that Mr Sargeson's offer might save my life. Already my future was bleak, with my living within a family yet feeling out of place, an extra, with my sister and her husband and family seeming like strangers to me. My sensitivity to my 'place' or lack of place and to the official judgments made about me was then extreme, and my security was shattered daily by the curious questions of the children — Who was I? Why didn't I live in my own house? Where were my children? And why wouldn't I sit with them at mealtimes? Experiences in hospital when I was once dragged by the hair to sit at the table, although I was greatly afraid of eating in the huge crowded room, watched over by the matron and her staff, waiting for orders to make any move, and feeling the tension as the knives were collected and the long counting began — these had made me reluctant to eat in company. Usually I ate alone, thus making myself what I least wanted to seem — an oddity. Also, my sister and her husband had many friends who sometimes came to the house. I stood by, like a stone pole, while they asked politely, 'Is she better now? How is she keeping?'

I arrived at Mr Sargeson's place with my 'things', including my rust-coloured skirt, my dull green twinset and the dull green overcoat I had finally bought from Mademoiselle Modes in Dunedin. I felt bound by the rules dictated by the colour wheel and the art teaching at training college and by the colour of my hair to choose dull greens and browns and yellows. Primary colours, bold bright colours, were 'bad', I had been taught, while the ones I chose were supposedly 'good'. There had long been an overflow of moral judgment upon articles of clothing, colours, shapes, with the 'good' linked to 'taste' and fastened with notions of superiority.

I was sure, then, that my clothes were in 'good taste'. In my state of extreme compliance as a yes-woman, a Simon Says woman, go there, come here, of course, I had even bought myself — at last — a corset or girdle, because the women at the Grand Hotel, and my sister in Auckland, had told me that my behind showed through my skirt, and in those days your behind was not at liberty to show. My only freedom was within, in my thoughts and language, most of which I kept carefully concealed, except in my writing. For conversation I reserved a harmless chatter which — surely — no one would label as 'peculiar' or 'mad'.

Once I arrived at Mr Sargeson's, however, with the prospect of living as a writer, with a place to work, to be alone, with no worry over money, and sharing meals and company with someone who actually *believed* I was a writer, the worry over colours, 'good' colours and 'bad' colours, the continued advice about my frizzy hair and the complaint that my behind showed through my skirt all became insignificant and far away. I had an army hut containing a bed, a built-in desk with a kerosene lamp, a rush mat on the floor, a small wardrobe with an old curtain strung in front, and a small window by the head of the bed. Mr Sargeson (I was not yet bold enough to call him Frank) had already arranged for a medical certificate and a benefit of three pounds a week, which was also the amount of his income. I thus had everything I desired and needed, as well as the regret of wondering why I had taken so many years to find it.

20 Mr Sargeson and the Army Hut

Mr Sargeson lived and worked to a strict routine which I adopted, although I could not change the habit of getting up in the very early morning and dressing at once. There had been no heating in the rooms of the Seacliff Brick Building, and in the early morning our bundle of clothes, outside the door during the night, was thrown in, and the air and the floor and the rusted wire netting in the small, high, barred window breathed frost and ice, and the caged light in the ceiling was misted over.

He did not get up until half-past seven, with breakfast at eight, and it seemed hours before I could pluck up courage to go up to the house with my chamberpot and my washing things, waiting until he was up and dressed. Usually I helped myself to my own breakfast of a yeast drink brewed overnight, home-made curds topped with honey, and bread and honey and tea. If Mr Sargeson had breakfast with me, sitting on his side of the counter, I was inclined to chatter. Within the first week of my stay he drew attention to this. 'You babble at breakfast,' he said.

I took note of what he said and in future I refrained from 'babbling', but it was not until I had been writing regularly each day that I understood the importance to each of us of forming, holding, maintaining our inner world, and how it was renewed each day on waking, how it even remained during sleep, like an animal outside the door waiting to come in; and how its form and power were protected most by surrounding silence. My hurt at being called a 'babbler' faded as I learned more of the life of a writer.

'What are you working on just now?' he asked me one day at lunch.

I was amazed and grateful at his acceptance of me as a writer doing daily work, particularly as I had not yet begun to write the novel I planned, and on some mornings I was so anxious to appear to be working that I typed 'The quick brown fox jumps over the lazy dog' and 'Now is the time for all good men to come to the aid of the party'; and my old favourite for unproductive moments, 'This is the forest primeval, the murmuring pines and the hemlock speak and in accents disconsolate answer the wail of the forest.'

'Oh,' I said mysteriously, 'I plan to write a novel but I'm working on other things just now.'

The 'other things' were poems and stories, some of which I sent to the *Listener*, although when one, a memory of Rakaia, was returned I became reluctant to send more. Having been told that the Education Department 'paid well' for work for the school bulletins, I wrote and published two stories there. I had written a story, 'Coal', about the male patients side by side like draughthorses between the shafts of the coal cart, hauling it from ward to ward, and how, when it was decided to 'modernise' transport and a lorry was used for coal, the men who, at work between the shafts, made yet another of the sad Dickensian pictures found everywhere in the hospitals, now sat drearily in the dayroom, locked in with nothing to do.

I also wrote a story called 'An Electric Blanket', exploring ways of giving warmth.

'Do you have any work for me to read?'

I was taken aback. I wasn't used to showing my work to others, unless I offered it to an editor for publication. I had secret pride in my latest story, 'An Electric Blanket', and so I rashly gave it to Mr Sargeson to read.

That afternoon, instead of resting and reading in the hut, following the example of Mr Sargeson's routine, I wandered the streets of Takapuna. I sat on the beach, looking out to Rangitoto, the island everyone in Auckland claimed as theirs, speaking of its perfect shape viewed from all directions as if they had helped to design and form it. 'See, there's Rangitoto,' they said. I thought, So this is the island in Charles Brasch's poem,

> Harshness of gorse darkens the yellow cliff-edge,
> And scarlet-flowered trees lean out to drop
> Their shadows on the bay below . . .

I had little experience of many people; I knew them only in my heart; I found endearing this eagerness of Aucklanders to claim Rangitoto.

I wondered if Mr Sargeson was reading my story. Was he thinking, 'Ah, this is good, a good ending.' I was cautious in my hopes. When I read the story it swept through me and had a finality of ending, like the right chord being played. I knew, though, that it was too loosely woven; I might even have said that it sagged in the middle. Oh, to have it stapled with bolts of fire to the sky!

I returned to the bach. He had been out shopping and was preparing dinner, a Spanish dish, paella, popular then as many of his friends had recently been to Spain and he liked to cook Mediterranean food. My story lay on the counter by the bunch of last year's red peppers. I took care not to fix my glance on it. Had he read it? In spite of my caution, I had been sure that as soon as I came into the room he would say, 'I've read your story. It's good. Congratulations.'

Mr Sargeson poured two glasses of his favourite Lemora wine and I sat on the high wooden stool opposite him while we drank our wine.

'I read your story,' he said. He took the pages, scanned them, and read aloud, '"Every morning she rose . . ."' He looked sternly at me. 'Rose? Went up to heaven, I suppose? Why not say, simply, 'she got up'. *Never* use *rose*.'

I listened contritely, realising that 'rose' was unforgivable.

'The story is quite good of its kind,' Mr Sargeson said. I felt a surge of disappointment. I resolved not to show him more stories, and I kept my resolve, later showing him only the beginning of my novel.

'If you are working on a novel,' Mr Sargeson said, 'you must have a plan.'

He then said that he always made a list of characters. He recalled how as a child, thinking he would write a book, he had begun to copy the pages of *Ivanhoe*, innocently believing he was now writing a book, when his mother found him and delivered a stern lecture on the sin of copying the work of others. He had thought that books belonged to everyone, going in and out of everyone's head, and anyone could write down any book and be a writer.

Those early months of my stay in the army hut were an unforgettable experience of sharing with Frank Sargeson (I learned to call him Frank) details of our lives, ideas and feelings, the reading of books, the evenings playing chess (which he taught me) or of my listening to the conversation between Frank and his many friends who came to dinner. Most of all we shared a working life, I learning, with his encouragement, to organise my day. I was still pursued by fears of hospital and nightmares of my experiences there. I was desperately shy, just emerging from a state of intimidation. Frank was protective and kind. I did not realise until much later, when I was writing many books, how extreme but how willing his inevitable sacrifice of part of his writing life had been. I realised also that protection of others, of one person at a time, one old or ill or disabled friend, with perhaps two or three others waiting their turn in the background, was a built-in necessity of Frank's nature, side by side with his writing.

He was a skilful relentless questioner, and when I had given him details of my formal education he said, slightly disappointed, 'So you're not a primitive after all!'

He talked passionately of his early life, of his dearly loved uncle and the farm in the Waikato. He talked of his journey through Europe, showing me the collection of postcards, and in his murmured, 'I'll never see those places again. That's all over', letting escape in his eyes and his face such a look of wild longing, almost of agony at what was gone, that I felt near to tears.

In all his conversation there was a vein of distrust, at times hatred, of women as a species distinct from men, and when he was in the mood for exploring that vein, I listened uneasily, unhappily, for I was a woman and he was speaking of my kind. I was sexually naive, unaware, and only half awake, and I was ignorant of such subjects as homosexuality, but I felt constantly hurt by his implied negation of a woman's body. My life with Frank Sargeson was for me a celibate life, a priestly life devoted to writing, in which I flourished, but because my make-up is not entirely priestly I felt the sadness of having moved from hospital, where it had been thought necessary to alter the make-up of my mind, to another asylum, where the desire was that my body should be of another gender. The price I paid for my stay in the army hut was the realisation of the nothingness of my body. Frank talked kindly of men and of lesbian women, and I was neither male nor lesbian. He preferred me to wear slacks rather than dresses. I, who now looked on Frank Sargeson as a saviour, was forced to recognise through the yearning sense of gloom, of fateful completeness, that the Gods had spoken, there was nothing to be done.

In exchange for this lack of self-esteem as a woman, I gained my life as I had wanted it to be. I gained also the joy of knowing a greater writer, a great man, and of meeting and knowing his friends. There was always a friend 'passing through' from Wellington or the South Island or overseas, or even across the harbour from Auckland: young men with their sheaf of typewritten poems, their first harvest; old acquaintances; loved friends, male and female, young and old. Friends came and went and were talked of and gossiped about, their past, present and future set, the gem-moments chosen skilfully, into the pattern of conversation. It was a world where appearance did not matter, where I was free at last from the ceaseless opinions about my hair and my clothes and the behind which showed through my skirt.

The time was ripe. I bought an exercise book, typing paper (green, Frank said, was easiest on the eyes), typing ribbon, and began to write my novel.

21 Talk of Treasure

Pictures of great treasure in the midst of sadness and waste haunted me and I began to think, in fiction, of a childhood, home life, hospital life, using people known to me as a base for the main characters, and inventing minor characters. For Daphne I chose a sensitive, poetic, frail person, who (I hoped) would give depth to inner worlds and perhaps a clearer, at least an individual, perception of outer worlds. The other characters, similarly fictional, were used to portray aspects of my 'message' — the excessively material outlook of 'Chicks', the confusion of Toby, the earthy make-up of Francie, and the toiling parents, the nearest characters to my own parents. The setting was W., a small town which the publisher later named *Waimaru*. (Later, when the book was published, I was alarmed to find that it was believed to be autobiographical, with the characters actual members of my family, and myself the character Daphne upon whom a brain operation was performed. Confronted by a doctor who had read the book, I was obliged to demonstrate to him the absence of leucotomy scars on my temples. Not every aspiring writer has such a terrifying but convincing method of displaying to others 'proof' that she has been writing fiction. Daphne resembled me in many ways except in her frailty and absorption in fantasy to the exclusion of 'reality'; I have always been strong and practical, even commonplace in my everyday life.)

The above invasion of the 'future' is inevitable in writing autobiography, particularly after one leaves childhood and the circle of being fills time and space and the lives of others, separated now from oneself and clearly visible. The process of the writing may be set down as simply as laying a main trunk railway line from Then to Now, with branch excursions into the outlying wilderness, but the real shape, the first shape, is always a circle formed only to be broken and reformed, again and again.

Each day after breakfast I went to the hut to work on my novel. I had not, as Frank suggested, written a list of characters, but I had set out in my exercise book a few ideas and themes, and the names of the parts of the book which I saw as a whole before I began typing. In my exercise book I ruled lines to make a timetable with day, date, number of pages I hoped to write, number of pages written, and a space headed *Excuses*. Each day I marked the number of pages written, in red pencil.

I was ever conscious of Frank's presence and of his place in his own routine. As he had charge of the household, with a few chores to do before starting work, be began later than I, who would hear him outside in his garden rustling through the bushes to attend to his plants, the young tomatoes or peppers. Even before he began his chores he sunbathed naked against the east wall of the bach for half an hour. He had once had tuberculosis, and he talked often of the scar and its need for oil and sunlight, which, like the colour green, were beneficial to the health of the body.

Hearing the crunch and rustle of his step dangerously close to my sanctuary as he touched or snipped a straying vine of chinese gooseberry, or playfully dropped the pollen from the male flower to the female, supposing the bees or the wind had not done their work, I, who had been dreaming about my day's writing, would hurry quickly to my typewriter and begin tapping 'The quick brown fox jumps over the lazy dog', my ideas frozen, as always, in the presence of another person. Only when Frank went inside to begin his own work was I able to settle, typing uninterrupted until I heard the door of the bach open, footsteps rustling in the long grass, a tap on the door and Frank's gentle voice saying, 'Are you ready for a cup of tea, Janet?' He'd put the tea on the built-in writing table, averting his gaze from the nakedness of my typed pages, then, retreating, make his way through the long grass to the bach. I'd hear the closing of the bach door. I then seized the eleven o'clock cup of tea and the rye wafer spread with honey as if I'd been starved. Then I'd continue my work until I again heard sounds from within the bach — Frank opening the door, fetching the mail, scraping and clattering sounds telling of lunch being prepared. Then promptly at one o'clock, again the rustling through the grass, the tap on the door and the gentle voice, 'I've made lunch, Janet.'

Eagerly, again as if I'd been starved, I hurried to the bach for my lunch. Frank would usually have a book in his hand or on the counter where we sat facing each other with our scrambled or poached egg or cheese and rye bread, and he'd read extracts aloud and discuss the writing while I listened, accepting, believing everything he said, full of wonder at his cleverness. I worshipped him and was in awe of him and with my now ingrained fear of authority or those 'in charge', I felt in need of his approval. He was twenty years older than I, and I thought of him as an old man. I felt trivial in mind and taste beside his rigid conscious sophistication. He informed me in a tone which said that working class was 'good', that I was 'working class'. And once again he described my sister and her husband, with whom I spent most weekends, as *bourgeois* and once again I marvelled at the use of terms that seemed archaic. Frank was able to place everyone within a 'class'.

After lunch he would have his 'nap', lying on the bed by the window while I, anxious to keep to the routine, also rested or read or wrote or perhaps walked around Takapuna. Then at three Frank would waken and there'd be another cup of tea with a rye wafer and honey. Then, slinging his canvas bag over his shoulder, he'd go out to buy food for the evening dinner, which we shared often with friends, our most frequent visitors then being Karl and Kay Stead, who had recently married, Karl a student at Auckland University, and Kay a librarian. Both were in a golden glow of youth and love and Karl was writing poetry and stories, and both became drawn with Frank into my web of worship. Their intelligence, their beauty, their love brought joy to Frank, who was often depressed by the general neglect of writers and by the fact that his own books were out of print. Fairburn was said to be ill, R. A. K. Mason was silent, and where was A. P.

Gaskell? Something was sadly amiss when writers wrote one acclaimed book and never spoke again. Speaking for ourselves, indeed! The message of silence was too depressing. Also, Frank felt subdued by my apparent ease of writing: he was not to know how often I was forced to make the quick brown fox jump over the lazy dog, all good men to come to the party, and to sit brooding in the 'forest primeval' while the 'murmuring pines and the hemlock' spoke and 'in accents disconsolate answered the wail of the forest'.

The friendship of Karl and Kay filled my life, giving me at last a place in my own years, for I felt I had lost so many years that I could not determine my 'real' age. I felt old beside the youth of Karl and Kay, and young beside Frank. I was not yet thirty-one.

My writing was accompanied by reading: I had many books to read.

'Have you read Proust?' Frank asked.

'No.'

When he was excited or nervous he had a habit of suddenly moving his arms and legs as if he were dancing. Now he 'danced' with the excitement of introducing *Proust* to my life. I was completely ignorant, even pronouncing the name incorrectly, although I remembered a remark of someone in Dunedin, 'It's like a scene from Proust.'

Dutifully at first, but inspired by Frank's enthusiasm, I began to read Proust, in the evening by the light of the kerosene lamp in the hut, the shadow of the flame wavering across the page. Entangled by the simplicity of the first sentence, 'For a long time I used to go to bed early,' I was soon trapped in Proust's world and each day Frank and I talked of the highlights of what I had read.

'And of course you've read *War and Peace*.'

I had not.

'It's time I re-read *War and Peace*,' Frank said, and once again I was impressed by his organisation of his life as a writer (remembering that he was perhaps the first professional writer living in New Zealand, an apprentice of ghosts in a world of distance). An accountant would say, 'I must study those old columns of figures.' A writer re-reads the classics, sweeping away present trivia, renewing inspiration, and marvelling at the imperishable truth and beauty; perhaps not every writer; but this was Frank's way.

As he had lately had a copy of *War and Peace* from Roy Parsons, who supplied him with books he couldn't afford to buy, often in exchange for reviews for *Parson's Packet*, he lent this copy to me while he re-read his original copy, with larger print. Frank was always aware that his eyes were precious, and as with the oil and the sunlight for his scar, he sought substances that were 'good for the eyes': carrots, certainly. Green typing paper and green shades on the lamps. He also wore an eyeshade, like that worn by tennis players. At his suggestion I too bought myself an eyeshade.

Together we lived through the events of *War and Peace*, Frank showing excited pleasure at my page by page discoveries, which we talked of together, analysing the characters, their actions and feelings, and every day at lunch he would say eagerly, 'Where are you now?'

When we had finished *War and Peace* we read *Anna Karenina*, *Resurrection* and the stories. Tolstoy inhabited Number Fourteen Esmonde Road, Takapuna, Auckland — both the bach and the dilapidated army hut. The characters lived there — in the room with the corner bed with its sagging mattress and threadbare blankets; with the high shelves of books, the rolled and tied faded manuscripts along the top shelf; the fireplace with the manuka logs, stacked ready for the evening fire; the collection of postcards, letters, small sculptures on the mantelpiece; with the paintings on the wall — *the sugar barge at Chelsea*; with the built-in table between the bookshelves, once used as a desk but now piled with yellowing copies of the *Times Literary Supplement*, the *New Statesman* and other journals, the electric light above shaded with its square of green cloth faded white around the edges, the room with the worn unpainted counter where we ate our meals, with the cupboards and sink and the hot-water cupboard, where the curds warmed for the next morning's breakfast; the small Atlas stove in the corner; the army-style tin kitchen utensils, the one or two or three white cups, two without handles; the huge wooden wireless built, Frank said, by 'Bob Gilbert', which Frank discreetly switched on when he used the lavatory in the small adjacent bathroom (he was a modest man, secretive; but his jokes were brilliantly lewd).

All Tolstoy's characters lived, and some died, in that room with its windows open to the honeysuckled front hedge, and, at evening, the windows shaded by placing a row of painted canvases against the glass; but the night sky always looked in, and for months the cicadas sang all day and the crickets sang all night.

The mosquitoes sang too, swarming from the mangrove swamp at the end of the road.

We saved *The Death of Ivan Ilych* for our last reading. Frank was shocked when he learned that I had never read it.

'The great classic,' he said.

I took the small dark blue book with its silken place-thread to the hut to read, and the next evening we talked of Ivan Ilych and of death.

There is a freedom born from the acknowledgement of greatness in literature, as if one gave away what one desired to keep, and in giving, there is a new space cleared for growth, an onrush of a new season beneath a secret sun. Acknowledging any great work of art is like being in love; one walks on air; any decline, destruction, death are within, not in the beloved; it is a falling in love with immortality, a freedom, a flight in paradise.

I cannot help remembering with love my days at Esmonde Road. There is the immediacy of sitting on my high stool facing Frank across the counter as we talked of *War and Peace*, and as we talk we are no longer in Esmonde Road, we are with Pierre, gone to see the war and looking on the face of Napoleon; or we are beside the stubborn slowly budding oak, the last to comply with the seasons, the last to give up its leaves; or at the deathbed of the old Prince, he, too, stubborn as an oak, in conflict with the season.

We also read Olive Schreiner's *Story of An African Farm*, becoming so steeped in it that we became Waldo and Bonaparte Blenkins. If Frank could not transform me into a male companion, at least he could give me a boy's name: Waldo.

Among my possessions was my radiogram from my days at the Grand Hotel, and my record of Beethoven's Seventh Symphony. I sensed at once Frank's disapproval of this 'luxury' item: 'If you need music, carry it in your head or listen to it first hand.' The radio was an 'excused' item. I adopted Frank's belief that radiograms, cameras, tape recorders were unnecessary, even *bourgeois*, and, ashamed, I hid my radiogram in the wardrobe under an old skirt. One evening, however, when Karl and Kay brought two records, 'A Little Night Music' and Beethoven's Violin Concerto played by David Oistrach, Frank said, 'We can play them on Janet's radiogram.' Accepting it. I can still see that room with the bare wallboard and the wooden floor, which Frank oiled each Saturday morning with a mop soaked in linseed oil ('it keeps down the dust'), with the canvas chairs ('the most comfortable type') with their wooden arms, the room that already held all the characters from *War and Peace*, *Anna Karenina*, the stories of Tolstoy and Chekhov, from Proust, Flaubert, Olive Schreiner, Doris Lessing, receiving now the music of Mozart and Beethoven while we listen. We play the record again. Karl and Frank begin to talk about Yeats. Karl reads 'Sailing to Byzantium', 'The Circus Animals' Desertion'. While I, bred on the 'old' Yeats, that is, the 'young' Yeats, of 'Had I the heavens' embroidered cloths' and 'The Lake Isle of Innisfree', listen, bathed in the words and the music. I think that I recite, then, the poem I knew by heart, Dylan Thomas's 'After the Funeral', and we talk of the meaning of 'the strutting fern lay seeds on the black sill'.

That evening I read in bed by the light of the kerosene lamp, Frank's copy of the *Poems* of Yeats:

> *We had fed the heart on fantasies,*
> *The heart's grown brutal from the fare;*

> *More substance in our enmities*
> *Than in our love; O honey-bees,*
> *Come build in the empty house of the stare.*

I finished *Talk of Treasure* two weeks before my thirty-first birthday, and taking my typescript, newly bound with tape in the way Frank had shown me, and a copy of William Faulkner's *A Fable*, which I had promised to review for *Parson's Packet*, I travelled home for two weeks to Oamaru and Willowglen.

22   The Pine Trees in the Cool of the Evening

The South Island was more reluctantly awakening to spring; frost lay on the grass; there was talk of snow and fear for the newborn lambs in the high country; the daily newspapers needed more space to record the usual winter toll of loved grandparents. At Willowglen the old lichen-covered trees in the orchard showed buds fattening into blossom, the may tree was already white and the wattle displayed its gold down by the tenantless fowlhouse.

Many-kittened Siggie greeted me with a baby rabbit, which at once sprang away unharmed into the next-door paddock. I found Siggie's Matilda, the once-kitten on which Isabel and I had practised our newly dis-covered psychology, defining her 'inferiority complex', lying dead, stiff and frosted under the bee-swarming flowering currant bush — for, as always on arriving at Willowglen, I explored 'outside' first, clambering up the bank at the back of the house among years of fallen composted pear tree leaves and fruit that stuck to the soles of my shoes and sent me skating down the dampened path. I explored the creek and the swamp and the daffodils in flower under the orchard trees, and I walked under the pine trees 'down on the flat', touching and smelling the blobs of sap-like pine-tree pearls glued to the trunks of the trees. The circumstances of our shifting from Fifty-six Eden Street, when we were 'turned out' of what I'd always believed was our home, and the anxiety of the time of the search for a 'place' made Willow-glen the equivalent of paradise, and it, not being human, was able to receive all the love heaped upon it, and survive and blossom.

I knew I was only a fair-weather visitor, that I could not bear to be reminded that the family season was winter, no matter how many fruit trees and flowers blossomed outside. Mother had lost weight and was clearly failing in health, while at the same time denying her condition. As ever she was full of hope, and her immediate delight was her success in persuading a clump of chives to grown in the small herb garden she had planted just outside the lean-to in the rich pear-composted soil. Although her inner life was full of sustaining joys and surprises, she expressed so few personal wishes and these were so seldom granted, that the clump of chives was an event in her life, with her moving gently and happily to the next phase of bliss, a 'chive sandwich with fresh bread and plenty of butter'. Faced with the prospect of her death, and now with the unusual action to grant herself a personal wish, my father, with fear in his eyes, turned to his refuge of mockery: 'Mum and her chives, just look at her!' I always knew that the 'outward' Dad was not he 'inward' Dad, and I felt pity for his inability to ally feelings with the right words instead of with words and actions seized in panic from an outer space of being human. There was such waste in his continued mockery.

My father had taught his children well. I too resented the inevitability of Mother's death. I felt helpless and hopeless and I spoke sternly to her, pleading with her to take her pills, to rest, to cease her everlasting fuelling of fires and cooking and caring, and come 'down on the flat in the cool of the evening in the last rays of the sun' as she dreamed of doing. Although I was a competent cook, having remembered the cooking lessons of junior high days, and experimented since when I had the chance, Mother's confidence was undone if another person cooked the meals or baked the cakes. (She still suffered from the reference to her as 'a bad household manager'.) If I baked bread or small cakes or cooked one of my 'specialties', Mother immediately baked 'her' bread, 'her' cakes, and 'her' speciality, attempting a kitchen counterpoint so transparent in meaning that I found it endearing and depressing, and withdrew my own floury melody.

During my stay I read to Mother selected pages from *Talk of Treasure*, naturally leaving out all reference to the death of the mother, Amy Withers. I read only the 'harmless happy' paragraphs, while Mother said faithfully, 'That's lovely.' She, and Dad, were more interested in 'this Mr Sargeson', but they appeared to be satisfied when I explained, 'He's an old man, a famous writer.' My parents had given up hope that their daughter, who had been years in a mental hospital, would 'meet her fate', but visitors often said slyly to me, 'Have you met your fate yet?' It seemed to me an old-fashioned, even a Victorian expression.

I spent time with Dad, too, down on the wharf fishing, and I was as amazed and grateful as I had been when I was a child and we had shared the crosswords and the detective stories, when he began to tell stories remembered from his childhood, of seafaring characters in Oamaru. It was cold down on the wharf with the sea wind. The green milky-murky waves lapped and sucked at the old wooden piles on the inner side of the harbour, where Dad waited for the cod to bite, while I sat facing north, the open sea, where the water was a clear stony grey lapping on rocks. We caught dogfish and a ling, which we used for bait to catch the blue cod. I really didn't care about fishing, but the chances to be with my father were rare. He fished in silence; we talked only when we had a catch to deal with.

'Never eat red cod,' he said, when I showed him the red cod on the end of my line. 'They're full of worms. The blue cod are the ones to keep.'

I listened obediently, wonderingly, as if I were being taught by a great teacher, while, always aware of a life of writing, I stored his words at the back of my mind for future use.

And while I was at Willowglen, in the midst of other activities, I was reading A Fable and other William Faulkner novels from the library. Spinning, spinning, awhirl, where am I? That might describe my feeling on reading the first page of William Faulkner. I read on and on, I read through the book, and when I had finished I was still awhirl in pools of words and feeling which affected me like powerful music where the meaning is seldom questioned. I was preparing a review — how could I write a review of a novelist who clouded my vision with feeling? I returned to the book, reading it again and again, slowly emerging into the clear fountain-light where the characters, the scenes, the meaning appeared starkly outlined, solid, real, good. This was William Faulkner's world, and I had found it to keep.

A few days before I caught the train to the north, I persuaded Mother to picnic with me 'on the flat', and so, late one afternoon, we made chive sandwiches and filled a thermos with tea; and carrying a rug and cushions we set out for 'the flat', walking slowly down the path beneath the old 'ghost' pine tree, past the old apple shed where the fantails danced in and out of the broken-hinged open door, past the cowbyre with its roof of sky and broken bail, the rotted pigsty where Siggy went regularly to have her kittens, by the old stables where furniture, pictures, boxes of photographs, most of the relics of Fifty-six Eden Street were stored, thrust without order on that wild, disorderly day of the shift; through the gate out of the cool shadow of the hill, at last where the stripling pines lay in the warm sun shining like another sun, not *our* sun, in another place. We spread the rug on the pine needles and leaned against the trees, the sticky resin clinging to our clothes. Feeling the warmth of the sun, I wriggled like a lizard come out to bask. We ate our sandwiches of bread and butter and chives and drank, with little black flies from the creek dropping in the tea. The pukekos watched us through the fence in the next paddock.

But Mother was restless. What if the phone rang? Surely we wouldn't hear it, down on the flat? What if 'your father' came home and found no dinner prepared? Besides, she had meant to phone the weekly order at the grocer's, the Self Help, and it might be too late for the order-boy to deliver it. We had moved our patronage from the Star Stores to the Self Help when the son of one of our Eden Street neighbours became manager. Having lived in Oamaru for many years, my family now had a faithful network of favourite shopkeepers, post office clerks, taxi drivers, many of whom were the 'boys' who used to dream, with Myrtle and me, of making the big time in Hollywood. Some of those who dreamed with us were now bones in the Western Desert, in Crete or Italy.

Our picnic was too soon over. Mother struggled to her feet, breathless with the effort, and together we climbed the path up to the house; and already the sun had gone from down on the flat, the driveway was growing dark, darkened more quickly by the presence of the pine trees, and we were once again where the frostbound hill leaned over the house, gripping it with a claw of everlasting winter.

Two days later when I boarded the Express for the north I knew I would not see Mother again, and in a burst of bitterness I said, 'I'm never coming back to Willowglen.'

My words hurt, as I knew they would. I said goodbye and the train pulled out on its familiar track, and even as it began its *Kaitangata, Kaitangata, Kaitangata, Winton, Winton, Winton, Kakanui, Kakanui, Kakanui*, I knew there was no use escaping anywhere, from family or frost or land, the escape made impossible anyway because, as the daughter of a railway worker, I had to accept the possession of and by every inch of railway track in the country: an iron bond of mutual ownership. The train continued to say a new word, *Willowglen, Willowglen, Willowglen*, as we crossed the Canterbury Plains.

23   A Death

Willowglen may have been the paradise of leaves, earth, dark water, swamps thick with green-for-danger bright grasses, but Auckland was still the paradise of light, full of swirling smoky clouds as if a volcano hid in the sky, erupting to another unseen world. Frank's garden was bursting with the spring plantings — tall columns of sweet corn growing outside the hut window, peppers shiny greenleaved on the east side of the house. He was planting Russian Red tomatoes, and he showed me the picture on the empty seed packet.

'Beefsteak and Russian Red, that's what I'm planting this year.'

There was a tiny pawpaw tree, too, near the hut. He nursed it carefully. He hoped one day to grow a custard apple. Barbara and Maurice Duggan, he said, had grown a custard apple. 'Perhaps the only one in the country.'

His wonder was endless; his eyes glistened when he talked of the custard apple (I was about to say 'his eyes *shone*', but the light in them was not a steady planetary shining, it was broken light coming through mist or dampness or plain tears).

'But what about your manuscript?' he asked. 'Have you sent it to Pegasus?'

When Denis Glover left the Caxton Press he apparently gave a handful of my stories and poems to Albion Wright of Pegasus, who sent them on to me. I promptly burned them. Among the papers was a letter from John Forrest to Denis Glover explaining that there was no hope for my recovery ('when I think of you I think of Van Gogh, of Hugo Wolf . . .'). Frank explained that Pegasus had taken over much of the Caxton Press's work.

I knew that after the cool reception of my story 'An Electric Blanket' I could not show Frank any of the book. I read, however, a token few lines from the beginning, which Frank liked so much that he suggested I send it as a poem to John Lehmann of the *London Magazine*. To make matters more interesting (we had been talking about the Australian Hoax of *Angry Penguins and Ern Malley*), Frank suggested I collect a few poems I had written and he would send them to John Lehmann. He chose a name for me — *Santa Cruz* — repeating solemnly as if I did not know, 'That means *Saint* and *Cross*.' His letter to John Lehmann explained that I was a woman from the Pacific Islands who was new to Auckland; he had been impressed with my writing. The reply was kind. The poems, John Lehmann said, were refreshing, new; he hoped that when I learned a little more English he might see more of my work.

In the meantime Frank helped me parcel the manuscript, and such was his care for it that he insisted on walking with me to the post office and watching while the clerk stuck on the correct stamps and thrust the envelope into the chute.

Two weeks later I heard that Pegasus Press had accepted my book. They enclosed a contract to be signed. I was bewildered, pleased, and scared, while Frank, having learned the routine of writing and publishing, and knowing the *etiquette*, said, 'We must celebrate.' Spending more than he could afford, he bought a bottle of Vat 69 whisky, which we drank that evening.

Summer came too quickly. The heat persisted day and night. I slept with the door of the hut open, the entry and the window by my bed draped with muslin to keep out the mosquitoes from the mangrove swamp and from Lake Pupuke. Having finished my book and being thrust once again into the ordinary factual world, I grew restless, unable to work in the heat. I wrote poems, a few stories. I played chess in the evenings or again listened to the anecdotes and conversation of Frank and his friends, or he and I talked over the books we were reading, but we both knew there had been a subtle change of emotional gear, we were no longer on the same path, the honeymoon was over. I knew it would soon be time to leave and I did not want to leave. Beginning, middle, end — how often we had talked of the fictional processes and how each could be expressed painlessly, invisibly.

Then one day early in December my sister and her husband came unexpectedly to see me. It was morning, working time. I heard Frank direct them to the hut.

June appeared at the door.

'I came to tell you,' she said. 'Mother died this morning. She had a stroke at about six o'clock and she died at half-past ten. Bruddie rang to tell Wilson and me.'

I tried to show as little feeling as possible. I said, 'She was worn out, anyway, and she was ready to die.'

On the deaths of Myrtle and Isabel we had embraced each other and cried, but that had been so long ago and I'd been on my own, alone with my feelings, for so many years.

'Her life was awful,' I said.

June agreed. They were not going to the funeral, she said. She asked would I be coming over as usual for the weekend.

'No, I don't think so,' I said.

'We'll see you some time then?'

'Yes.'

'They didn't want to worry you with the news, they told us to tell you.'

The mixture of sadness and relief at Mother's death was strengthened and sharpened by my familiar feeling of anger and depression at being treated as the 'frail, mad' member of the family, who must be sheltered from unpleasant news. The well-meaning consideration of my family served to emphasise and increase my separation from them. I was jealous of my sister's first knowledge of the death, almost as if it were a treasured gift chosen to be given to her, then passed on, used and soiled, second-hand, to me. It was partly a reawakening of the former childhood rivalries in being first to know, to see, the first to embrace the cherished secret; in fact, the rivalry had never reawakened for it had never slept!

I told Frank my news.

'So what?' he said, showing his bitterness towards his own family. 'Parents are better dead.'

Bravely, I agreed with him.

That night in the privacy of the hut I wept, and the next morning, faced with Frank's scornful reproaches about 'all those tears', I explained that I was weeping for Mother's life, not for her death. I regretted that with our parents' lives spent almost entirely in feeding, clothing, sheltering us, we had little time to know and be friends with them. My life had been spent watching, listening to my parents, trying to decipher their code, always searching for clues. They were the two trees between us and the wind, sea, snow; but that was in childhood. I felt that their death might expose us but it would also let the light in from all directions, and we would know the reality instead of the rumour of wind, sea, snow, and be able to perceive all moments of being.

I stayed the weekend at the hut, and so on Sunday I shared the meal that Frank always cooked for his friend Harry, while Harry, at first silent as a speaking plank of wood, soon lost his suspicion of me and talked to me while Frank, more nervous than usual and showing it by the excessive gesturing and waving of his hands, stirred and tasted and measured and dipped and finally served his usual perfect meal. After the meal I returned to the hut, leaving Frank and Harry to talk over old and new times. They had known each other so long that they used half-sentences or single words for conversation, and when I came to know Harry a little I realised how much Frank prized him, not only as a lasting companion, but as a source of information about the 'other' world of racecourses and sleazy city hotels and sad derelict wanderers down by the Ferry Buildings and lower Queen Street. Frank had staged his own life perfectly, with himself as a writer, and he made sure that while he lived within the act of writing he was surrounded by characters who would bring him news from the world he could no longer explore in reality when the physical demands of fiction mean a seat at a desk or table, all morning or all day, and silence, solitude, and sleep.

No one expected me to go to mother's funeral; I fulfilled my family's expectations of me by not feeling able to go. Instead, I asked my father to send me the letters and telegrams of sympathy, which I answered. Then I celebrated and mourned Mother in a handful of poems. Their movement is not good but they do give details of what I was thinking.

> Burn the dirty clothes she died in,
> the sour stockings, the stained dress,
> the holey (holy) interlock
> she wore to greet the sad surprise
> the sad morning surprise of death.
>
> Put her costume on a hanger
> on the clothes-line for the wind
> to blow the shreds of sick disaster
> into the trees or the next town.
> Lay the death-sheets on the lawn
> for dew and sun to bleach and clean.
>
> I say that only fire and air
> are kindly charities, so give
> to them your pennyworth of grief
> refusing earth and water who buried
> her body, drowned her with too many tears.

Another poem —

> Whose death will never kill its moment, smoke out
> from her heart the small dire ferret of time
> will not walk again, her heavy body in garment
> outsize, sunflower hat; in seven-league shoes
> across bog, byre-mud, snowgrass after her runaway
> rabbit of God who bred deep, his warren
> burrowed secret from the hawk beneath her paddock
> of stone and thistle, flaglily and bracken.
>
> Though my chisel of salt will not curl or reshape
> her stone, my tears increase no flight of thistledown
> or tell its time of travel, though night flay her lilies,
> her blue bog-sunrise, her palpitating Gods
> breed in darkness, still let the crazed hawk refugees
> fly down to her bed of bracken, sleep safe.

What else could I write, having the examples of George Barker's, 'Most near most dear most loved and most far', and 'After the funeral, mules' praises, brays . . .' by Dylan Thomas?

My preoccupation then was with condensed imagery and the use of general terms — love, death, charity, heart — which are like small grenades set within a poem — the feeling, touching them, explodes itself into power-less fragments and so at the end of the poem the feeling has either been destroyed or dispersed, and nothing remains. The condensed imagery also has the effect of jet travel — you see nothing of the landscape beneath and thus are unaffected by it, and when you arrive at your destination — or the end of the poem — you are as fresh — apart from the tedium of travelling — as when you set out, and the poem might as well be nothing, a shadow.

Trying to write poetry, I did my best, although I knew the poems were not 'good'. I spent much feeling (which might better have been used in strengthening the poems) in hoping they were good, while knowing they were not — the ice-cream indulgence of a dream.

I wrote one other poem about Mother's death, 'Their eyes pleading the light are mocked by light', which I read to Karl Stead, and although he was years younger than I and had written less poetry, his judgment and sense of rightness were keener than mine. He listened and said little, but when he repeated the words, frowning, 'The sun is death's lawyer', I knew the poem was a failure because I then had the urge to say, like one caught in the misdemeanour of a poem, 'Oh, I can explain everything.'

I could, too. The metaphor was worked out, but it did not strike.

> Their eyes pleading the light are mocked by light
> if scribbled nought beyond, within, themselves —
>   the doom or flame-encircling litigant
>   paid by decay to prosecute their lives;
> for now in magnitude of mourning, relatives
>   beachcombing, probe my mother's body,
>   gull through binoculars of fear and grief
>   above the coast to seek her hieroglyph,
>   where death's most ardent lawyer, the sun
>   of December, in this her sixty-third year
> has awakened early for darkest work, has written
>   client signatures across her skin
>   like tributaries dry without cipher
>   bedded on bone, on gaunt and decaying bone
>   misled, tongueless, to the tasting-edge
> of her stopped blood-this, who could have foreseen?

I was strongly affected by the fact that Mother died in the morning, the work-time, that she had got up (never 'risen') early and gone to the kitchen and had lit the fire, and when Dad found her she, half conscious, whispered to him, 'I thought I'd make a cup of tea . . .' These were her last words; she never regained consciousness. As a statement of her life they could be judged, without cynicism, as her best literary effort.

My continued feeling of betrayal that Frank had shown no sympathy at Mother's death melted when I overheard him say to Kathleen, our neighbour, 'A mother's death is hardest to take. It's a sad time for Janet.' Frank, too, had secret feelings to hide!

24   The Silkworms

When the summer is over, I thought, and the weather is cooler (a dream: in the cool of the evening) I shall write another novel. Emerged from my fictional world, I can see clearly that my staying in the hut was using more of Frank's time, energy and feeling than he had bargained for, as I was not his only *charge* (the word in all its variety of meaning), and each (Harry, Jack, old Jim next door, Frank's two elderly aunts, one of whom was blind, who lived near the beach in an old gabled house full of high dark furniture) had to be visited and listened to and comforted, with the poorer 'charges' receiving vegetables from the garden, or a ten shilling or pound note. The visit to the aunts most consumed Frank's energy, for their tongues were sharply critical, while he remained patiently docile. When he returned from seeing them, he always said, in a tone of amazement, 'My *fat aunts, my huge aunts.*' And they were huge aunts, with a kind of solidity that would seem to be incapable of ever melting: I think they were Frank's mother's sisters; and I think they were like the past, his past, in being unable to vanish: they were not snow-women; they were without season or time; and when the sick blind aunt lay in bed, one day when I visited with Frank, she was diminished not by her blindness or sickness but only by the tall oak bookcase that loomed by the bed.

The heat of the summer persisted. Frank began to talk of the 'golden time' in his childhood when he kept silkworms. It was a remembered summer, like 'That Summer' of his short perfect novel. It happened then that one day I was walking in Karangahape Road (a 'possession' of Auckland, like Rangitoto) when I noticed silkworms displayed in a pet-shop window. I bought half a dozen and that evening I nervously unwrapped them and set them on the kitchen counter. The sensitivity between Frank and myself was now so extreme that every movement had to be planned for fear of hurting or implying by one a state which could not be borne in the other. I had seen Frank come near to weeping over his postcards of his early European journey; I felt that the golden time of his uncle and the silkworms belonged only to him, and I did not want him to think that I, listening to his constant remembering of a childhood happiness, had dared to try to provide him with a replica of the past. I was casual about the silkworms. He was delighted, with an immediate, not a recollective delight. He, in his turn, viewed the silkworms as a means of absorbing *my* attention while he and I planned my next 'move', which, according to Frank, was for me to 'travel overseas' to 'broaden my experience', a convenient way, both he and I realised, of saying that I was 'better out of New Zealand before someone decided I should be in a mental hospital'. We both knew that in a conformist society there are a surprising number of 'deciders' upon the lives and fate of others. Frank even suggested that he become my next of kin in a marriage of convenience, which I then found insulting, and he, on overnight reflection, decided against.

We concentrated on the silkworms, I roaming the neighbourhood of Takapuna until I found in an old-fashioned garden overlooking the beach and the pohutukawa trees, the mulberry tree with leaves to feed our 'charges', and a kindly owner willing to give me supplies of leaves. Frank brought home a shoebox from Hannahs shoe store, nestled the mulberry leaves inside and gently lay the silkworms upon the leaves. At once they began to eat. During the day we kept the box on the end of the counter near the bookcase, and at night I took it down to the hut and set it on my desk-table. We knew the silkworms were eating for *dear life*. In the silence of the night as I lay in bed I heard a sound like the turning of tiny pages in a tiny library, which I've heard only since then, slightly magnified, in the library of the British Museum as the readers steadily consume page after cherished page of their chosen books. The silkworms' consuming was literal, the sound of steady chewing and chomping all night and all day, although unlistened to during the day, without pause until that stage of their life was over: a lifelong meal. Frank explained what would happen next, and we watched as the silkworms entered their next life, as they began to wave their heads in a circular motion, with a thread like a golden spiderweb being drawn from their mouths. Frank had placed each on a strip of cardboard which they used as their anchorage, enclosing themselves and the cardboard in a golden cocoon, and when all was still within, Frank gently cut through the silk, removing the naked grubs and wrapping them in nests of cottonwool — the usual intrusion based on the belief that we own the world, its creatures and its produce. The golden thread of plaited silk hung on the wall by the window in that same room where Ivan Ilych and the old Prince died, and Pierre saw Napoleon, and the oak tree budded and shed its leaves, and Mozart and Beethoven had their music played: a rich gold room.

In time, the grubs, cosy in their cottonwool, became moths, which in their first moments sought each other, male and female, the males mounting the females for mating that lasted, like the eating and spinning, all day and night until the males fell torpid, dying one by one, while the females, again with their furniture provided, laid tiny rows of white eggs, like Braille dots or stitches, neatly upon the sheet of cardboard; then they also died, whereupon Frank, who in all the stages of the silkworms' development had repeated his actions of years ago, explaining each stage, describing how it would be, set the sheet of cardboard with the silkworms, enclosed in their own past, present and future, in the shoebox, which he buried, lowering it like a makeshift coffin into the earth.

'That's the cycle,' he said, his words and his glance capturing other references, other species.

'They'll stay there the winter, and when the warm weather comes, I'll dig them up, they'll hatch, and the cycle will repeat itself.'

The completeness, perfection, and near-indestructibility of the cycle did not escape us.

That evening, like gods, we celebrated with Vat 69 the lives dedicated to eating, spinning, mating.

The next day we planned a letter to the Literary Fund applying for a grant for me to 'travel overseas and broaden my experience'. I was now free to accept the invitation from one of Frank's friends, Paula Lincoln, known as P. T. Lincoln, or Paul, to stay at her bach at Mount Maunganui while we awaited the outcome of my application.

25 Miss Lincoln, Beatrix Potter and Dr Donne

I had met Paula Lincoln when she once visited Frank, and I had seen her as a small grey-haired woman with a voice full of tears as she talked of how her body had 'changed' and of how she had been deprived of her share of peace. She was in distress that afternoon. I could see Frank's movement away from her as he, disliking displays of feeling, tried to escape the fountain of inexplicable misery where she seemed to be the central figure, the statue, receiving all.

If only, I thought, she didn't go on so.

I could sense that her past and Frank's were bound up in her feelings. I never solved the mystery of that afternoon. When she had gone Frank murmured sadly without explaining, 'Poor woman. She gets in a state. Every time she comes here she's in a state. By the way, she has invited you to stay at the Mount whenever you feel like a holiday. Poor woman. I'm very fond of her.'

He showed me a photo of a young Frank with three friends, one a small pretty dark-haired woman. 'That's her. Paul.'

He explained about her life, how she had been educated at a famous public school for girls, how she had broken away from her 'upper-class' family to come to New Zealand when she was thirty, and how she had worked as a physiotherapist, and during the war, with the Pacifist Council; how she readily became interested in causes, how they had met, she became interested in writing, how a small inheritance gave her a private income with freedom to write, but she had written only a few stories. She had helped Frank with money for the building of his bach and the publishing of his first book.

I said that I remembered her story in *Speaking for Ourselves*.

'She's a wonderful person,' Frank said. 'She's a lesbian, you know.'

Even with my growing knowledge of the varieties of sexual preference, I was unaware of the meaning and implication of lesbianism, and when Frank explained it to me, I found that I, like Queen Victoria, didn't believe it!

I set out for Mount Maunganui. The train journey lasted most of the day and was one of a number of train routes then where the journey took so long and was so much a part of the natural surroundings of bush, waterfalls, ferns, wet clay, a glistening world of wet, that the heart of the land entered the railway carriage and there was the feeling of the loneliness and strangeness of a personal exploration. There were few passengers, some lying sleeping on the seats, others like myself sitting alone in a double seat, all a prey to the wild world beyond the carriage windows. Once when the train was forced to a stop before a landslide of clay covering the line, the driver and fireman and a trolley of gangers worked with shovels clearing the line while the passengers sat silently immersed in the green dream, and when the train at last began to move, creaking slowly around narrow bend after narrow bend where rainwater oozed from every pore of earth and bark and leaf and fern, there was the privilege of knowing, like being favoured with a secret, that this was not the 'main trunk line', accepted by use, with refreshment stops and cities along the way, this was a 'branch line', with all its mystery, neglect, vague atmosphere of exile which is the nature of branch lines everywhere, even in dreams, thinking, and history.

Finally the train stopped at Tauranga, and although it was to continue along the isthmus towards Mount Maunganui, Paula Lincoln had arranged to meet me in Tauranga so that we might take the evening launch across the harbour. It was already dark with a wintry full moon. Paula Lincoln was waiting on the platform, dressed as she had been the day she visited Frank — grey flannel slacks, white cotton blouse like a school blouse, grey cardigan, and gaberdine raincoat. Her shoes were black lace-up 'sensible' winter shoes. She was eager and nervous, speaking in the English accent which we used to call 'Oxford', heard in teachers, doctor and royalty, which therefore gave it an association with authority, a hint of admonishment. P. T. L.'s voice had a defensive note as if holding a permanent thread of *This is why it is so and it can't be helped.*

We walked from the station to the jetty, with Miss Lincoln bright-eyed, steeped now not in a fountain of misery but in the moonspray and moonlight, for suddenly the clouded sky cleared and the light poured down on the harbour. Even the silkworms had consumed time with their mulberry leaves: the cold of the night was winter, May, cold.

We boarded the launch, and as we moved on to the expanse of harbour, Miss Lincoln trailed her hand over the side, touching the water, and murmuring, 'liquid lumps of light'.

'That's how Greville described it,' she said. 'Has Frank talked about Greville Texidor? Have you read her stories?'

I said I had seen *These Dark Glasses*, Greville's stories. I had been impressed and quietly depressed by their assurance and sophistication. Frank had talked, too, of Greville and her life, giving the condensed biography that accompanied talk of each of his friends and acquaintances, and stressing the personal marvel of nature, talent or experience that each held like a dazzling lure: Greville's was the fact that she had once been married to a contortionist and had toured the world with him. '*Very early in her life.*' Frank admired her writing, too, but it was her 'experience of life' that captured him: where she had been, what she had seen, and what she had done — with her contortionist husband!

As the launch neared the Mount, Miss Lincoln continued to talk of Greville and of Frank and his early life with his friends. Then we were silent, enjoying the moonlight, and when the launch pulled in to the jetty, Miss Lincoln said, 'I like to be with someone and not have to talk all the time.'

'Oh, so do I,' I said with new-acquaintance enthusiasm. Frank had told me that Paul didn't 'take to' people easily. 'She'll like you,' he said. 'You'll be good for each other.'

Frank sometimes dispensed people as if they were medicine and he were the doctor in charge of the case. He prescribed for himself, too. Cooking Sunday dinner for Harry and hearing him talk about his world of horse racing, and listening to Jack's woes and dreams, and looking after Jim next door were seen by Frank as being, among the pleasures, 'good for him'. I was wondering what would happen if Frank's friend, Miss Lincoln, didn't 'take to' me, or in her language, which held a number of words used in school stories and in Somerset Maugham, if we didn't 'click'.

'Everyone calls me Paul,' she said, as we walked towards the beach road. 'I've been Paul since my school days.' (I had been mumbling at intervals, 'Miss Lincoln'.)

'Well . . .' I said.

Mount Maunganui was like a sandy settlement in the middle of the sea, with the sea as the only horizon, and as we walked past the cluster of beach stores where Miss Lincoln stopped to buy bread and fruit, we came suddenly into Ocean Beach Road.

> *Round the cape of a sudden came the sea*
> *And the moon looked over the mountain's rim*

we quoted together.

'I always think of it, every time,' Miss Lincoln said excitedly, her Oxford accent spear-sharp.

'I love "A Grammarian's Funeral",' I said, straying in search of further means of operating the 'clicking' mechanism.

'I can't place that just now,' Miss Lincoln said.

The beach was wild, lonely, a long stretch of surf rolling for ever, with the moon staying in Tauranga across the harbour on the other side, yet following us, looking down with its hint of shadowy peaks, making a path across the open sea towards Ocean Beach Road. Miss Lincoln pointed to a dark mass now sharing the horizon with the sea.

'That's Matakana Island, planted with pine trees; and next is Rabbit Island.'

She pointed to our left, behind us.

'That's the Mount.'

I had grown used to the North Islanders' reference to hills as mountains.

'And beyond the end of Ocean Beach Road, around the corner, you can see White Island, on fire with volcanic eruption.'

I looked intelligently towards where White Island would be visible.

We arrived at a small whitewashed beach cottage, which I immediately likened to Haworth Parsonage. Only the gravel road and the sandhills lay between the cottage and the wintry ocean. The front of the section was an expanse of sand, where a few plants, grey-leaved, stunted in growth, leaned away from the wind towards the cottage.

Once inside, Miss Lincoln showed me to a book-lined room with a big sagging bed in the middle and a wooden sandstrewn floor. It was cold, stark The rusted window felt frozen with the dark massed beyond it, for the moon, having followed us home, had retreated, leaving pitch dark except for the flashes of light made by the crashing breakers.

'I've already gathered pipis,' Miss Lincoln said. 'For the special meal.'

All the ingredients were there, once described faithfully by Frank Sargeson in his *Up on to the Roof and Down Again* when he and the woman he called K. (Miss Lincoln) had eaten the meal here at Mount Maunganui. And as Miss Lincoln cooked our meal she quoted from Frank's description, word for word, 'Oh God, I hope not too much' as she added liquid to the rice. That paragraph from Frank's description belonged indisputably to her, and she flaunted with delight the scene where she and Frank had shared the stage.

She opened a bottle of wine. 'Keats' favourite wine,' she said. 'You'll be visiting his house in London, won't you, if you get the grant?'

I had a sense of being borne along on the wishes of others, but that was not unusual in my life. The momentum frightened me; I had no desire to travel anywhere . . . but where could I live? I knew it was time to leave Esmonde Road, and there was no hope of my having a small house of my own with enough money for necessities, for if I had applied to the Literary Fund for money to spend thus, surely it would be denied. The magic enticement was 'broadening experience overseas'.

'I suppose you have all kinds of plans for overseas?'

'Well . . .' I felt ashamed of my simple desires — haunted by Wordsworth's sonnet

> Tax not the royal Saint with vain expense,
> With ill-matched aims the Architect who planned
> (Albeit labouring for a scanty band
> Of white-robed Scholars only) this immense
> And glorious work of fine intelligence!

I dreamed of seeing King's College Chapel, Cambridge. I wanted to roam the countryside of the Scholar-Gipsy, and that of the Hardy novels; to see, in Shakespeare country, the 'bank whereon the wild thyme grows'; and even to walk in Kew Gardens among the lilacs! — all unfashionable dreams in a new age of *Speaking for Ourselves*. I longed also to wander in the *Euganean Hills*,

> Many a green isle needs must be
> In the deep wide sea of Misery,
> Or the mariner, worn and wan
> Never thus could voyage on
> Day and night, and night and day . . .

and to see

> The blue Mediterranean, where he lay,
> Lulled by the coil of his crystalline streams . . .

These romantic images of countryside and academic seclusion were balanced by those of 'dark satanic mills' and the squalor of the cities, for I'd heard again and again of how we in New Zealand could never imagine the squalor of cities like London, Paris, Glasgow, and when I tried to imagine being in, say, London, I furnished my images with darkness and poverty and wild-eyed medieval characters set against tall grey stone buildings.

'I haven't really thought where I'll be,' I said.

That night for dessert we had gritty strawberry-tasting guavas from the bush growing outside the back door beside the dunny, and as this was my first taste of guavas, Miss Lincoln watched anxiously while I tasted — savoured — the new fruit, and when I declared my approval, she looked pleased, as if I had been judging her. She was sensitive also about her house and her possessions, I told her that I loved her place by the sea; there was a feeling that it lay in the middle of the sea, while the book-lined room was ideal.

'I shall read and read and read.'

I was slightly nervous, however, of Miss Lincoln — Paul — for she had announced soon after our meeting that she always 'said honestly what she thought'. Although I value honesty, I am sometimes fearful of the sharpness, the hint of aggression with which it is often expressed.

'I say what I think,' Miss Lincoln repeated. Her English voice had a quelling effect. I resolved to be careful not to make myself the target of disapproval or censure, for it is usually only in such climate of conversation that people proclaim they are being 'strictly honest'.

'Have you read *The Well of Loneliness* by Radclyffe Hall?' she asked as I was going to my room. I had not read or heard of it. She said that if I wished to read it I would find it on the bookshelf, that it was one of the earliest books written about lesbianism, and that there had been a scandal over its publication.

'You know I'm a lesbian,' she said.

'Yes. Frank said something about it, I think.' I spoke lightly, out of my depth.

I read the book that evening, in a curious turmoil of distaste and wondering as I tried to imagine women making physical love to women — I, who had never made love to anyone! The next day I believed and felt sympathy for Miss Lincoln when she explained that she'd had a lifelong passion for a schoolgirl at her former public school. She talked of Lily as if Lily were there in front of her and the passion were still alive. Tears came to her eyes.

'Lily was so beautiful.'

Lily had been her lasting, only love. Although there had been friends since who 'clicked', there had been no love as with men and women.

I decided that I liked Paul, that she was just another of the misunderstood misfits of the world. I was repelled by the idea of both male and female homosexuality yet I was learning slowly to accept the sacred differences in people, although I was then ignorant of biological and hormonal facts. I knew then only that such sexual differences threatened and hurt those who loved the opposite sex.

I understood the way Paul was distressed in recounting past experiences, her longing for what had been and what had not been, and I knew that like all outcasts she would need to struggle doubly hard to survive the daily raids on her sensitivity. It occurred to me that she was almost the same age as my mother had been — two or three years younger, and here we were talking to each other as two persons. This, more than sexual confessions, occupied my thoughts during my stay, and each time we found a new topic of conversation — literature, Frank and his early life and friends, the Mount, New Zealand as it appeared to an English woman, I thought to myself, What would mother have talked about, had she and I ever been

273

simply two persons talking? Mother, her thoughts glued to her family, so that when she might have tried to speak as a person she would find among her thoughts fragment-fibres of 'your father', 'the kiddies', 'the cows', 'the grocery order from the Self Help', 'the bill from Calder Mckays for the blankets' . . . I couldn't believe that Miss Lincoln and Mother would have shared historical memories and thoughts about them. When had mother time to read a book?

I could do as I wished, Paul said, during my stay. There was a bike I could ride and the sandy flat terrain was excellent for biking. Also, she wondered if I would like to meet some of her friends? There was Michael Hodgkins (the nephew of Frances Hodgkins), who lived in a small bach across the harbour but came to the beach to walk and find shells. There were also the Gilberts, Mr Gilbert a well-known conchologist and his wife Sarah a connoisseur of interesting people. They were a clever family, 'one of the old families', and their daughter in London knew several poets.

I was impressed.

'The only thing,' Paul said with a slight note of complaint, 'is that when I bring my interesting friends to the Mount, Sarah Gilbert is inclined to steal them, and eventually they become *her* friends rather than *mine*.' At that stage of my life I could not quite imagine the importance of some of the territorial urgencies and restrictions of human friendship. How could I have forgotten so quickly all the tricks of desperation that people will use to assure and reassure themselves of their place, their p(a)lace? The desperation of people in their 'ordinary' setting was no less intense, though less visible, than among people classed as abnormal; and in both cases the desperation may be increased by the surroundings!

Here was the sandy bleak Mount Maunganui, where few came in winter, where even the plants had to be bedded in sacking to help them survive; the lonely sandswept roads, the few households, where the occupants waited as they wait on islands and peninsulas everywhere for news from the mainland, for interesting visitors to remind them of the continued existence of themselves and their three-sided world leased at the sea's pleasure. I could perceive now that the enticement of friends from one household to another might be something to be feared, and if the friend were lost, then the loss would be bitter.

Fortunately, the Mount's acknowledged eccentric, treasured for himself and for being the nephew of the famous painter, was shared by all. He came one day to the bach, waiting outside for us to walk with him on the beach. He was perhaps in his mid-forties; tall, dark, thin, greatly unwashed, with piercing blue eyes that looked always elsewhere. We walked on the beach, gathered shells and returned to the bach for a cup of tea, and although he did enter the sitting room, he showed his unease at being within four walls, and quickly moved outside again within sight of the surf, and once again at home on the beach, he relaxed, partly with us, partly with the sea and sky. He appeared almost to be a relic which his aunt, the famous painter, might have arranged to leave, as some painters may paint a mysterious figure within their canvas or leave an unexplained reference of colour and light that remains a source of wonder.

I met also Miss Lincoln's friends, the Gilberts. Mr Gilbert sat in a corner of the room by the fire knitting a jersey with wool that he himself had gathered, spun, and carded. Sarah, his wife, served afternoon tea of scones and cakes from a tiered fancy plate with a handle, and while Mr Gilbert spoke little, although now and again exchanging an amused glance with Miss Lincoln ('we understand each other,' Miss Lincoln said later), Mrs Gilbert, having learned of my application for a grant to travel overseas to 'broaden my experience', talked of her daughter in London who knew several well-known poets and was a close friend of one in particular. She mentioned a name. Had I read his work? Yes, I had read a poem in a Penguin anthology.

I listened with awe, a sense of failure, a pang of envy, as she explained how much her daughter was part of the literary life of London.

(And I was secretly trying to subdue my panic at the thought of the buildings, the city itself!)

Still talking of her daughter and the poet, she said securely, comfortably, 'They're very close.'

Sarah Gilbert was a woman of strength. I could see how she had 'lured' (using the word in its original sense of bait) some of Miss Lincoln's friends. Even Miss Lincoln had responded to the lure.

'She's a member of one of the *earliest* families,' she reminded me. 'Both she and her husband — they're *the* Gilberts.'

My stay with Miss Lincoln (I couldn't really say 'Paul' to her face) was made more memorable by the books I read — *Alice in Wonderland*, *Alice Through the Looking Glass*, the Borrower tales, the books of Beatrix Potter — none of which I had read before; and the *Complete Sermons* of Dr John Donne. At night I lay in bed reading while the waves crashed just beyond the cottage and the wind raced the sand along the dunes between us and the beach, leaving a layer of sand in the front gardens of Ocean Beach Road, in the guttering on the roof, the cracks in the walls, down the chimney, with always a small drift of sand just inside the door as a promise and reminder of invasion.

And each day, in her plain white blouse and grey flannel slacks, like a refugee from an old-fashioned girls' school, Miss Lincoln knelt by her battered hedge plants, binding them with strips of sacking tied to the manuka stakes — the right dress, I thought, for plants living here by the sea; for Miss Lincoln, like Frank Sargeson, had an intense dislike of 'frills and fripperies', and so even the plants were clothed to her taste. Not being able to give up my lifelong fascination with clothes which I longed for but never had, yet might some day acquire even if it were by the ultimate magic of unfolding layer upon layer of silk from a small brown hazelnut, I usually felt slightly ashamed when Frank or Miss Lincoln began their tirade against what they called 'feminine fripperies'. They reminded me of my father and his, 'What do you want clothes for? You've got a perfectly good school uniform.'

In spite of their plain dress, however, the Mount Maunganui, the *Haworth Parsonage* hedge plants wore proudly a special, glittering ribbon of salt and rainbow light borrowed from the ocean.

A few days before I was to return to Auckland, the telegram came from Frank.

'Privately informed. Three hundred pounds granted. Congratulations.'

So my journey away from New Zealand was to be a reality. I had so little notion of the value of money that I could not judge whether three hundred pounds, which to me seemed like a fortune, was much or little, or how it would provide me with fare and expenses, and for how long.

Miss Lincoln shared my excitement at the news. The evening before I left, we celebrated as we had done on the first night, with pipis and rice ('Oh my God I hope not too much!') and the red wine of Keats. And as I was packing my small suitcase, Miss Lincoln brought in a carefully folded pair of grey flannel slacks.

'They will fit you,' she said. 'Take them, for your journey.'

I tried them on. They fitted. I could not tell her that I disliked wearing slacks, that I thought these were ugly with baggy legs, and the grey flannel reminded me too much of our old junior high uniform.

The next day I travelled again through the wilderness of bush-enclosed railway track to Auckland and its wet wintry world and upper-sky light, and as I now had an almost visible 'future', my life took on a new excitement as Frank and I waited for the official announcement of the grant and the cheque for three hundred pounds.

26 *Advice to the Traveller*

I received official notification of my grant but before the cheque was sent the Advisory Committee requested that I be interviewed by one of its members, Miss Louden, a former school headmistress living in Auckland. This was to be the beginning, after my known length of stay in hospital, of a number of investigations of my sanity by people who would try to find out for themselves whether I was incurably ill as the medical diagnosis would imply, or whether (as was later proved during my time in London) there had been an awful mistake even in my first admission to hospital, and from then a continued misinterpretation of my plight. The general opinion of the literary world then is confirmed by the reference in *The New Zealand Encyclopedia* to my 'tragic disordered power' and 'unstable personality', an opinion repeated many times by people unknown to me.

Frank, as usual, tried to cheer me when I learned of the interview.

'It'll be nothing,' he said. 'Just put on the schoolgirl act, being agreeable and polite in front of the headmistress.'

He assured me that Miss Louden was a pleasant, sensible, intelligent person who would realise that, whatever she thought of my 'history', the best move for me was to get away from New Zealand.

A few days later I travelled on the bus to Remuera for my interview with Miss Louden, where, in between drinking tea and eating scones and cakes from yet another fancily tiered plate, I tried to impress with my 'normality', presenting myself as a happy healthy woman. Miss Louden, like most retired women teachers I had heard of, lived in a house packed with furniture and books in rooms with carpets patterned rose and dark red, like cinema carpets; while she herself had the air of being packed with Culture. I spoke in what I hoped was a fearless manner about my trip overseas, whereupon she began to talk of my schooldays and in reply to her questions on topics closed centuries ago — sport, prefects, the sixth form — I listed my long-past activities — captain of the B basketball team, Physical Training shield, House Captain, Proxime Accessit to Dux . . . and so on, playing her chosen game of yesterdays.

It was a pleasant if perspiry afternoon; and I knew that I had succeeded when Frank, through the eternally pruned, fertilised, growing and fruiting literary grapevine of which he appeared to be the Auckland keeper, heard that Miss Louden had judged me to be a 'normal, happy, healthy *girl*'.

The cheque arrived. I gazed unbelievingly at it. I showed it to Frank.

'What shall I do with it?' I asked. I had never had a bank account, for, like so many other facilities, bank accounts were thought to be for 'other people'. In our family only Myrtle had ever had a bank account, a Post Office savings book, with three and sixpence entered one week and two and sixpence withdrawn the next, leaving the magic shilling which was said to keep the account 'open'. When Myrtle died, the shilling and a few pence were returned, and the face of the page stamped *Cancelled, Withdrawn*.

That afternoon, instead of taking his usual rest, Frank went with me and the cheque to the Bank of New South Wales, where he introduced me to the manager. I was a highly recommended client, he said, praising me as a writer.

My next move was to pay seventy-eight pounds for a berth in a six-berth cabin in the *Ruahine* sailing from Wellington to Southampton at the end of July. I then applied for a passport and arranged for a primary vaccination for smallpox. I was on my way overseas!

The advice poured in, the first and most valuable from Jess Whitworth, who had twice travelled to Europe on the savings from her pension and who knew a place in London where I might be able to stay. I visited her and her husband, Ernest, at Northcote and spent the afternoon listening to her disarming accounts of her travels. She had made her first journey when she was seventy, sailing alone while Ernest, who was not interested in physical travel, stayed at home with the stereo record player he had built, and listened to his collection of Schubert and Mozart. Anyone who knew Jess will say that she was a remarkable woman. She had a talented family from her first marriage with Oliver Duff. She had written a vivid account of her childhood as the daughter of a pubkeeper in Central Otago, and her girlhood in Dunedin, in her book *Otago Interval*, which even then was out of print and so unknown to many. Jess had been a music teacher and shared her love of music with her second husband. She was eager, wise, literate, adventurous and soft-hearted, while Ernest, some years younger, was everlastingly devoted to her.

It was a curious chance that six months after Mother's death I was befriended by two women of her generation who perhaps in their late childhood were alike in their fondness for the arts and their possession of an extra store of imagination, yet whose lives were notable for their differences, and for what remained in each in the long struggle for survival. Jess, too, had had the time of many children and many nappies in a household without too much money. Paula or Paul Lincoln had broken away from her family; Mother's marriage had estranged her from her disapproving family. Listening to Jess and her tales of travel, I couldn't help thinking of the lifetime of words that Mother never spoke: I saw them marching in single or double file (as words do) to the tip of her tongue, then being turned away because the time was not right or there was no one to receive them, and even her hastily written poems and letters to the editor and prayers to God could not have released all the furious prisoners crowded in the anterooms of her thoughts. If only she had been able to *speak for herself!*

Jess was full of advice. I should buy one or two metal dishes for cooking, and a small metal cooker to use with solid methylated spirits, so that if I had to stay in a hotel I could save money by making my own tea, boiling eggs, and so on. There was a woman who kept a boardinghouse in Clapham Common, with a row of garden rooms at the back of the house, Jess explained, and there were always rooms vacant for seventeen shillings a week. For my first few nights in London, she recommended that I stay in the hostel of the *Society of Friends* in Euston Square, and that I write to them at once, booking my room. As she travelled only in the European summer, with her cooking utensils, two dresses and a petticoat also worn as a night-dress, two or three pairs of pants, that is, with as little luggage as possible, she wasn't able to advise on winter clothes. She suggested a money belt.

'A money belt?'

'You put your money in it and fasten it around your waist; or make a small bag and tie it around your neck, dropping it down your bosom.'

'Oh.'

Jess always visited Salzburg, staying in a pension 'around the corner from Mozart's birthplace'. Before I left her home that afternoon, she sat at her old walnut-gold piano and played two early pieces by Mozart.

She laughed. 'Early! He composed these when he was six!'

Next, Frank's friends, returned from Spain, also gave advice.

'If you want to make your money last,' they said, 'Ibiza is the place.'

'Ibiza?'

'It's spelt with a "z" but you say it the Spanish way, "th".'

'Oh.'

'You can live on the island of Ibiza for three or four pounds a month.'

Frank reminded me that Greville now lived at Tossa, with a flat in Barcelona, and he would write to her, and they'd meet me at Barcelona and see me on to the boat to Ibiza.

'I suppose Ibiza would be the place to stay, then, as I shan't have much money.'

'See, here it is on the map, just below Majorca and Minorca. Majorca where *Robert Graves* lives.'

'Robert Graves!'

We'd been reading his prose and poetry. Frank's friends told how friends of theirs had visited Majorca and called on Robert Graves! They met Freya Stark, too.

'Freya Stark?'

'The travel writer.'

'Oh.'

Everyone had tales of travel! Everyone talked of what to do, where to go, what to expect, while I listened proud, pleased, and frightened. One evening Una Platts arrived with hilarious stories of sailing through the Suez Canal to London. The Suez Canal. The white slave traffic! Una wore a pleated skirt which she identified as 'terylene'.

'It's new,' she said. 'You never have to iron it. The pleats are *permanent*.' (Oh for a permanently pleated skirt!)

The question of clothes for the journey had begun to occupy me. My images of all factors in the Northern Hemisphere, including weather (the descriptions gleaned from the Anglo-Saxon 'Wanderer' and 'Seafarer'), were extreme, stark and terrifying, and I saw my clothes as at least a first protection against the northern danger.

'All you need,' Frank said (beginning his counsel exactly as my father would have done), 'is Paul's slacks and a blouse. Plus the cardigan you knitted.' During the recent weeks of waiting, like a woman expecting a child, I had begun to knit, making an outsize grey pullover for Frank, and for myself a large fawn cardigan with a hood, the fawn chosen because I was not brave enough to choose a *real* colour. Lately I had been studying the brochures from the shipping company, with the impressive photos of women wearing glittering evening clothes and fashionable sunsuits, with one special photo of a woman in a slinky backless dress getting ready for dinner while a handsome man in a flared jacket fixed her zip; they were laughing, she glancing at him in a romantic way, over her shoulder. Shipboard life was portrayed as a whirlwind of sexual ecstasy, with meeting eyes and hands and the promise of meeting bodies, with all passengers handsome and beautiful and dressed in the highest fashion and during the day so constantly active with games, walks, dining at tables laden with roast turkey, lobsters, trifle, champagne, dancing the moonlight hours away, that one might have wondered if there were enough energy left for the remaining night's activities. I could scarcely believe that I was to be among these passengers, even perhaps wearing a backless evening dress while someone, laughing, fixed my zip.

My fantasies perished as soon as they were born. I· was to live the Spartan life. Clothes did not matter.

Yet, seeing my three hundred pounds fast diminishing, I collected a suitcase of my fairly new clothes, and taking the ferry to town, sitting among all the morning shoppers in their white gloves and hats, for everyone in those days 'dressed' to go to town, I hawked my clothes in the second-hand shops where I quickly found that my pleas of 'but they're almost brand-new' brought the same response, 'They're worth almost nothing.' I could feel the growing misery and panic of being face to face with the 'real' world, where nobody cared, where people were hard-faced — mercenary — city people; and I couldn't even console myself by thinking it doesn't matter, because it did matter, I had to supplement my money. I wanted to give my radiogram and records to Frank, but he insisted that I sell it; yet one more hard-faced shopkeeper gave me ten pounds, and I gave the records to my sister. Then, miraculously, an 'anonymous donor', whom I guessed correctly to be Charles Brasch, sent fifty pounds to Frank 'for Janet to buy some clothes for her journey'. Surprisingly, I was now the Spartan, insisting that fifty pounds was too precious to waste on 'mere clothes'. All the same, I again took the ferry to Auckland, where I hoped to sell my new *Mademoiselle Modes* olive-green coat. Surely, I thought, remembering the struggle to save the ten pounds, and the pleasure of buying the coat, surely it is worth something.

'Two shillings, no more,' the shop assistant said.

I decided to keep it rather than see it thrown among a heap of shiny baggy cast-off clothes in the dingy sweat-and-mothball-smelling shop.

Then, wanting to make my own plans for my journey, I bought an old *Fodor's Guide To Europe*, which I took back to the hut without showing it to Frank, who might have thought me extravagant to buy it. As I read the guide I found myself becoming more dazed, confused, excited and alarmed. Was travelling overseas really like this? The guide was packed with information all presented as important, much of it in lists of what to buy and where to buy it, details of the best bargains in leather, silk, woollen goods, furs, china, jewellery, with the names of the shops, the cities, the countries where the goods were held, the assumption being that every traveller was a merchant in search of prized bargains. The guide also contained lists of sights to see, museums, galleries, cathedrals; tours to take; clothes to pack for the tours; and finally, *Common Words and Phrases in Many Languages* (which I quickly dealt with by tearing out the pages and pasting them on a cardboard folder to consult during my journey).

I studied the advice on clothing. The traveller to wintry Europe, the books stressed, should wear a heavy coat with a warm removable lining that would double as a dressing-gown.

I promptly bought four yards of cheap molleton cloth, striped blue-grey, and tried without success to sew a coat lining: the result bunched and would not 'hang' and parts of it drooped beneath my coat. I also bought from the Army Surplus store a green canvas haversack, an army cooking pan with a folding handle, and three small green canvas bags, like a child's marble bags, for use as money bags. Frank had said that a haversack was better than a suitcase. His friends had reminded me that if you travelled by sea you always took a *cabin trunk*. How deprived was I, I wondered, not having a cabin trunk?

My visits to my sister's at Northcote also resulted in gleanings of advice. When my sister's English friend heard that I was planning to stay at Clapham Common, she stared at me in horror.

'Clapham? Surely not! I wouldn't recommend it. It's terribly *urban*, so *urban*,' with her feelings centred on the word *urban*. I wondered if perhaps I had mistaken the meaning of urban, if it now meant more than 'of the city'.

'What do you mean, "urban"?'

'You know, *urban*. Factories and so on.'

From that moment I had my image of where I would be staying in London. I saw a street without people, with a succession of factories, huge buildings like aerodromes, each with a small grey door opening on to the street. My garden room would be set between two factories, down a narrow alley with another small door leading to a square of concrete, with no sign of a real garden, the name having been given only in a burst of wishful dreaming. I was completely alone in the street of factories where the machines worked noisily day and night without the attendance of people. I thought of Jess Whitworth's description of her 'tackling' a big city, how she first found her place to stay, then left her luggage and set out to 'find her bearings', noting the names and streets and the different shops where she would buy her provisions, then after her preliminary exploration, returning home to 'gather steam' (many of her metaphors were nautical) for venturing further afield. I tried to picture myself walking miles and miles with no sign of people or shops, then returning along that narrow alley to my 'Garden Room'. During those weeks before my journey, my mind swarmed with so many foreboding images of the Northern Hemisphere that I wonder, in retrospect, if I was as clear-headed as I thought myself to be, and I can partly explain when I remember that I was again surrounded by people who were planning my future.

I was again living the submissive, passive role which in hospital had been forced upon me but which my shy nature had accommodated with ease: at its best it is the role of the queen bee surrounded by her attendants; at its worst it is that of the victim without power or possession; and in both cases there is no ownership of one's self, for all have a stake in the planned future.

My passport arrived. I had my ticket (with return travel guaranteed by the anonymous donor of the fifty pounds for clothes), and I'd booked my sleeping berth on the night express to Wellington.

Then I became ill, very ill, with the effects of the smallpox vaccination. I felt as if I were dying. I lay only half conscious in the hut while Frank spoon-fed me with *Farex* mixed with milk, the kind of food given to babies and kittens separated early from their mother. And just when I was recovering from the vaccination I was stricken with the influenza, called the '1918 flu', that spread over Auckland that year. My recovery was slow as I was now dreading the prospect of travelling anywhere. Frank, ever kind and patient, tried to cheer me as one would cheer a sick child, bringing items to distract and please — a glass globe enclosing a snowstorm, a Japanese paper flower that opened in water. He hung Chinese wind chimes at the open door of the hut, where they played a tinkling tune as the breeze passed through the window and out into the space of garden by the pawpaw tree.

Neither Frank nor I could disguise our feeling of gloom as if it were the end of a century or the extinction of a race that had survived over millions of years; there was an exaggeration of time as if like a creature deprived of its shell, it quivered, being touched or even glanced at; it was like the silkworm cut away from its mass of silk.

Our friends Karl and Kay had gone from Auckland. We missed them greatly and looked forward eagerly to their letters from Armidale. Maurice Duggan was despondent, not working. Frank took me one day to see Maurice and Barbara and the custard apple tree and we sat in a largely airy room listening to Victoria Los Angeles; and copies of the *Paris Review* lay on a small table. *The Paris Review*. I looked at Maurice (described by Frank as 'the suffering romantic') and Barbara and it seemed to me that they were clever and literary and their subtle colours would have delighted the art lecturer at training college. I was still overendowed with the capacity to gape with wonder, to marvel at everything and everyone, and the world.

Fragments of tasks remained: Albion Wright of the Pegasus Press disliking my title, *Talk of Treasure*, suggested I choose another. I thought of *Within Sound of the Sea* but he said no, there had recently been a book *Within Sound of the Bell* (by a school teacher). What about *When Owls Do Cry?* I said. No, *Owls Do Cry*, he said.

In the evenings now I sat listening to the latest topic of conversation. 'Janet is going to Ibiza to live until her money runs out . . .'. 'Janet plans to go to London first, then take the train south . . . she will probably stay overnight in Paris . . . then to Barcelona . . . then take the boat to the Balearic Islands . . . Janet is . . . Janet will be . . . Janet has . . .'

Beneath my gloom was a rising sense of adventure. I knew that Frank's gloom concealed a feeling of relief that he would be free to continue more peacefully with his writing. I could not even remember how it had been decided that I would leave the country; I knew only that there was no way back, that if my path did lead back there would be no second chance for my survival, that it was best for me to escape from a country where, since my student days, a difference which was only myself, and even my ambition to write, had been looked on as evidence of abnormality.

But — oh, I was daunted by the length and unfamiliarity of the path forward, the sea journey across the immense Pacific, across the English Channel, the night in Paris, travelling through France, Spain, across the Mediterranean! Why? I was sustained then, as ever, by the prospect of seeing through 'Shelley's eyes' the landscape and

> *The blue Mediterranean, where he lay,*
> *Lulled by the coil of his crystalline streams.*

27   The Traveller

Like a mythical character about to embark on a long voyage, I had first to undergo a test, a refining process supervised by my family and lasting four days until my ship sailed. I was to stay with Aunty Polly and Uncle Vere in Petone while my father, who usually travelled north at this time of year for rugby matches, would also be in Wellington at Aunty Polly's. Mother's two sisters, Elsie and Joy, hoped to see me in Wellington. After a long train-sick journey from Auckland I dreaded the polishing process that is a result of the natural friction within families.

At Petone Aunty Polly showed me to my bed, a low canvas camp stretcher propped just inside the door of the sitting room, low enough to receive the icy blast from beneath the back door.

'Your father, of course, will have the bed in the spare room.'

'Oh, of course.'

She looked sternly at me. 'I can't understand why you're leaving your father to go all that way overseas. Your mother has just died, and your place is at home looking after your father.'

I had no answer to that. We were meeting Dad the next morning at the ferry wharf.

Then Aunty Polly turned her attention to my clothes. (Aunty Polly the clever dressmaker who even now had her small workroom spread with 'difficult' sewing — men's coats, trousers, suits and women's dresses with fancy sleeves and bodices.)

'What on earth are you wearing that horrible cardigan for? It's far too big and it's an awful colour, it's just no colour at all. You look a piece of earth or something, wearing it. And you can see your whole shape through your skirt!'

'I knitted this cardigan,' I said proudly. 'And the colour goes with everything.'

'It's drab.'

Once Aunty Polly had made her criticism she became kinder. 'So you've had the 'flu. Well you don't want to catch cold.'

That evening when Uncle Vere, tall, gentle with cowlike brown eyes, came home from the motor works Aunty Polly submitted him, in his turn, to her judgment of his appearance, 'Just look at your scarf, it shouldn't be that way. What have you done to your coat, the way it hangs?'

Dressmaker to the world! Like an artist who is constantly framing the view, isolating and freezing objects in order to transform them with imagination.

When Uncle Vere had been transformed to Aunty Polly's liking, there was ordinary conversation once again, even kindness and laughter.

Next morning Aunty Polly drove me in her frog-green car to meet Dad at the ferry, and when I saw him coming down the gangway, with his greying hair even greyer in the wintry light of sky and sea, and his forlorn look stemming from an inner dishevelment of grief (though he was outwardly smart with his polished shoes and spic and span best suit), I burst into tears and went towards him. I hadn't seen him since Mother's death. His lip, pouting in infant shape, trembled, and we embraced each other and cried. Dad, unlike Aunty Polly, was proud of my grant and my journey overseas, and his sense of pride, when aroused, could always quell other more painful feelings.

'So you're going home,' he said.

I was startled. I had never heard him call the Northern Hemisphere *home*; he had usually laughed at people who still talked of the United Kingdom as *Home*; I had heard him say scornfully, 'Home, my foot. Here's home right here. Or I'll go hopping sideways to Puketeraki.'

During my stay I heard him repeat several times, 'Janet's going home, you know.' I found myself acquiring a prestige which almost covered my identity as the 'mad niece'. I was now the 'niece who is going overseas, *home*'.

I realised suddenly that my father's use of the word 'home' was in defer-ence to Aunty Polly and Uncle Vere and the other relations, for it was *their* language which he, with an intuitive courtesy or a dislike of appearing different, had adopted. He also used his knife and fork in a different way, Aunty Polly's way. And he didn't fart once. Aunty Polly and Uncle Vere, as I have said, were thought of as being 'in society', a nebulous fluctuating area bordered by a few mayors and councillors and other acknowledged 'important' people. 'He's someone, you know,' Aunty Polly used to say. I never heard her say of a person, 'He's no one', but she did imply that not everybody was somebody.

Mother's sisters Elsie and Joy took me to morning tea at Kirkcaldies. They, too, were critical of my clothes and of the fact that I had not 'met my fate', that is, married, but their kind of criticism was without sharpness or bitterness. They were beautiful women who melted into laughter as they reminisced about Kirkcaldies as it had been in their youth. They were gentle, kindly, concerned, Aunty Joy's brown eyes showing flashes of appre-hension and startle like the look in a wild creature's eyes, and because I did not know her well, I could not guess at the origin of that glance.

Both, insisting that I would need a heavier coat for the northern winter, went 'halves' in buying me a warm brown coat.

'Now you look smarter,' they said.

And even Aunty Polly approved of my new coat.

'At least it covers up that awful jacket.'

I forgave her; it is a responsibility being a dressmaker to the world.

The *Ruahine* came into port. It was the evening of my departure. Aunty Polly, Uncle Vere and Dad saw me on to the ship, helped me find the six-berth cabin down several layers from the main deck, then, almost as if they were afraid to be captured, as if the ship were a prison, they went ashore on to the wharf.

'We won't be staying to see her go out.'

Dad spoke proudly of the ship as he used to speak of the train engine, calling it 'she' and 'her'. He used to call the rivers 'she' also, looking at them with a weatherwise eye and warning, 'She's coming down dirty . . .'

I stood on deck among a crowd of passengers, all throwing streamers that were caught by the watchers on the wharf, for in those days travelling by ship was a momentous occasion. There was a brass band playing old tunes, Maori songs and a few military marches. I stayed on deck to catch one more glimpse of Aunty Polly, looking fraiily neat in her blue coat, Uncle Vere, tall beside her, and Dad, huddled against the wind, in the half-shelter of the wharf shed, then with a final wave, and clutching the five-pound note that Aunty Polly had pressed into my hand with a whispered

'Something from Uncle Vere and myself', I went towards the stairs, just as the band was playing 'Now is the Hour', and the music reached down like a long spoon inside me and stirred and stirred.

I came to my six-berth cabin, with my lower berth by the door. Accepting the advice of those who knew better than I, I had brought with me a small oval bottle of lavender smelling salts and a small tin of water biscuits and tube of *Kwells* seasick preventative. I put these in a locker drawer; rather disdainfully, for I knew I would not need them. I felt the throbbing of the engines and the slow movement of the ship as it sailed out of Wellington Harbour.

'It's good,' I thought, all fears of seasickness vanishing. 'My first ocean voyage and it's running smoothly.'

I went up on deck. It was too soon for the appearance of the passengers dancing and wearing evening dress, but somewhere there was music playing, and the sound of talking and laughter.

The lights of Wellington now shone in the distance. I leaned over the deck rail and I felt like weeping with fear and delight. Then suddenly the motion of the ship changed to a steeper rise and fall and rolling from side to side: we were on the open sea. My voyage had begun.

VOLUME THREE

The Envoy
from Mirror City

This third volume
is dedicated to my friends and family,
whom I've mentioned, and in particular to
Professor Robert Hugh Cawley and his colleagues.

CONTENTS

Part One   Triple Witness

Part Two   At Home in the City

PART ONE

Triple Witness

1 Earthless, the Sailing

Far from the New Zealand coast the *Ruahine* pitched and rolled through the wintry July seas.

The six-berth inside cabin had none of the spaciousness pictured in the tourist brochures: there was scarcely room to move, while only the privileged faces of the women in the top end bunks could receive the air (warm, stale) churned in by the cream-coloured 'blower' or ventilator angled from the ceiling. Isolated from sky, earth, light in a rich element of time, I lay on my lower bunk by the cabin door and listened to the excited voices of my fellow-passengers — two office girls from Hamilton making their first visit overseas; a dark-haired small woman from Australia who had been 'around the world' several times and was eager to display photographs taken on her travels; a schoolteacher returning to the Midlands after a year's visit on exchange to New Zealand; a quiet middle-aged woman, the daughter of a famous Norwegian writer, and herself a writer, returning home to Norway. In the sickeningly warm, throbbing cabin where even the walls seemed to surge and sway, in the claustrophobic atmosphere of bodies stacked as if on shelves, of the odours and shadows of the draped newly washed or dry underwear and stockings, limp disembodied legs over every railing, in the swarm of words circling a frantic excitement of anticipation and anxiety, my head whirled while my stomach heaved with every roll and pitch and plunge of the *Ruahine*. The discomfort could be eased neither by the Kwells tablets recommended by Jess Whitworth, a seasoned traveller and friend of Frank Sargeson, nor by the lavender-perfumed, lavender-ribboned smelling salts in their heart-shaped cut-glass bottle. Unable to eat meals, I ate water biscuits that Jess had given me with the assurance that I would come to look on them as my 'best friends'.

After three days of continuing seasickness and a return of a recent attack of 'flu, I was taken to the ship's hospital where, in a state of great weakness familiar to those who ever have suffered from motion sickness I lay almost helpless for nearly two weeks until as the ship began to slow down preparing to enter the Panama Canal, I was able to sit in a chair and watch the theatre of the Panamanian jungle with its basking crocodiles; the gaudy parrots flitting among the trees that leaned, burdened with blossoming vines, to touch the water; to the accompaniment of the American guide announcing the dollar worth of everything within sight. By the time the ship reached Curaçao, and the engines and the movement ceased as we anchored for the day in Willemstad, my sickness had gone, and with the ship unmoving except for a gentle swaying, I was able to eat the buffet lunch, and to go ashore at Willemstad, my first landfall in a foreign country. How clearly I understood the travellers' custom at the end of a long voyage of stopping to kiss the earth! In Willemstad however, the immediate earth was concrete, and the smell was not of fresh grass but of oil from the refinery, yet the light was new, otherworldly above and upon the dull reds, browns, cream of the buildings, and the foliage glittered paintbox green with a poisonous brightness. I wandered alone through the streets of Willemstad. I sat in the Museum grounds watching unfamiliar lizards basking on unfamiliar stones, and birds that I'd never seen before or heard singing, flocking in the trees. Then I walked by the river and, noting the empty bottles and tins, I was aware of the 'other country' comparison — were not our rivers pure and swift, not sluggish and polluted? And the people walking by the river, how poor they seemed to be, and sickly, unlike the robust New Zealanders! A small travelling zoo had set up its Sunday entertainment on a plot of waste land: cramped cages housing a miserable fur-patched bear and a stinking brown-yellow lion, each confirming my opinion, acquired in New Zealand, that people 'overseas' had little compassion for animals, also that overseas was poor, not as civilised as New Zealand. In my first foreign country I still wore the old clothes of prejudice. I'd also seen for the first time a group of people whose skin was not shades of brown or yellow but dusky black. At school I had been taught that Maori and Pakeha had equal opportunities and I believed what I had been taught. I had also learned that Chinese people excelled in gardening and fruit-growing, the Greeks were excellent fishermen, while the Maoris were the best drivers of heavy vehicles.

'Maoris are very mechanically minded,' a lecturer at Training College had told us, a class of Pakehas. Now, faced with Afro-Americans and Indians I dismissed from my mind the comparison with teams of slaves. I said 'Hello', heartily, to show my lack of prejudice but I became alarmed when my greeting was followed by an attempt at conversation, for I had nothing to say. And here I was, travelling overseas to 'broaden my experience' and already undergoing the change forced on every new traveller and accomplished by examining not the place of arrival but the place of departure. The years of cowboy films, of white-horsed fairhaired 'goodies', and dark-skinned dark-horsed and hatted 'baddies', the Mexican bandits and rustlers against the honest hardworking American ranchers, the American Indians intent on destruction and massacre while the cowboys and cavalry sought 'peace and a fair deal for all', these films seen in childhood, all goodie-baddie drama including detective drama, while letting reason function, had stored feelings that lay undisturbed, perhaps unknown and unsuspected, but ready to overcome the guardian reason to try to direct the unwary traveller in the new land.

Before I returned over the Willemstad pontoon bridge to the *Ruahine* I performed a ritual that also had its origin in what I had heard or read or thought in New Zealand where, it seemed, everyone had been singing

> *Drinking rum and Coca-Cola*
> *Waiting for the Yankee dollar . . .*

The American guide through the Panama Canal had used the word 'dollar' in almost every sentence: here, in Willemstad, advertisements for Coca-Cola were everywhere. I completed my first visit to a foreign land by drinking my first bottle of Coca-Cola with as much reverence as if I were sipping wine in church. One needs to be reminded that in the late 1950s Coca-Cola had an aura of magic, of promise, as a symbol to many outside the United States of America of all that was essentially American, generous, good, dollar-flavoured, new-world, bathed in the glow of a country's morning that was not yet tarnished by the scrutiny of daylight.

For the final week of my journey, still unable to visit the dining room once the ship had begun to sail, I took my bedding on deck and slept in the cool air beneath the sky returning only when the early morning deck-scrubbers began sloshing their buckets of water. Much had happened on board during my stay in the hospital: the mixture of passengers had swirled to form new compounds: the comics, the leaders, the gossip targets, the wonderful and the beautiful, like viruses, had been isolated, identified and studied. The enterprising Pacific and now the Atlantic were not so busy with their own drifting of objects on distant shores that they had not been able to cast upon the decks of the *Ruahine* these special passengers that rise to the surface on every long voyage. Much talked about and admired in our cabin was the beautiful brilliant blonde scholarship winner on her way to Oxford; she was envied, too, for her many escorts, her dinners at the captain's table, her dances with the ship's doctor, while the others, like the 'others' on land or sea, had to be content with partners of lesser glory. There was also the young pianist who surrounded by admirers, practised confidently in the lounge. Oh how I longed to be admired for any accomplishments I might have! Oh how I longed for everyone to know that I was travelling overseas on a literary grant! How could everyone appear to be so self-assured? And there were the two office girls with their store of purchases from Panama and Willemstad (everyone except the Norwegian writer and I had bought silk kimonos, pyjamas, scarves, glittering purses), why they talked and behaved as if they owned the world and as soon as they set foot in Great Britain the ownership papers would be handed to them at a special ceremony. Perhaps the Australian woman with her photographs and her tales of travel was not as confident as she appeared for the more she talked, the more I began to compare her with a character who has been set in motion and is unable to stop, for she had been to and fro, to and fro, from north to south and east to west and there was occasionally panic in her eyes when someone asked where she planned to live 'finally' 'in the end', for, obviously, she couldn't travel for ever . . . or could she? Sometimes she appeared to feel that she had no choice, it was too late to turn back, there was now no 'back' to turn to. I wondered, briefly, what if I became like her, a doomed traveller with no feeling of home?

And as I watched and listened I comforted myself by trying to feel superior as I said to myself, 'Little do they know that I'm recording everything in my mind, that I can see through them, beneath their masks, right to the bottom of their heart, for if I'm to be and stay a writer I must follow all the signs in everything they say and do, and in the silence and inactivity, reading their faces and the faces and the eyes that are mapped with their private isobars and isotherms above the fertile lands, the swamps secret with marsh birds, the remote mountains sharp with rock formations, softened with snow. I must forever watch and listen.'

That voyage has not stayed in my mind in complete detail. I remember only the nightmare and the envious longings. I remember the day in Willemstad, the groupings of the passengers, their excitement and anticipation. I remember the serious doctor who advised me never again to travel by sea. I remember the red-faced captain with gold braid encircling him or seeming to as if it were markings on a teapot — these details stay like small ships tossed on my own waves of seasickness where as those who have suffered this will know, the abiding dream is for the ship to stop moving, for the sick passenger to be put ashore at some island, any island, any land that happens by as if land ever happened by in search of a lone castaway. In the past I had practised endurance. During the voyage I had not been prepared, I was unable to organise my defence against the awful diminishing of my human power where every move was a nauseating effort and the seconds, the minutes, the hours, the days became a mountain of oppressive time. The reward of surviving the crossing of the Pacific became the vision of the gradual melting of the terrible mountain until the final handful of rock and earth was buried by the looming Destination.

After thirty-two days at sea, on the day after my thirty-second birthday, the *Ruahine* berthed at Southampton where the passengers boarded the waiting train to Waterloo Station, London.

2 · The Gentleman

Waterloo Station. I am standing with my two suitcases, my green haversack containing my typewriter, and I'm holding fast to my *Traveller's Joy* handbag as I propel my luggage towards the street and the row of taxis. Repeating almost dutifully to myself, 'so this is London', I watch as the other passengers are swept away by welcoming groups of friends and relatives. It's raining and grey and the black taxis are like hearses. With a sense of sweet satisfaction in knowing that soon I shall be safe in a room in the Friends' Hostel, and able to claim at last a bed on earth, I hail a taxi (as I have seen it done on films) and say boldly, 'The Friends' Hostel in Euston Road, please.'

The taxi sways sickeningly up and down rain-splashed streets to Euston Road and the Society of Friends' Hostel. And here I stand, my luggage on the footpath beside me, outside the building that will be my home for at least a week. Overtaken by the joy of having arrived at last, I herd my luggage closer to me as I climb the steps to the front door and press the bell. Footsteps. The door opens.

'I'm Janet Frame from New Zealand,' I say quickly to the grey-haired woman. 'I wrote to you, reserving a room for a week.'

The woman frowned. 'Your name again?'

'Janet Frame, from New Zealand.' I emphasise *New Zealand*.

'Will you wait one moment, please.'

The woman studies a book at the reception desk and returns, frowning more deeply.

'There's been a mistake. We have received no letter from a Janet Frame in New Zealand. We are fully booked. It's the end of August, you know.'

'Oh yes.' I think, 'Of course I know, all those books with descriptions of Bank Holidays. "August for the people and their favourite islands."'

The woman repeats, 'I'm sorry. There are no vacancies. Your letter did not reach us.'

Disbelieving, fighting off panic, I play what I think must be my winning card.

'I've a friend in New Zealand who *always* stays with you. Jess Whitworth.' (Surely she remembers Jess Whitworth!)

'I'm sorry, Miss Frame. I don't recall her. And we are fully booked. Perhaps next week . . .'

I'm in tears now.

'But next week's too late. I'm *all the way from New Zealand*. I'm just off the boat.'

The woman smiles patiently.

'We have guests coming from all over the world. Every day.'

'But I did write to you. And I'm just off the boat. I've never been to London before,' I add bleakly. 'I've never been to London before, and I don't know where to stay.'

I can still see myself surrounded by my remnants of New Zealand — the two old suitcases, the green canvas haversack that Frank Sargeson had insisted I would need because thirty years earlier he had carried a haversack on his walking tour of Europe, the leather Traveller's Joy handbag costing an enormous ten pounds that had been the gift from the Gordon Family. As I stood uncertainly at the door of the hostel, I remembered how Frank and I had pored over his old yellowed copies of the *New Statesman*, reading the advertisement on the back page — Rooms to Let: St John's Wood, Swiss Cottage, Hampstead Heath, Earls Court — names then unknown, romantically enticing, but now seeming like stark cliff faces without hand or foothold, inhospitably plunging me into the dark unknown.

'You have no friends in London?' the woman asked.

'No,' I quavered.

'There's the YWCA Hostel not far from here. I'll phone and see if they have a room.'

Minutes later she returned with the welcome news that there was a 'share room' vacant for two nights.

The woman offered to ring for a taxi.

'Please. And thank you.'

Standing with my luggage on the grimy London steps I felt fleetingly at the back of my mind the perennial drama of the Arrival and its place in myth and fiction, and I again experienced the thrilling sense of being myself excavated as reality, the ore of the polished fiction. The journey, the arrival, the surprises and problems of arrival. And even in my first experience in London there'd been also the reminder of the *Letter* in fiction — the missing letter, the discovered letter, the letter of such portent that lives are lost and destinies changed as in Macbeth's 'They met me in the day of success; and I have learned by the perfectest report, they have more in them than mortal knowledge . . .' and the role of the bearer of the letter, of the successful or failed messenger. For a moment the loss of the letter I had written seemed to be unimportant beside the fictional gift of the loss, as if within every event lay a reflection reached only through the imagination and its various servant languages, as if, like the shadows in Plato's cave, our lives and the world contain mirror cities revealed to us by our imagination, the Envoy.

In spite of fictional possibilities and enthusiasms, that first day in London was dreary and uncomfortable. Already, in late August, London was drawing down the blinds for a darkening winter. The YWCA where I found a room for two nights reminded me of a mental hospital without the noise, without the constant jingling of keys and the attempt to control the guests, although there were efforts at control in the sheet of rules pinned inside the doors of the bedrooms and bathrooms and lavatories that were in rows, institutional in appearance and smell. The baths were cavernous, the floors were set with chilling black and white tiles.

Please leave the bath as you would wish others to find it. A suitable hostel translation of the Golden Rule, sensibly moral and assuming altruism and the practice of Christian principles. The office downstairs held a cage where luggage could be left. A stern-faced woman supervised the entrance and exit of guests and distributed mail as if the letters were holy tablets, and, aware of the power of letters, I know they may have been.

Although I found the YWCA intimidating with its continued presence of authority, I observed that the guests were happy, friendly; there was an atmosphere of excitement as arrivals, departures, excursions were discussed. The cafeteria food was cheap and plentiful and I quickly became one of the group of excited 'strangers to London'. I shared my room with a woman from Singapore who, as innocent as I, dreaming of visiting Piccadilly Circus, travelled there by Underground and not only discovered the truth of Piccadilly Circus (that it was not, as we believed, a real circus) but spent the day trapped in the Underground.

I marvelled at my freedom, especially as the Victorian atmosphere and appearance of many of the London buildings had released a fountain (of fear) from my recent past. My drenching was temporary: again the contemplation of the parallel, the mirror dream, sustained me, proofed me against the nightmare of the past.

On my first evening I telephoned the address in Clapham Common where Jess Whitworth had stayed in the Garden Room. In spite of disillusionment with the reality of romantic names, I still hoped for a pleasant stay in a *Garden Room* that would be as I dreamed, and when a Patrick Reilly, one of the tenants of the main house, explained that he was in charge while the owners were in Scotland, and that a Garden Room was vacant for seventeen and six a week and that I could move in any time, I forgot the many miseries of my arrival in London and began to look forward to a measure of paradise.

I could move in the next day, Patrick Reilly suggested. He'd have a day off work and could meet me and see me settled in the room. How kind of him, I thought.

The down-under accent, he said, had proved I was a genuine enquirer.

My departure from the YWCA was made through the ritual of censure because I had undertaken to stay two nights.

'Rooms are hard to get at this time of year. Refunds are not usual,' the warden said.

I accepted the necessary underlining of my imperfect behaviour and lack of forethought. I apologised. I understood how institutions thrive on accuracy of moral edicts and on judgments which must be made as plain as the credit and debit of those who use the institutions.

The next afternoon I arrived by taxi at Cedars Road, Clapham Common North Side, to find Patrick Reilly waiting to escort me to my Garden Room.

And here was Mr Reilly carrying my luggage through the side gate to Garden Room Number Three. There were four rooms set in a row against a tall brick boundary wall, facing towards the back garden of the main house. They appeared to be shacks rather than rooms, with their floors set directly upon the earth with no damp course between.

'I hope you won't be in this room for the winter,' Patrick Reilly said. 'A woman died of pneumonia here last winter.'

He pointed to the end room.

'There's a Russian ballet dancer there now. And we had a European Prince last year.'

Patrick Reilly was talkative with a pleasant Irish accent. He was sturdily built, not tall, with greying hair, a large smooth pale face and brown well-spring eyes. His occasionally tightly pursed lips gave me a sign of a certain restriction of inward horizons: setting the limits, as it were. His step was agile and sure. He thrust the key into the lock of Number Three and with some urging and pushing he opened the door into a small damp-smelling room containing a narrow bed with some bedding, a curtained wardrobe, a chair, and on the rush-mat-covered floor a single electric plate connected to an electric meter, fed with shillings, just inside the door. There was one small square window by the door and one light suspended from the ceiling. A pile of assorted dishes and pots and pans stood on a box beside the electric ring.

'I need a place for my typewriter,' I said.

'I'll fetch a table from the cellar. It's full of old furniture and junk. And I'll show you the bathroom and the geyser in the main house. Like a cup of tea?'

And so I then inspected the cramped bathroom and tried to absorb Patrick Reilly's instructions on the working of the geyser that heated the bathwater. He warned me to be careful, or the geyser might explode.

Someone had been killed, he said, a year or two earlier. And the house was almost wrecked.

'They were injured, anyway,' he corrected. 'It happened before my time.'

Patrick Reilly was beginning to acquire mythical attributes as The Greeter who was also The Warner: even during this first meeting he began to list the lurking dangers of Cedars Road, Clapham Common North Side. I supposed that he would deal later with London and the World.

He took me to his room next to the bathroom in the main house and I sat silently watching while he filled a kettle from the tap on the landing and lighting a gas ring on the table, boiled the water for a cup of tea. I knew I was seeing for the first time the ritual of a way of living that was new to me, where people lived alone in one room of a large house of many rooms, each self-contained except for the shared bathroom and lavatory and the water tap above the basin on the landing where Patrick had filled the kettle for our tea. Already I had noticed two men with buckets fetching their supply of water either for washing or for drinking.

'Women are not popular with landladies,' Patrick explained. 'They leave hair in the bathroom and are always washing clothes.'

He set two cups and saucers at one end of the large oilcloth-covered table, and lifting a full bottle of milk from a basin of water and grasping the bottle at both ends he gently rocked the milk to and fro, then lay it sideways on the table beside the cups and saucers.

'Bluetop. Jersey Island milk. I buy the best,' he said. 'That's how you spread the cream.'

He made the tea.

'I wait five minutes, no more, no less for the infusion.'

He said 'infusion' in self-admiring way, like a surgeon who has diagnosed and will operate correctly.

He then probed apart the wrapping from a tube of biscuits, holding them for me to examine before he tipped three or four on to a plate.

'Digestive. Chocolate digestive. The dark kind.'

The tea was now brewed. I bit into my chocolate digestive and began to drink my tea.

'It's Tetley's Tips,' Patrick Reilly said. 'And the biscuits are Peek Frean.' Peek Frean.

He spoke in a satisfied way as if he had achieved another point on the path to perfection.

I repeated the name. 'Peek Frean.' It fascinated me. I listened, marvelling, to Patrick Reilly's accent and the occasional Irish idiom that I knew from the Irish stereotype and from the Irish playwrights but had never heard spoken.

'I'm after going shopping,' he said. He appeared to be equally fascinated by my New Zealand accent. There was a bond between us, he said. Neither of us was English. He spoke with a dislike of English. And as a colonial, he said, I would understand what the English had done to Ireland.

'They eat our pork and our butter and race our horses and we come here for jobs.'

The Republic of Ireland, he said, was God's Own Country and it was full of poverty. I thought, surprised, 'But isn't New Zealand God's Own Country?' It hadn't occurred to me that other countries, perhaps every country made this claim. In New Zealand, particularly among people who could see clearly, there had been jokes about our claim to be God's Own Country, and although I, too, had mocked the claim, I believed it since my childhood when I recited fervently the poetry of William Pember Reeves:

> God girt her about with the surges
> And winds of the masterless deep,
> Whose tumult uprouses and urges
> Quick billows to sparkle and leap . . .
>
> Her never the fever-mist shrouding,
> Nor drought of the desert may blight . . .

So Ireland was God's Own Country, I said to myself, grasping this new fact of my overseas experience.

We finished our tea.

'If there's anything you want help with, just ask me,' Patrick Reilly said. 'You may call me Patrick.'

'Patrick. I'm Janet.'

He was impressed when I told him I was in England on a 'literary grant'.

'But I'm really on my way to the Balearic Islands . . . as soon as I can make arrangements here.'

'You're not going alone?'

'Oh yes.'

He frowned.

'You'll be in danger,' he warned. 'Foreign places are all dangerous. Even more than London.'

He was a member of the Catholic committee, he said, trying to rescue young Irish girls from prostitution. In his work as a bus driver he saw many such girls.

'They get into trouble,' he said sharply. 'I direct them to the Irish Hostels.'

He paused.

'And I'll look after you, Janet, while you're in London. But you mustn't go to Europe on your own. By the way, are you fancy free?'

'What an old-fashioned expression,' I thought. One that might have belonged to my mother's girlhood and not to Patrick Reilly who had said his age was forty-four.

'Oh yes, I'm fancy free.'

'Good. And think again about going abroad.'

'I must go,' I said.

'Writing isn't a very good occupation,' Patrick said.

'I once trained as a school teacher.'

'A school teacher! Now that's the sort of work you should be doing.'

He said excitedly that his sister was a school teacher in Ireland while his cousin was Archbishop of a northern town. Also, the woman who had once been his sweetheart had been a school teacher.

'M. stole her from me,' Patrick said. M. was an Irish correspondent much in the news in the late 1950s.

A person's belief, with its implication of possession and ownership, that others could be 'stolen' from him, interested me as it had in New Zealand when Paula Lincoln accused a neighbour of 'stealing' her friends. Yet such facts of ownership are written into the legal description of 'enticement' where 'enticement' is a misdemeanor against property, the property here being a person 'owned' by another. Patrick did not explain particulars of the robbery that had left him without a fiancé.

As I was leaving the bedsitter he again warned me.

'Watch out for the blacks in London. They're everywhere. They're stealing all the work. Clapham's full of them.'

He drew his lips back from his gums and bared his teeth in an apparently unconscious gesture. I was repelled. I wanted to love the World and everyone in it ('the fullness thereof, the World and they that dwell therein . . .').

Feeling insulted on behalf of those referred to as 'black', I said carefully, 'You mean the people from the West Indies and Africa?'

'Yes, the blacks.'

'I don't think people should be referred to by the colour of their skin,' I said anxiously.

'They're lower than us. They're the blacks,' he said almost viciously.

I let the new unpleasantness wash over me. He was ignorant, I decided. He didn't know and he didn't understand. Also, he was afraid. Nothing would make him change his mind while he was afraid.

'See you tomorrow,' he called as I went down the stairs.

'Yes,' I said, echoing, 'see you tomorrow,' realising that for weeks I had been in a world where no one said, 'See you tomorrow.'

I was grateful to Patrick Reilly. He was a natural helper. He was also dependable, self-satisfied, bigoted, lonely, religious, with an endearing Irish accent. In spite of his largely disqualifying prejudice he was what my mother would have called 'a gentleman'. He was my first friend in London.

3   Keats and the Storytellers of Battersea

The reader may laugh at what I, in all my naivety, imagined I would find when I boarded the bus number 137 to *Crystal Palace*. During those early weeks in keenest anticipation, I made other long bus journeys to places with haunting names — Ponders End, High Wycombe, Mortlake, Shepherds Bush, Swiss Cottage, each time arriving at a cluster of dreary-looking buildings set in a waste of concrete and brick and full of people who appeared to be pale, worried and smaller in build than most New Zealanders.

'The Picts and the Scots,' I said to myself, dredging items and images absorbed in early history lessons. The Angles. The Saxons. The Picts and the Scots. The Romans.

And the words of London fascinated me — the stacks of newspapers and magazines, sheets of advertisements in the windows of the tobacconists and newspaper shops, the names on the buses, the street signs, the illuminated advertising signs, the menus chalked on blackboards outside the humble Transport Cafés — Giant Toad and Two Veg., Shepherd's — the posters in the Underground stations and the graffiti in the public lavatories and road tunnels; the numerous bookshops and libraries. I had never had so much opportunity for public reading.

Nearer home, I enjoyed my Garden Room and the helpful company of Patrick. Each morning I crouched on the floor of the room waiting for the colour to surge into the electric plate to boil the kettle for washing and coffee, saving a shallow swill for rinsing the dishes, and then, following the example of a neighbouring tenant, I'd throw the dirty water into the gooseberry bushes that screened the rooms from the back lawn where the tenants from the main house hung their washing and on the rare fine afternoons sunned themselves in the company of the landlady's tortoise, it also trying to attract the smoke-filtered warmth of the now faraway sun.

The nights were cold. The stretcher bed placed low near the floor caught the night air that seeped with a taste of London fog between the cracks and beneath the ill-fitting door. I'd clear the resulting railway taste from my mouth and snuggle under the thin bedclothes with my warm coat spread on top. I was not too worried by the cold — I was in London, wasn't I? I had been to Crystal Palace, Ponders End, Piccadilly Circus, High Wycombe. I had walked on the Common and looked up at the city's second and third storey of trees and the September sun filled with blood. My destination of Ibiza now seemed years rather than weeks away. I had much to do: also I needed to find a job for a few weeks to earn more money. And so, listening to the distant roar of the traffic that I honestly thought was the sound of ocean waves breaking on an invisible shore, I planned my remaining time in London.

And as a cherished dream had been to visit Hampstead Heath and the neighbourhood where Keats had lived, one day I caught a bus to Hampstead Heath where I walked as far as the pond. The sky was grey, a mist hung over the city below, flocks of birds hurried through the sky in narrow formation as in a corridor, going somewhere towards the light; and the leaves trembled and tugged on the golden trees; and at the sight of the tall brown rushes growing at the edge of the pond I began to repeat to myself, naturally,

> O what can ail thee, knight-at-arms,
> Alone and palely loitering?
> The sedge has wither'd from the lake,
> And no birds sing.

I knew that I must have been one among thousands of visitors to London who had stood by the withered sedge, remembering Keats, experiencing the excited recognition of suddenly inhabiting a living poem, perhaps reciting it from memory, and then, as if rejecting a worn-out gift, with a sense almost of shame, banishing the feeling, then, later, going in search of it, reliving it without judging, yet always aware that too often everyone must read the thousandth, millionth, seldom the first early layer of the world of imagination. Yet only the first day and night on earth could ever be thought of as the first layer on which the following secondary makers wove the shared carpet that in the peculiar arithmetic of making allows no limit of space for the known and unknown works of past and present and those, unfashioned, of the future. Looking down at London I could sense the accumulation of artistic weavings, and feel that there could be a time when the carpet became a web or shroud and other times a warm blanket or shawl: the prospect for burial by entrapment or warmth was close. How different it appeared to be in New Zealand where the place names and the landscape, the trees, the sea and the sky still echoed with their first voice while the earliest works of art uttered their response, in a primary dialogue with the Gods.

On Hampstead Heath I did not know whether to thank or curse John Keats and others for having planted their sedge, basil, woodbine and nodding violets, and arranged their perennial nightingales to sing in my mind. Misgivings (mis-givings) could not detract entirely from my first literary experience of London. That evening in my Garden Room I read and recited Keats and others (I having followed the advice of Jess Whitworth and joined the local Clapham Library and greedily accepted the rule — 'as many books as you wish').

Already, in practical pursuit of my literary aim I had bought copies of the *New Statesman*, the *Times Literary Supplement*, *John O'London's Weekly*, the *London Magazine*, the *Poetry Review*. (One wet day I visited the rooms of the Poetry Society where I gazed and gazed but did not enter.) I read exciting new poetry and prose by writers from the West Indies, some written in literary English, others with a West Indian version of English but all charged with a morning vision of London and the United Kingdom. I was much influenced by the West Indian writers and, feeling inadequate in my New Zealand-ness (for did I not come from a land then described as 'more English than England'?), I wrote a group of poems from the point of view of a West Indian new arrival and, repeating the experiment that Frank Sargeson and I had made with the *London Magazine* when I pretended to be of Pacific Island origin, I sent the poems to the *London Magazine* with a covering letter explaining my recent arrival from the West Indies. The poems were returned with the comment that they were 'fresh, original' and the editor would like to see more of my work. The poems submitted did not quite come up to the standard of English required. I did realise that such literary pretences were a safeguard against the discovery by others than my 'real' poetry was worthless. They were also a reflection then of a New Zealander's search for identity beyond her own country where being thought 'more English than the English' was felt to be more insulting than praiseworthy. In a sense my literary lie was an escape from a national lie that left a colonial New Zealander overseas without any real identity.

Other practical matters, however, interrupted my poetic dreams. I had booked on the ferry to Dieppe, the train to Paris, a night in a Paris hotel, the train to Barcelona, the ferry across the Mediterranean to Ibiza — the journey was simple and done with if I said it quickly!

Next, I found work for two weeks as a housemaid/waitress at the Battersea Technical College Hostel where from six in the morning until noon my duties were to empty the ashes from the huge fireplaces, like brick altars, to clean and polish the ash-splattered floor, where, as it was now eight or nine in the morning, students walked to and from breakfast and lectures imprinting their footsteps in ash as if each trod unknowingly the slopes of Vesuvius, while I knelt, like a mountain-housemaid, scrubbing and polishing the world. When the students and staff had gone I cleaned the bedrooms that were often rich with incense as the hostel catered for Africans, from many countries, Indians, Egyptians, Arabs, each with a special religion, as as well as for students from the British Isles. The household staff were mostly from London, of English or West Indian origin. At the hostel I found myself unexpectedly living as if during the days of the Second World War.

When the meal known as 'lunch' (a substantial morning tea) was served at eleven o'clock each morning the household staff sat eating 'doorstep' bread and cheese sandwiches, drinking tea, and talking, first about the television programmes of the evening before, next about their experiences as Londoners during the Blitz. The discussion of the television programmes was clearly seen as an introduction to the major topic, and perhaps as a reassurance that the events to be so vividly recounted were now also in a shadow world of the past. Yet day after day the women talked of the war, reliving horrors they had never mentioned and could only now describe, while I, with a shuddering eerie sense of the overturning of time that one is often persuaded may flow so neatly from past to present to future, sat silently listening, feeling a growing respect for the relentlessness of experience that like a determined, pursuing, eternally embracing suitor will at last secure its match with speech, even if the process, as here, takes fifteen years' work in its refining, defusing, washing, drying of tears, change of content and view, preserving, discarding, undergoing death and rebirth. Perhaps if the war had not been a shared experience the memories might not have had the combined force that enabled them temporarily to abolish the present, 1956, the long wooden dining table, the students, the technical college, and replace the group of household workers, mostly women between forty-five and fifty, with their former thirty-two-year-old selves, my contemporaries.

During those days I began to relive the war as the Londoners had known it. The relics were evident: bombed sites not yet rebuilt, overgrown with grass and weeds and scattered with rubble; the former Underground station with its hundreds of entombed Londoners caught in an air raid; squares and streets where death and destruction had now been given a place and names. My interest in the storytellers of Battersea made more tolerable for me the early morning waking in the now cold damp Garden Room, the walk through damp fog to the hostel, the thankless task of emptying the ashes, and in the evening, the waiting at the High Table, for tea during the week and high tea on Sundays. How old-fashioned the English are, I thought, as I stood by the 'low' tables waiting for a summons to attend to the High Table on its platform above the level of the rest of the room. The hierarchy was respected: no one dared make a mistake in identifying rank or choosing the mode of address. I knew that in my past I'd witnessed similar behaviour in the mental hospitals where the doctors, matron and senior staff were regarded as gods; while I had looked thus on university lecturers and professors. At the hostel the fact that the surroundings were tailored to fit the superiority of some and the inferiority of others gave the system a permanence, locking everyone in place in a season of calm with not even the prospect of storm to dislodge and rearrange, while the argument against rearrangement lay always in the secure rewards of being already in place.

On days when I collected the mail from the Bank of New South Wales in Berkeley Square, I exchanged opinions with other New Zealanders and Australians.

'What do you think of it all?' we'd ask.

The answer would be, 'The class system? They're in the Middle Ages.'

I felt, however, that the storytellers of Battersea were quietly arranging their own revolution, even without thought of past uprisings . . . the Picts and the Scots . . . the Angles . . . the Saxons . . . the Romans of Londinium . . .

4 Three

One afternoon when I was travelling on the now familiar 137 bus from Central London to Clapham Common (final destination Crystal Palace), I noticed a passenger staring at me, staring all the way to the Common, and when I left the bus he followed and fell into step beside me.

'I'm Nigel N.,' he said. 'I'm a law student. I live in Cedars Road.'

'I live in Cedars Road too,' I said primly but less primly than if he had been an apparent Englishman. I thought he looked old for a student, perhaps thirty-five, until I remembered that many of the students at the technical college were men in their forties. Nigel was dressed in the manner of 'someone in the city' — dark striped suit, white shirt, white handkerchief, bowler hat, neatly furled umbrella used and flourished as a walking stick. There was a ludicrous striving about his appearance that roused my pity and made me ashamed for him.

'I'm from West Africa,' he said. 'Nigeria.'

'I'm from New Zealand.'

'Oh, New Zealand,' he exclaimed, beginning to list the facts of our landscape, bays, rivers, waterfalls; exports and imports; cities and their notable features. He was one of the few I had met in London who knew facts about New Zealand.

I listened admiringly to his recital and when he had finished, my silence told him the humiliating story of my ignorance of Africa and its peoples. Tarzan films. Painted warriors dancing about an intended human sacrifice intoning words that sounded like 'The Far Far Jungle, The Far Far Jungle . . .'. My adult life had little reference to life in Africa and thus I was forced to reach into childhood for myths and a curiosity that had been shut, like jewelled gates, from later education and daily experience and reopened only slightly by the works of Olive Schreiner, Doris Lessing, Dan Jacobson, Alan Paton, Nadine Gordimer, who despite their imagination and empathy were not writing from the unique point of view of native Africans.

And so when Nigel invited me to the cinema that weekend I accepted, a little nervously as I'd begun to feed on a range of London papers including *News of the World* and the *South London Press*, both lurid with detail of local domestic and street life. Nigel could be a pimp trying to lure me to Leicester Square, I thought. I'd already met the kerb-crawlers beckoning from their limousines, following persistently until I escaped into a less deserted street or well-lit shop. I had a feeling of disquiet that I had allowed myself to be 'picked up' and I was thankful that I had chosen an afternoon session for our date at the cinema. I remembered how Nigel had stared at me completely focusing his attention during the whole of the bus journey: perhaps in his culture this was a natural way of meeting people? I knew I was ignorant, colonial born and taught, yet passionately intent on learning about the rest of the world, 'them', the people who until now had been only statistics, stereotypes showered with equal concentrations of curiosity, fear, prejudice, mixed with the main brew of 'love your neighbour', 'we must love one another or die' — then why was I not looking forward to my Saturday afternoon at the cinema with Nigel?

We arranged to meet at the bus stop at Clapham Common where we took the 137 (coming from Crystal Palace) to near Leicester Square. Nigel was dressed smartly, again as a Londoner working 'in the city' and all he lacked to identify him as a city Englishman was the narrow leather briefcase initialled with gold, and the city-pale skin. I too wore the uniform of my group, the woman traveller who had listened to advice and read the brochures: I wore my jersey and skirt and coat and carried my Traveller's Joy handbag with its many compartments for travel documents, and no doubt, like Nigel, in time, once I felt safe in my new world I would discard my false uniform — already my handbag was more a burden than a joy with its heavy linings, brass buckles and clasps and extra straps for over the shoulder; why, it even had a lock and key.

I don't recall the name of the film except that it was a wide-screen epic popular then. We sat in the best seats, in the *Dress Circle*. The blue ceiling of the theatre, representing the sky, glittered with silver stars while music from an electric organ set on a platform beneath the stage played melodies from Rodgers and Hammerstein. During the interval (which I, rugby-bred, knew as 'half time'), Nigel, instead of rushing out to the foyer to smoke, bought ice creams, the best, with a swirl of chocolate on top, and as I sat licking my ice cream I looked around at the audience and as I noticed others doing the same, I felt a growing self-consciousness followed by a feeling of my own 'worth', a snugness because in 'going out' with someone from Africa I had shown myself free from racial prejudice. During my few weeks in London the newspapers and the radio referred constantly to 'racial prejudice' and so for the first time I was forced to consider my own feelings, and realising the nature of my smugness I gave it sad recognition: I was no better than Patrick with his open bigotry. Why did it have to be?

The film ended. Nigel and I had sandwiches and coffee in a nearby 'Lyons' where again I felt self-consciousness, having read the London scandals about black women and white men and white women and black men, with the implication that the women were prostitutes, the black men, pimps, the white men unfortunate victims: the newspapers explained it all so neatly.

Trying to dissolve or dismiss my unpleasant feelings, I enjoyed Nigel's company. We shared much. We were both 'colonials' with similar education — heavy doses of British Empire, English history, products, rivers, cities, kings — and literature. He too had been given lists of the good, the strong, the brave, with friends and enemies clearly, permanently identified. He too had read of other places, other worlds, with a mantle of invisibility cast upon his own world. I was more favoured, however, in having my ancestors placed among the good, the strong, the brave, the friendly, in the position of the patronising disposers, the blessed givers. We waited for the bus at Lower Regent Street.

'Let's sit upstairs,' Nigel said in a burst of eagerness.

I said primly (aware too of my tendency to motion sickness on the swaying upper deck of a London bus), 'No. I prefer downstairs.'

We sat downstairs, side by side on the long seat just inside the door —
he, stiff-necked in his starched collar, I making casual conversation now and
again, trying too hard to atone for my past unpleasant feelings. I sneaked
a sideways glance at Nigel, just to look, a secret stare. His hands were lightly
clenched, the sooty black rims closing upon a palm of black-smudged pink
as if he had rose buds in each hand. Any feelings of 'duty', of necessary love,
of sentimental contemplation of the abstract 'humanity' vanished when I
saw this aspect of beauty. A cynic might remark, with Nigel wearing his
English clothing, what more could bring him nearer to his apparent desire
to be English, denying his origin, than a handful of rosebuds, the English
flower? I wasn't cynical: I also was adopting English clothes, the word-
clothes of Keats, 'Beauty is truth, truth beauty.'

We walked home beside the Common to Cedars Road.

'Come home and dance,' he said. 'We roll back the carpet and dance
and dance.'

Feeling threatened, I said quickly, 'No thank you,' while a glance at his
face told me that he thought of me as yet another racially prejudiced person.

'It's not that,' I said hurriedly. 'I've so much work to do. And thank you
for the lovely afternoon.'

He smiled gently.

'You need to dance,' he said. 'You all need to dance and enjoy yourselves more. You English don't know how to enjoy yourselves.'

I didn't make the obvious reply, 'I'm not English, I'm from New
Zealand,' for his observation was correct. I felt ashamed of my timidity. I
knew I could have dined and danced and danced but I sensed also that the
distractions of 'living' might threaten my desire and time to write. I was
unwilling to take the chance.

Nigel and I parted coldly. I received a note from him saying he was sorry
I had been unwilling to take the time to dance. I did not see him again. I
remembered some lines of the verses returned from the *London Magazine*:

> *Now you light fires.*
> *The dancing woman wears amber beads*
> *and snip-snap the scissor cold*
> *shortens the hem of summer . . .*

and

> *He came from a far country*
> *where they sit under lemon trees and ask*
> *riddles of giant vermilion cattle with white faces . . .*

The next week I accepted another invitation, again to the 'cinema', from Jack, an English physicist who lived in a basement room of the Main House and lectured at the Technical Institute. We went in the evening to a theatre in Clapham Junction where we sat in the back stalls. Again, I don't remember the name of the film. When the interval began, Jack, opening his mouth economically above small white teeth, said in a low voice, through his teeth, 'Would you like choc ice or plain?'

This ordinary question, 'Would you like choc ice or plain?' spoken with a London accent, seemed to be as full of revelation for me as had Nigel's recitation of English kings and queens and New Zealand mountains and rivers.

'And would you like a cornet?'

A cornet!

Cornet, high tea, indoors, pavement, Bear Right, Bear Left, Giant Toad and Two Veg. Do you travel by tube? Crystal Palace, High Wycombe, Tooting Bec, Wandsworth . . .

'She do look pretty, don't she?'

I was startled to find that Jack had lapses of grammar with usages that I'd been taught with such sternness were equivalent to criminal acts. I had not realised how deeply I had been persuaded that breaking the rules of language was a crime to be punished. I thought it unlikely that Londoners in all their races and cultures might live in fear of a split infinitive, a dangled participle, a misrelated clause, all of which might bring upon them a *sentence*.

Jack and I ate our choc ices, oblong blocks covered with a brittle layer of chocolate and wrapped in silver paper, and sipped our orange drinks, then, when the film was over, we walked home to Cedars Road where, after drinking coffee in his room, I returned to my Garden Room. The next day, Saturday, when the sun came out and I was sitting by the gooseberry bushes, he came into the garden. He was formally dressed as many Londoners appeared to be, even at leisure, and he looked out of place lying in his city clothes on the rug I had spread on the lawn. He began to try to persuade the landlady's tortoise to come out of its shell, and as I watched the schoolboyish teasing and prodding of the tortoise I wondered could this tall pale man with his choc ices and cornets, his lapses in grammar, and how his pestering of the tortoise, really be a lecturer in physics? I had certain notions of how different professions must be and appear and my knowledge of people in the 'world' was still so meagre that I believed that such experts as physicists, doctors, lawyers were beyond displaying childish traits, and thus I found the behaviour of Jack, the physicist, almost incredible. I remembered the story of one of Tennyson's admirers who was shocked when Tennyson opened the conversation with a complaint about the price of coal.

Jack's behaviour depressed me by its ordinariness. I was shocked, too, by the way everyone at Cedars Road appeared to accept their dreary lives in gas-smelling rooms, their stained slop bucket and the 'good' water bucket, their seldom-confessed loneliness that showed in the lingering way they clung to casual conversation as if words drifting by on stairs and in doorways must be snatched as a last hope. Although I was now one among them, I felt that I had a resource, an aim.

I also had the *Envoy*.

Had the tenants of the house in Cedars Road an Envoy, I wondered? I watched Jack, the physicist, as he jabbed at the tortoise.

'You'll hurt it,' I said.

He smiled, his lips opening slightly, like a door being opened yet alert for the intrusion of hostile air, debt-collectors, strangers.

'He doesn't feel it.'

The sun vanished then behind the gathering clouds. Evening came earlier each day. It was no use pretending that summer was not over. The leaves rattled harshly brittle in the trees. The gooseberries had long been gathered and the bushes were bare. I returned to my Garden Room to study the maps for my coming journey to Europe. The lengthening, darkening days, the damp chill of early morning and evening, the comforting presence of the many buildings in London, even the massed dreariness of the Cancer Hospital next door with its high wall backing on to the Garden Room, seemed to paralyse my desire to travel into the European winter. Perhaps, I thought, Spain, the South, would be different. I was deceived again by literature:

> *Oh for a beaker full of the warm South . . .*

and

> *Swallow, swallow flying south . . .*

My third encounter was with the artists of Parliament Hill Fields.

Letters from Frank Sargeson kept reminding me to visit the address given to us by the young couple who'd lived in Ibiza, and so one afternoon I telephoned Parliament Hill Fields and was invited to dinner that evening. I talked to Ben, a poet, who gave instructions about getting there, and again impatient with expectation aroused by names such as Parliament Hill Fields, Crouch End, I took the bus to a street of brick houses where Ben, a slim dark young man with thin hunched shoulders and long arms swinging to and fro like pendulums, guided me from the bus stop to the house.

His eyes were an intense brown, his face pale and moist.

'So you're from New Zealand?' he asked, looking at me as if to read the signs. He spoke with a Scottish accent.

'And are you Scottish?'

'Nay.'

'You sound Scottish.'

'Aye.'

He laughed then, explaining that he'd not long returned from his first visit to Scotland where he'd met *Hugh McDiarmid*.

'Hugh McDiarmid.'

'Oh?'

I knew that I should appear excited, perhaps amazed, admiring certainly but, sadly, I did not know of Hugh McDiarmid. I sensed that he was a poet. I remembered then a haunting poem in my *Golden Book of Modern English Poetry*, a reference to 'Stony Limits'. Hadn't that been written by McDiarmid?

'McDiarmid and James Joyce are my favourite poets,' Ben said in his soft Scottish accent, adding, 'Aye, Aye . . .'

'I am Polish,' he said as we walked to the front door of the house in Crouch End.

There were several tenants, male and female, all in London to further their artistic careers. They welcomed me, and after I had made my usual claim of being 'all the way from New Zealand', they asked me why I had come to London.

'I'm a writer,' I said with more certainty than I felt. 'I've a travel grant from the Literary Fund to further my experience.'

'Have you written any books?'

'Two,' I said, trying to sound casual.

'But have you had anything published?'

I realised that my new friends were not used to connecting writing with publication.

'You mean you've published a *book*?'

'A book of stories. And I've a novel being published soon.'

'Only in New Zealand,' I added hastily, trying to diminish their shock and restore plain curiosity to their faces. 'I'm hoping to get my novel published here some day.'

We were about to sit down to dinner. A young woman, an ample house-mother, put a huge bowl of fruit in the centre of the table. She returned with another of salad and one of cooked rice. She too stopped to stare when someone said, 'She's published a book!'

She called to the others in the kitchen as if summoning them to deal with an emergency. 'Quick. She's published a book!'

Those who were to share the meal came hurrying in. All stared at me. One explained, 'I've never met anyone who's published a book. I mean, someone like us.'

We began to eat.

'It's paella,' someone said. 'The Spanish dish.'

'Oh yes, I know,' I said eagerly. I was back in Sargeson country.

My friends impressed me; they were gifted, intelligent, learned, more than I could ever hope to be, and, anxious to represent myself honestly in case there should be a misapprehension, I repeated that my book had been published 'only in New Zealand', while the novel would be available 'only in New Zealand'.

They asked the name of my publisher.

'Caxton for the first,' I said, 'and Pegasus for the novel.'

Their excitement about meeting a published author lessened as they admitted that already they had chosen their one and only publisher: Faber and Faber. Nothing less than Faber and Faber.

I confessed that I, too, dreamed of Faber and Faber.

'There's Deutsch, of course . . . and Michael Joseph . . . and Calder . . .' Solemnly we raised our glasses of red wine in a toast to Faber and Faber, the supreme publishers of poetry.

They talked late into the night while I listened with wonder to their hopes and dreams of exhibition, performance, publication, for not all were poets; and when it was too late for me to catch a bus home to Cedars Road, they suggested I stay the night, sleeping in Mary's room. Mary had been Ben's girl, he told me, until he walked in one night to find her in the arms of Dora. He was sleeping alone now, Ben said, since he returned from Scotland and meeting Hugh McDiarmid. There was a flurry of midnight excitement as everyone focused on Hugh McDiarmid. What a great poet, he was! The greatest, with Joyce, Yeats, T. S. Eliot . . .

'And Auden?'

'Oh, Auden! Yes.'

'And T. S. Eliot is the *head* of Faber and Faber!'

The excitement of the evening kept me awake when all had gone to bed, most with their chosen sleeping partners. Mary slept with her girlfriend, Dora, upstairs. I lay marvelling at the poetic dreams and the apparent confidence of those who seemed to become poets and painters simply by the spell of utterance: 'I'm a poet, I'm a painter.' I was impressed by the communal living, the freedom, the absence of demanding authority. I was surprised to find that some of the tenants were Londoners with their families living in London. Two of the girls were scholarship students at the Slade School of Art, while those without formal work while they pursued their chosen career, earned money (like Ben) as models in the art classes, and found much of their food by visiting the free sample areas of the Oxford Street and Knightsbridge stores where they munched crackers and caviar and tasted various pâtés and cheeses while no one dared turn them away as they might have been eccentric millionaires in disguise.

Waking into the uninterested spurning light of day, I felt like a stranger in a household already preparing for the day's routine. Had I really toasted Faber and Faber among these self-possessed clever people whom in New Zealand I would never have dared approach unless I were safely in a corner at Frank Sargeson's while he took charge of the conversation?

I said a shy good morning. No, I wouldn't wait for breakfast. Then with promises to come again I said goodbye and hurried to the bus stop, losing my change purse on the way. Ashamed, panicking, I returned to the house.

'My purse, I dropped it. My money, my keys!'

I felt myself in a disarray that somehow might lessen my chances of ever being published by Faber and Faber or having my novel published in the United Kingdom, as if I had scattered words as carelessly as I scattered my purse, keys and money.

The artists of Crouch End had begun their day with that immuring process contracted by morning, already advanced, while I, exposed, felt unfixed and strange as I cried out again, like an intruder from a play, 'My purse! My keys! My money!'

Ben shook himself free to return with me to the bus stop and give me enough money for my fare.

Arriving at Cedars Road, unable to get through the locked gate, I rang the doorbell of the main house and Patrick Reilly came to my rescue by finding a spare key and, later, replacement keys.

'The landlady need never know,' he said. 'Though it's not something I'd do every day.' Patrick was a man of judgment who referred all actions, including his own, to an unalterable set of rules, a first generation of rules with some of the second generation allowed occasional change or compromise. He was satisfied, I perceived, that my night away from the Garden Room had been innocently spent, although he frowned his disapproval when I said that my new friends were artists and poets.

'They're not the type for you,' he said. 'They hang around and do no work. And their morals are no better than they should be.'

'Oh no,' I protested, 'They *do* work.' And touched with their golden confidence I reminded him that I was a writer.

'You're different. When you come back from Spain to live in London, you'll be getting a *real* job.'

'Oh?'

'Yes. Peek Frean's are always looking for workers. Or you could be a shorthand typist.'

'Peek Frean's?'

'Peek Frean's.'

It seemed to me as if Patrick Reilly had sprouted from a handful of New Zealand earth that had found its way in my green haversack and spilled into the garden at Cedars Road. Patrick Reilly had helped me. He was now trying to take charge of me. He had accepted, against his will, that I was leaving for Ibiza, but he was firm in his plans for me to return 'fancy free' to London where I would find a decent job.

'We can look at our future then,' he said.

I said nothing. I did not really like Patrick Reilly. He reminded me of those I had lunched with in my far-off schooldays because there was no one else available. Although he behaved with confidence and had firm opinions on almost every subject he impressed me as being yet another reject of a demanding world, although he might never have thought of himself this way. He knew he was a successful bus driver who had refused promotion to inspector because he did not care to stand at London bus stops freezing to death, flapping his arms to get warm while the buses passed with their drivers cosily sheltered from the weather. He preferred to be active, up there driving the bus, receiving messages from the conductor up top (one stamp with the foot, go, two stamps stop). All the same, he knew he was 'manager material'. He said so.

'There's no doubt that I'm manager material.'

He was clever, he spoke well, he could command attention, give orders. At home in his bedsitter with his best bluetop and Peek Frean's dark chocolate digestive biscuits and best Irish bacon and Irish butter, he retained his assurance and certainty.

Except, now and then, for a flicker of unease in his deep brown eyes, a wondering was it all so, as it seemed to be? Or was there perhaps something he had missed?

5 A Game of Chess

During my last week in London I finished work at the Battersea Technical and said goodbye to the storytellers of Battersea. And on my last day in London, Ben, the poet, paid me a visit and after we had our tea and Peek Frean's dark chocolate digestive biscuits we began to talk about chess and discovered that we shared a delight in playing although neither of us had had a game for many weeks. I readily agreed when he said impulsively, 'Let's buy a set and play chess.'

We went in search of a chess set. The Clapham shops were closed, Clapham Junction was closed. We walked to Battersea, Chelsea, towards Sloane Square and still we could find no chess set for sale. Returning we tried Balham, Tooting, and the further we walked and the less likely our prospects became of finding a set, the more desperate our search grew. We both knew but did not say that the need for a game of chess had long ago delivered up its original impulse to become a symbol of those indefinable longings of one young man and one young woman, both aspiring poets, on an autumn afternoon in London. A game of chess would have anchored our longings, postponed our questions, for the time being ended our search. I remember clearly that strange afternoon. Ben with his long arms propelled in a kind of rowing motion was a quick walker and I hurried to keep up with him so that our pace was almost a run. An onlooker might have wondered, 'Why are that man and woman running through London on this autumn afternoon? What have they lost that they hope to find or who or what is pursuing them?'

We finally gave up. Still hurrying, we came to the flat where Ben's mother lived, a tiny upstairs flat in Hampstead. I felt disbelief and wonder that the small black-clad woman, the Polish emigrant who spoke no English, could be the articulate Ben's mother. Young men and women keep their parents so well hidden as if they stitched them in a sack inside their heart.

Upstairs in Ben's room we talked about books. He lay on the large double bed.

'My marriage bed,' he explained. 'When I find a Jewish girl to marry.'

He read from Hugh McDiarmid's poems and from *Ulysses*. And when I said it was time to leave, there was a feeling of regret, resignation, loss, as when we had failed to find our game of chess. He walked with me across the Heath to the bus stop and as we passed the pond I pointed to the withered sedge that was now one of my early memories of arriving in

London, as if I had lived there now for many years. 'It was like this,' I said. 'And this.' Aware of the distortions of time that accompany departures.

My bus arrived. We said goodbye and promised to keep in touch. Our day had been a time of private intensity. We were acquaintances becoming friends. We sensed poetic movements within each other like two houses side by side where lights were turned on in different rooms and the occupants of each house, going their separate ways to different destinies, pause to recognise the neighbouring pattern of illumination.

I returned to the Garden Room to spend my last evening there. Patrick Reilly whom I'd not seen for several days was watching out for me.

'Let's go to the Common for a meal on your last evening,' he suggested. 'Well . . .'

We walked across the Common past the Outsize Dress Shop which Jess Whitworth, small in build, had patronised during her visits from New Zealand, as brochures addressed to her were delivered regularly to the Garden Room. Latest news from the Outsize Shop.

We passed the huge second-hand bookshop, the ABC, the stationer's with the dusty fountain pens in a row in the window overlooked by the briefcases, the plastic toys, the dust-covered jigsaw puzzles. Finally we came to the restaurant which unlike the transport cafès where Patrick said he usually had meals, had tablecloths and a menu printed, not written on a blackboard outside.

I let Patrick choose. Steak medium rare with vegetables, followed by apple pie and cream.

The steak was large with shreds of thick fibre that displeased Patrick who complained, 'I expect it's horsemeat.'

I churned my mouthful and pulled a face.

'Surely not!'

'Oh yes, they often serve horsemeat if they can get away with it. I was hoping for a good Irish steak.'

I smiled to myself. Here was I, bred on the worship of the New Zealand butter god, and asking when I bought butter, 'Is it from New Zealand? I'm *all the way from New Zealand*,' while Patrick in his turn kept asking for Irish butter, bacon, steak.

Our conversation was dull. Patrick was homely and ordinary with little trace of romance or excitement, yet sometimes in the evenings when we had walked on the Common where the owners of the toy boats gathered to sail their craft by remote control, pressing buttons and switches as they stood in their mackintoshes and sou'westers, although the evenings were mostly fine, Patrick had begun to talk dreamily of Ireland and the leprechauns. He'd seen them, he said, with his own eyes. I believed him, especially in the evening when the blood-red sun was dying, its edge balanced on the earth, and the leaves of the plane trees lay spread like withered hands relit, revived, on the paths and under the trees. When I became bored with Patrick or oppressed by his bigotry, I remembered the leprechauns and thought kindly of him.

The next day he took time from work to say goodbye at the station. 'Keep in touch,' he said. 'And stay fancy free.' His brown eyes were shining darker than usual, and I, softhearted, overcome by many goodbyes, felt tearful and sad to see him like another lost soul seemingly unaware of imprisonment or freedom.

The ferry where I had booked a sleeping berth steamed out into the Channel where it stopped halfway in a fog too dense to navigate. The sea was calm. I heard the measured lapping of the waves and the foghorns calling one to the other like distressed seabirds.

At noon the next day, in slowly clearing fog, we anchored at Dieppe where I boarded the train to Paris.

6   Plaza Roma

My first day in Paris is remembered for the tears I shed trying to make myself understood, and for realising as I finally bought my bread, eggs, butter to cook on my small stove in the tiny attic room of the hotel over-looking the site of the old Bastille, that bread is indeed *pain*. I had been so well schooled in the mechanics of travel by Frank Sargeson remembering his walking tour of Europe and Jess Whitworth sharing her more recent overseas experience, that I obeyed their instructions exactly. The object, wherever I might be travelling, was to save money by cooking my own meals and, if possible, to stay in camping grounds or Youth Hostels, and so I had arrived in Paris with my pots and pans, a Girl Guide set of cutlery, tin-opener, pocket knife, cooking stove fuelled with sticks of methylated spirits, and sleeping bag with sleeping sheet. I'd also accumulated many books, secondhand and new, during my time in London, with a *Teach Yourself Spanish Part One* and a *Teach Yourself Spanish Phrase Book*. These, and my huge hooded fawn jersey, exercise books, a rug ('all travellers have a rug'), a supply of clothing, packed into my now bulging suitcases, with my typewriter in the green haversack, made my luggage a wearisome burden. I had chosen the hotel because it overlooked the Bastille and I wanted my two days in Paris to be spent not merely in organising my travels and worrying over my pieces of luggage. I consoled myself by whispering loved passages of French prose and poetry and looking out of the tiny window at the wintry sky and reminding myself that I was in Paris. Who ever thought I'd be in Paris? I sang to myself part of the folk song 'Duncan Gray'.

> *You may go to France for me,*
> *Ha Ha the wooing o' it . . .*

And the next morning, refreshed and determined to purify in advance my memory of Paris I set out before dawn to explore the streets and after a time I found myself lost in the vegetable market of Les Halles, surrounded by cabbages, tripping over them, sliding on cabbage leaves, and unable to escape, for it was no use my reciting passages of Daudet, *Contes et Légendes*, Pierre Loti, Victor Hugo . . .

At last I found my way to the hotel where I prepared to take the night train to Barcelona.

At the station I stood in the queue at the counter marked *Consigne* where I hoped to *consign* my luggage to Barcelona, although I was surprised as I surrendered all but a small shopping bag and my Traveller's Joy that I was given a small numbered ticket without any inspection of my train ticket. Wasn't this unusual?

'Vous ne voulez pas regarder mon billet de voyage?' I recited clearly, triumphantly.

'Non.'

Willing to accept that this must be the French way, I went to the platform, found my seat on the train, and waited, looking out now and then, as anxious travellers do, to try to identify my luggage among the trolleys being wheeled to the goods van.

On the long seat opposite me were an elderly man and a small boy, very frail, who lay covered with a blanket, his head in the old man's lap. The boy had been in Paris for an operation on his heart, the man said. Now and again throughout the journey he selected grapes from a bag and fed them one by one to the boy who opened his mouth for them, like a young bird.

'These are good for him,' the old man said. 'They will make him well.'

The other passengers in the compartment, two middle-aged Spanish women travelling to Perpignan, talked in Spanish to each other for several hours, then fell asleep, while I drowsed now and again. The old man stayed awake, vigilant, upright, occasionally adjusting the blanket over the boy, so that even when I drowsed I'd open my eyes to see the old man's alert pale face and his intent dark eyes. The women glanced often at the two and made sympathetic murmurings about the sleeping boy.

Morning came, and we approached the Spanish border, and I was content to abandon my own description of my journey in remembering the acute observation of Maurice Duggan's *Diary of a Journey*. For me, this was Duggan country. I remembered Duggan's description of train, guards, sea, sky, earth. The landscape was his, and these were his border guards (with occasional contributions by Lorca and Lawrence Durrell) moving with flashing guns, polished buckles and boots, ushering the passengers into the customs hall, where the experience again became uniquely my own.

I inspected and re-inspected the unclaimed suitcases. No familiar green haversack, no two old suitcases with their straps of New Zealand leather.

'Mes bagages,' I said wildly to no one in particular. 'Je les ai consignés de Paris.'

I approached an official.

'Mes bagages?' I said.

The official shrugged.

'Consignés,' I said.

After a halting exchange of phrases I realised that I had deposited my luggage in the left luggage department at the Paris Station and the ticket I held was my ticket of deposit.

A sweeping cloud of tears threatened but did not fall. I gulped. Then, in spite of growing apprehension and a feeling of lonely misery, I was overtaken by the delight of being free of luggage. I watched the other passengers struggling to climb into the high Spanish train and my sense of freedom increased. Lighthearted now, I could have flown on my own wings to Barcelona and Ibiza.

Frank Sargeson had written to his friend, the writer Greville Texidor, who lived in Spain, telling her of my visit. I was met at Barcelona by Greville's daughter, Christina, who with her husband, the painter Paterson, took me to lunch at La Plaza Roma, remembered as an old square lined with grey eucalyptus — or were they olive? — trees with the surrounding buildings standing like ancient earthforms, earth coloured, with their roots deep in the red soil. There appeared to be a dust of sun fallen over everything, with the square enclosed in quiet, like a private pathway to other times. Unburdened by ridiculously beleaguering luggage, I felt my being untethered, my senses sharpened by my night of waking. I was aware not of the noise and traffic of Barcelona but of this background of overflowing quiet that enveloped me with a feeling of being at home, in place at last, like a piece of human furniture that has been shifted and reshifted and re-arranged, never before exactly right, in all corners of the world. I did not know yet whether this was the common experience of travellers, in response to foreignness, difference, an abrupt removal of all tethering and bonds to a native land.

Later I met Greville and her husband and their twelve-year-old daughter at their city apartment where I sat smiling, empty headed and shy. I met also Colin, introduced as an English poet, who was returning to Ibiza on the same boat and who had kindly offered to make sure I found somewhere to stay.

'A room for a few nights,' he said. 'Una *habitacion*.'

'Una habitacion,' I repeated nervously, aware that I knew nothing of Spanish.

That evening I saw Colin, briefly, as I boarded the ferry. The boat seemed frail, a cockleshell, the Spanish night was dark, *obscure*, the sea was dark, calm with small clumps of waves rocking and glinting white like a rooted bed of flowers, asters or Queen Anne's lace. I hurried to my sleeping berth and waited, sleeping most of the night until morning.

7 Calle Ignacio Riquer

When I woke the ferry had already entered the harbour of Ibiza and was preparing to anchor. Colin was there waiting for the gangplank to be put in place. Some passengers had already leapt ashore without waiting.

And twenty minutes later there was Colin revving his scooter and calling to me, 'Climb on the back. I'll take you to a small hotel I know.'

Boldly I climbed on the back saddle and clinging fast to Colin's waist and with some alarm as I'd never ridden a scooter, I swayed back and forth as we roared up and down the narrow cobbled streets stopping in front of a small pension.

'Here,' he said. 'You can stay here for a few nights, there's sure to be a vacant room.'

He led me to the reception desk where he spoke fluently in Spanish, received a reply, and turned to me.

'Two nights?'

'That's fine,' I said.

Then, his duty discharged he returned to his scooter, restarted the engine and roared away up the street while I, feeling lost with my vanity hurt, watched him go. He might at least have said he would see me again or it was nice to meet me or good luck with my writing. Well, he knew Spanish and they'd said, with respect, that he was a *poet*. And who was I? Only a friend of a friend of a friend.

I stood in my room smelling the pervasive Ibicencan smell that I could not yet identify, feeling tired, anxious about finding a *permanent* place to stay, inferior because I was not a poet, but, overturning all these feelings, was my eagerness to begin my new life in a foreign land.

First, I needed a phrase book that was not directed entirely at the rich buying, skiing, photographing, share-accumulating traveller likely to be a paratrooper going bankrupt, being measured for a new suit, who is struck by a thunderbolt while suffering from a fractured skull at the railway station.

And so, joyously, because I had no luggage to take care of, I went in search of a bookshop where I bought a tissue-paper-thin edition of the *Daily Telegraph*, several Spanish newspapers, Paris newspapers, and a phrase book of Catalan, *Learn Spanish With Me*, which I then used to buy bread, butter, cheese, an apple and a banana. I bought also a cake of chocolate costing more than the sum of the other foods. It had creatures inside it, waving their tiny heads from their tiny nests.

When night came I discovered that the one small ceiling light in my room was so dim that I could barely see the outline of the furniture, and when I looked into the street below, I saw that the shops were candle-lit, with all lights dim. I slept then, and woke full of anticipation for my first 'pure' morning in Ibiza. I would walk, I decided, in search of a place to stay.

I walked towards the old city on the hill, along the narrow cobbled streets to the remains of the Roman wall with its stone figure of a Roman warrior at the entrance to the tunnel leading to the upper city. Walking carefully to avoid the piles of dog and human mess in every corner, I came into the daylight of the hill where I looked down on the harbour and the buildings across the harbour, perfectly mirrored in the clear tideless ocean. At the top of the hill I could see the other side of the island beyond the fields and olive groves to the transparent Mediterranean. I sat leaning against a grey rock that was massed like an accumulation of layers of ancient olive leaves. I shared the solitude with a small herd of wild goats, and the silence with the distant sound of the fishing boats. The grey-leaved olive trees with their twisted branches and trunks turned in defence against the sea wind, and the white-grey stones like long-fallen snow that had refused to melt, on the red soil beneath the trees, drew from me a feeling of tenderness as if this land were mine and I had known it long ago. It was, of course, Shelley's world, and I had known it in poetry, and they were Shelley's phrases that came first to mind allowing me the — parasitic — indulgence of reunion with 'Ode To the West Wind'.

> *Thou who didst waken from his summer dreams*
> *The blue Mediterranean, where he lay,*
> *Lulled by the coil of his crystalline streams,*
> *Beside a pumice isle in Baiae's bay,*
> *And saw in sleep dim palaces and towers*
> *Quivering within the wave's intenser day . . .*

before clearing the space where I wanted my 'own' thoughts to be. It was tempting, however, to sit remembering my first ice-clean exposure to poetry, like the first spring of all time, and for the moment I was happy just to *be* where I had always felt most at home — outside, under the sky, on a hilltop overlooking the ocean; and I might have sat there, as I used to sit for hours had I not remembered the purpose of my walk — to find a place to stay.

I followed the narrow path along the bowed ridge of the hill where the storms had struck more harshly and the bowed vegetation showed its agonised struggle to grow in the face of the wind with little roothold except in the crevices in the snow-grey rock.

As I walked I saw two figures in black shawls, stockings and shoes, bending to gather twigs and branches to heap into their large woven baskets, and again I recognised them because I had known them before — in paintings depicting the toil of peasants or as casual onlookers in the midst of a miracle, or in descriptions by Victor Hugo and Pierre Loti and Daudet. The two women furnished the landscape as if it were an interior long ago formed, decorated, occupied with no prospect of change.

Consulting my new phrase book, I murmured, 'Buenos dias.'

'Buenos tardes,' one replied, pointing to the sun.

I spoke hesitatingly, 'Jo soy de Nueva Zealanda. Janet. Quiero habitacion.' I placed the palms of my hands together and rested them against my cheek.

The two women began to talk excitedly together. They turned to me. 'El Patron,' they said. 'El Patron.'

I gradually understood that they were *Catalina* and *Francesca* and I was *Janetta*, and they would take me to their *patron* who would rent his house to me. I dissolved any suspicions they might have had when I explained that I was not a *tourist* — 'No soy turista,' I said firmly. 'Soy *escritora*.'

Grasping me lightly by the arm, Catalina led me down the hillside through the narrow cobbled streets to *Ignacio Riquer* where, they said, the house was next to theirs. El Patron was in charge of the Museum and his brother *Fermin* was in charge of the house where I might be able to stay. At Number Six Ignacio Riquer they pushed open a heavy unlocked front door. A starved-looking cat sitting on the wooden table in the kitchen lashed at us with its claws as it vanished in a streak of grey.

'Los gatos,' Francesca said angrily, explaining that they were wild cats who would attack me if I left the door open. Would I wait, Catalina asked, while they fetched El Patron?

Within five minutes they had returned with El Patron's brother, Fermin, slightly built and in his mid-forties, who appeared to be agreeable to my staying in the house and who named a rent comparable to that mentioned by Frank's friends in New Zealand who had stayed on Ibiza, and after Fermin had shown me the room where I could sleep, and the lavatory at the end of the terrace, and the kitchen (there was no bathroom), I said I'd return to my hotel to pick up my shopping bag. I understood that I was renting the entire house. Later when I arrived with my shopping bag and my Traveller's Joy, Fermin was in the sitting room overlooking the terrace, playing a violin. He stopped playing as I entered. He looked surprised by my lack of luggage. I hastily turned the pages of my phrase book.

'No hay equipages,' I said. 'A Paris.'

At last I was able to explain that my luggage had been deposited at the Paris railway station and I'd be sending for it and if all was well it should arrive within two weeks. I explained that I was an *escritora* and my typewriter was in my luggage. I came from New Zealand, Nueva Zealanda, I said, the land of sheep, wool, butter . . . I tried to give the impression that New Zealanders were unlike the rest of the world in being clean, pure, unprejudiced, well disposed towards all members of the human race. And New Zealand was a beautiful country. It was *God's Own Country*.

Fermin understood. He frowned. Ibiza, he said, was also *God's Own Country*.

I knew that in speaking thus of New Zealand I was showing little sense or perception, but to affirm New Zealand in this way was habitual to one who had been taught so insistently to equate survival with sheep, wool, butter, or, rather, death with the failure to export sheep, wool, butter: *export or die*.

Fermin was sympathetic about my luggage. He undertook to make it his duty to inquire each morning at the waterfront for news of it. He came to the house each day, he said, to practise the violin as he played it each evening in a nightclub. Other members of the household also came to the house, he said, while the servants Catalina and Francesca who lived next door would use the kitchen for their cooking, as usual.

At least, I thought, in spite of the comings and goings, I'm the only occupant.

My bedroom was large and airy with a wide window overlooking the harbour and the distant shore where the buildings lay like those of another city, a sea or mirror city reflected in the clear water. I arranged a table and chair for writing and I thought with some excitement of the new book I'd begun in Auckland, *Uncle Pylades*, and the one I planned to write following that. My first task, however, was to write to American Express in Paris enclosing my left luggage ticket with instructions to them to collect and forward my luggage. Next, I needed a change of clothing.

I wrote and mailed my letter to Paris, then I shopped for underwear, stockings, a skirt, jersey, nightgown and writing materials and when I arrived home, laden with parcels but bewildered that the shops would no longer accept my money, Fermin, inspecting the limp pile of pesetas, explained that someone had given me 'old' money, pre-1935, that was no longer legal tender.

'It's worth nothing,' he said. 'You've been tricked.'

I sat again at my desk. I wrote poems and some letters, the kind of inspired letters travellers send from a new country where everything glistens with marvel. For me, that marvel was the light, the sky, the colour of the olive trees and of the buildings thumbed and worn like old stone pages, with none of the restlessness of New Zealand buildings, none of the sensed fear of sudden extinction by earthquake or volcano. These rose like opened books on a lectern of earth and were turned perhaps once in a hundred years, their certainty lying in their age and their openness. And crowning the marvel was the receptiveness of the tideless ocean admitting to its depths the entire world standing on its shores, creating a mirror city that I looked upon each day.

Without my typewriter I felt limbless, and it was good news when I heard that my luggage was on its way to Ibiza. I happened that day to be walking past a café when I saw Colin, the English poet, sitting with friends at one of the tables on the footpath, and I did not realise until I saw him how miserably lonely I'd been feeling without my typewriter and my luggage and with my several hundred worthless pesetas. Mildly self-conscious but trying to hide it, I strolled past his table and looked towards him. 'Oh,' I said, in a tone of surprise. 'Hello again.' Then in a burst of excitement, I said rather more loudly that I had meant to, 'My luggage is coming soon! And I've found a place to stay!'

His friends stopped in their eating and drinking to stare. At first Colin did not seem to recognise me. Then he said coolly, dismissively, 'Oh, hello.'

He simply stared, showing no delighted response at my news.

I may have exaggerated his coolness; I certainly remember it. I felt a chill current swirling about me and I wished I had said nothing. He and his friends were so much in place there, drinking at the kerbside cafè table, just as Maurice Duggan, sophisticated and clever, had described, and as Frank Sargeson had recalled to me, saying, 'It's the continental way.'

I hurried away from Colin, the English poet, and his friends, and after my rebuff I made no attempt to mix with or meet the English-speaking colony. I therefore spoke only in Spanish and French, coached by Catalina, originally from Algeria, who also spoke French, and by Francesca, Fermin, and José, the twenty-year-old son of El Patron, a law student, who came each week to the house to bath in the tin tub in the kitchen and who, after his bath, came to my room to try to teach me Spanish.

Each morning when Fermin finished practising his violin he also taught me a few words and phrases of Spanish, and sometimes he reminisced about his past. He unlocked one day a large cupboard, drawing out the double doors to reveal a lit interior with carvings of the crucified Christ, on shelves, and pinned to the inside of the door, a poster of a young handsome General Franco, El Caudillo.

'He saved us from the Communists,' Fermin said. 'He was younger then. And I was young.'

He shrugged and looked ashamed.

'Things are different now. It was long ago. Mirra.'

He led me to the window that like my bedroom window overlooked the city and the sea and, nearer, the road leading from the Roman tunnel to the church on the hill. He pointed to the stone wall bordering the road.

'The Stations of the Cross,' he said. 'El Caudillo lined up all the Communists there and shot them. I saw it. But I was a young man. It's different now. And El Caudillo . . .'

Fermin shrugged and went to the cupboard. I thought he was about to spit on the poster. Intead, he ripped El Caudillo from the wall and thrust the crumpled poster on the lowest shelf of the cupboard. Then he shut the door and locked it.

'Those are my carvings in there,' he said. 'I'm an artist too. But it's different now.'

As each day passed and I occupied myself with writing poems and letters and stories, telling myself that when my luggage arrived with my typewriter I'd begin work on my book, Fermin would bring news of my luggage, for each morning he inquired at the wharf. My luggage and his secret cupboard locking away the dreams of a younger man became our bond. And one day he came to me with a small box closely packed with small religious pictures.

'This is another treasure,' he said. 'Which Saint would you like, Janetta?'

I hesitated.

'Oh. St Francis.'

He found the picture of St Francis and gave it to me.

'These are long ago too,' he said . . .

So what have I seen in memory? Memory is not history. The passing of time does not flow like a ribbon held in the hand while the dancer remains momentarily still. Memory becomes scenes only until the past is not even yesterday, it is a series of retained moments released at random. I am remembering Fermin's face as he spoke of his once-passionate hate of the Communists, how in showing me the Stations of the Cross where the executions had taken place, he talked not of distant enemies with a vaguely fearful ideology but of friends and neighbours, even relatives, and how he had approved the killing because the orders came from his beloved Caudillo. Now he was shocked, saddened, and unsure whether the killing had been necessary.

He could not even tell of his doubts through the medium of his violin. He may have known that his family laughed at his violin playing, or smiled tolerantly when they happened to hear him. I smiled politely, murmuring a phrase that might have been 'Bueno, Bueno.'

I still see Fermin's troubled face as he stares from the window at the Stations of the Cross.

8   Soap-New People

The time of waiting for my luggage and typewriter became my apprenticeship to the life of Ibiza and the family of El Patron.

With gesture of poetic greed I bought a book entitled *Las Mil Mejores Poesias de La Lengua Castellana (1154–1954)* which I showed to José, asking, 'Where are the poets of Ibiza? Has Ibiza anypoets?'

The island of Formentor, covered with pine trees and lying just south of Ibiza, had a poet, José said. Miguel Costa Llobera. I therefore found the one poem by Llobera, 'El Pino de Formentor', which José read aloud and I later learnt by heart. It became my 'set piece', my focus, even more than the poems of Lorca included in the anthology, for an Ibiza that I found to be so old, touched by the Moors and the Romans, and as young as childhood's blue-sky days.

> Hay en mi tierra un arbol que el corazon venera;
> de cedro es su ramaje, de cesped su verdor,
> anida entre sus hojas perenne primavera . . .

And

> No asoma por sus ramos la flor enamorada,
> no va la fuenticilla sus plantas a besar;
> mas banase en aromas su frente consagrada
> y tiene por terreno la costa acantilada,
> por fuente el hondo mar.

Laboriously I searched my new dictionary for definitions before I wrote my poetic translation of 'El Pino'. Llobera was a 'safe' poet, a patriot, not a rebel. Fermin and José approved of my choice of a poet who wrote of pine trees, and I wondered if I had not, in part, come home to my own childhood when I remembered other times I had never known by writing, twenty years earlier.

> A memory, a forgotten day
> so full of spring sunshines.
> Told by trees that gently sway
> and whispered by the pines.

The traveller to new lands has a rare opportunity to revisit or visit other times, for

> soap-new people come and go
> washing away the stale time's flow
> in an heap to eternity . . .

José's mother and sister rarely came to the house: their lives were sheltered. Although I was a single woman, alone, I was still a foreigner, and everyone knew that the ways of women from foreign lands were not those of Spanish women. I was approved of, however, because I was not a tourist, I was not American, I was an industrious *escritora* who did not have foreign friends, while there was a homelessness about me because my luggage and my typewriter had gone astray: my misfortune had become my advantage. Catalina and Francesca therefore took charge of me, and each morning when the fishing boats came in with their catch, Catalina and Francesca taught me how to choose the best fish, what to ask for, how much to pay. The tiny silvery fish, like sardines, cost one peseta for five. Later, the two women showed me how to cook the Ibicencan dishes, and I was now able to think back in astonishment and some embarrassment at my early purchases of butter and chocolate. Early in my stay, arriving home with butter, I met Francesca cooking her tea and I was dismayed and saddened by the way she stared at the butter in my basket.

'Mantequilla!' she said in awe.

Only the rich bought *mantequilla*.

I had also bought a strip of steak.

'*Carne*. Oh Janetta!

I shared my butter and meat and when Catalina came for her tea I heard them talking excitedly about *Janetta* who had bought *mantequilla* and *carne*!

As I learned to live on the Ibicencan diet there was no longer cause for amazement and curiosity about my food. I copied Francesca and Catalina, also, in the fuel I bought for the fire. Whereas in New Zealand, I thought of coal and wood arriving in sacks on laden lorries, here I took my woven basket with the long handles to queue with the blackgarbed and shawled women for a small basket of coke and perhaps two or three small blocks of wood. Yet Francesca's eyes still glittered as she watched me arrive home with my full basket, as if I had a natural permanent abundance granted me. Even when my supply was low, her glance made me ashamed, reminding me of the hungry state of the alley cats that still waited outside the door for a chance to get in, and each morning followed the rubbish collector as he led his donkey, the paniers overflowing, up the narrow street to the hilltop and the other side of the island.

This was my first encounter with the feelings of the really poor, and with my own awareness that I had the means to travel, I could support myself for several months, I could return to New Zealand to the world of plentiful electricity where people lived in houses surrounded by gardens of fruit, vegetables and flowers; and that in spite of my constant refrain, *No hay mucho dinero*, I belonged to a rich nation. I may not have been a rich *turista* spending money on hotels, wining, dining, clothes, but my homeland was then rich in opportunity, in compassionate legislation that took account of everyone's need for food, shelter and for health as distinct from ill-health. Before I left New Zealand, Frank Sargeson had said, 'There'll be the poor, and the beggars. If you start thinking about them you'll go mad. You have to try to forget them. There's nothing you can do.'

What could I have done to improve the lot of Francesca and Catalina? Butter and meat every day? I could not bear the way they searched my clothes with their eyes as if I might be wearing concealed jewels. Francesca's dark eyes, in particular, had an alertness I'd not seen before in a human being — she was the hungry one eager for goods as well as food she could not buy. And yet there was seldom a sign of discontent unless it was revealed one day when, riding my hired bicycle along the dusty white country roads by the olive groves, I met Catalina and Francesca who must have walked many miles, gathering the olives that had fallen from over-hanging branches into the road. There were others too, families from the city who had come with their baskets to pick up the olives. Catalina and Francesca explained that this was their chance to supply themselves, and when Catalina said wistfully that El Patron had a farm in the country and I asked if the family gave her vegetables, eggs, fruit, she said, 'Oh no, we buy them from the market. The farm is for El Patron and his family; but we are always allowed to collect the olives that fall in the road.' I glanced into their basket at the small, hard, pitted fruit, and I constructed for myself a proverb that, in the way of proverbs, would try to solve everything: the olives that fall to the side of the dusty road are the tastiest, the most treasured. Words again came to the rescue.

Imagining that the Balearic Islands, the *Spanish Islands*, were by defi-nition always blessed with sun, perpetual summer, I had given little thought to winter clothing, and as the days, still blue and sunny, became colder I was glad to have my outsize fawn jacket with its big pockets and hood, and once I had explained to Catalina and Francesca that wearing slacks did not make me a female devil (*diablas* was their word for the foreign women in their black slacks), I began to wear the grey slacks I'd been given in New Zealand, and the warm brown coat bought by Aunties Joy and Elsie.

It was near Christmas when my luggage arrived by sea. When Fermin brought the news there was great excitement and when the truck delivered the two suitcases and the green canvas haversack, and Fermin carried every-thing through to the sitting room, Catalina and Francesca and José, fresh from his bath, came to stare, expecting me to open the cases at once. Con-fronted with goods that, except for my typewriter, I had now convinced myself were no longer necessary I felt embarrassed as if I were meeting friends I no longer wished to know because we had outgrown the friendship. I felt I should compensate the family for their obvious disappointment: three months of waiting and wondering and asking, and now these old battered cases, crushed at the corners, one lid askew, as if, like some objects in old fairytales, they had manoeuvred themselves miles along roads and across seas to reach Ibiza.

When later in the privacy of my room I opened the suitcases, I looked distastefully at everything I had packed. Then, as I saw again my books, the small stove, the Girl Guide cutlery, the army pots and pans, I felt more kindly towards my outcast luggage. Ah, there was the blue 'tube' dress I had sewn from a length of jersey silk, the material that 'everyone' in New Zealand was wearing. Now the colour appeared too bright and out of place in a land where clothes were black.

And because I could not deny Catalina and Francesca the chance to see the 'goods', I invited them in. I showed them my typewriter. And here was the green velvet dress that my sister had made from a curtain.

Catalina and Francesca laughed.

'Janetta's cortina, Janetta's cortina.'

I retrieved my rug and hot-water bottle to make good use of both for apart from the kitchen fire there was no heating in the house and the vast marble floors were now permanently chilled, and the nights were very cold. And now that I had my typewriter, I felt that I could *really* begin work instead of writing poems and letters and stories. I was aware, however, that I had invested more in the arrival of my luggage than it could ever acommodate, that I had been practising the oldest form of self-deception, appeasing the present by clinging to an event in the future: I was in good human company.

9   *The Pine Trees*

In the days that followed I sat wrapped in my rug, nursing my filled hot-water bottle while I typed my novel, *Uncle Pylades*. I looked out of the window at the children playing hopscotch under the eucalyptus trees, the markings for the game drawn with a stick in the white dust. I listened to the chanting

> *Tengo tengo tengo*
> *tu ne tiene nada*
> *tengo mantequilla . . .*

and I watched the elder sisters sitting in the doorways, their lace pillows propped on their knee, working their lace bobbins, hands swiftly passing one bobbin over the other, and I thought of that time in hospital when I had made French lace, gathering from the French instructions a feeling that although I was being denied books and writing and ordinary human conversation, new life was being channelled to me through those instructions in the *Manual of Lacemaking: Plantez un épingle au point Deux . . . jetez trois fois . . .* Language that had betrayed, changed, influenced, could still befriend the isolated, could help when human beings had withdrawn their help.

Thunderstorms came crashing above the house. Lightning played vividly in the room, and winds wailed, cried, screamed as I'd never heard winds, reminding me of the ancient gods, creatures born of thunder, lightning, storm, raging up and down the windowpanes as if trying to get in, clawing the glass, mouthing it as if it were an instrument of music. Often, in the midst of the storm, I'd walk outside, up the street to the other side of the island and I'd sit on the grey rock among the battered silver-grey plants and trees, and I'd think that I had never felt so much at home. I rejoiced that I was alone on a Mediterranean island, speaking no English, with my Spanish welcomed as my English had never been, for my struggle to express my thoughts was attended by the kindness of those who were proud that I was trying to speak their language and who were eager to explain, suggest, help, and teach, whereas in speaking one's native language to others who also speak it one is alone, struggling to meet the expectations of the listener.

As I sat at my table typing, I looked each day at the city mirrored in the sea, and one day I walked around the harbour road to the opposite shore where the *real* city lay that I knew only as the city in the sea, but I felt as if I were trying to walk behind a mirror, and I knew that whatever the outward phenomenon of light, city, and sea, the real mirror city lay within as the city of the imagination.

I thought much about islands and seas. I wrote a verse,

> Pity the banished continent estranged from sea
> where people longing for mirror capture
> behind their eyes a mountain plain or valley
> that shifts with the tides of seeing
> in snowshapes and masses of cloud, never wholly
> growing apart from the shadowy ponderous
> land stopping, itself in shadow, to drink the day's light.
>
> Small are islands, forever fluid in image
> known best once only, over the shoulder
> as birds flying or rabbits crouched, thumping the sea;

> *each day a stranger shape within the mirror,*
> *more completely shining and misting over*
> *than broken shadows from centuries, than moveless wings*
> *of a giant bird or the one whole leaf discarded*
> *from a tree whose whole form and seeking*
> *of invisible sky are held flickering*
> *beyond the communion of water*
> *even on a calm day of a quiet inland sea.*
>
> *Small are islands, a tyranny of completeness,*
> *a fear of meeting too many selves in mirrors.*

Oh how seriously I took my dream of being a poet! I'm on my own now, I told myself. I'm living the life of a writer. I felt at peace within my own mind, as if I were on an unearthly shore, seeing the creation of scenes from the great paintings of the world, the people of Ibiza moving as if directed by the painters, with the houses, the plants, the day and night skies each the colours the painters would have chosen. In my afternoon walks or cycling I marvelled at the way the clear perimeter of the island unfolded before my eyes. I wrote ecstatic letters to Frank Sargeson. Ibiza, I said, was all they claimed it would be and all I dreamed. I felt it contained within me and when I had explored the beaches and the salt mountains I cycled past the fields of clay where the clay surface opened its red vein, at the pottery works, and leaving my bicycle, walked to the wooded interior of the island, to a mass of light-green pine forest where, Catalina and Francesca warned me, the bandits and wild men roamed, and although I did not believe them, I discovered later that they spoke the truth — Ibiza, like Sicily, had its bandits.

Sometimes during my walks in town I saw and heard the foreigners laughing, talking, and I wanted to cry out to them, 'I'm here, I also speak English. I'm from New Zealand, *all the way from New Zealand.*' Instead, I passed haughtily by as if I knew everything in the world.

I could not believe the gentleness of Ibiza. In the evening when the supply of electricity was reduced and the shops were candle-lit. I'd walk without fear around the dark streets of the city. When I had asked for a key to the front door, Fermin, Catalina and Francesca had stared in surprise, explaining that only foreigners locked their doors, the secretive, possessive foreigners guarding their wealth, their large supply of *dinero*. My front door, therefore, was always unlocked.

Christmas came with a letter and a food parcel from Patrick Reilly in London. He sent corned beef and Irish stew and he hoped I was still fancy free.

With Christmas also, the sound ceased that had persisted for many days, a cry like a small sharp succession of cheers, a chorus of 'Bravo, Bravo, Bravo,' which had puzzled me and which I thought were the cries of the island dogs that like flesh-coloured almost transparent shadows ran at intervals through the streets. I learned that the cries had been those of the turkeys in the small yard beneath the house where now there was silence. I wrote:

> Christmas and Death are hungry times
> when only the foolish and the dying
> with circumscribed vision of Here
> learn complete praise, saying
> Bravo Bravo to the Invisible.

> Who knows to what in the small yard
> the turkey gives violent praise?
> Or the sick man spread
> on a white plate in his diminishing world?

And with the bitter cold came a new sound, the almost ceaseless tolling of the church bells and I'd look out to where the small white coffins were carried in the many funeral processions. Each days as the tolling began, Catalina or Francesca would sigh, murmuring, 'Ah, un crio, un crio.'

Many *crios* died that winter: it seemed to be usual. The cypress-bordered cemetery on the road to the interior was lined with new graves.

And so I wrote, and I walked — in the evening to the hilltop where I watched the small dark shapes of the bats swinging to and fro like threads out of the sky.

And once, cycling, I stopped to rest at a small pine-bordered beach where I lay under the trees and listened to their hush-hush, and the light fell like blue and green snow around and upon me, and the sea glittered through the pine branches. Not an unusual scene but, as in my visit to the pine forests of the interior, it touched the antenna reaching from childhood, just as childhood contains its own antennae originating in conception and the life of the dead and the newly begun; and feeling the sensation at the nerve ending and its origin in the past among the pine trees and sky and water and light, I made this scene a replacement, a telescoping with the trained economy of memory, so that from then and in the future the memory of this scene contains the collective feeling of those past, and now when I listen to pine trees by water, in light and blue, I feel the link, the fullness of being and loving and losing and wondering, the spinning 'Why was the world?' that haunted me in childhood, the shiver of yesterday, yet I remember the pine trees of Ibiza.

Christmas that tends to block the view ahead having passed, I began to think with a nagging anxiety of my 'future'. When my grant had been used, I supposed that the accepted move would be a return to New Zealand, yet I felt so much at home away from New Zealand that I was reluctant to return. Also, Frank Sargeson and I had talked of the advisability of my consulting a psychiatrist in London so that I might discover whether the New Zealand doctors had been correct in the diagnosis of schizophrenia. I knew I had not suffered from it. My claim, however, was naturally looked on with disbelief by almost everyone. Since the publication of my book of stories *The Lagoon*, John Forrest, my friend of distant student days, had written from America where he now lived. Not having seen me for eleven years, and unaware of my real story, my determination to live up to his expectation of me as 'kin to Hugo Wolf, Van Gogh', he also very likely had few doubts about the validity of the diagnosis. In answering his occasional letters I delivered with a casual touch, myself in my former role of supposed 'cleverness', 'difference', a dreamer of dreams, maker of fantasies. When John Forrest's inevitable 'Dear Everyone' letters arrived I smiled at my new maturity. With a touch of snobbery I had sometimes referred to him as 'My friend, the doctor in America.' I mention him because he had lately written to say that if I wished he could arrange an appointment with a doctor at the famous London hospital, the Maudsley.

10   *El Americano*

I had been told that spring came early in Las Baleares. Even so, its outbreak of blossom in early January encircled the island with a new bond of sweetness so excessive that it forced dark pleats of pain to be folded within the pleasure.

With the black-and-white beanflower filling acres of fields, the orchards pink and white with colours, never reproduced in paintings, that remain locked within certain flowers, with the spring wind warm, full of the scent of the wild flowers, the almond and avocado blossom, and the beanflowers, I prepared to tolerate the poetry I knew I would try to write in the midst of writing my novel. Often I remembered with a feeling of strangeness that

I hadn't spoken English for three months, although I was aware of my English speech tucked away in corner of my mouth with the key turned in the lock, but I did not realise how rusty with disuse were the key, the lock, and the speech until, arriving home from my walk one afternoon, I met Francesca who repeated excitedly, 'El Americano, El Americano,' while I listened mystified until I saw a tall brown-haired young man coming down the stairs into the sitting room.

He was equally startled to see me.

'Hi,' he said. 'I'm Edwin Mather. I've rented the studio upstairs. I'm a painter.'

I had to search for my English words. (My words indeed!)

'I live in the front room,' I said. 'I'm a writer.'

'I guess we share the kitchen and the john outside?'

El Americano. Just as Francesca had warned. Hadn't she told me that she left Algeria because Los Americanos came and took all the oil and perfume?

I felt sick with disappointment and a sense of betrayal for I believed I had rented the entire house and I could not understand how El Patron could now rent other rooms. Perhaps I had been mistaken. I had looked on Number Six Ignacio Riquer as *my place*, shared of course with El Patron and his family and Catalina and Francesca, but not with a *foreigner*, an American painter who spoke English! I felt hostile and unprotected as English thoughts and English words crowded into my head as into an auditorium, each ready to perform its role. There was no one to appeal to. Number Six Ignacio Riquer had been *my place*.

I recovered a little. At least Edwin Mather would be living upstairs. He would share the house, though, the kitchen, the fire, the front door to the street, the hallway, the sitting room opening on to the patio, the lavatory on the patio, and I'd always be aware of a presence in the house and part of me would be tuned to that presence and distracted from my writing. I felt that the link between the world of living and of writing resembled a high wire needing intense relaxed concentration for the barefoot journey (on knives or featherbeds) between. In such a life the presence of others is a resented intrusion and becomes a welcome joyous diversion only when the attention must be directed away from words, if only briefly, during times of travel and sickness.

On this first meeting Edwin and I, like candidates for a post which both had to accept (for he, too, may have thought he had rented the entire house) explained our presence in Ibiza — his funds were from a scholarship which he collected from Andorra where the money market was 'free'. Ignorant of the ways of international currency, I listened attentively as he advised me to change my foreign money in Andorra. He could arrange it, he said.

'Oh,' I said dubiously.

He showed me his studio upstairs, a large airy room with white stone walls, a skylight, and a door opening on to the roof with a panorama of the city, the fields, the ocean, and the mirror city. I felt suddenly disappointed in my restricting of my spirit of adventure — why had I never explored this upper storey of the house? Passing through the sitting room on my way to my bedroom I glanced always at the stone stairway as if it were a place forbidden, without realising that it was I who had hung out the trespass warning, not aware that I was denying myself a richer view of Mirror City. This revelation of the panorama from the rooftop when I had spent day after day huddled in a rug in my chair in my room, my typewriter on the table before me, my gaze when it strayed from the typewriter fixed only on the mirror city across the harbour, had the effect of an earthquake, shifting my balance, opening depths beneath me, distorting yet enlarging my simple view, as simple as the stare of the blinkered horse I had seen harnessed to circle the well hour after hour, to draw water. No doubt the water was pure and sweet, bearing little relation to the routine of the imprisoned agent working at the well, but I was not so sure that what had appeared on my typewriter was so fresh and sparkling.

Suddenly also I was forced to make a new routine that took account of Edwin. Up early, lighting the fire, I now set aside Edwin's shaving and washing water, and by the time he was out of bed I had breakfasted and begun work. For the evening meal he usually ate with friends at a café or stayed home and cooked his specialty, French onion soup, or shared what was now my specialty, paella with *saffron* which I mention only because I took delight in thinking of myself as 'eating crocuses'. Edwin painted most of the day while I wrote and at times we'd have spontaneous or contrived meetings in the kitchen when he or I asked, 'Quiere el fuego?'

And soon the kitchen shelves became crowded with luxury food that set Catalina and Francesca aquiver with excitement. Edwin's first meeting with them prompted the remark, 'Who are those two old women wandering around prying into everything?'

I explained. Edwin appeared to be unsympathetic towards them while I, who felt that I 'understood' them, sprang to their defence, reminding him that they were poor and could not afford the kind of food he was buying and its was natural for them to help themselves from his bountiful larder.

'But they're wandering in and out all day.'

I told him they lived next door and our fire was their only means of cooking. They had one room, I told him, and they kept bantam hens on a small balcony off their bedroom. 'They might give you a fresh egg now and then,' I said.

He also complained, not unreasonably, about the light bulbs. Although his studio had natural light from the skylight he wanted to be able to paint whenever he wished and to read at night. (I was managing by lighting three or four candles at my table.) Edwin searched the town for new light bulbs which instantly blew the fuses in the house and brought rebuke from Fermin whom Edwin described as 'that interfering little guy with the violin. Have you heard the awful sounds he makes on that violin? I didn't know he would be using this house to practise!'

I pointed to the locked cupboard in the sitting room.

'He has carvings in there. The cupboard lights up when you open the door. He's a sensitive soul.'

Edwin's view of Francesca, Catalina, Fermin, depressed me for to me they were my new family who had looked after me and waited for my luggage to arrive and taught me to shop and cook, and when my three-month visa expired it had been Catalina who had taken me to the police station to introduce me as her friend the writer from Nueva Zelanda who needed her visa renewed. I felt that El Patron and his family needed protection against El Americano. He and his English or American language were the intruders.

For a time I could not adapt to what I saw as the destruction of my perfect world, and I still found writing difficult with a 'presence' in the house, yet gradually Edwin and I began to talk to each other about our work. Each day when he'd finished painting he'd invite me to his studio where he explained his morning's effort and talked about his ideas and art in general, his favourite artists, his life, and in return, although I did not discuss my current work, I lent him a copy of my novel, *Owls Do Cry*, which had now been published and had recently been at the correos when I collected my mail. Edwin liked *Owls Do Cry*. 'It should appear in the States,' he said. He knew someone in New York who worked for a publisher; perhaps he could send a copy there?

I said I'd 'see'.

Apart from professional talk and the phrase spoken often during the day, 'Quiere el fuego', we lived our separate lives. Then one afternoon when I returned from my walk I was met by Catalina and Francesca in a state of excitement: Edwin had a woman visitor who'd be staying the night . . . in the same room . . . in the same bed. And that evening I met Dora, a flute-player from the mid-West, studying music in Paris. She was small, dainty, with black hair. She wore the 'right' clothes — black *pantalones* and sweater. I longed wistfully to be as full of secrets as she seemed to be, that would prompt a man to discover them, but for so long I had blocked all exits and entrances that I knew or felt that I was as sexless as a block of wood. I had smoothed myself away with veneers of protection.

That evening Edwin and Dora dined out while I, uneasily, with a nagging sense of loneliness and an unwillingness to return to my writing, prepared my self-sufficient meal, read for a while in the half-darkness, looked out dreamily at my Mirror City, then retired to bed. I heard Edwin and Dora come home, laughing and talking as they went up the stairs to his studio, and I felt the sudden unfriendly chill of being just myself and no one else: not dainty but with legs that my sister had said were like footballer's legs, and wristbones that reminded me of railway sleepers.

11 *Figuretti's*

The next morning, Dora was gone even before I was up. She was catching a boat or plane to the mainland or the north. Edwin and I had a late breakfast and he talked casually of her as if she were just anyone. Catalina and Francesca could not stop talking about her, *la diabla*, who had stayed the night with El Americano, and the bedsheets had to be washed and what a disgrace. A female devil! They turned to me, 'You're not like her, you're not a female devil! Los Americanos!'

I knew I had played that role before — as a child at home, at school, at university and college: the keeper of the rules, the 'good' person delivered from evil, never led into temptation. Where then the praise had given me a feeling of syrupy self-complacence, now it gave me little satisfaction for in the arithmetic of my thirty-two years it was now a subtraction from rather than an addition to my self-esteem.

For a while my life returned more or less to its usual routine. Then one evening when I was in my room typing I heard the sound of voices in the kitchen, men's voices punctuated by hearty laughter, and with the pretext of fetching hot water, I went to satisfy my curiosity and found Edwin and a friend whom he introduced as *Bernard* whose thirty-fourth birthday they were celebrating. I said hello (unable to bring myself to use what I thought of as that ridiculous 'Hi!'), shared a toast with a glass of rosé (the best on the island, according to Bernard), and then, explaining that I had work to do, I returned to my room, and as I left, I heard Edwin say, 'Janet has had a book published.'

Later, in bed, I still heard their laughter grown slightly drunken now as the hours passed. I thought Bernard's laughter was the most joyous I had ever heard. The sound seemed to have the right assembly to connect with a jagged shape inside my heart. I could not otherwise explain the delight of listening to his laughter.

The next morning, a blue and white and green spring morning, leaving my work untouched and with a surge of domesticity, I prepared to cook the marmalade from the recipe Edwin had cut from the *Observer*, and the blood-tinged fruit was bubbling in the big pan Catalina lent me, and I was leaning over the pan, stirring the golden blood-streaked syrupy liquid when the door opened and Bernard walked in.

'Hi,' he said. 'I couldn't work this morning. I thought I'd take a walk. Care to come?'

I felt nervous. 'What work do you do?' I asked, remembering that Edwin had said something about Bernard helping to bring Freud into Spain by working on the oil pipeline in Northern Spain.

'Back home, I'm a history professor. I was working on the pipeline until I fell off a horse and broke my arm — it's healing now. I'm really a poet. I've written several poems since I've been on the island.'

He was of medium build with fair hair, grey eyes, and a rich voice that sounded like chords of music to my already enchanted ears. I thought his eyes, intent in their gaze, looked slightly glazed and mad: in my innocence it never occurred to me that he might have been taking drugs. He watched while I poured the marmalade into the six prepared jars, and now and then when I leaned forward I saw him staring down my dress at my breasts. He kept staring at them. He stared at me, too, with his bright, mad-looking eyes.

We talked of ourselves.

'I couldn't work either,' I said. 'This beautiful day.'

'Let's go for a walk along the beach past Figuretti's.'

'Figuretti's?'

'Yes. Don't you know Figuretti's?'

I said no, I didn't, and he didn't explain and during the rest of my stay on the island I never discovered the nature or meaning of Figuretti's. At times I thought it was a café on the beach, then I thought it must be a bay, then a patch of sky, for in the weeks that followed Bernard and others I came to know would say, 'Figuretti's is beautiful today,' or 'It's just past Figuretti's,' or 'When I first went to Figuretti's.' Once, Bernard pointed to a café, a group of buildings, the church, the sky, 'Look,' he said in a satisfied tone. 'There's Figuretti's.'

Strangely, I cherished my ignorance and never inquired.

I sealed the last jar of marmalade and set the six in a row on the table. Edwin will be pleased, I thought, listening in vain for the sound of him working in his studio, and I wished that I lived in the days of pen and quill when authors, too, were silent workers and none knew, listening, what sound of words they might be mixing and stirring and applying to the parchment or paper.

'Edwin is busy,' I murmured.

We walked along the narrow streets, uphill through a grove of tall cacti with their calloused spiked palms upward. Bernard pointed to the entrances of the caves where some Ibicencans lived. I was aware of myself now making another journey, a first, as I had when Ben and I searched London for a chess set that in spite of the occasional surfacing of dreams and desires, remained a literal chess set on which to play a real game of chess. This beach walk with Bernard was recognised by us as an intention like the preliminary movement that birds make when determining their final flight. Bernard and I also laughed and talked and quoted our favourite poets (I was slightly disappointed when he quoted Kipling's 'Gunga Din'), but I was again entranced with him when I learned that he spoke fluent French and Spanish and at once I drew out my favourite quotations, like confessions being cooked, shaped and set for tasting. Picture, then, a woman of thirty-two, fresh-complexioned, blue-eyed, dressing in a blue jersey 'sack' which Edwin (a painter who should know) said was a 'beautiful colour', and Roman sandals. (Frank Sargeson always wore Roman sandals in summer. He had only to say to me, 'Roman sandals are best and cheapest for summer. You need Roman sandals,' for me to make Roman sandals part of my spring and summer existence wherever in the world I might be living.) Picture me by the 'blue Mediterranean' beginning to quote a fable learned years ago, quoting to share my pleasure in the verse and to show my cleverness in remembering it,

> Maître Corbeau, sur un arbre perché,
> Tenait en son bec un fromage.
> Maître Renard, par l'odeur alléché,
> Lui tint à peu près ce langage:
> Hé! bonjour monsieur du Corbeau.
> Que vous êtes joli! que vous me semblez beau . . .

and then, done with La Fontaine, turning for good measure to Alphonse Daudet, I shook the dust from 'Si vous avez jamais passé la nuit à la belle étoile, vous savez qu'à l'heure où nous dormons un monde mystérieux s'éveille dans le solitude et le silence. Alors le source chante bien plus clair et il y a dans l'air les frôlements, les bruits imperceptibles si l'on entendit l'herbe pousser, la branche grandir . . .' followed by a helping of Victor Hugo, 'C'est pour renaître ailleurs qu'ici bas on succombe . . .'

I had thus hinted at my supposed cleverness and now it was Bernard's turn to impress me.

'What about Auden?' he said.

I was rapturous. 'Oh! Auden!'

I began, 'He disappeared in the dead of winter/The brooks were frozen . . .'

> Follow, poet, follow right
> To the bottom of the night.
> With your unconstraining voice
> Still persuade us to rejoice . . .

Bernard responded with a quote from Edna St Vincent Millay while I listened with polite attention, snobbishly aware that my poets were 'better' than his, and wishing he would quote long passages of Yeats as I tried to preserve my image of his perfection from my realistic impulse to destroy what I had created from the day, the circumstance, and the person who talked longingly of the mysterious Figuretti's. We walked on, our spirits rising as we looked about us at the sea, the sky, and smelled the bean-flowers, the almond blossom and the innumerable unnamed flowers growing everywhere in an everlasting springtime.

We passed a gaunt cow grazing at the end of its tethering rope, its circle of earth bare of grass, and with a gesture of magnanimity towards the world, Bernard withdrew the post and led the cow to a new pasture, but after he had sunk the post in the earth he picked up a stick and struck the cow's hide sharply twice in a burst of unprovoked anger that reminded me of the gesture of the pale physicist assaulting the tortoise on the lawn at Clapham Common. Again I fought to mantle and not to dismantle the perfection of the Ibicencan day.

We walked on. The light wind blew a bundle of grass across the sand to the water.

'Look,' Bernard cried with delight. 'Tumbleweed! Do you know tumble-weed?'

Ashamed, I said I had believed that tumbleweed was a roaming cowboy. With my childhood of Western films my mind turned easily to Texas, New Mexico, Arizona and their flora and fauna and the cowboy songs I used to sing, among them

> Drifting along with the tumbling tumbleweed . . .

My response was ecstatic. So this was tumbleweed! I watched as the bundle of grass, its roots enclosing itself, rolled on and on towards the sea where it stopped and partly propelling itself, partly in the hand of the wind, it zig-zagged along the shore, never pausing to rest or take root. Although I did not want to indulge in anthropomorphism or pathetic fallacy I did invest in the tumbleweed a power of detachment, of protective isolation: I looked sympathetically on it. We had walked the length of the beach passing on the way the white stone villa Bernard had rented, a few yards from the water. We talked of ourselves and our lives and when Bernard asked if I were married I said no, but, unwilling to reveal myself as sexually but not technically a virgin, I gave dark hints of liaisons of former days.

Bernard had married at an early age and was now separated.

I had no one special, I said. I had one or two men friends but I was so busy with my writing that I had little time or inclination for affairs of the heart.

My attempt at mystery amused Bernard. He laughed heartily and each time he laughed I felt within me a reverberation of his laughter as if I were a vast empty palace awaiting the guests and the feast.

We climbed the hill at the far end of the beach overlooking a triangular sea and the neatly terraced land with every inch cultivated to yield its fruit. We spread our picnic on the grass and ate and drank and talked and as we looked down at the fields and the sea, I stood with his arm encircling my waist. We had been away for hours. It was growing dark.

'Let's go to my villa,' Bernard said, 'and build a log fire.'

Hand in hand we retraced our steps among the beach to the white stone villa. A villa on the beach! The fairytale image of life lived like a shellfish within reach of the sea and within sight of the tumbleweed that now took its place as a special plant beside my loved matagouri!

When Bernard and I had eaten a meal and were sitting in the twilight beside a blazing log fire, enacting a cliché drawn from all the *True Romance* magazines I had read in my girlhood, I felt the satisfaction of having yet another first experience — merely sitting, talking of interesting matters as well as exchanging hints of feeling, underlining, signing an invisible contract without speaking of it, in an atmosphere of mutual excitement. I, unlike Bernard, was new to seduction.

The night wind from the Mediterranean brought a chill into the room and I reached to shut the window. Bernard leaned forward, gripped me tightly around my waist, pressing our bodies close. I struggled free.

'Oh no,' I said primly. 'I've only just met you. I don't know you. I don't believe in . . . I mean I've just met you.'

Then, adopting a calm, reasoned objective approach, I not only successfully extinguished the spark but washed it over, becoming my own sea, with a dampening regret; and no store of kindling in sight.

For a while, then, we talked, still excitedly exchanging details of our lives, our beliefs, opinions, all punctuated inevitably by romantic quotes from poetry.

It was early morning when we walked along the cobbled streets towards Ignacio Riquer and as we stood outside 'my' house, he again clasped me tightly while his practised hands sought the 'right' places, and he kissed me until I responded and we stood, breathless, in the dark street. I then freed myself, said a prim goodnight, and went inside to my room, with my body feeling as if still enclosed by him in an embrace that lingered all night, like a phantom, and when it began to recede like a slowly vanishing dream, I willed it to return.

I spent a restless few days.

'I don't hear your typewriter,' Edwin said in a complaining tone as if the sound of my typewriter were a necessary accompaniment to his own working; and it may have been, for a state of restlessness can be infectious and any departure from an artist's planned routine can be a trigger to anarchy as the ideas, looking in, find nowhere to come home to.

'Aren't you working these days?'

I 'laughed lightly' (as I had read it described in novels when laughter is heaviest and most melancholy) for like the place on earth where the giant has lain, the memory of Bernard left its deep print, and, waking one morning with a haunting thought that I (shy, in my thirty-third year, travelling overseas to 'broaden my experience') might never have another such experience, I dressed, prepared Edwin's shaving water, then walked out along the street towards the hill and the sea and Bernard's villa. I stopped at the *pastelria* to buy breakfast cakes. I walked through the grove of tall cactus trees by the white windowless houses and the caves. I came to the beach, the 'blue Mediterranean where he lay lulled by the coil of the crystal-line streams.'

I looked for tumbleweed but saw none.

I knocked on the door of Bernard's villa.

He was not surprised to see me. He was wearing a dressing-gown and had a scrap of paper in his hand.

'I've been writing a poem,' he said. 'About spring in Ohio.'

He began to read, 'Only spring in Ohio . . .'

I thought it was a slight, almost a nothing poem, and when he had finished reading it I murmured, 'Oh. Spring in Ohio. It must be lovely.'

'It is. It's like no other springtime. You wake one morning and it's there. The suddenness of Ibicencan spring reminds me of it.'

'Spring in Ohio,' I murmured fatuously, looking shy when Bernard turned his attention from his poem to me.

'I haven't had breakfast yet,' he said. 'I write best on an empty stomach.'

It reminded me of an old radio joke and I wanted to snigger but I thrust my bag of breakfast cakes on the table and said, 'I brought your breakfast.'

And so we sat facing each other, eating our breakfast cakes and continuing our conversation where it had lapsed several evenings since, punctuating our prose with quotes of our favourite poems with each silently judging the poetic taste of the other until, our breakfast over, we sat on the sofa facing the wide window looking out at the beach. The Mediterranean, I thought to myself, aware that I had moved into a permanent cliché.

And then Bernard was slowly undressing me and I was unbuttoning his buttons and we both knew this was the reason for my visit. Naked, we went to the bedroom to the big double bed while the sea hushed and washed and hushed outside and the morning sun dazzled and glittered in the room. Bernard was about to draw the curtains when I said, thinking I sounded very experienced, and remembering a sentence from the book *Meeting and Mating* that my sisters and I had studied years ago, 'It is a good idea to make love in daylight,' casually as if I knew it all.

I lay on the bed. I stared at Bernard's large erected penis. I did not dare say that this was the first time I had been with a naked man. I continued to stare at the red-roofed dovecote full of white doves ready to fly into the sky and never return; and I was the sky; and how strange that was, I, with all my conversation during our walk, about the 'men in my life' was having a first experience and only I knew. And there was Bernard suddenly two beings, himself, and the manikin that resembled a dovecote. I felt the sadness and finality of being in the midst of a *True Romance* ('then he . . . then I . . .') in a white stone villa by the Mediterranean.

Bernard then went to the bathroom and returned with the dovecote dressed in a condom while a vague unhappiness came over me as I asked myself, 'Why is he so prepared, carrying them about like indigestion tablets?' I quelled my momentary chill: I did not want to forgo my new experience. Oh why, I thought, must I touch up my feelings to make them acceptably *love* as it should be without doubts and suspicions. And thus I apply cosmetics to what may be already a corpse?

We spent the morning lovemaking. In spite of my reading in the subject, I, limited in my knowledge to the 'missionary' act, suffered or enjoyed shocks and surprises that were lessened by the addicting sensations. Besides, I felt I could not undo my lies about myself as 'experienced'. I, who supposed I was always searching for the 'truth', was I now searching for the truth within a lie? I knew the lies were those of vanity and cowardice, of unwillingness to see my life as it had been and not as I supposed or hoped it might have been.

In the afternoon, newly entwined in a strong swiftly sealed bond, arms around each other, hand clasped tightly, we walked out in the daylight through the streets of the town. We passed Figuretti's.

'There's Figuretti's,' Bernard said while I stared about me at the mysterious world of sky, stone, sand, sea.

'Figuretti's,' I repeated as if it were game, a contest I had engaged in all my life and could never know the answers.

We came to the Post Office where I found a parcel waiting for me. From England. Who could have sent it?

Later, at the villa, we opened the parcel to find four tins of corned beef from Patrick Reilly.

And a letter that ended, 'I hope you are still fancy free.'

I savoured the feeling of transgressing as Bernard and I lay in bed making love and later eating our corned beef and French loaf.

From that day I spent every night and much of the day at Bernard's villa. I'd steal home at breakfast time, trying to keep up the pretence of the innocent *escritora* from Nueva Zelanda and knowing I had failed when I saw the disappointment in the eyes of both Catalina and Francesca when I met them one morning as I came in the door.

'El Americano?' Francesca questioned with a sly smile. 'Mucho dinero?'

I lapsed into my mixture of French and Spanish.

It was generally accepted, then, that all Americans were rich, chiefly because they appeared to take for granted and buy the most costly food and goods. Even Edwin, with his scholarship, lived in luxury with purchases beyond the reach of Catalina, Francesca and myself. And there was Bernard living in his 'villa by the Mediterranean'! I could sense the subtle shift in the feelings of Catalina and Francesca towards me; I was no longer the bewildered Janetta all alone, waiting for her luggage and her typewriter; I had become, not without a sense of triumph for myself as well as a feeling of loss, one of the female devils, and, being one, I knew I had now sacrificed the rare pleasure of again being invited to Catalina's and Francesca's tiny apartment to share, say, a fiesta party, sitting around the table laughing and talking while the brazier burned beneath.

Now, I had joined Los Americanos. I was Bernard's 'woman'.

Bernard and I called on other Americans, many of them exiles from the McCarthy regime — the film director turned painter who had built himself a villa in Ibiza and who conducted us through his personal gallery of the American Civil War where each of the portraits of the Generals were portraits of himself. We attended recitals of music and poetry at the French

Prancing on the beach at Stewart Island. Myself second from left.

The Frame house at Willowglen from the 1940s on.

Isabel, the day before her death by drowning.

Jess Whitworth on one of her London trips.

Cottage in Braiseworth, East Suffolk, where I lived at reduced rent in return for helping with the garden and the dog.

Apt scenes from Andorra the day I left, during the snow.

The Italian gentleman of Andorra.

Right: *At Willowglen after hospital days.*

Below: *After my hospital days.*

Left: *Sitting at the door of Frank Sargeson's hut.*

Below: *At the Auckland Show with June in 1955.*

Dad with June and her children (Pamela, Ian and Neil), in the 1950s.

Dad photographed at Aunty Grace's in Kaikoura, 1958.

Dr John Money (Forrest), late 1950s.

This photo was taken in London in the 1950s.

George (Bruddie) and his cat.

Willowglen in blossom time.

The day the cow looked in the front door at Willowglen.

Dad and the old sheepdog in the 1950s.

Mother.

Mother feeding a fantail at Willowglen.

Mother with a cow in the 1950s.

Left: George (Bruddie) selling race books at the race course in the 1940s. He was about 20 years old and working at the freezing works.

Below: George working at the Oamaru baths, pumping water out, about 1955.

Dad trying out a new train at the Oamaru sheds, about 1950.

Mother wearing her best straw hat, with two cows, in the 1950s.

Left: *After my return to New Zealand, in 1964.*

Below: *On board the* Corinthic, *returning to New Zealand in 1963.*

June revisiting Picton in the 1960s.

June near the family graves at Picton, April 1985.

Institute. We wined and dined with Edwin's and Bernard's friends, mostly Americans, with the men and women living with their chosen partners in the sensuous sensual kind of luxury enjoyed by the lotus eaters. Now and then I found myself in alarming situations — the time I arrived at a dinner party to discover I was the only guest while my host, a stranger, sitting at the far end of the table suddenly collapsed with malaria and I wondered as I helped him to his bedroom and undressed him if his sickness was a version of the 'etchings' we had often laughed about in our girlhood. He was genuinely ill. Aware that I was indeed fulfilling the purpose of my literary grant by 'broadening my experience', I sat all night by his bed, preparing and feeding him medicine.

During our calls on the Americans I learned much from what was said and unsaid. I heard of the mechanics of drug-running. I was not aware that anyone I knew was drug-trafficking or taking but my innocence in this was so complete that I wonder now if I misread signs or neglected to notice them. I simply listened, fascinated by all the stories as if I were a child allowed to stay up late to listen to the exploits of the grown-up world.

I was unable to ignore some real intimations of the future of others and in turn to wonder about my own risks when I heard that Barbara, a painter living and painting happily with Greg, another painter, was suddenly alone, in distress. Greg had gone to Paris and would not be returning and people were asking Barbara how would she manage when the baby was born. Would she stay on the island? How would she provide for herself? Would she return to America to have the baby or would she choose not to have it? There was still time . . . someone knew someone who knew someone . . . Everyone felt sorry for Barbara. It had happened to others, too, they said.

On one of my rare meetings with Edwin at Ignacio Riquer when I murmured out of habit our classic phrase of — centuries ago, in my life — 'Quiere el fuego?' he replied with, 'I hope you know what you're doing?'

'Of course I do,' I said.

'But what about your writing? I never hear your typewriter these days. What has happened?'

'Well . . .'

Bernard occupied my mind and my body. We explored the island, hiring bicycles and spending the day on remote beaches. We talked and quoted and sang and made love. Once, we visited his friends on a yacht in the harbour (Mirror City!). Their supply of guns frightened me.

Then one night when we were in bed Bernard said, dismayed, 'I've run out of supplies. I meant to get some.'

I felt distaste for his concern. In such moments one does not care about such things.

'What does it matter?' I said recklessly.

Later, I said dreamily, 'What if I do have a baby?'

Bernard's reply shocked me.

'That would be terrible,' he said.

He meant it. That would be terrible. His words haunted me with a reality that until then had been unable to reach me. A baby, a loving replica of Bernard and me; a gift from Bernard for whom I'd felt a determined kind of love that, during the past weeks as soon as there were signs of disarray, I had quickly straightened and smoothed to preserve in perfection — wasn't a baby the fulfilment of our love?

His words, 'That would be terrible,' effectively destroyed that perfect love. Quite suddenly the place on earth marked — as I thought indelibly — by the giant resumed its former shape and growth. I felt my life, like the grass, resuming its place, responding to sun and light and wind: my longing and love and passion for Bernard were gone. His cold words, 'That would be terrible. A baby would be terrible,' how could he have thought and spoken them? A baby would be terrible.

That night was the last I spent at the villa. I returned to live and write in my room at Calle Ignacio Riquer. I found a key for the front door and locked it and refused to answer when Bernard called. Edwin and I returned to our routine of painting and writing and each afternoon I went to his studio to see his morning's work. He had named one of his paintings 'The Street Where the Children Don't Play Anymore'.

'Remember?' he said.

I remembered. We had been walking late through the streets while someone played the flute and the flute-notes fell sharp as broken cobblestones, glittering in the moonlight and the children who had been playing all day in the street had long since vanished.

'It's like a street where the children don't play any more,' I said.

Then one day Edwin told me that Bernard was leaving the island. I was missing him. We had nested in each other and there's no warmer nest than skin.

The day Bernard left, I gave Edwin a bunch of wild flowers to take to him at the ship.

Catalina and Francesca were both pleased to learn that El Americano had gone.

'Los Americanos,' they said. 'They disturb everything. Everywhere. Even the light.'

And that was true, for Edwin was in disgrace again having blown the electric fuses with his high-powered lamps.

'They disturb the light,' Francesca said. 'And make everything dark.'

I stayed six more weeks in Ibiza. Not being with Bernard hurt more than I had supposed it would for he had taken over my life and my self and now, in his absence, searching the empty places, I found only a blank uninhabited darkness with fleeting glimpses of Bernard. My love had been awakened partly through my deliberate engineering of my feelings and partly through my delight in the sound of Bernard's laughter. I had nurtured the love and even in the short period I had known it, its complexity, its light absorbed everything I knew or felt or had been or would be.

True Romance indeed! So much for poetry and music! I was beginning to suspect that I might be pregnant. I was overtaken by an alarm that did not quite match my image of perfect love. Also, my money would not last for ever. Edwin, whom I did not tell of my possible plight but who knew my funds were low, suggested I might try living in Andorra, the 'free' money-market he had spoken of before. He sensed that Ibiza had become an intolerable place for me — Ibiza, my island now in its warm balm of blossom with the interior and the gentle hills shining with the forests of light-green pine trees, their branches tipped a glossier lighter green with new growth — Ibiza was suddenly changed, steeped in my own feelings, destroyed by my glance. Where before my surroundings (I supposed) had existed in their own right, the sky and the sea and the weather and the Mirror City, and I too had existed in my own right, with the island and its features as my companions, now all suffered an effect, not the Midas touch but the touch of ash: I could almost see the trees decaying, the olive blossoms withering; also, I was invaded by knowing others on the island, I was no longer alone, creator and preserver of my world, in harmony with other worlds because I could interpret them as I wished: I was tasting the sour and bitter of absence and lost pleasure, bound to a magnet of reality.

(When autumn is over and the leaves have fallen from the trees with only·the dark evergreens retaining their bulk which is at once a shelter and an obstacle to the passage of light, we see that we have never been alone in the forest. Shapes of houses emerge, people going about their daily lives; there's a new perspective of distance, a discovery of horizons one could never see during spring and summer and guess at only, throughout autumn. Look at those tall chimneys rising from fires we never knew were lit but that still burn, fuelled in secret! Look at the newly revealed paths! Now I, more clearly looking through this and that world and its seasons become also more clearly looked at. My own surroundings lose their camouflage; I myself lose my camouflage. There is even the possibility of nests, new or abandoned, in my own tree!)

12   *Andorra*

I left Ibiza on a grey day when the Mediterranean was whipped mountainously by a gale into waves thirty feet high and I and the other passengers had to be helped on board the violently tossing ferry. There was a kind of recklessness, an embracing of doom in the way I ignored what would formerly have terrified me. I said goodbye to Edwin, faithful Edwin who still hoped to see *Owls Do Cry* published in New York. I then went at once to my cabin and was seasick all night and in the morning, in the glassy calm when the ship, scarcely moving, berthed at Barcelona, I collected my suitcases, my green haversack, and grasping these and my bulky Traveller's Joy handbag, I sat in a classically forlorn pose, on an upturned suitcase, on Barcelona wharf as I recovered from my seasickness and wondered where to go and what to do. I knew only that my *destination* was Andorra.

Later, I found a room in a small hotel and as I walked into the hallway and smelled the pervading smell of olives and olive oil, I felt a wave of homesickness for Ibiza, Catalina, Francesca, Fermin, José, all my Ibicencan family and myself as the innocent *escritora* with the quiet uncomplicated daily chores and the simple stack of typing paper and the communion with Mirror City.

And now it was Bernard whose presence stayed, like a phantom. He was there beside me, around, within me. Hearing his laughter in the street I'd look out to see a stranger laughing and talking among strangers.

The next morning I was told that no buses travelled to Andorra at that time of year. It was still winter on the mainland and the months of Ibicencan spring were like a mirage, a dream remembered in the cold wind of Barcelona. The roads to Andorra were impassable except for one used by private cars. I could hire a taxi, someone suggested.

The taxi was cheap. I could not believe that I, a New Zealander who never went anywhere by taxi, was travelling late that morning from Barcelona to Andorra with two other passengers, through the villages of northern Spain, past the fields and ancient monasteries and the miles of red earth. The other passengers soon left the minibus, for such it was, leaving me marvelling alone at the small villages growing like dark-red fruit and flowers out of the earth, or like old wounds, still open in places, covered with congealed blood that beneath the brilliant blue sky were unrelieved by the usual benison of green. I tried to seize and hold the memory of those villages for I knew that this would perhaps be my only journey through northern Spain. I knew also that whatever I remembered I would see the country's wounds opening as in the Civil War and I'd think of my Ibicencan

friends and Fermin pointing to the place of the executions beside the Stations of the Cross.

Soon the bus began its ascent through the foothills of the Pyrenees where the light became choked suddenly by the forests of dark green pines, almost black in the afternoon. The contrast between the gently light-green trees of Ibiza, their foliage soft, clouded, sometimes yellow in the falling sunlight, and the stark black of the northern trees against the snow seemed to be part of the natural regression from southern spring to northern winter and in tune with the mood of the inescapable present that sooner or later besets a woman of thirty-two who is alone and may be pregnant. (Undoubtedly during that journey I performed an exercise in emotional pollution by transposing the outward to the inward scene, back and forth until I might have believed that I became the dark winter-embraced pine tree.)

By late afternoon we had arrived at the village of Andorra La Vella where I unloaded my increasingly burdensome luggage, paid the driver, and once again sat on an upturned suitcase while I pondered my next move. I had supposed that Andorra would be a large town of the principality, but here was a village square lined with buildings and, beyond, the mountains. I therefore began to walk along the street and I had just turned a corner on the road out of town when I met a young man.

'Por favor,' I said. 'Quiero una habitacion.'

Without replying at first he beckoned me to follow him until we came to a carload of workmen leaving Andorra for their homes in other villages. The young man, Carlos, explained that he would take me to his home in Les Escaldes where he was sure his wife and he could give me a room.

'Come with me,' he said.

A short drive away, at Les Escaldes, Carlos and I left the car and walked through the main street towards the river, a roaring mountain torrent that washed at the basement walls of the tenement buildings lining its banks. We climbed the narrow stairs of one such building to the third floor, an apartment overlooking the street where Carlos, his wife Donna, their two children, six-year-old Antoine and four-year-old Xavier lived, and as Carlos was explaining to Donna that I was hoping to find *una habitacion* with them, the children, shy, large-eyed, clung to their mother's skirt and stared at me. The stare changed to angry bewilderment when they learned that their bedroom was no longer their bedroom, but Mama's and Papa's also, while I was to sleep in Mama's and Papa's room, in the big double bed with the feather mattress. I did not learn at once of my disruption of the family's sleeping arrangements but I soon understood that, struggling in poverty, they were grateful for extra pesetas. The remaining small bedroom was rented to another lodger, El Vici Mario, whom I met for the first time that evening.

The other rooms were a tiny kitchen, a lavatory with a washbasin and two taps, hot and cold, with only the cold giving water as the town's hot water, drawn from hot springs in the mountains, could be freely used at the basins and taps in the square and the municipal bathing and washing house.

My room looked on to the street, closely overlooked by the snow-covered Pyrenees, and the night air in the room tasted of snow and was so cold that it had the effect of pain, not endless, but mingled with the pleasurable anticipation of daylight and, perhaps, the sun's warmth. I snuggled into my featherbed like a bird in its nest with the mattress heaped around me, and there I tried to plan a future that included a child, for it was almost certain that I was pregnant. I remembered how my small eight-year-old friend, Poppy, had said that if Hollywood stars didn't want their babies they drank gin or ate quinine or ran up and down mountains . . . well, I was in the Pyrenees, wasn't I? How had Poppy collected such folklore? And why did I think so swiftly of childhood solutions? I knew that in hospital I'd had a serious enduring lesson on what may happen when one person in a group or community has power to decide the life or death of others, and giving myself such a right was abhorrent. Yet, trying to enter the nearer reality, I became trapped in it. I did hurry up and down the slopes of the Pyrenees. I also swallowed quinine tablets. At the same time, I prepared for the baby so as to clothe and warm it. I bought wool, knitting needles, a French book of instructions (explaining, 'ma soeur . . . son bébé . . .) and I began knitting for 'le premier âge' from the section 'de la naissance à trois mois . . . pour tous les soins du bébé . . . ensemble d'exécution simple et rapide . . .' I knitted a tiny matinée jacket and bootees, placing them neatly in the bottom of my suitcase.

Another month passed. I had begun to fit in with the family's routine, each morning taking the tin bucket along the street, over the ancient stone bridge to the dairy for the day's milk, returning in time to share breakfast with the children, now up and dressed, and El Vici Mario and Donna and Carlos. We sat around the table with the big bowl of bread and milk in the centre while each fed from the bowl and passed it to the next person. Then Xavier and Antoine left for the Spanish school (Andorra had both Spanish and French schools). Even at four, Xavier was reading in the first sentence of his first book, of earliest violence — 'Cain mató a su hermano Abel . . .'

During the day when Carlos and El Vici and the children had gone, Donna and I talked about 'this and that' — the children, Carlos, El Vici, how hard it was to earn a living during the winter when there was little work for a carpenter, and how Carlos therefore earned money during the winter by waiting at a restaurant on Sunday evenings, bringing home wages that he could not count for he could neither read nor write nor calculate, and that Donna who had been to school counted for him, trying to teach him by arranging coloured counters with the coins on the dining room table. This was why it was important, she said, for the children to go to school each day in all weathers; and perhaps one day the family might emigrate to Canada to start a new life. Their neighbours in the apartment opposite, overlooking the river, were emigrating to Canada. The woman's husband had left ten months ago promising to send the fare for his wife and children when he had earned enough money and found a permanent place to live. He'd written at first, and he'd even sent money for the house-keeping, but for months there had been no word·from him and sometimes Lola had cried wondering what would become of her and the three *crios*.

In the afternoons and evenings I'd tell the children stories using both the French and Spanish versions of 'Once upon a time' — 'Il y avait une fois' and 'Hay en tiempos muy remotos . . .' phrases that always transport me to the mirror world like the Mirror City where civilisations live their lives under the light of the imagination instead of the sun. Lured always by that world and by the fascination of trying to describe it in words that may not even exist for accurate description, from a limited vocabulary, I realised increasingly the extent of its treasure, discovered during visits to the Mirror City where the great artists had lived and returned to describe what they had seen and felt and known. I knew that some had visited and never returned. And here was I with yet another key to the city — 'Hay en tiempos muy remotos', an entrance through the past to the present and the future with stories picked like flowers from the wayside as the traveller moves to and from the City.

As in Ibiza, I became one of the family in Les Escaldes. On Sundays, wearing my black mantilla, I went to church with the family. On Sunday evenings we went to the local cinema where we watched an American film, usually a Western, with Spanish subtitles. And while in the morning I tried to type my book, I was becoming more worried about the pregnancy and myself as the mother of a child: occasionally I was happy, thinking I'd have a replica of Bernard, picturing a boy with Bernard's face and build and laugh, or a girl with his eyes; while of myself reproduced I could see only another fuzzily red-haired Shirley Temple-dimpled child as I had been and I could not imagine Bernard's contribution to another myself. Perhaps, I thought, our grandparents might emerge, effectively cancelling or setting aside our characteristics, or heredity might reach further into the past to retrieve some abandoned trait waiting like a railway coach on a siding to be returned to the main line.

Such romantic dreams were soon dismissed as I recklessly wandered in the mountains, climbing steep slopes, and vaguely wondering about the signs, *Perigo, Danger, Avalanches*. I climbed to the warm lake nestled in the peaks, and I sat gazing down at the dark pines below the snowline, and again I thought of the pines of Ibiza 'que el corazon venera' contrasting them with the dark grief-bowed heads of the pines of Andorra. I passed villages of stone that seemed to be growing out of the rock, huge barns full of cattle, the smell of their manure lingering around the entrance but freezing to nothingness in the mountain breath of the snow. Soon, I was told, the sheep would be driven home through the passes from France where they spent each winter. I learned much about these mountain passes from El Vici who knew the routes by heart and who earned his living, in winter, both as a smuggler and a guide. My naivety was such that El Vici's smuggling gave him a romantic aura: I never wondered about the nature of the goods smuggled: I simply imagined a group of wild-looking men, El Vici among them, trundling packhorses laden with boxes of contraband across the rugged mountain passes.

After my daily walk I swallowed my quinine tablet as I hoped and denied my hope and grew increasingly fearful and pleased at my condition. It was the need for light that brought a solution to the problem. Although Andorra, unlike Ibiza, had plentiful electricity from the mountain rivers, the inhabitants like Carlos and Donna were too poor to use it and therefore, as in Ibiza, the electric light bulbs were too dim for reading and writing. As Edwin had done in Ibiza (El Americano who 'killed' the light), as Francesca described him, I bought a bulb of higher wattage and standing on a chair, and reaching to change the light to a higher intensity, I became dizzy and sick and fell, and blood flowed reminding me of that first time it had flowed, in the daffodil, snow, World War and birthday time in Oamaru. The blood was bulky. I collected it in a towel and flushed it down the lavatory, pulling the chain several times before it shredded (a quick horror-filled glance told me) and vanished.

Weak and sick I lay in my featherbed and looked at the snow on the mountains.

'You're very pale,' Donna said that evening.

'It's one of those days,' I said.

She smiled, recognising that we were two women in a male household. I did not realise until the baby had gone that I had accepted it and was preparing for it. I knew a feeling that was stronger than regret but not as intense as a bereavement, a no-woman's land of feeling where a marvellous sense of freedom sprang up beside hate for myself, longing for Bernard and what he had given me and never knew, sadness for a lost path, vanishings, with the sense of freedom and the prospect of living a new life in Mirror

City, triumphing like the rankest, strongest, most pungent weeds that yet carry exquisite flowers, outgrowing the accepted flowers in no-woman's land.

The physical loss, like widowhood, of Bernard and the loss of the tiny envelope of growth, his 'share', made me turn naturally to accept El Vici's offered company, urged by the delighted Donna and Carlos who already had plans to see us married in the new church. My few days' sickness aroused less attention because the two boys had developed chickenpox and were kept home from school in their darkened room and given drinks of *tisane*.

And in my newly clarified and fused and perhaps con-fused state I accepted El Vici's invitation to go with him for a picnic in the mountains, and so one morning, aware of the approval of Carlos and Donna and of the glances of El Vici's friends along the street, we set out with our picnic along the mountain paths towards the snowline. I had learned that El Vici had been a Resistance worker during the war, later a prisoner in a French concentration camp, and after the war he came to live in Andorra as his knowledge of the mountain pathways was intimate and detailed; in the autumn he picked grapes in the south of France or worked in a fur shop in the south. Like many Italians he was a skilled bicycle racer and so had brought his wonderful blue and white bicycle to Andorra where it was kept in his bedroom, for although he did not ride it, he polished it, oiled it, and turned it upside down on the landing while he spun the wheels and fiddled with the gears. He had given me this information about himself in French which, with Italian and Spanish, he spoke fluently.

I, always an admirer of those with a gift for language, was prepared to like this tall handsome man. I admired his fight against the Fascists led by Il Duce, Mussolini, I sympathised with his suffering and torture in a concentration camp; the fact, however, that I could not accept his wearing of two-tone black and white shoes, and particularly his wearing them in the photograph he gave me, is more a comment on me and the influence of my early life than upon the character of El Vici. In my past and lost world any man wearing 'two-tone' shoes was a 'spiv', a 'lounge lizard', possibly a gangster.

As we walked towards the snow El Vici pointed out landmarks and we talked in French although occasionally we would speak Spanish. We stopped a few yards from the snow that I, enraptured always by snow, heralded with quotes from French poetry in what seemed to be an alarming, even a pathetic, repetition of my first walk in Ibiza with Bernard. I felt that I was playing an old record, perhaps my only one, and I thought, would it always be like this, in these circumstances, up and down the same worn pathways of the brain?

As I spread the food on the bare patch of rock, El Vici told how he had been born and brought up in Milano, and how his father was a quiet man and his mother was huge in build (he spread his hands apart to depict the width of his mother). He explained that he'd not had 'la bonne chance' with women.

As we began to eat our salami and bread and drink our wine, he suddenly leaned forward to grab at my breasts. I, the prim young woman again, struggled free.

'Oh no,' I said, adopting the manner of a counsellor on affairs of the heart. 'Let's talk about this.' I didn't kiss and cuddle those I didn't know well, I said.

'But you have come walking in the mountains with me,' El Vici protested. 'No woman goes walking in the mountains with a man unless they wish to be lovers.' Women did not go out alone as I did, walking and walking by the river, through the streets, in the mountains. In future, he said, someone should walk with me. He would walk with me and when he was working, Donna and Carlos and the children would escort me. I was Andorran now, he said. Andorra was my home.

El Vici's feelings were more serious than I had gauged. After the day of the picnic he made sure that I did not walk alone, and as it was now the beginning of the Andorran spring, although the road into France was still closed, the mountain flowers were coming into bloom and Donna and the children and I went picking flowers — white violets, primroses, freesias, lilies, their scent still frozen within them by the snowfilled air. I still managed to have my solitary walks, sometimes following the path of the Andorra river or walking into Andorra La Vella to collect parcels sent by Patrick Reilly from England — tins of corned beef, Irish stew, creamed rice, as if I were living in a land of hunger. I had nostalgic letters from Edwin, too. Ibiza was not the same. The old crowd had left, the house was lonely, and Fermin still came to play squeaky music on his violin and the two old servants still pottered around prying into everything and complaining about the terrible crime he was committing by increasing the power of the light bulbs. He had applied for another scholarship, Edwin wrote. Based in Paris. He had not heard from Bernard.

Then one evening when El Vici and I were talking in his room, El Vici suddenly knelt before me, murmuring as he tried to put a ring on my finger, 'Voulez-vous me marier, moi?' The ring, he said, had belonged to his grandmother in Milano.

I was flattered, alarmed, and melancholy, for it was Bernard who still occupied my thoughts and dreams. I realised also that because I'd had the years of my twenties removed from my life I was now behaving in some ways like a woman in her early twenties who had recently left school and home and was exploring for the first time the world of men, women, sex, love. Although I did not accept El Vici's ring, I did not reject him. Was I prompted perhaps by an impulse of greed, for love at any cost? He and the family therefore concluded that we were 'engaged' and would be married in the church in Andorra. My response had been wait and see. Then, with a sense of panic, I explained that I would first need to return to London where I had 'things to see to' (as if I were arranging my life in preparation for my death), and I would then return to Andorra.

And so it happened again that during the remainder of my stay in Andorra I found myself assuming my most accustomed role, that of the passive person whose life is being planned for her while she dare not for fear of punishment or provocation, refuse. After spending so many years in hospital I was beginning to learn that in the years that followed, this role waited always for me, and much of my life would be spent trying to escape from a prison that I had entered because I was 'used to it and use is everything.'

And so I went walking with El Vici at the proper time for 'promenading'. We attended church, preparing for the late Easter Festival. Donna talked to me of what I would wear at the wedding. Introduced to me, El Vici's friends shook hands heartily and spoke friendly words. And at night curled in my featherbed nest and looking out at the snowcovered mountains behind the buildings of Les Escaldes, I thought of the day's conversation with El Vici, the plans he was making, the answers he gave to my questions, and I felt a chill alarm spreading through me at the prospect of my future life, first in Andorra, then in the south of France working in vineyards, or helping in the fur shop, perhaps living in poverty, trying to take care of *los crios*. I found myself thinking like an 'Englishwoman' going to live in the 'colonies' — 'What about the children's education, the schools?' And what of books, and reading, and my writing? What of music and art? I did not want to become one of the characters that I had seen so romantically as living figures from the paintings of the great artists. Nor did I want to repeat what I had now done several times — used poetry to put myself in human danger and to try to force a flow of love towards me. I was learning that the uses of poetry are endless but not always harmless.

El Vici went with me while I bought a return ticket to London. While he waited outside the travel agency I asked urgently, 'If I don't use the return ticket will my money be refunded?' The clerk assured me it would be.

The Easter celebration was solemnly joyful with the traditional chocolate cake in the shape of a house, the large golden wheel of cheese distributed by the priest from the food parcel from the American government, fondants and biscuits and canalones that I helped Donna make. The table was dressed with a white cloth and candles, like an altar, and even Antoine and Xavier who had been in disgrace for having thrown their Palm Sunday palms out the window into the street, sat quietly and obediently wearing their white lace collars and their best clothes. Everyone glanced lovingly at everyone else with special glances for El Vici and me, and again I felt myself under the spell of the Spanish and Italian faces with the dark glowing eyes that belonged in the paintings of the masters who 'about suffering were never wrong'. Oh why could I not be there, too, in the painting? I, in spite of my Celtic red hair, my birthplace an antipodean world where the trees like the pines of Andorra, were a serious evergreen, the colour of eternity, of sovereignty, of the forest ruling naturally with the sea, the sky, the land, the weather. My desire to belong (and how much closer may one be to belonging when one is within both the real city and the Mirror City?) increased my willingness to allow others to decide my life.

That evening I sat in my room, my typewriter balanced on my knee, typing. I heard the murmur of voices as Donna worked with Carlos and the coloured counters. I knew that El Vici was in his room, perhaps polishing his blue and white bicycle. It occurred to me suddenly that I did not know whether he could read or write . . . I was the Englishwoman again among the 'poor peasants' who could never escape, while I could escape to London. I thought again of the *crios*, his and mine, loved and wanted but poor, barefooted, unable to go to school — how far did I wish to go, I wondered, in this 'broadening of experience' I had promised to the Literary Fund Committee when I applied for my grant to travel overseas?

And my writing? In a future where I was never alone, where I worked all day picking grapes, caring for children, cooking for my family . . . how could I ever be alone again, able to enter that world of imagination to explore it and try to describe it? Certainly I would be living within it in the world of the old masters but in a world where the cherubs cried and wet their nappies, where bunches of grapes moved and grew and must be picked, in millions, not merely enough to fill a bowl lit by an everlasting shaft of golden light, where dimly lit rooms with all their wonderful play of light and shadow must be lived in, cleaned and repaired and made weatherproof.

And I did not love El Vici: he simply fitted willingly into a vacant space that would soon have its natural overgrowth more suitable to the kind of life I wished to lead.

In mid-May, the very morning the road to France was re-opened, I waited with Donna, Carlos, El Vici and the children for the small mountain bus to Perpignan. There were sad farewells, much hugging and kissing and tenderness. No, I told El Vici as we kissed, I would not take his ring with me for perhaps I might lose it. The solemn wise-eyed children who perhaps knew everyting (*Cain mató a su hermano Abel*) said their goodbyes. I had bought Antoine a mouth organ with blow-draw instructions; he tried to play a tune for me. I gave Donna my green cortina and the warm brown coat bought for me by my two laughing aunts, Elsie and Joy, mother's sisters. Then, with kisses again for everyone, last for El Vici, I boarded.

The snow lay in two high walls each side of the road. I sat entranced by the blue light, the unreal mountain road brooded over by the snow and the pine trees, and the way that the bus, the first vehicle on the opened road, struggled with its snowplough to clear the path for the snow was falling again. Then, arriving in Perpignan I felt as if I had emerged from a vale of darkness for suddenly the trees were light green, the earth was bathed in a soft cloud of green spring, the *right* springtime. I spent two and a half hours waiting for the train, walking in the village, sitting on the stone seat outside the cemetery, enjoying a luxury of solitude and silence, and the peace, lapped by the desolation of a small wayside station where nothing is coming or going very often, where the posters advertise other places — cities, cathedrals, oceans, other suns and skies full of bright yellow sunlight. I thought of the small railway stations on the main trunk line in the South Island of New Zealand — Winton, Gore, Balclutha, Milton, Clinton . . . and of course walking through the cemetery recalled for me the French poems and prose that were never far from my thoughts . . . 'Qu'il était triste, le cimetière de La Semillante . . . Que je le vois encore avec sa petite muraille basse . . .', sentences that, like music, tastes, perfumes, colours, define and isolate the brooding memories, seeding the clouds, as it were, with pearls. Why do such memories unfailingly return me to my lifelong preoccupation with the sky, with alternating moments of the sun's warmth and the chill and despair of losing the sun and waiting for its return, of a life supervised, blessed and made lonely by the sky?

I boarded the train to Paris where I spent the night in the hotel by the Bastille. The next day I arrived in London to find Patrick Reilly meeting me at the station with the news that he had found a new place to stay in Clapham Common South and had he been presumptuous in renting a room for me also? The landlady, he said, wished to be called, simply, Ma.

I thanked him. What work had I to show, I wondered, for my time in Ibiza and Andorra? I quote Albert Camus for I cannot express it so well myself, 'Living is slightly the opposite of expressing. If I am to believe the great Tuscan masters, it means bearing triple witness, in silence, flames and immobility.'

PART TWO

At Home in the City

13 *London*

In London I planned to find work and to discover by objective means whether I had ever suffered from schizophrenia. I hoped to take advantage of the offer from John Forrest to arrange an appointment for me at the Institute of Psychiatry. Although I was still inclined to cherish the distorted 'privilege' of having schizophrenia because it allied me with the great artists more readily than my attempts to produce works of art might have done, I suspected that my published writing might destroy that tenuous alliance, for I could not people, everlastingly, my novels with characters suffering from the 'Ophelia syndrome' with details drawn from my observations in hospital. I knew that the Ophelia syndrome is a poetic fiction that nevertheless usefully allows a writer to explore varieties of otherwise unspoken or unacceptable feelings, thoughts, and language.

I planned also to find an agent who would submit *Owls Do Cry* to English and American publishers while, supported by my earnings from a job, I continued writing my poems, stories, and the novel I had begun before I left New Zealand — *Uncle Pylades*.

My next preoccupation, as a result of my love affair in Ibiza, my parting from Bernard, my shortlived pregnancy, and my too ready acceptance of El Vici Mario as my future husband, was my need to gain more than an elementary knowledge of female and male anatomy and sexual practices: my ignorance even in my pretended state of 'sophisticated woman' had been appalling.

And so with Patrick Reilly's faithful and sometimes misdirected help, I began to study the Situations Vacant columns of the *South London Press* while Patrick, as before, like a conformist New Zealand conscience that had somehow travelled with me and assumed human shape, kept reminding me, 'You want a good steady job. A typist or secretary. You don't want to spend your time writing. There's no money in it. And it's not savoury.'

Obediently I went with him to the Labour Exchange in Vauxhall Road ('for the better type of worker, temp. or permanent') where my nervousness made me unable to pass the typing test without making too many mistakes.

'What about Peek Frean's then?'

Ah, Peek Frean's! Perhaps to Patrick the London equivalent of Figuretti's. I thought nostalgically of my early days in London of Patrick's dominating kindness and his continued reference to Peek Frean's — the biscuit (digestive, dark chocolate), the biscuit factory, even the factory premises, and how I'd been haunted by the name — Peek Frean's, with the other London names Tooting Bdy, Hatfield North, Crystal Palace, High Barnet . . . these names returned with renewed power.

I murmured, knowing Patrick would reply, 'Peek Frean's.'

'Yes, Peek Frean's. You could work in the biscuit factory.'

I did not take Patrick's advice; instead, I answered an advertisement for a writer of a fashion catalogue with a mail order firm in Brixton, and after an interview with Mr Jones when I flipped through a copy of *Owls Do Cry* saying casually that I had written the book and noting that he appeared to be impressed, I was given the job, with a copy of an old catalogue for me to study and learn the descriptions of clothing. I would work with others in a large room; writing from 'nine till five'.

It was the presence of 'others' that deterred me. I explained that I had found other work.

Next, as I was now living near the South London Hospital for Women which advertised constantly for domestic help, I applied for work as a part-time wardsmaid but my interview with the matron resulted in her advising me to apply for nursing training as she considered me to be 'good nursing material'. The older students in their late twenties and early thirties, she said, were more able to apply themselves to study and practical work: she was sure I would make an excellent nurse. I would need a medical certificate of course, but that would be no problem as I appeared to be a healthy, intelligent, capable young woman.

The ideas and the flattery lured me. I made an appointment for a medical examination, choosing a doctor with rooms nearby, and with a name that sounded absurdly fictional, and that I now reduce, for obvious reasons, to initials. Dr C. S. My medical examination was never conducted because I made the mistake of disclosing my 'mental history' whereupon Dr C. S., instantly alarmed and horrified, her horror mixed with sympathy, exclaimed that nursing was not for me. She scanned my face for 'signs' of my prolonged incarceration and what had caused it; I knew better than to say it had been a 'mistake'.

Quickly she began ushering me to the door where she paused, perhaps slightly ashamed of her haste and her ill-concealed fear. She did have a friend, she said, who wanted a maid for light domestic help, and perhaps I could work there . . . under supervision, of course. Otherwise . . . with my history . . . my condition . . .

She ushered me quickly out the door.

I remember that interview vividly: its essence is contained in the peculiarly fictional name of Dr C. S. Among my memories of London names it has a place beside Peek Frean's, Tooting Bdy, Tufnell Park . . . except that unlike these it enclosed a small globule of horror.

It was not only the evil of conformity in the shape of Patrick Reilly that pursued me; my own past, too, continued to loom. How could I regain my confidence when I had never been able to tell 'my side' of the story? I knew it was time for me to find out 'the truth'.

Therefore I arranged through John Forrest an appointment with Dr Michael Berger of the Institute of Psychiatry.

In the meantime I found a job, a literary agent, and I bought an encyclopaedia of sex.

14 Questions

I became an usherette at the Regal Theatre, Streatham (women were known by the diminutive form of the word — *usherette*), where I began each day at half-past ten to prepare for the eleven o'clock session, with a break in the afternoon, and on alternate days I'd work the five o'clock or the seven o'clock session; sometimes both, finishing after eleven o'clock at night, after the routine search of the theatre for stray patrons, lost property; and newborn babies in the lavatory. I tried to enjoy the work for it was no doubt a 'broadening of experience' but it was not pleasant being in charge of a theatreful of children during the Saturday morning sessions or trying to control the teddy boys and girls in the Sunday afternoon sex-and-horror movies, or, during the intervals, playing the role of ice-maiden with my tray of orange drink, choc ices and plain ices strapped around my waist and over my shoulders and my hands in the half-dark trying to choose the correct change from my 'float', and then, later, having to pay money because I had confused the massive two shilling pieces with New Zealand halfcrowns. The staff and the audience fascinated me. In my role of 'developing writer' I 'studied' them carefully while I learned the language and ways of usherettes, how ushering in the counties was simply another job but ushering in the London suburbs was a prelude to ushering in the theatres like the Leicester Square where premieres were staged and film stars, directors, producers, made personal appearances and where an usherette at the right place and time and creating an interesting impression might find herself noticed, spoken to, perhaps on her way to Hollywood, stardom . . . the big time. This was the dream of all the young usherettes who worked with me and no doubt it was a sustaining dream for those living in the bedsitters of Streatham, Brixton, Clapham, and there was always an imagined or real example of the usherette — 'you remember her . . . only two years ago . . . who'd have thought?' — who 'made good'.

I found the work tiring and depressing: cinemas were being closed, replaced by bingo halls, and with each change of programme the managers of the Regals, ABC's, Odeons and Gaumonts, threatened with the loss of their jobs, tried to devise a more spectacular promotion. One week fake lions roared in the foyer, children took part in impossible competitions that they could never win, reminding me of the games arranged by the picture theatres in my childhood in the days of the Depression when a letter missing from a sentence to be completed with a set of letters, meant, for us, almost life or death. During the three weeks that *The Curse of Frankenstein* played, vampires, stakes, silver bullets, a model of Frankenstein, all in a mixture of horror folklore, were displayed in the foyer. And all the while the manager, a short middle-aged man with an upward gaze and sandy hair looked increasingly anxious; and the usherettes dreamed of the time in Hollywood.

One free day after having chosen from the *Artists' and Writers' Yearbook* an agent, A. M. Heath, who had been the agent of e. e. cummings, and therefore I reasoned, must be willing to deal with experimental writing, that is, sacrifice money for faith in a writer, I went to Dover Street to keep an appointment with Patience Ross, of A. M. Heath. I found the office near the top floor. The general air of disorderliness surprised me — manuscripts everywhere, some piled on the floor, some on shelves, newly published books with the gloss still on their jackets displayed on stands and upon the walls, in cases, on bookshelves; photos of authors, many authors, men and women, all unknown to me.

Patience Ross, wearing black and grey with grey short hair, grey eyes, and a kindly manner, greeted me.

My first literary agent!

She reached into a large handbag crammed with books and drew out the copy of *Owls Do Cry* that she had been reading. She had been impressed by it, she said, although she did not suppose it would be of popular interest. If I agreed to allow them to be my agents they would begin submitting the book to English publishers and, through their agent in the United States, to American publishers, although I must bear in mind that publishers preferred to handle manuscripts and not books already published in another country. Did I realise, she asked, that under my contract with Pegasus Press they would be entitled to fifty percent of all my earnings from overseas? The prospect of royalties being so distant I merely smiled with an air of 'who cares?'

After the interview we left the office together in the openwork cast iron lift which Patience Ross compared to 'something out of Kafka' whereupon I, eager to appear 'like a writer' to match those daunting literary portraits on the office walls, murmured knowingly, 'Yes, Kafka . . .'

I caught the 137 bus back to Clapham South.

My next task was accomplished swiftly. I walked in to a shop in Charing Cross Road and bought a large volume, the *Encyclopaedia of Sex*, advertised in the window as having 'hundreds of diagrams and photos in colour'.

I then prepared to keep my appointment for the following week with Dr Berger.

It was my first London summer with the heat oppressively full of fumes and the pavements burning. On the day of my appointment with Dr Berger at the Maudsley Hospital, Denmark Hill, I walked from Clapham South to Clapham North along Clapham Park Road and Acre Lane, through Brixton along Coldharbour Lane to Camberwell Green, past the rows of dilapidated brick houses; everywhere was grim, dirty with an air of poverty; the voices were strange, the woman in the shop said 'luv', 'Here you are, luv,' when I bought a packet of peppermints, *Curiously Strong*; the women wore headscarves, their faces looked tired; the men were pale, of small build, like burrow animals; beggars sat on the pavement, with cap or tin beside them, waiting for money to be thrown in response to the placard propped against the wall beside them — *War Wounded, Stumps For Legs. Blind From Birth. Born This Way. A Wife and Five Children*.

I passed a shop that advertised *Horse Flesh For Human Consumption*. I read the notices in the newsagents, and the chalked menus outside the uninviting transport cafés. I arrived at a square of dried grass bordered with a few shrubs and seats and surrounded by traffic going to Peckham, Forest Hill, Central London, Clapham. I walked up the street to the outpatient department of the Maudsley Hospital where I hoped to find at last the answers to the questions I still asked myself about my 'history'. I had to know whether my own views, usually met with polite disbelief or sometimes with sceptical agreement, held any truth or were merely another instance of self-deception.

During my first interview with Dr Berger I found myself again in the familiar role of using my long stay in hospital as a means of holding his attention. I knew that such a long stay with such drastic treatments performed and planned, usually gave the conclusion that my condition had been hopeless, as well as the surmise that it could recur: I knew the effect on strangers of learning about my past. I also knew that their response could be used to accomplish my wishes. The fact that, invariably, I was forced to go to such lengths to uncover my 'secret, true' self, to find the answers to questions that, had I the confidence and serenity of being myself 'in the world' could have been asked directly, was evidence to me of a certain unhealthy self-burial. Often, after repeated earthquakes, there is little sign of what survives beneath the ruins, and if there are survivors they must first attract attention before the authorities decide to investigate and explore the remains of the city, whether it be a real or a mirror city that moves when the wind moves and is subjected to ocean and sky.

Dr Berger, a tall dark pale man, with a chillingly superior glance and quellingly English voice, made another appointment to see me. Feelings of past unpleasantness and fear had been roused in me by this visit to a psychiatrist: attracting his attention and observing his serious face had reduced my store of confidence. I knew, however, that if anyone could discover the 'truth' it would be he, alone or with his colleagues.

I continued to work at the Regal Theatre. My supply of money was fast running out, and ushering became more tedious and depressing as each afternoon during the coffee break I listened to the confidences of the younger usherettes. One had been going to bed with a famous singer whom everyone thought of as perfect, you could see his kindly face on the television each evening: he had promised her a contract and, perhaps, stardom, she said. Another, learning that I hoped to be a writer, brought her collection of poems for me to read and I winced as I followed her golden moon to the month of June and looked into her lover's eyes that were blue as skies; yet perhaps I need not have winced had I thought of my own experiences.

Sometimes my father in Oamaru sent a bundle of five shilling postal notes bought on separate days and 'saved' during the currency restrictions. Miss Lincoln at Mt Maunganui also sent her bundle of five shilling postal notes.

And in the evening when Patrick Reilly and I were not working, we walked on the Common as in the days when I first came to London, and it was nearing that time of year, the blemished summer finally promising to give way in a cloud of dust and withering leaves, with the suddenly blood-filled sun stalking the city in and out through the thinning branches of the plane trees; and soon the grass on the Common would lie sparse, brown, with no hope of further growth.

I kept my second appointment with Dr Berger. I, who had been absorbing the city of London in its seasons, spoke as if I were the city, revealing myself as tired, looking towards winter. I talked of suicide. Such talk came readily to me as a shortcut to ensure action when the paths to real communication had been overgrown. I knew that talk of suicide must always be taken seriously, that it is only the uninformed who do otherwise or respond, to their later regret, with calm acceptance of the fact and the possibility of the deed. Such acceptance, an assurance that all is well, is enough to precipitate the act in a desperate person who then has no other way of making known the desperation.

It was Dr Berger's opinion that I should become a patient at the Maudsley for observation and tests. My plan had succeeded. I would now have my questions answered. Although I had many fears, I supposed that this famous Institute of Psychiatry would have few of the shortcomings of New Zealand hospitals, that it would have many doctors trained to make thorough diagnoses after learning all the facts of each case; also that, unlike in New Zealand, the 'case' would have a chance to speak, to be known at first hand. I expected much.

Dr Berger allowed me to return to my room in Clapham South where I collected a few personal belongings, and explained to Patrick who offered to store my suitcases in his room for the six weeks I'd be in hospital. In spite of my growing apprehension I did feel my action was necessary: I would at last find out 'the truth'.

15   The Investigation and the Verdict

I had not known what to expect from the Maudsley. What I found impressed me and gave me cause for gratitude that I still feel. There was then an abundance of medical, nursing, domestic staff with many of the nurses from Europe, Africa, Ireland, the West Indies, and one or two from New Zealand. In the admission and observation ward the ratio was one nurse to five patients with domestic duties given to ward-maids, kitchen-maids, cooks, leaving the nurses free for professional nursing. Remembering my days in Seacliff Hospital in New Zealand, in the 'back ward' where the nurses were forbidden to talk to me (I was told this later by two nurses, now retired), I was amazed to discover that here at the Maudsley it was the nurses' duty to talk to the patients, to get to know them — how else could a correct diagnosis be made? I was impressed also to find that the patients were interviewed by their doctor several times a week, at first daily, and not, as happened in New Zealand, once on admission, once on discharge, with occasional fatuous 'Hellos' between, no matter how many years the interval 'between' may have been. At the Maudsley I would have no reason to complain that decisions were made about me without anyone having taken the time and trouble to speak to me and try to know me. The Maudsley also gave numerous standard 'tests' as an aid to diagnosis (another method unheard of or at least not practised during my years in New Zealand hospitals).

There was an element of luxury, even of self-indulgence, in having a personal doctor and nurse. I was assigned a Dr Alan Miller, a young American graduate to whom I gave my personal history (omitting the large mass of the untellable) during frequent interviews. The Maudsley had already obtained from New Zealand details of my period in hospitals there, of diagnosis, treatment, prognosis.

Dr Miller was a tall burly man who was feeling the cold of the approaching English winter, and so appeared to be wearing many layers of clothes, increasing his bulk. He worried about his weight. He often ate chocolate bars during our interviews. For recreation he played the viola and was proud to correspond once a year with Pablo Casals. He had brought his wife, his children and his American Ford station wagon for his year at the Maudsley, and was lamenting that his year would be over soon. Although finding out such details about a psychiatrist was not usual, Dr Miller talked freely about himself and his feelings and opinions in contrast to the serious sober Englishmen who stared, frowned, half-smiled, and uttered only 'M-m, I see.' I was grateful to have as my doctor someone who was not afraid to acknowledge and voice the awful thought that he belonged, after all, to the human race, that there was nothing he could do about it, and pretending to be a god could never change it. And how enthusiastic Dr Miller was! 'You've never suffered from schizophrenia,' he said. 'Schizophrenia is a terrible illness.' The verdict had to be objective, however, the result of the tests and observations and interviews with the team of doctors supervised by Dr Berger, with the results to be given at a meeting chaired by Sir Aubrey Lewis, then director of the hospital. Infected by Dr Miller's enthusiasm I performed and underwent tests of many kinds, mental, manual. I had my first electroencephalogram (a test which should have been given as routine years ago) and I was disconcerted when Dr Miller, always eager to communicate the results, announced that my brain-waves were 'more normal than normal', thus shattering my long-held acquaintance and kinship with Van Gogh, Hugo Wolf — inspired to blossom by the unforgettable words of the handsome charming young lecturer of years ago — 'When I think of you I think of Van Gogh, Hugo Wolf . . . Janet you are suffering from a loneliness of the inner soul . . .'

Finally I was summoned to the interview room where the medical team sat at a long table with Sir Aubrey Lewis at the head. The team had already had its meeting and formed its conclusions, and after a few minutes' conversation with me, Sir Aubrey gave the verdict. I had never suffered from schizophrenia, he said. I should never have been admitted to a mental hospital. Any problems I now experienced were mostly a direct result of my stay in hospital.

I smiled. 'Thank you,' I said shyly, formally, as if I had won a prize.

Later, Dr Miller triumphantly repeated the verdict. I recall his expression of delight, and the way he turned bulkily in his chair because his layers of clothes appeared to hinder his movement.

'England's cold,' he said. 'I have this thick woollen underwear.' The latest fashions, short overcoats, narrowed trouser legs, added to his discomfort. Perhaps I remember so vividly Dr Miller's layers of clothes worn against the winter season because I myself had suddenly been stripped of a garment I had worn for twelve or thirteen years — my schizophrenia. I remembered how wonderingly, fearfully I had tried to pronounce the word when I first learned of the diagnosis, how I had searched for it in psychology books and medical dictionaries, and how, at first disbelievingly, then surrendering to the opinion of the 'experts', I had accepted it, how in the midst of the agony and terror of the acceptance I found the unexpected warmth, comfort, protection: how I had longed to be rid of the opinion but was unwilling to part with it. And even when I did not wear it openly I always had it by for emergency, to put on quickly, for shelter from the cruel world. And now it was gone, not destroyed by me and my constant pleading for 'the truth' allied to an unwillingness to lose so useful a protection, but banished officially by experts: I could never again turn to it for help.

The loss was great. At first, the truth seemed to be more terrifying than the lie. Schizophrenia, as a psychosis, had been an accomplishment, removing ordinary responsibility from the sufferer. I was bereaved. I was ashamed. How could I ask for help directly when there was 'nothing wrong with me'? How could I explain myself when I could no longer move cunningly but necessarily from the status of a writer to one of having schizophrenia, back and forth when the occasion *suited*? The official plunder of my self-esteem was eased by the attitude of the staff at the hospital. As Professor Lewis had said, I did need professional help to free myself from the consequences of my long stay in hospital; in the meantime I would remain in the Maudsley while my interviews with Dr Miller continued. Once he had learned of the background of my life we talked mostly of everyday matters of the present, in a formless kind of therapy that allowed inclusion of worries of the present and of the past. We calmly dragged the lake, as it were, and watched the fireflies and the sunlight on the water, and usually let the old dead rest and the discovered dead return to their depths, while the water, momentarily clouded, cleared and became still. The one prolonged difficulty in our talks was my panic, scarcely comprehended or admitted, at the loss of my schizophrenia and my unwillingness to let it go, my urging, out of habit and a need for warmth, that maybe it was there after all, forever a part of my life?

I spent the winter cocooned in the warmth of the Maudsley. I became friends with the nurses and patients and with the kitchen-maid from Germany, *Gerda*, who enveloped everyone with kindness — 'Oh Janet, mein goodness kinder,' she'd say, smiling.

I have heard that the time when the hospital was fully staffed did pass; then, in the late nineteen fifties the staff were all highly qualified and diverse with the foreign nurses and psychiatrists bringing an extra dimension of their culture to their work. A particular example of the strength and wisdom of the management of the Maudsley was the inclusion of doctors who were themselves handicapped by disabilities, and it was often these doctors who became more easily able to communicate with their patients.

I was now preparing to leave hospital to continue with my 'own life'. It was early spring, with occasional snowstorms. Rather too directly for my comfort, Dr Berger explained that as a prelude to my 'holding down a job' he had asked Miss Baer, the librarian, to give me work in the medical library. Although it was known that I'd had two books published in New Zealand and I had an ambition to write full time, there was little evidence in the harsh publishing world of London that I would be able to make a career of writing. I had heard from Patience Ross of A. M. Heath that up to fifty publishers in the United States and the United Kingdom had admired my *Owls Do Cry* but declined to publish it, and therefore, in some dejection, but maintaining my 'poetic' stance, I went to work in the medical library only to find, a few days later, that I was pronounced 'unsuitable'. Dr Berger then gave me the task of cataloguing medical papers in the brain museum. The brain museum! Blissfully alone, I spent many days sorting through medical journals in the company of glass display cases filled with preserved, labelled tumours and brains. I learned from studying the journals that ECT (Electric Shock or Convulsive Therapy) was commended as a means of provoking *fear* in the patient, the fear being as it were a *bonus*, and salutary — for the psychiatrist no doubt and not for the patient! Sitting there among the labelled, bottled brains I ventured to hope for the quality of strength and vigilance in psychiatrists, their continued examination and testing of their humanity without which they might become political operators infected with the endemic virus of psychiatry, politics, and some other professions — belief in the self as God.

I wrote a poem in the brain museum.

Dobson's tumour, nineteen fifty-five.
You could not see it through his balding head
or in his clouded face, or hear it speaking
from his wild cries though it fanged forth speech
in snakely blossoming unreason. He spent his last years hiding
under a fliff of circular beetles and raging sunlight. One day
a landslide of weightless rock fell, and Dobson died.

Cremation was at Golders Green, a service held
in the private chapel, solemnly his virtues extolled
(the flotsam of vice as yet concealed by the full tide of grief).
His widow rented a niche for his ashes in the church wall,
and gave the wreath money to tumour research.
But few at the ceremony ever dreamed they burned
and buried less of Dobson than it seemed.

Another lantern-slide, another joke. Nightfall.
The room empties. Layers of cold cling to the varnished furniture.
Once more the labelled and bottled thing is set aside
on the cluttered desk among files and case histories.

For three years now it has told how Dobson died: with my double tongue
I spat at God. In formalin
my prestige grows fat. I survive
as Dobson's tumour, nineteen fifty-five.

After I had worked two or three weeks in the brain museum it was decided that I should take daily leave from hospital to find somewhere to live, as I did not wish to stay in the same house as Patrick Reilly who, no doubt at my unconscious invitation, had threatened to take over my life with his behaviour as a bumptious parent. On his regular visits to me he spent the time warning me against the perils of the world, and in particular the perils of sex, for he had discovered my *Encyclopaedia of Sex* among my possessions. I was a fallen woman, he said, brandishing the book. 'No one should know so much about their body. All those diagrams and photos!'

He opened the book at a diagram of a woman's sex organs.

'Is a woman *really* like that?' he asked, answering his question, 'I don't believe it.'

He was vehement. 'This book goes in the rubbish can tonight.'

That day, with the cooperation of Dr Miller, I told Patrick Reilly that it would be better if he no longer came to see me. I was soon to leave for America, I said, where I had friends.

Although I was disappointed that no one suggested I continue my writing career, I hoped to find time to write, as the social worker had arranged an initial National Assistance payment until I was settled enough to 'hold down a job', as Dr Berger again expressed it. And so one wintry afternoon, not without a surge of self-pity and a feeling of isolation, I searched for living quarters. My sense of misery was increased by the thought that Dr Miller would soon be returning to the United States and I would have another doctor to talk to at the outpatient department. Along Camberwell Road I boarded a bus for Chalk Farm. I'd find a room near there, I told myself; on the map, it wasn't far from Primrose Hill. Surely a pleasant place to live! Chalk Farm was perhaps near a disused quarry on farmland with fields and *primroses* in spring.

The bus turned past Elephant and Castle, past Westminster, round Trafalgar Square, up Charing Cross Road, Tottenham Court Road, Goudge Street Station, Mornington Station, Camden, with the scene growing drearier and grimier until we came to Chalk Farm Station which, as far as I could see, was a high brick wall concealing the railway line out of Euston or Kings Cross or Paddington, with a row of dilapidated brick houses lining one side of the road. I left the bus at Chalk Farm and walked back towards Kentish Town and into Fortess Road which I read mistakenly as *Fortress* Road, and there before me was a sign, *Room to Let*.

Somewhere to live.

I rented the room. The rent was low. A basement room in an old house where every room was let as a bedsitter, it was dirty, with broken furniture, smashed window glass replaced by wire netting with the snowfilled London wind blowing through. A small anteroom by the bedsitter had a hole in the roof (the roof being the pavement at street level) to receive deliveries of coal and any other objects that might be thrown in. If I looked through the street window I could see and hear the wheels of traffic and the feet of walking people and dogs. I stayed one week only in that room. The building was cold, without heating, and when one day the electricity was cut off because the landlord had not paid the bill, I discovered, exploring, that the other tenants were poor, overcrowded, depressed by the damp, cold and dark and by the bedbugs. I spoke to a woman upstairs, at street level; her baby lay asleep in bed while the woman sat by the bed with scores of dolls' heads heaped beside her, laboriously painting the eyes in the blank faces. And now there was no light for her to work by.

As it was useless for me to try to type in a dark basement, I went into the street in search of another place and found to my delight a room advertised directly opposite, but a room in a flat, described enticingly in the advertisement. What good fortune, I thought, at once enquiring to inspect the room. I was shown to the third floor of the building, to a small room opening into a corridor with a kitchen and a bathroom at the end, and although the outlook was dreary, overlooking another of North London's brick walls, I rented the room at once, knowing that I could quickly move in from my basement room across *Fortress Road*. Perhaps as in Ibiza I misinterpreted the information: I had thought I was the sole occupant of the tiny flat, but I had moved and settled in and was rejoicing at my good fortune when I was surprised to hear one, then a second, then a third person entering and moving about the flat. Why had I not noticed that the narrow corridor held three other small rooms with my room second from the kitchen? I went to the kitchen where I found three women in various stages of preparing to cook a meal: Jane, pretty, fairhaired, a schoolteacher in her early twenties; Gloria, darkhaired, an office worker; Millicent, a librarian in an industrial firm. It was Millicent who, putting herself in charge, introduced the others and herself. I was a writer, I said. Perhaps, I said, when they asked if they could read my work, perhaps I would show them my book. I was reluctant to say the title for so much had happened since the book had been written and published that I was beginning to think of it as disintegrating, dissolving, and soon it would be nothing. Although I knew that words and ideas and their expression may disappear, I had not realised the fragility of a published book, I had imagined that its form, presence, and multiplication might give it power and weight and permanence. And now even the title of my book was retreating from being voiced.

In my room in the new flat I again began my life as a writer, sitting each morning trying to type while I stared at the oppressive brick walls of Kentish Town. And each week I kept an appointment at the Maudsley Hospital with Dr Miller, each time realising with growing gloom that his departure was weeks away, and when one day he introduced me to his replacement, a Dr Portion, I felt my heart sinking as I heard the crisp English accent contrasting so strangely with Dr Miller's rich cheerful voice with its accent that I had known for years, in Hollywood films. I wondered how I could possibly talk to Dr Portion.

After my discharge from hospital I renewed acquaintance with the poet Ben who introduced me to a friend, Lawrence, recently returned from living for twelve years in the United States, and as both Ben and Lawrence, like myself, had no regular work, and as they lived north of Kentish Town, they formed the habit of 'dropping in' to the flat in the early morning on their way to town, that is, to their haunts in Soho where they usually met other unemployed poets and painters and sat and talked in the *French* café where the customers always pointed with pride to the famous Ironfoot Jack, reputed to be a member, past or present, of the underworld. Often after giving Ben and Lawrence a cup of coffee, and feeling reluctant to face the Kentish Town brick wall, I'd go with them to Soho where we met an assortment of people whose ambition was to write or paint or compose, and I felt at home with them, yet saddened by their everlasting dreaming, their talking about what they hoped to produce when they knew clearly (as I knew) that while they talked and dreamed, their work stayed untouched in the loneliness of their bedsitters or their poky gas-reeking flats with share bathroom share kitchen share everything. My Kentish Town wall wasn't the only formidable opponent to my working — dreaming was easier, though I did not voice my dreams. I regularly bought the weekly literary magazines and the *London Magazine* that had begun a series entitled 'Coming to London' recording the experiences of famous writers in their early days. I read eagerly of their experience with editors, agents, publishers while mentally composing my own 'Coming to London' which I would write one day and which would be full of references to poets and novelists I had met, with casual references to 'my publisher' (preferably Faber and Faber). 'Having lunch with my publisher one day . . .'

Indeed I dreamed.

When Lawrence began to look on me as his 'girl' I was agreeable but lukewarm, refusing to put myself again in danger of another pregnancy but willing to be comforted and to comfort, naked body to naked body. When Lawrence began arriving at the flat at half-past eight in the morning on too many mornings, Millicent expressed her disapproval, Jane also did not think I should entertain a man so early in the morning. Only Gloria, in the end room and apart from the others because she, too, had 'entertained men', understood, and she and I, like two sisters, had many confiding talks. During the day Lawrence and I would take the usual route to Soho followed by a 'gallery crawl' inspecting the new paintings in each gallery. This was his duty, he said. Someone must take the responsibility of looking at new paintings otherwise they hung there, with people perhaps glancing at them, but few getting to know them, and it was a dismal experience for a painter to realise that no one bothered to look at his work. The painting suffered too, Lawrence said. Just ten or fifteen minutes was enough to restore life and hope to an abandoned painting and through it, renewed life to the painter alone in front of his easel.

Through Ben and Lawrence I met many of the 'outsiders' of Soho. Following the publication and popularity of Colin Wilson's *The Outsider*, there was some prestige in being 'outside', quite unlike my experience in New Zealand when the prestige lay in being 'inside', although when one has the prestige of being 'outside' one is then 'inside' the 'outside' . . . I visited sleazy clubs, becoming a member for the evening to gain admission. I met prostitutes, male and female and I listened to their stories, gaping impolitely as I cherished my growing 'experience of life' and quoting to myself on many occasions, 'I sit in one of the dives on Fifty-Second Street . . .'

The direction I had set myself, however, was too clear for me to be waylaid for long. Wasn't it time I applied myself to my writing? The words of Dylan Thomas came readily to mind.

> Oh no work of words now for three months in the bloody
> Belly of the rich year . . .
> I bitterly take to task my poverty and craft . . .

Three months only and he was in despair! Perhaps I was not 'really' a writer? My doubts returned. Perhaps the desire to journey back and forth from that Mirror City was merely an abnormality after all? Oh why had they robbed me of my schizophrenia which had been the answer to all my misgivings about myself? Like King Lear I had gone in search of 'the truth' and I now had nothing. 'Nothing will come out of nothing.'

Dr Miller decided that I should begin seeing Dr Portion now that I had met him, and so we said a brief goodbye and good luck to each other, and I felt as if all the griefs I had ever known had surfaced within me. I felt completely alone in the world, in a grey world where for months the colour had been drained from the faces of Londoners and the face of the earth, and in such a mood I found ludicrous the idea that I would ever be able to communicate with a doctor who during our first interview, with a well-meant cheerfulness and a desire to prove perhaps his wide range of interests, talked of the coming world heavyweight championship and asked me if I thought Floyd Paterson would win. Other remarks he made were just as remote from what I felt to be the centre of concern. Knowing the ways of psychiatrists I was ready to suppose that his approach was planned, scientific . . . but my feelings were that everything he said was out of tune, prompting me to select from my repertoire the more striking examples of behaviour guaranteed to command attention, with the result that he suggested I enter a North London hospital, and so after our first interview, when Dr Miller had gone from the hospital, I left with an admission form to one of them.

How well I remember the bus ride I took the following afternoon to 'inspect' the new hospital! It was a High Barnet bus, a name that then carried romantic possibilities — High Barnet, Tooting Bec, Friern Barnet . . . The bus arrived at the outskirts of London, at a point where the green buses are suddenly numerous and the red no longer travel to and from Central London but from Outer East to Outer West, Outer South to North, as if denying the existence of the London metropolis; here, near High Barnet, there were fewer people in the streets of now semidetached and detached houses. And then, near the corner, I saw the hospital I had been directed to — tall, of grey stone, menacing, like an old workhouse or prison. A feeling of terror came over me. I must keep calm, I thought, trying to subdue my rising panic. I don't have to go there. I must remember the investigation and the verdict, and not return to believing what I have believed in the past. I shall simply return to Kentish Town, face the brick wall, and continue with my writing. Yet the desolation of having no-one to 'tell my story to' surged through me. Perhaps I should never have left New Zealand. I did not long for any special place in New Zealand. I yearned, painfully, for sight of a straggly cabbage tree in a front garden, anyone's front garden, and for a sight and touch of a hillside covered with golden tussock.

Sitting in the bus, I felt as if I were a child again with memories that I had never identified and that I could only think were part of the vision of 'the light that never was on sea or land', the kind of world spoken of in the Book of Revelations, and in Thomas Traherne's *Centuries of Meditation* where 'eternity was manifest in the light of day' and 'the city seemed to stand in Eden or to be built in heaven'. My feeling of isolation began to recede then as I reminded myself that London, of all places in the world, was full of poets, that the poems appearing in the slim and fat volumes of Faber and Faber and in the periodicals and journals were written by men and women who were now walking in the streets of London, entering bookshops, buying books, or just sleeping, talking, loving, eating; living their everyday lives in London. And writing their poems.

They may not have known it but they were *company* for me, their very breath kept me warm and dispelled my grief.

16   Dr Cawley and the Luxury of Time

I returned sobered and frightened from my bus ride to High Barnet. The next week I was again admitted to the Maudsley Hospital. Now, without my schizophrenia, I had only my ordinary self to use to try to explain my distress. More importantly, others, the genuine 'experts' knew that I had only my ordinary or extraordinary self with which to explain myself, and this was the first such opportunity for me since I had been an adult. The prospect was a luxury as the reality would be. I know that so many live and die without tasting this luxury. I do not know what marvel of insight — or was it a gesture of impatience? — prompted Dr Berger, the consultant, to try to help me unearth myself. And who was I to suppose that I had the special right to experience a clear vision of myself and the world? Some obstinacy, some persistence in myself pursued this right until at last with the help of a combination of circumstances, coincidence, providence, and good friends, I arrived at the point of knowing the agony of the luxury of trying to tell my story, of demanding and accepting the luxury of 'the truth'.

Dr Berger assigned me to a young recently qualified psychiatrist who had been a zoologist and mathematician and was therefore above the usual age and experience of a junior registrar. I found, however, that for the Maudsley, difference was part of the usual and the practising motto may have been, 'All care in diversity'. I think I was able to accept Dr Cawley because I was aware that his view was wider, over a range of studies and disciplines and personal experience, just as I had readily accepted Dr Miller because I knew he was interested in music and art. The qualificiations of medicine and psychiatry were extensions of these men, not starting and ending points. I had felt that although Dr Portion was a qualified psychiatrist, he may have superimposed life upon psychiatry and not psychiatry upon life.

I was also pleased to discover that Dr Cawley, like myself, was interested in the Here and Now and not in theories about the past, and our talks were largely at first an accounting process, an examination of my emotional, personal, and even financial budget with a view to balancing all so that I could survive in spite of the bankruptcy imposed during my long stay in hospital, and my existence since then on unreal notions of myself, fed to me by myself and others, and now my sudden extreme poverty of being myself following the Investigation and the Verdict: the wastage of being other than myself could lead to the nothingness I had formerly experienced.

I know that Dr Cawley found me a difficult patient for I was 'against psychiatry' and I disapproved of all psychiatric gods, with perhaps more tolerance of Jung; but my interviews were not an excuse for the psychiatrist to test any theories he might have had. I was disconcerted when during our first interview Dr Cawley sat with a pen and paper and wrote or appeared to write everything I said, sometimes without looking up. At first I said little. Dr Miller at least, I thought, rebelliously, 'talked' to me. Dr Cawley, however, was 'different' from Dr Miller, and if I were to preach the importance of difference my first need was to accept it in others, and so I told myself that this was Dr Cawley's 'way'. I guessed that he might have been a shy man. Like Dr Portion and Dr Berger, he spoke with an 'English' accent that chilled me when I heard it in the distance but in his presence it could not frighten me for he was not aggressive, his manner was excessively polite, his smile kindly as if these were more a protection for himself than a gift for me. I felt that he was a clever, uncertain man whose sole triumph in our interviews was the accuracy of his recording the content. Sometimes he had a cold; he sniffed, he took out a large white handkerchief like a conjuror's aid, and blew his nose. He wore black-rimmed spectacles, magnifying, I thought, much of what he saw; and his shoes were black, well polished. He dressed as for a day in the office.

I stayed many months in hospital, and each time it might have appeared to Dr Cawley that all my problems had been solved, I would immediately present a new emergency, either through fear of being abandoned or because there was another problem I dared not mention. With time, the marvellous luxury of time, and patience, Dr Cawley convinced me that I was myself, I was an adult, I need not explain myself to others. The 'you should' days were over, he said. *You should go here, go there, be this, be that, do this, do that — you* should *you know — it would be good for you*! Lifelong, largely because of my own makeup I had been a target for the *You should*-ers, with a long interval of *You must Or Else*: it was time to begin again.

Perhaps I had sensed a new beginning or tried to advance it because one day during the past summer I had changed my surname, recording it on the necessary document. I had been issued with a new passport.

Dr Cawley's view, supported no doubt by his assessment of our interviews of many months, was that I genuinely needed to write, that it was a way of life for me, and that the best practical help for me was to arrange a National Assistance weekly payment and for me to find accommodation near the hospital so that we might continue our talks. It was his opinion also that as I was obviously suffering from the effects of my long stay in hospital in New Zealand, I should write my story of that time to give me a clearer view of my future. In his response to this lifelong urging of others to me that I should 'get out and mix', Dr Cawley was clear: his prescription for my ideal life was that I should live alone and write while resisting, if I wished this, the demands of others to 'join in'. There had never been any question of my not being able to exist in the 'real world' unless that existence also deprived me of my 'own world', the journeys to and from Mirror City, either by the Envoy who is forever present, or by myself.

The progress of healing and preparation for my life as myself in the 'real' world was such that one day I again began to look for accommodation — near the hospital, in Camberwell. I was to receive a National Assistance payment each week. I was discharged from hospital. These arrangements were made by the team supervised always by the consultant, Dr Berger, with the social worker, and with Dr Cawley who would continue to see me each week. I now had confidence in Dr Cawley, for I had not only seen myself developing and growing in his care, I had observed his own development as an assured psychiatrist who, I felt, would always respect the human spirit before the practice, the fashions and demands of psychiatry. I was influenced also by the persistence of Dr Cawley in being 'himself' and not some 'image' of a psychiatrist: he did not patronise or pretend, and when he talked of my writing, he confessed modestly, with an old-fashioned air of a character from a Somerset Maugham story, 'I'm not a literary chap, you know.'

No longer, I hoped, dependent on my 'schizophrenia' for comfort and attention and help, but with myself as myself, I again began my writing career.

17 Grove Hill Road and the Life of a Writer

For twenty-seven shillings a week I rented a large front room on the second floor in the home of Ted and Joan Morgan in Grove Hill Road, Camberwell. The Morgans' daughter, Myra, and a middle-aged boarder, Tilly, slept on the third floor, while my room was next to the main bedroom, with a small kitchen (to be shared with Tilly) and a bathroom and lavatory (to be shared with all) on the same floor. My room, overlooking the street, had a large mirrored wardrobe, a dressing table, a large dining table covered with a green and white checked oilcloth that I remember affectionately as I spent most of my time writing at one end, eating at the other: two chairs, one a fat armchair with outsize padded arms and floral covering, an old stretcher bed dipping in the middle beneath a mattress full of hard unevenly distributed parcels of kapok. There was a disused fireplace and a small kerosene heater.

At first, Mrs Morgan showed alarm on discovering that she had rented her room to one of those tenants frowned on in the letting world as being 'home all day' when any reader of newspaper columns and the notices in tobacconists' windows would know that the ideal tenants then were 'business woman only . . . business couple only . . . out all day' with, often, 'away weekends' as well as the usual 'no children, pets, coloured or Irish'.

I explained that I was writing a book.

'Oh, a journalist,' Mr Morgan said with some deference.

'More a book writer.'

'We'll say you're a journalist,' he said.

He was about forty, sleek, with a coat buttoned to show his continuing sleekness, handsome, with a small moustache and a plausible manner suited to his work as a television salesman, but reminiscent for me of my idea of a con-man. Joan, in her middle thirties, was small, dark, businesslike, the part owner with her sister of a hairdressing salon 'down the Green'. Myra, who practised the piano each afternoon in the room beneath me, was at the serious stage of English life known as the 'eleven-plus year', with an examination looming, followed by her 'streaming' into grammar, comprehensive or high school. Myra's parents told me that one day Myra would be a clever journalist.

'You should see her essays. The talent is there.'

Tilly, the boarder, nearing sixty, who worked assembling electrical plant at the General Electric factory, and was away to work early and home late, was another Londoner whose memories of the war had matured for harmless telling. She too had come home one day to find her street, her home, her family destroyed by a flying bomb, a 'buzz bomb'. She talked often, too, of her 'post-war credits' and how their payment had been delayed by the government. 'If I'd had my post-war credits,' she'd say as she stood in the kitchen stirring her scrambled egg or her collard greens, 'life would have been different for me.' The government had failed her: she was bitter, and wary of being betrayed, and when her doctor suggested removing one of her toes to alleviate her arthritis, she saw the betrayal as extending to her own body.

Tilly was a clever dressmaker. Her whirring machine made Myra's clothes, and sewed for me a woollen skirt. 'You need it, in the English winter.'

The Morgans were naturally curious about my income. At first I did not disclose that I received three pounds seventeen and six a week from a book of National Assistance cheques to be renewed or cancelled after six months when a National Assistance inspector would call for an interview, first sending a window envelope through the post with the advice, *An Officer of the Department will call*, giving the time and date. *Please be at home to receive him.* As the mail for the house was delivered early in the morning through the letterbox in the front door, on days when I expected a letter from the National Assistance Board, I, trying to preserve my secret, contrived to be first to pick up the mail. One morning I was too late. Mrs

Morgan picked up the mail. I saw her glancing at the easily identifiable window envelope where some of the printing of the notice could be read through the ample window. 'It's for me,' I said, bursting into tears. 'I'm on National Assistance.'

My secret was out.

To my surprise, Mrs Morgan smiled sadly.

'I suppose you know my secret by now.'

'No,' I said truthfully.

'It's Ted — Mr Morgan. He's an alcoholic. He falls in the door most nights of the week when he's been drinking.'

She too burst into tears, and together we went to her small sitting room where she made a cup of tea and we sat talking with the intimacy that follows a newly shared secret. She explained that Ted didn't keep jobs for long, but he'd been good lately with two months working as a salesman and repairman at the television shop in Peckham Rye. (Peckham Rye. Goose Green. Dulwich. Camberwell Green.)

Later, Mrs Morgan ('I'm Joan. Call me Joan.' 'Call me Janet.') showed me the small back garden where I could hang my washing. ('I wouldn't ask anyone to use it.') She also introduced me to the grey tomcat, and as I was returning upstairs she gave me a privileged glimpse into the front sitting room with its polished piano. 'Myra has a future at the piano. And I've told you about her essays, haven't I?'

'Yes.'

We did not speak again of our broken secrets. Instead we sealed them with a new formality until it might again be necessary to break them and inspect the contents and sweep away more tears in a process similar to a periodical airing and restoring of bed linen that lay too long against our skin.

And when late one evening the door bell rang and I answered it and Ted Morgan fell through the door at my feet, Joan appeared, and not acknowledging my presence, she helped Ted to his feet and guided him into the back sitting room while I returned upstairs.

With my novel, *Uncle Pylades*, now abandoned, although the theme remains after many years, waiting, I began to write the story of my experiences in hospitals in New Zealand, recording faithfully every happening and the patients and the staff I had known, but borrowing from what I had observed among the patients to build a more credibly 'mad' central character, Istina Mavet, the narrator. Also planning a subdued rather than a sensational record, I omitted much, aiming more for credibility than a challenge to me by those who might disbelieve my record.

The book was written quickly. I kept to the routine I began when I was living in Frank Sargeson's hut in Takapuna. I also continued the method I had adopted of buying a new school exercise book, carefully writing my name in the space provided on the cover, with the word 'Novel' in a juvenile, laborious hand beside the *subject*, then ruling various columns to record timetable, progress, with spaces for *Excuses*, now called *Wasted Days* as I did not need to identify the known excuses to myself. I had already made, in my mind, an entire book from which I chose chapter headings to remind me of the whole. There was more enthusiasm than usual in my working: each week had an impartial observer in Dr Cawley to talk to and complain to and tell of my progress. Also I had news from Patience Ross, the literary agent, that an American publisher, George Braziller, with a new small firm, had decided to publish *Owls Do Cry*, while in England, W. H. Allen had shown interest and would most likely publish. As I had 'signed away' to Pegasus Press in New Zealand most of the rights of the book, the contracts would be the affair of Pegasus and not myself.

Now that I was again writing, I was sensitively aware of interruptions and each Wednesday morning when a woman came to clean the Morgans' house, I, with much complaining to myself, would take my exercise book and pen and walk or bus to Dulwich Library where I wrote, watched over by the bust of Robert Browning. My morning's work at Dulwich meant that I saved a morning's kerosene for my heater — kerosene here known as 'paraffin' and sold either as 'pink' paraffin or by a rival firm as 'blue' paraffin. One of my childish delights was to watch every second week for the 'pink paraffin man', and in discussion with shoppers at the Green or the Rye, to remain loyal to 'pink' paraffin while listening to the arguments for 'blue'.

I finished *Faces in the Water*. I showed it first to Dr Cawley whose comment was, 'It's not brilliant but it will do,' reminding me as he observed my disappointment, 'You know, I'm not a literary chap.'

I suspected that he was being modest.

He persuaded me to show the typescript to Patience Ross who liked it and when Pegasus had read it, A. M. Heath suggested I did not sign the Pegasus contract which again removed most of my rights to the book. My advance for *Owls Do Cry* was 75 pounds divided with Pegasus after a deduction of ten per cent for the agent. My advance for *Faces in the Water* was 100 pounds similarly divided. George Braziller of New York gave similar advances, in dollars.

After writing *Faces in the Water* and existing through the inevitable few weeks of 'Wasted Days', I began to write *The Edge of the Alphabet*. My routine remained the same, with regular visits to Dr Cawley where I usually described the happenings of the week, and how my work was progressing.

I was now awaiting the publication of *Owls Do Cry* and I knew that I was excited. I had never known a publication day in New Zealand and I wasn't sure of the English routine, although since I'd been in London I had read avidly in the newspapers of theatre first nights, art gallery private viewings, launching of books at an author's or publisher's party, with the newspapers the next day proclaiming the play, 'A hit, a palpable hit', or perhaps burying the latest works of art. Music first nights were important also, with the response to a performance in Wigmore Hall awaited eagerly by young Commonwealth musicians. The newspapers presented a world of vicarious excitement where authors, painters, sculptors, playwrights, especially if they were sons or daughters of lords or had some unusual distinguishing feature, not directly related to their work, were wined, dined, romanced, gossiped about. What if . . . ? I dreamed briefly, dismissing such dreams. I did wonder, however, how I would feel on publication day when I opened the newspaper and there were the headlines. *New Author of Fine Novel.*

My problem was, I didn't really think that *Owls Do Cry* was 'fine'!

On publication day I took the bus to Westminster, bought newspapers at the Westminster Station, took them to the lavatory in the subway, and began to read, as I thought, of my *publication*. I searched the book pages. I could find nothing. I think there was one newspaper with a small note at the foot of a 'continued' column, about a novel of poverty in New Zealand, *Owls Do Cry*. I don't think it gave an opinion.

I learned my lesson, satisfying to a person like myself who is always seeing 'sermons in stones'. Not every book published in London is reviewed, whereas in New Zealand if you were a New Zealand author your book was always reviewed. *New Zealand author writes novel*, as if you had won the Melbourne Cup or first prize in Tatts, an event that would never happen again.

Later, there were some favourable reviews of *Owls Do Cry*.

I continued with my routine of writing. If I had any practical problems Dr Cawley was always quick to help me solve them even if the solution were only a telephone call by him to the Camberwell Library to explain that I was a resident and entitled to borrow records, or recommending a dentist when I had toothache. He also became part of the routine of my work and when a typescript was finished he always allowed me to borrow a 'punch' from the hospital office to make holes for threading tape through the pages. One might ask, 'Surely it's a waste of precious time for a psychiatrist now a senior registrar to bother about minor details like lending office equipment to his patient or making it possible for her to borrow records from a library?' My biased answer would be that nothing is unimportant unless the person seeking help admits and believes it is so. I know that at my age then, in my early thirties, most women would have the help of a mate, husband, companion. I know also that there are no 'most women' and not to be one, through disinclination or disability even is not to be a personal failure: the failure lies in the expectations of others.

In the afternoon, in winter and summer, I'd go to the local cinema and sit in the warm dark planning my next day's work and watching the one-and-sixpenny double feature B movies usually made by ABC (Associated British Cinemas), black-and-white films full of murders, with opening and closing of squeaking doors, and with the camera moving cautiously around apparently empty rooms until it stayed focused on the shocking sight behind the sofa or 'slumped' over a desk! The popular advertisement of the time was that ending 'You're never alone with a Strand' with the man in the raincoat walking the wet deserted street. Cadburys also filled the screen with their multicoloured chocolate wrappers. At half-past four I'd leave the cinema, noticing as the lights came on that many others in the audience had discovered a place to keep warm and to hide on a dreary afternoon — poor Londoners, middle-aged men alone, young women with babies who cried and cried until the audience began to murmur and the usher to shine a torch on the offender; West Indian immigrants, men and women; most were alone and, suddenly illuminated, they looked like plants set the required distance from one another in some unkempt allotment by the railway line. I was such an avid cinemagoer that I travelled to all the outer suburbs seeing all the films that were shown, and each afternooon coming out into an unfamiliar place — King's Cross, Holloway, Shepherd's Bush, Tooting (the Classic cinema), Balham — where I'd venture before taking the bus home to Grove Hill Road where I'd be faced again with my writing. On many afternoons also I went to the art galleries, the Portrait Gallery, the Museum of Musical Instruments, the Victoria and Albert Museum, the Museum of Natural History where like a character in one of my stories, I used to sit for hours among the life-size reconstructions of the extinct mammoths, looking up at them, wondering about them and their world, imagining their lives.

Lately as I worked I began to hear bursts of loud music as Ted Morgan repaired radio and television sets he had brought home. When he discovered that I'd not seen much television he insisted on putting a set in my room and showing me how to work it, and sometimes in the evening I'd watch the programmes. Although the set was black and white, the people always appeared elongated, snowed upon and coloured maroon, yet I continued to watch, thinking that this was normal television, until the images grew darker and fainter.

'How's your telly?' Ted asked one day.

'My television?' I was shy of the familiar word, 'telly', as if it were a person I'd just met.

'Yes. How's it going?'

'The picture's very dark.'

'It's your tube,' Ted said.

That evening Ted replaced the tube and when he had finished tuning the set he seized me and kissed me.

'Just a token,' he said. 'Just a token.'

He had been drinking. He stayed away from work the next day, spending the time exploring the volume of his collection of televisions, and later in the week Joan Morgan told me he'd lost his job but he'd applied for another as a telephonist on the Continental Exchange. It would mean night work, she said. And he'd be sleeping during the day.

'I know you won't mind,' Joan said, 'if I ask you not to type during the day.'

I had to say I wouldn't mind: it was their home.

Then, coinciding with Harold MacMillan's election slogan, 'You've never had it so good,' Grove Hill Road became noisy as one by one the residents could afford to buy televisions and record players. My room was now penetrated by the daytime endless flow of radio talk and music, all tuned to full volume, and during the evening, the sound of gunshots from war and cowboy films. The morning offered record players that could be heard from one end of Grove Hill Road to another, that is, from the Hostel for the Blind to the pub at the corner.

Panic came over me — what would I do? Where would I go? I tried to build myself a soundproofed booth, like a telephone box, in the middle of my room, draping blankets around screens, shifting the wardrobe between me, the typewriter and the Morgan's bedroom where Ted was now sleeping during the day, but it was little use: the noise from the street and the adjacent rooms increased, and Ted was still wakened by my typewriter.

I therefore boldly bought a record player with records of Beethoven's Ninth Symphony and Schubert songs, including 'To Music' and 'Shepherd on the Rock', and when Ted Morgan had finished his daily sleep and the television and radio and record player sounds rose to full volume, I'd add my chosen music to the din while I typed. To add variety to my listening, I borrowed records from the Camberwell Library. In my struggle to get my writing done I realised the obvious fact that the only certainty about writing and trying to be a writer is that it has to be done, not dreamed of or planned and never written, or talked about (the ego eventually falls apart like a soaked sponge), but simply written: it's a dreary awful fact that writing is like any other work with the marvellous exception of the presence of the Mirror City and the constant journeys either of oneself or of the Envoy from Mirror City.

During this time *Faces in the Water* was published and I finished writing *The Edge of the Alphabet*. Again, I bought newspapers to discover what 'they' were saying about *Faces in the Water*, and I was startled to find my photo on the book page of the Sunday papers and relieved that I had changed my surname as I preferred to live anonymously in Grove Hill Road. I was amused by the *Manchester Guardian*'s comment, 'Surely the use of the first person was a mistake. A woman who has been what this woman has been would never be able to remember and write about it in this way.' It was assumed that the character of Istina Mavet was a portrait of myself.

Faces in the Water was a success with reviewers and sold more copies than *Owls Do Cry*. There were foreign translations with advances less commission divided equally between myself and Pegasus Press in New Zealand, but for *The Edge of the Alphabet* the agents at last persuaded me to sign separate contracts with each publisher. *The Edge of the Alphabet* before publication was among those from which 'Book of the Month' was chosen and therefore, published, was entitled to wear a gaudy yellow sash. The sudden attention to my work (not personally as the agent protected me, the supposed character of *Faces in the Water*) brought new lessons for me. When the agent and publisher received the typescript of *The Edge of the Alphabet*, the agents suggested I omit one chapter, the publishers that I enlarge the same chapter; there were other conflicting suggestions some of which I diffidently tried to follow. When the book was published, some reviews said of the now diminished chapter, 'It could have been longer,' while others praised parts criticised adversely by the agent and publisher but which I had not changed, while yet others criticised parts that had been praised. This confusing experience reminded me of what I already knew, and strengthened my resolution never to forget that a writer must stand on the rock of her self and her judgment or be swept away by the tide or sink in the quaking earth: there must be an inviolate place where the choices and decisions, however imperfect, are the writer's own, where the decision must be as individual and solitary as birth or death. What was the use of my having survived as a person if I could not maintain my own judgment? Only then could I have the confidence to try to shape a novel or story or poem the way I desired and needed it to be, with both the imperfections and the felicities bearing my own signature.

Another lesson was as personal: reading praise of me and my writing, I could feel within myself an inflation of self-esteem similar to my feelings as a child when I won school prizes or had poems published in the newspapers, and I thought as I walked along Thames Street, Oamaru, North Otago, New Zealand, the South Pacific, the Earth, the World, the Universe, 'Everyone everywhere will know how clever I am!'

Now as I walked along Charing Cross Road I thought to myself, I wonder if these people know it is I whose photo was in the paper today, it is my writing they were praising, my book described in headlines? I'd glance at the literary types in Charing Cross Road and I'd think, 'If only they knew! I know I don't dine in fancy restaurants nor am I mentioned in the "About Town" notes of the *Evening News* and the *Evening Standard* ("promising novelist seen . . . etc"), but I'm in London, I'm here, I'm secret, and I'm in the reviews and some have compared me to Virginia Woolf!'

This self-inflation lasted until, reading the inevitable adverse criticism that hurt, that seemed not to 'understand' what I had written, that seemed 'unfair', and that sometimes described me as 'a woman who had been insane', I experienced the anguish of wondering who I thought I was that I could aspire to be a writer: I, with little talent, few words. I knew I had feelings and I could see inside people without having learned about them, but these were too few qualifications: I should never have begun writing.

Once *Owls Do Cry, Faces in the Water, The Edge of the Alphabet* were published I'd had enough experience of opposing reactions to make a deliberate effort to smooth my feelings about all reviews, to allow myself to believe neither the praise nor the adverse criticism, become neither overjoyed nor depressed, and if possible not to read reviews unless it was obvious that the writers had read the book and not just the blurb and a few biographical notes (not provided by me) that referred to 'insanity', and who, understanding or not understanding the book, made intelligent comments about it.

These early lessons remained with me and helped to simplify the complex mechanism of publication where the author is in danger of being trapped and even disabled.

During the snowbound quiet of the London winter I wrote two volumes of stories from which the *New Yorker* and other magazines that I learned were known as 'glossies' chose stories. When my cheque arrived from the *New Yorker* I was amazed and guilty that what had seemed an enjoyable exercise had been rewarded with so much money. I now had over six hundred pounds in my bank account — the magic number for those on National Assistance; soon, with fragments of advances being paid, I knew I would not longer be eligible. I planned to try to move to a quieter room.

18 Friends in London

One day I had a letter from John Forrest whom I'd not seen for nearly twenty years although we had corresponded from time to time and it was he who had arranged my initial appointment with Dr Berger at the Maudsley. He was now passing through London, he said, and he wondered if he could say hello.

He arrived one afternoon at Grove Hill Road bringing the gift of a Mexican bracelet that, in the continuing war of some jewellery with my body, would not fit on my large wrist. Bracelets always broke, necklaces were too small, brooches came apart, earrings unclasped or were too tight.

'Never mind,' I said. 'I'll fix it later.'

Our mutual apprehension melted. We talked of ordinary matters, his work and my work. We exchanged copies of books we had written. And later we dined at the restaurant on the South Bank overlooking the Thames. We might have been on an English pier in winter. There were few patrons, an icy wind blew from the Thames, the chairs and tables had been quickly overlaid by rust in a world where the effective substances are still blood and salt and water. The next day John Forrest flew home to America knowing we were now in a level state of uncomplicated friendship and would stay there. He was still perhaps unaware of many facts of my life and of the influence of his words spoken twenty years earlier, 'When I think of you I think of Van Gogh . . .'

Another friend, more recent, also influenced my life: the National Assistance man who, I felt, decided my very existence. Even in writing my books I planned each one to be written within six months because my supply of cheques lasted six months before the dreaded notice came in its window envelope, 'An Officer of the Department will call . . .'

I knew I'd not be able to work that day. I grew apprehensive. Would I be granted my six-monthly lease of life? I'd had the small advance from my books, and the postal notes for five shillings each, sent by my father, and now almost six hundred pounds in the bank. Not ever being sure if I would be allowed to keep my typewriter, and fearful at first that the National Assistance man would seize it, I used to hide it in the wardrobe with my reams of paper.

When I first met the National Assistance man, I was surprised and saddened by his appearance. He was tall, thin, with a pale face that made him seem ill. His clothing, his shoes, his briefcase were shabby and he himself might have been an applicant for National Assistance. I discounted the thought that the Department arranged his appearance to make his clients feel at home with him! Yet if he had been dressed like a stockbroker he might not have been received so warmly by those he had set out to 'inspect'. There was nothing officious about him; he was apologetic, mournful, and efficient.

Declining my offer of a cup of tea and a digestive biscuit he smiled gently, 'I've just had morning tea next door — the top floor where the Polish family live, and then the Italians on the ground floor gave me a feast. I think I must have clients in almost every house in Grove Hill Road.'

He spoke with pleasure and some pride.

When he had finished examining my bankbook, he glanced across the room while I waited in suspense as he looked again at the television. I said hastily, 'My landlord, Mr Morgan, used to work in a television shop. It belongs to him.'

The National Assistance man smiled.

'Do you watch "Coronation Street" and "Dixon of Dock Green"? And "Emergency Ward Ten"?'

'Sometimes. I like watching the new performers. Russ Conway.'

'Oh yes, Russ Conway. My children watch it too much, I think. I've two boys at High School. Comprehensive.'

I knew that in the English world he was immediately 'placed', for schools as well as accents placed people here.

He shuffled his papers into his briefcase, buckled it shut, and walked towards the door.

'I'll see you in another six months,' he said gently.

When he had gone, I put my typewriter on its mat on the table, and the paper beside it, ready. Then I went out for a walk to breathe the air and rejoice that I was safe for another six months; and in two or three days when my book of cheques came through the mail I'd buy a bun covered with coconut icing, split it open, butter it and eat it. I had six months to write, until the next window letter came — 'An Officer of the Department will call . . .'

When *Faces in the Water* was published, I gave a copy to the National Assistance man, writing simply, 'To the National Assistance Man with thanks . . .'

John Forrest, the National Assistance man . . . and Patrick Reilly. One day when I was boarding a bus I met Patrick Reilly who was as surprised as I at our meeting.

'I thought you were in America,' he said.

'Oh?' I'd forgotten the lie I told to get rid of him.

'I went to America too,' he said.

He then described how, shortly after he thought I had arrived in America he had seen an advertisement for a salesman in Illinois, based in Chicago, how he had applied for the job, he had been accepted, and had spent the winter trying to avoid burial in snowdrifts. He had learned that the company always placed tantalising advertisements in other countries because salesmen in the United States avoided travelling through Illinois in winter. He had thought it would be exciting, and the pay was high, Patrick said. He had looked up Illinois on the map. The gateway to the West. Money, a car, accommodation . . .

'Well,' I said. 'I didn't go to America. I changed my mind.'

'Where are you living?'

I told him. He frowned sternly when I said I was living on National Assistance.

'That won't do,' he said. He was working in the stationery store at Selfridges. He could visit me in the weekends, he said. And so we drifted together again.

The next weekend was to be the first of many when I, trying to make my National Assistance payment last, used to look out of the window to see Patrick, faithful Patrick, still with his jaunty walk and his bumptious air, coming down the road past the hostel for the blind, past the house next door where the Italian and Polish families lived, to the Morgans; and always he'd be carrying his Woolworths paper bag with the string handle: packed with food. I felt like a child at Christmas as he set the bottles and jars and packets on the table.

'I thought you might like this,' he'd say. 'Or this.'

There was always an assortment of Peek Frean's biscuits, Irish bacon and butter, a Hovis loaf, tinned creamed rice or white grapes: Patrick's channel of communication was food. Usually he brought enough to supplement my ordinary supply for a week. He brought me notebooks, too, as my father had done when I was a child, from his workplace. His resemblance to my father, particularly when his lips pursed with disapproval, was uncanny and caused me to wonder about myself and my life. Dr Miller had said frankly that he thought my father was a bully; he had a similar opinion of Patrick Reilly. My life had been erased, almost, by expert bullying while I played the role of victim that like any other repeated role, resists a change.

Patrick became the provider, the companion. He gave no sign of wanting to touch or kiss me; if he accidentally touched me he said, 'Excuse me, I'm sorry.' I depended on him yet I found him repugnant; I felt no sexual desire for him. I liked him best when he talked of the leprechauns and the Irish language, and we shared a love of weather, of sky and sea and green, and as we had done in my early days in London, we walked in Ruskin Park or on Clapham Common where he now had a single council flat on the ground floor.

And when Patrick learned that I'd never been to a circus and there was a circus booked to appear on Clapham Common, he bought tickets for us, but on the morning of the expected performance he appeared with the news that the circus had been rained out in one of those local storms that strike separate suburbs of London. The circus had gone north, Patrick said.

We walked on the Common where the tents and caravans had been. The ground was like a Southland cowbyre in winter, churned with mud and hoofmarks. And it was not Patrick but I with my didactic leanings who suggested that perhaps I had been 'meant' not to see a circus.

Patrick and I had a memorable Whitsunday during those Grove Hill Road days. He arrived for his usual Saturday visit. 'Next week's Whit,' he said while I listened with delight at the abbreviation — *Whit*. 'What are you doing for Whit?'

'Nothing,' I said.

'Oh you can't be alone for Whit.'

He was cooking a turkey, he said, and I was to come to his flat and share the Whitsunday dinner.

The next Sunday I arrived at one of those tall apartment buildings that replaced the bombed houses and were named after various Englishmen — Tennyson House, Milton House . . . Patrick's flat was tiny like the corner of a cardboard box of the kind my sisters and I used to divide into a house for our kewpie dolls.

A large cooked turkey crouched on a plate in the middle of the table beside a dish of tinned peaches, a jug of whipped cream, chocolate digestive biscuits unwrapped and parted from one another in a semi-circle on a plate. There were ABC scones freshly buttered with Irish butter; and two Lyons individual fruit pies to eat with the peaches.

The meal was the thing, as if Patrick were a marksman arrowing in on it. I followed his example. We started on the turkey and when dinner was over much of the turkey and the dessert remained, and when I left for Camberwell Patrick walked me to the bus stop, inviting me to the church nearby where we sat subdued by turkey and peaches and individual fruit pies before the crucifix. I admired Patrick for his fierce protectiveness towards *his* church, and the fervent way he tried to persuade me to belong, to give up all evil. We could go to the priest for instruction, he said.

'But I believe in divorce,' I said.

We argued over divorce. I was full of platitudes in many of my arguments as if I were again an ignorant student trying to discourse on 'free love', determinedly opposing all beliefs of the 'older' generation, for, in my view,

Patrick was an older generation because he came from an older civilisation where it was not so easy to be rid of embedded belief.

The next weekend, as he unpacked his carry bag of food and I asked how he had spent the rest of Whitsunday, he looked ashamed.

'I ate the whole turkey. The whole turkey. As soon as I got home I started on it and ate and ate.'

He looked uncomfortably surprised by his actions. Gluttony was a sin and sins were serious.

'To tell you the truth,' he said, 'there was nothing else to do.'

His words were an admission of such awful emptiness that I felt helpless, imagining him stifling time with a cooked turkey. The dreariness depressed me. I knew that London was full of people like Patrick. Didn't I, too, spend all afternoon in the cinema, to get warm, certainly, but also to *mark* time, to disguise time, *mask* it, when I needed to escape from my work when it frightened me; I, too, paying my admission fee in daylight, emerging in darkness, feeling robbed of the hours between but grateful for their passing, as if Time and I were partners. And later, home at Grove Hill Road, regretting the vanished hours, I'd think, 'I can't believe I deliberately banished so much time.'

Poor Patrick! He may not have been happy with his consuming almost a whole turkey, but I, in my turn was unhappy and guilty over using him as a provider, continuing to accept his gifts while feeling irritation and dislike for him. He thought always of what he might give me, his giving taking the form of *goods*. We'd be walking along the street and he'd say suddenly, peering into a shop window, 'Look, that's what you want. That's what I can give you.'

Or he'd stop and gasp as an idea came to him, 'I know what I can give you. I know what you would like.'

Books, a fountain pen, underwear . . .

I accepted all with a voiced gratitude but with a feeling of dislike both for him and myself that we were apparently so unskilled or inadequate that we relied for our human trading upon the currency of a world of commerce. Perhaps it was enough. Men and women have always used the materials around them to supplement, enhance or replace or transform the material within themselves. My laborious journeys to and from Mirror City were another instance of the politics of use.

It was Patrick's renewed attempt to select my friends that finally parted us. I had kept in touch with the poet and painter of North London. They too had been marking time with their desperate signatures. Ben who had visited me regularly in hospital bringing the comfort of books, ideas, news about the world of Soho and Charing Cross Road, had now embraced a 'new' psychology which was old to me as I had studied it nearly twenty years earlier. Uninhibited expression was the thing, he said, although he knew and I knew that this was only another way of avoiding the responsibility of creating order, and when I questioned him on this he assured me that order came naturally from chaos. I was more sceptical. What if it remained chaos and you were caught in chaos and *Time* passed?

Ben smiled ruefully. 'Oh, time,' he said, adding thoughtfully, 'Aye. Aye,' as if perhaps because he had been to Scotland and had met Hugh McDiarmid, then Hugh McDiarmid, with Time obviously in his control, would take care of time for Ben, too. 'The thing is to be free, to do as you wish when you wish.'

I admired Ben's persistence. In a café, he'd suddenly get to his feet and begin whirling his arms like a windmill and calling out words that came at random, then he'd meow like a cat, or perhaps sing the line of a song, or begin hopping. Then he'd sit down, saying, in an aside, 'Free expression.'

When Patrick arrived at Grove Hill Road one Saturday afternoon to find Ben there, and I introduced them, and later Patrick said, 'Poets and artists are no good. Have nothing to do with them,' I felt like a clinging insect that had glued itself to the wrong plant in the wrong garden in the wrong world. Wrong for the insect, the plant, the garden and the world.

I shook myself free of Patrick.

I retreated again into my own habitat, looking out at all worlds. Working day by day, and still hoping that I might be able to find a quieter room, I finished *Scented Gardens for the Blind*. Dr Cawley, advancing in his profession, was transferring to a post in Birmingham; he was not lost to me, however, for it was arranged that he retain a post at the Maudsley where he would see me during his frequent visits to London.

And while I was absorbing this change I answered an advertisement to rent a cottage in Suffolk at a reduced rental in return for looking after the property and a dog. I had a letter from my London publisher ('my London publisher'!) arranging a meeting, and a letter from Patrick Reilly to say that London was too evil therefore he was returning to Ireland. I never saw him again.

19   Meeting the Publisher

When my landlady knew that I was to have my first meeting with my publisher, she made an appointment for me at her hairdressing salon 'down the Green'.

'I've never said anything to you before, but you must do something about your hair. We could wetten it and straighten it.'

The old echoes. I smiled to myself. Well, I said, it was time I had a haircut and the publisher had asked for a photo.

Meekly I fell into the preparations for the occasion. I even took the bus to the West End where browsing in Marks and Spencer's for a dress, I bought a patterned green and white and black jersey silk, shortsleeved with a tie belt, and as soon as I arrived home and paraded in front of the wardrobe mirror with my newly washed, cut and flattened hair that gave me the appearance of having had the top of my head sliced off, I knew that I had chosen the ugliest dress I had ever worn. Seen in daylight, the colours were dreary, the pattern busily confused. I stared at the stranger in the wardrobe mirror and saw myself as I had been years ago — trapped, miserably, obedient, and I was relieved that writing a book did not entail a visit to a 'writing salon' where one's words were cleaned and snipped by someone trained for the purpose. I tried to roughen my hair to its old mop and halo of curls but it was useless.

I set out to the Strand and the publisher W. H. Allen in Essex Street. I sat in the bus enjoying the familiar route — around the corner past the world headquarters of the Salvation Army with its statue of Gore Booth, opposite the Denmark Hill railway station; I remembered the train crash in the first November smog after I had returned to London — my first experience of local drama in the focus of every London newspaper, the radio and television news with their lists of the dead and injured, the names of the stations — Forest Hill, Dulwich, the pictures of the fleet of ambulances ferrying to and from the South London hospitals, the comparison to the blitz, all in the first choking swirling smog of winter, the accepted signal then of the season's arrival and for the increasing daily tally of the deaths of the frail old and the cold poor.

Now down past the Institute of Psychiatry, the Maudsley Hospital, King's College Hospital, to the 'Green' with its Odeon painted an ugly dog-mess brown, past the new council flats, the dilapidated shops, the surge of the East Street market and cluttered pavements, past the Elephant, the Eye Hospital, the Old Vic, Waterloo Station, Waterloo Bridge to the Strand.

A number 68 bus, its destination still, mockingly, *Chalk Farm*.

I had my photo taken in a PolyFoto studio at Charing Cross. Then I walked back towards Essex Street, loitering as I was too early, by looking in shop windows. And then I had turned the corner from the Strand and was in Essex Street, standing in front of W. H. Allen. Having observed in my early London days the various publishing houses of London when Ben and Lawrence and I used to walk up and down outside the publishers in Great Russell Street, trying to imagine the activity within and wondering, would we ever?, I knew that publishing houses were not as I had supposed they would be — palaces equal in majesty to the influence of their complete book list — and were more often like any other place of business, perhaps seedier, more unkempt. My disappointment at this discovery was tempered by knowing that within the buildings, books outnumbered people and maintained power and influence, ruling from their floor-to-ceiling shelves while the stack of untested manuscripts sat confidently waiting their turn.

Mark Goulden's office was suitably booklined with windows facing the street; a thick carpet, and a large desk where Mark Goulden sat while I sat in the deep easy chair and thought, so this is my English publisher. I thought he looked like a bookie or a 'spiv', a small grey-haired wiry man with a 'weathered' face. A gambler-publisher. His voice was rich, musical, his eyes quick, lively. He said that although my books had excellent reviews, they did not sell: he was hoping that some day I would write a 'bestseller'.

He then began to reminisce while I listened fascinated as he referred to the current controversy over who had 'discovered' Dylan Thomas, and the recent published statement by Edith Sitwell supporting Mark Goulden's claim that *he* had discovered Dylan Thomas when, as an editor of a small poetry magazine, he received a number of poems which led him to want to meet the author who was then invited to London.

Mr Goulden waved his arm in the direction of the Strand.

'We put him up at the Strand Palace,' he said.

Yes, he repeated, he had discovered Dylan Thomas.

He then described other authors while I listened enthralled by his charm and his power as a raconteur. He was evidently a joyful man, delighting in himself and others.

'Where are you living?' he asked, adding that he didn't care for his authors living in a waste land like Camberwell.

'I think I'm going to stay in a cottage in Suffolk,' I said.

'You don't want to bury yourself in the country, either . . . We could give you an apartment in London while you write your new book.' Shyness overcame me. I was also wary of apartments that I couldn't afford, and he hadn't said he would pay.

'I'll see,' I said.

'Remember, if you get tired of living in the country and want to come to London, we can give you an apartment.'

'Yes.'

What did 'give' mean? Was it used in its general sense?

Mark Goulden walked to the window and looked down at Essex Street.

'When Wanda Lyons comes here she comes in a Rolls Royce. You're a better writer than Wanda Lyons. You should have diamonds and furs, and when you come to see me again I want you to be able to arrive in a Rolls Royce.'

As I was leaving he gave me two novels to read.

'These have been bestsellers,' he said.

He had painted a picture of such impossible glory for me that I felt afraid. I walked along the Strand to Charing Cross Station where I went to the ladies lavatory and cried.

When later I described to Patience Ross my meeting with Mark Goulden, I was surprised that her voice held a note of awe.

'You've met Mark Goulden?'

'Haven't you met him?'

'Oh no. Agents don't usually meet the publishers.'

I had not understood that in the United Kingdom literary agents were looked on by the publishers as intruders rather than allies.

'What do you think of him?' Patience Ross asked.

'Oh he's a wonderful man,' I said. 'A wonderful storyteller.'

'Yes, I've heard that about him.'

Was I mistaken in detecting envy in her voice? I knew that Patience Ross, now nearing retirement, had a high reputation for integrity, judgment, literacy, literary knowledge, and I felt sad that another instance of 'class' in London had denied the publisher the rewards of meeting her.

When I returned to Grove Hill Road, I found that Joan Morgan, anticipating my probable move to the country, had already found a new tenant for my room. She would increase the rent also, she said. And before I left would I do a favour for the Morgans? Myra who had passed her eleven-plus and was applying for a place at the Mary Datchelor Grammar School, specialising in music, needed a reference from outside her family. Would I kindly sign a reference for her?

'Of course.'

I had watched Myra growing. I had written verses about her and her family. I had travelled with Myra to parts of London during the music competitions where I heard her play her 'piece', followed by the inevitable prodigy, the small boy (dressed like young Mozart) who had to be lifted on a cushion and whose tiny fingers played a Mozart sonata . . .

Ted Morgan brought the reference for me to sign.

I wrote my name, and in the space, *Occupation*, I wrote, *Author*. Ted Morgan produced another form.

'Would you mind filling it in again?' he said. 'This time say you're a journalist.'

Dutifully I wrote, 'Journalist'.

Ted Morgan beamed.

'Authors are thought to be unreliable,' he said. 'But when they know we've had a *journalist* staying in the house . . .'

That evening I had a phone call from the owners of the cottage in Suffolk. Would I go to their place in *World's End* for an interview?

20 A Cottage in the Country

World's End? I caught the bus to Chelsea, along King's Road past the gasworks to the house where the owners of the cottage lived, and as they showed me into the cosy downstairs sitting room and prepared to serve afternoon tea, they told me, echoing each other, how they had bought and renovated the Suffolk cottage and were now renovating their home here in King's Road. They were a Miss Wilson and a Miss Collins who asked to be addressed as *Will* and *Coll*, and they worked as receptionists in the Moorfields Eye Hospital. Coll who was English, perhaps in her late thirties or early forties, was daintily built, darkhaired and obviously fastidious about domestic matters: her interest was antiques, she said. Will, from Australia but an English citizen for many years was less contained with a personality more easily ventilated: one might compare two pine cones, one dark, shiny and closed, the other, easily ripened, with open shutters. They were enthusiastic about the Suffolk cottage that had now had its roof rethatched, its furnishing replaced in keeping with the period, and they were eager for me to know that both the cottage and the house had been paid for by savings out of their salaries, and they themselves had undertaken renovations, working long hours in weekends. Their problem was that they were unable to use the cottage until they retired and it needed a tenant, the right tenant to care for it all year. There was also a dog to be walked and fed.

They'd had many replies to their advertisement, including a telegram from a retired Colonel, *Will accept cottage. Arriving weekend with five hounds.*

The idea of a writer living in the cottage seemed to appeal to them. They had even planned where I would work — at an old sewing machine placed directly before the picture window looking out at the rose garden, the lawn, and the ninety-foot lilac hedge.

'There's a rose garden that you'll be looking after. The ninety-foot lilac hedge also. And we'd like a vegetable garden. And there's the dog, actually a mongrel bitch, Minnie, belonging to an old woman living in a cottage down the road, but we've taken over Minnie for her.'

So I was suddenly the appointed caretaker, at a third of the normal rent, of a thatched cottage at Braiseworth, near Eye, in East Suffolk. (As I had recently finished writing *Scented Gardens for the Blind*, I felt bemused by the women's work at the eye hospital, and this postal location of the cottage, *Near Eye*.)

They explained how I should get to the cottage. They were enthusiastic pronouncing the place names in East Suffolk like incantations.

'Stowmarket is the place,' Coll said.

'Stowmarket?' I too was captured by the names.

'Stowmarket. When you have your belongings put on the train, remember they travel only as far as *Stowmarket*, and from there you hire a carrier to deliver them.'

'And remember, you're not going to Suffolk *proper*.'

'Not Suffolk *proper*?'

'No, it's *East* Suffolk. It's apart and different and quite *unspoiled*.'

Their voices were rich with the satisfaction of praising East Suffolk.

They would go to East Suffolk that weekend to prepare for my arrival in three weeks, they said, and they'd be waiting for me the weekend I arrived, to welcome me.

'And if you're coming by bus you ask for the Braiseworth turnoff and turn right down the oak lane . . .'

'Turn right down the oak lane,' I echoed as I caught the bus home to Camberwell. The words had the magic of directions given and followed in fairy tales, myths and legends.

Three weeks later I took the train from Liverpool Street Station to Ipswich where, changing to an Eastern Counties bus, I travelled to the 'turnoff at Braiseworth' and 'turned right, down the oak lane', walked down the oak lane to the cottage where Will and Coll waited to receive me and instruct me in my duties as caretaker.

They had prepared a bedroom upstairs below the sloping roof, with a dormer window and dark exposed beams and a view over the fields surrounding the cottage, and the ninety-foot lilac hedge just beginning to bud. Downstairs they had thoughtfully cleared the top of the old sewing machine and arranged a likely place for me to work where, as they said, I could gaze out of the window 'for inspiration', at the ninety-foot lilac hedge. They kept noting its length and describing how it would appear in flower, and remembering that they had both fallen in love with the cottage but when they saw the lilac hedge they knew the cottage would be their home. They'd installed hot water, with the Raeburn stove, a flush lavatory, and a bath. Coll, with her special feeling for roses, had planted the rose garden while Will had cleared the paths and repaired the front gate and searched until she found the heavy oak door to replace the too modern glass-panelled door with its frosted picture of a stag beside a mountain. East Suffolk had been the most wonderful discovery of their lives.

'Can you believe it?' they asked ecstatically as they toured the garden.

Later the next day Will and Coll drove back to London, leaving me alone with Minnie the mongrel bitch, my typewriter, the country quiet, and my plans for my next book.

I now thought of myself as living the life of a writer, for my two books of stories had been published and *Scented Gardens for the Blind* was about to be published, and during my time at Grove Hill Road I had been aware of a subtle shifting of my life into a world of fiction where I spread before me everything I saw and heard, people I met in buses, streets, railway stations, and where I lived, choosing from the displayed treasure frag-ments and mo-ments that combined to make a shape of a novel or poem or story. Nothing was without its use. I had learned to be a citizen of the Mirror City. My only qualification for continuing this autobiography is that although I have used, invented, mixed, remodelled, changed, added, subtracted from all experiences I have never written directly of my own life and feelings. Undoubtedly I have mixed myself with other characters who themselves are a product of known and unknown, real and imagined; I have created 'selves'; but I have never written of 'me'. Why? Because if I make that hazardous journey to the Mirror City where everything I have known or seen or dreamed of is bathed in the light of another world, what use is there in returning only with a mirrorful of me? Or, indeed, of others who exist very well by the ordinary light of day? The self must be the container of the treasures of Mirror City, the Envoy as it were, and when the time comes to arrange and list those treasures for shaping into words, the self must be the worker, the bearer of the burden, the chooser, placer and polisher. And when the work is finished and the nothingness must be endured, the self may take a holiday, if only to reweave the used container that awaits the next visit to Mirror City. These are the processes of fiction. 'Putting it all down as it happens' is not fiction; there must be the journey by oneself, the changing of the light focused upon the material, the willingness of the author herself to live within that light, that city of reflections governed by different laws, materials, currency. Writing a novel is not merely going on a shopping expedition across the border to an unreal land: it is hours and years spent in the factories, the streets, the cathedrals of the imagination, learning the unique functioning of Mirror City, its skies and space, its own planetary system, without stopping to think that one may become homeless in the world, and bankrupt, abandoned by the Envoy.

With these preoccupations I allied the more earthly duties of caretaker of the cottage in the oak lane, Braiseworth, near Eye, with my morning beginning, not as planned, in availing myself of Will's and Coll's promised inspiration, but in walking Minnie, and in performing other tasks — cleaning the cottage, preparing the vegetable garden, riding the three miles on the old bicycle to Eye for groceries and dog meat, and making a regular all-day visit to London to talk to Dr Cawley. My time was consumed. I spent spare moments gazing with admiration at my newly dug and planted garden and with horror at the nettles that grew twice as tall after I had scythed them. Nor was there time in the evening, for unfamiliar with the gas lighting, I used it seldom after trying to light the lamps and finding their mantles collapsed in my hand when I touched them. And so in the evening I took a candle upstairs and tried to read while Minnie lay on a rug near the door, her everwatchful glance divided between me and the door. She had quickly become attached to me, although I had been warned that she was savage with strangers and indeed was under a court ruling which ordered her to be destroyed should she again attack.

Tired enough by my daily routine as caretaker, I was not prepared for the exertions of the weekends when Will and Coll came to stay, determined to enjoy every minute and every delight of their cottage which they called, simply, *The Cottage*. Their first weekend was an alarming, exhausting intrusion. Certainly the terms of my tenancy were that I should care for the house, the dog, the garden, but I did not expect that on Saturday afternoon Will and Coll would set up their deckchairs in the sun while they suggested (ordered would be a more suitable word: they had met in the army) that I climb the ladder and remove all the dead lilac blossoms from the ninety-foot lilac hedge, working my way along each side. Otherwise, they said, the lilac wouldn't last, it would vanish in a few weeks, and what would they do, knowing they had wasted the precious lilac? My next task was to prune the rose bushes and to weed the garden borders ('you must keep the garden free of weeds'), and while I toiled most of the afternoon, snipping, pulling, tearing; redfaced, breathless and hot, I watched them lounging in their deckchairs as if they were passengers on a cruise ship observing the fascinating work of the crew. Now and again they gave more directions or pointed out weeds that I had missed, or a bunch of dead lilac, 'See, right on top of the hedge, up this end.' Sometimes they closed their eyes and basked; or they caught up with the news and the advertisements in Will's favourite magazine, *The Lady*.

Their abundance of plans fascinated me. But how could they find time, they asked. 'We've taken on too much in the cottage,' they admitted. They were glad to have a caretaker; in the winter they'd not be able to get to Braiseworth.

My experiences and impressions of East Suffolk, the inhabitants, the countryside, were absorbed to emerge later when I returned to New Zealand and wrote *The Adaptable Man*. And because my life had shifted, as I have described, to Mirror City, I now watch the story of myself receding also to Mirror City, for under the light of the ordinary sun and the ordinary day, the 'real' experiences hold diminishing interest for me, for these are the scraps only of the ultimate feast. The more I lived as a writer, the less interesting to outward eyes my life became, ruled by routine, and even in Braiseworth near Eye, with my writing crowded out by domestic duties of *garden*, *clean*, *walk the dog*, *shop*, the Mirror City stayed in my mind as the true desirable dwelling place.

On the days when I had an appointment in London I woke early, cycled two miles to the nearest railway station, Mellis, left my bike with the stationmaster, and caught the train from Norwich to London; or the bus to Ipswich and the train from Ipswich. Approaching London, I felt the excitement of coming home, the train gathering speed, the countryside left behind for the brick oceans, the dirty city, the squalid warehouses and factories of East London — ah the delight! — and Liverpool Street Station, just in time to step out to the marching tunes played over the loudspeaker and encouraging the ten o'clock city workers to a brisk pace.

Then I'd make my way to Camberwell; to see Dr Cawley who'd also made a journey, from Birmingham; and we were like two who come from distant lands for a summit conference, to discuss important plans and futures. And after we'd had our talk I'd just have time perhaps to browse in Charing Cross Road or the Strand before I caught the one-thirty train to Ipswich, and the bus to Braiseworth. I'd arrive home to be welcomed by Minnie, and feeling tired and wondering why I was living in the country when it was the city that attracted me, and wondering where my writing day had gone, I'd go to bed in the twilight and watch the blossoming of the country dark and listen to the creatures outside, and hope for the sound of the nightingale. And alone in the cottage I was surprised to realise that

I was afraid. For the first time in my life I was living alone in a house and I was afraid. If at any time I was in one room, who occupied the other rooms? I'd open the doors and look in. Nothing. I could have been adrift on an ice floe. Sometimes I heard the fluttering of a bird caught under the mesh that covered the thatch. How different the night was from my childhood night in Wyndham when the dark was as dark and I listened, afraid, to the night sounds, and thought:

> Hark, Hark, the dogs do bark
> the beggars are coming to town,
> some in rags, some in bags,
> and some in velvet gown.

But then I was surrounded by the warmth of people and I knew that in the kitchen the fire was burning, the room was lit by the lamp and the candles and the firelight, there was laughter and singing, and the baby was asleep.

In Suffolk I always welcomed morning and light. I was as eager as Minnie to go walking in the dew-wet lanes, watching the hares in the corn, seeing the wildflowers, primroses, cowslips, bluebells, blackthorn; but my heart was in London, I wanted to return there where I was happy to be alone in the crowd, surrounded and sustained by the immensity of people, of the human race, who, although it — we — had destroyed or crippled much of the natural world, including my northern hemisphere sky, could still send representatives to explore the Mirror City, and though some might be lost there and never return there were always those who struggled home to create their works of art.

And so when my publisher wrote reminding me of his offer of 'an apartment in the city' I thankfully accepted it, provided I could pay my usual rent. I knew from the nature of gifts, the contract between giver and receiver, that no gift is 'free', and so I thought it better to remove the apartment from the complex status of 'gift'.

I explained truthfully to the owners of the cottage the reason for my abrupt departure and I hoped they would understand: I would remain at the cottage for a few weeks until they found a replacement. I had been growing increasingly alarmed at the thought of spending a snowy winter alone with a dog in a dark house full of collapsed gas mantles, for even under the supervision of Will and Coll I never learned to touch the mantles and leave them unharmed, as each time I touched them they dissolved into powdery substance in my hand and I was reminded of my attempt at writing poems that behaved in the same way when I fingered them or tried to set them alight.

Will and Coll tried to be understanding about my betrayal of them, and I could see my alarm about a winter in Suffolk — East Suffolk — transferred to them as they wondered how they could lure a tenant without first offering the luxury bait of summer in the oak lane and the fields of Braiseworth near Eye; and when they warned me I'd be returning to the noise of London I did not list the corresponding noises of Suffolk — daylong shots as the farmers tried to scare the crows from the crops, the roar of tractors and harvesters, the loudspeaker that sounded as if from a perennial fairground that I searched for and could not find. I did not describe to them the exhaustion of spending each day walking, planting, weeding, pedalling, instead of, as they and I had imagined, sitting at the old sewing machine table gazing through the picture window at the well of inspiration, the ninety-foot lilac hedge.

Their disappointment was lessened by the sight of the bountiful garden with its many varieties of vegetables and herbs. They were impressed, too, that I had dug a larger, deeper plot, presumably for further planting before winter. I did not explain that, discovering that the straight road at the end of the oak lane was originally a Roman road from Ipswich to Norwich, and having already unearthed a collection of stones that I washed to reveal pretty colours and designs and — with little effort of imagining — pictures, I had been seized by the fever of finding ancient relics, and thus each day I had extended the original garden till it grew wider and deeper and longer as I dug my pieces of flint, my imagined household gods and Anglo-Saxon jewellery . . .

For my first night in London before moving to the South Kensington apartment rented for me by my publisher, I stayed at World's End, with Will and Coll. I ate their perfectly cooked meal. I listened again to their marvelling at what they had done with a small house at World's End and a three-hundred-year-old cottage in East Suffolk, and I apologised again for cutting short my tenancy.

'Perhaps you'll put us in your book?' they said.

'I'll help with your suitcase,' Coll said as the next morning I walked to the bus stop on the way to Kensington. 'It feels as if it's full of stones.'

Half-full of English, Roman, Saxon, Danish stones, relics from another city.

21   An Apartment in the City

It was a basement apartment with windows looking out over two streets, the large sitting room and kitchen facing the busier streets, the large bedroom beside the quieter 'place', with the bathroom enclosed in the hallway. The pebble garden at the back was planted with spiked shrubs of the kinds that, growing by the sea, suffer the salt spray and winds by bending their backs and heads forward away from the storm, and, growing in a city, adopt the same pose to avoid the fumes, soundwaves and odious smells, and in both cases they survive and bloom with thorn crowns and small blue and pink flowers. When the trucks passed along the back street the apartment shuddered with grindings, slammings, squealing of brakes, while outside the bedroom the traffic though quiet, was unceasing.

The apartment was luxurious for me. For the first time since I had been in London I had hot running water and a bath and bathroom and kitchen to myself. The furnishings were luxurious also, with striped Regency sofas and chairs with round bun-like seats, and dark polished chests of drawers. The double bed had sheets and blankets wide enough and long enough to tuck in and the mattress was as level as a wooden shelf and as unyielding, while some of the towels in the linen cupboard were labelled *Bath Sheets*.

At first I arranged my workplace in the bedroom only to find the room was too dark and I felt I was missing events in the sitting room, therefore I tried typing there beside the inner wall but the sounds of traffic intruded. I was also intimidated by the fine furniture. In a half-hearted way I leafed through the poems I had written during my East Suffolk days, and the book I had begun but my mind was occupied by the publication of *Scented Gardens for the Blind* and the sentence from a review that I could not ignore: 'This book is unreadable in the worst sense.' I struggled against losing my small supply of confidence. In another journal someone had described the book as 'likely a work of genius.' The two opinions, extreme yet balancing, shifted from me like alternatingly oppressive and buoyant waves, leaving me a damp survivor, jetsam of yet another flow of reviews.

In South Kensington I learned more about life in London, of the ease of living in SW7 compared to SE5, for a miracle seemed to occur in libraries, museums, shops as soon as I gave my address: I was treated with kindness, I was offered credit; and could they call me a taxi? The tendency to questioning and suspicion by the keepers of Camberwell had vanished. And when I walked along the streets of Kensington and Knightsbridge, jostled by the beautiful and the rich, I found myself remembering the dream of my

Aunt Polly in Petone, New Zealand, to be 'someone'. 'I'd like to be some-body,' she'd say, reminding herself that she had relations, town clerks or mayors, lawyers or doctors, who were 'somebody'. In Kensington I too was 'somebody', but not because of my actions or works or some remarkable personal trait: I was 'somebody' because my address was South Kensington SW7. I had a luxury apartment with a bathroom, a white entry phone as well as an 'ordinary' telephone, a tradesman's entrance and a private entrance . . . I was out of step, however, with the dwellers of South Kensing-ton. In Grove Hill Road SE5, getting up very early and starting work, I'd know a feeling of being at home as I saw the lights in the houses and imagined the hasty breakfasts, and watched the workers hurrying through the half-dark to catch their buses, and, later, the groups of children on their way to school, swishing and tapping and knocking their sticks in an unknowing rehearsal of age. Here in Kensington few appeared to be awake before ten in the morning. The mail was delivered late. If there were children they were driven silently to school in large dark cars. I might have felt stranded had I not known that other writers lived in Kensington. I liked to think they were working near, unseen, never forgetting or abandoning the Mirror City.

In the centre of my dining table I put the bowl of planted flowers sent by the Gouldens to welcome me on my first day in the apartment. They had also sent an invitation to their home to meet the author Alan Sillitoe and his wife, Ruth, at afternoon tea, and on the day, in spite of the heavy rain, I chose to walk to their place in Mayfair, planning a route where I might arrive fairly dry. The rain persisted. I did not find the verandahs I had hoped to find. My shoes filled with water, my stockings, the lower part of my dress, the back of my cardigan were soaking when at last I stood out-side the Gouldens' apartment and watched the Sillitoes arriving warm and dry by taxi. I was hot, red-faced, flurried; my bladder was full, and my visit was just beginning. I waited 'in the shadows' as it were until the Sillitoes had gone into the building, then I took the lift to the top floor, rang the bell, and was admitted by Mrs Goulden, tall, dark, regal (with a remarkable resemblance, I thought, to the Queen of Spades in the film I had lately seen, *The Manchurian Candidate*). She wore black and had an air of having lived inside her skin as if it were a house, polished, prepared daily, with herself the mistress in total possession. She was not an immediate person; there was a porch, an entrance hall where one waited to be received. She introduced me to Alan and Ruth Sillitoe. ('I've read your books . . . etc.')

The introductions over, there was consternation that my clothes and shoes were saturated. Mrs Goulden took me to a bedroom where she found dry clothes and shoes for me to wear while mine dried, and so I began my visit wearing a tight-fitting black dress and black evening shoes with gold borders, peep toes and two-inch heels.

Presently Mrs Goulden rang a silver bell and a servant, a darkhaired buxom woman named *Columba*, appeared with the afternoon tea and when she had left the room, Mrs Goulden explained that Columba had been brought from Portugal and spoke little English. This caused excitement between the Sillitoes (Alan, the latest star of the northern writers, deep in realism, poverty, struggles for food, work and sex in the slums of the north) who had been living in Morocco and had brought a servant home with them, they said, but when they arrived in England, they discovered they had purchased and paid for her as if she were a slave.

Oh, the servant problem!

I listened, quietly amazed, while Mrs Goulden and the Sillitoes ranged from the servant problem to the *au pair* and back to the servant problem; there in the Mayfair apartment with its Persian rugs, Turkish cats, exquisite paintings, dark knobbly furniture.

I had little to say. I smiled a lot and said 'Yes, yes.' My evening shoes were pinching. And when the time came to leave and I changed into my dry clothes and shoes Mrs Goulden parcelled up the black dress and evening shoes.

'You're welcome to keep them,' she said.

The rain had stopped. No, I said, I'd walk home and not get a taxi. As I left, carrying my new black dress and evening shoes, I thought, with excitement and satisfaction, I have met Alan and Ruth Sillitoe. My second *real* writer. (The first had been John Silkin who had given me a poem inscribed to me, but that is another story.)

Living in South Kensington I could not rid myself of the idea that I was playing house, playing at being someone who lived in an apartment with a white entry phone and a white telephone in the bedroom, beside the bed, for me to answer calls in the middle of the night, 'Oh is that you darling. Don't bother me now.' Playing at having a real bathroom and bath with hot water and cupboards full of linen and huge towels labelled *Bath Sheets* for me to wrap around me when Nigel and Gerald came (opening the door with their private key) and I called, 'Just a minute, *hunny*, I'm in the bath,' with the imagined dialogue the same as that used when I and my sisters played Hollywood with our kewpie dolls. The apartment was a game, beginning with my role as tenant to the unrealistic rent that I would never have money to pay.

And each day I sat at my table trying to write my new novel, *Letter to a Sculptor*. Then I'd get up and walk around the apartment and gloat over it as I used to gloat over the garden in Suffolk, as if producing it had been 'all my own work'. And instead of returning to my typewriter and shaping a batch of sentences, I'd experiment with the new stove in the kitchen, producing an unusual dish from *Aunt Daisy's Recipe Book* sent to me by my father for my last birthday. He'd also sent me a case of New Zealand butter which, after giving some away, I had packed in the snowy refrigerator.

Then one day a friend of Frank Sargeson, Paula Lincoln, who had left New Zealand after thirty years and bought a cottage in a small village in Norfolk, wrote to say that she and her sister Rachel who were ardent cricket fans were coming to London to see the cricket at Lords and they'd like to accept the invitation I had given them to 'stay any time'.

I met them at Liverpool Street Station. They were to sleep in the bedroom while I slept on a folding bed placed half in and out of the hall cupboard with just enough room for passing into the kitchen. I found both Paula and Rachel overwhelming, eager, enthusiastic, moving abruptly in what seemed like a physical attack on the space around them; and as they were sisters who did not see each other often, their voices were high-pitched with excitement and their Oxford accents, sharply edged, sliced through the apartment, furniture, fittings, air and my ears. At Lords I sat watching a tedious game that I knew nothing about, and when a newcomer whispered urgently to me, 'I say, who's first man?' and I echoed meekly, 'First man?' the woman looked at me with disgust.

Halfway through the morning I left Paula and Rachel and returned to Kensington where I found a letter from my sister in New Zealand telling me that my father, cycling to his work as boiler attendant 'out the North Road' had collapsed near Willowglen, our home, and had been admitted to hospital where a diagnosis was not made at once, and the next day he was being x-rayed, still in a state of collapse, when he died. He had been suffering a haemorrhage from a stomach ulcer.

Poor difficult, bullying, loving Dad, I thought, sighing my tears. Later when Paula and Rachel came home from Lords, I told them my news. What could they say? They began to reminisce about their father, a distant man who when they were children had visited them occasionally in the nursery. They remembered his 'twinkling, kindly eyes' and his shyness. They had called him 'Father'. He was a clergyman at a girls' public school, and because he was employed there the Lincoln family was educated there, and, later, they were at school in Switzerland. They had called their mother, 'Mother'. Their parents came rarely to the nursery, they said, and it was their elder sister to whom they looked for guidance and help.

'Poor Mother,' they said. 'Poor Father.'

And they said to each other, 'Do you remember? . . .' using words and phrases that were of the nineteen twenties and before and that I'd read only in books. Some of the girls at school had fathers who were 'rotters', they cried. 'Rotters and cads. But Father was tophole, wasn't he?'

That evening as I lay in my foldaway bed I thought of Dad alone at Willowglen and I remembered Aunt Polly's criticism of me for going 'overseas' — 'You are single and it's your place to stay home and look after your father.' Poor Dad with his five-shilling postal notes, and his stinking fish-bag, the inside covered with old fish scales, hanging inside the back door, and his trouser clips for his bike hanging on their hook behind the door, and his face wobbling with tears when he said goodbye at the Wellington wharf.

A few days later I had a letter from the lawyer in Oamaru to say that my brother and I were now joint owners of Willowglen and that I had been left all the contents of the home, and would I be returning to New Zealand as I was the sole executor of my father's estate? My father's estate! There were the home and its contents, enough money for the funeral, a small sum of money for my sister, and a bank book containing six shillings and fourpence. The cash for the funeral and the small bequest came from money won a week earlier in a lottery or on a racehorse, otherwise there would have been nothing.

I consulted Dr Cawley whom I still visited regularly. Should I return to New Zealand? A shocked angry letter from my brother said that Willowglen had been locked up and no-one would let him in, and although he was not living at Willowglen, he was hurt by the idea of not being allowed into his old home.

Should I return? Perhaps I had already made up my mind. The opinion was that it might be unwise to live in New Zealand after my past experience there, and that I might even be in danger from the mistaken diagnosis for few there had questioned it, and now that my books were being published there was constant reference to me as 'unbalanced, insane' with a tendency to ally this to my writing and even make it a reason and explanation for my writing. Perhaps I had already made up my mind, for I realised that I wished to return to live and work in New Zealand. Although I was now being referred to as an 'expatriate' writer, my reasons for leaving New Zealand, apart from the desire to 'broaden my experience', had not been literary or artistic. My reason for returning was literary. Europe was so much on the map of the imagination (which is a limitless map, indeed) with room for anyone who cares to find a place there, while the layers of the long dead and recently dead are a fertile growing place for new shoots and buds, yet the prospect of exploring a new country with not so many layers of mapmakers, particularly the country where one first saw daylight and the sun and the dark, was too tantalising to resist. Also, the first layer of imagination mapped by the early inhabitants leaves those who follow an access or passageway to the bone. Living in New Zealand, would be for me, like living in an age of mythmakers; with a freedom of imagination among all the artists because it is possible to begin at the beginning and to know the unformed places and to help to form them, to be a mapmaker for those who will follow nourished by this generation's layers of the dead. I was strongly influenced in my decision by remembering, from time to time, Frank Sargeson's words to me, 'Remember you'll never know another country like that where you spent your earliest years. You'll never be able to write intimately of another country,'

My argument had always been, 'What of the writers forced into political exile who never had or have the choice of returning, who live and work and bring new insights to the language of their adopted country? And what of those who have had to go more deeply into the unknown by changing their language? Conrad, Nabokov . . . and what about James Joyce . . . and Samuel Beckett . . . ? All writers — all beings — are exiles as a matter of course. The certainty about living is that it is a succession of expulsions of whatever carries the life force . . . All writers are exiles wherever they live and their work is a lifelong journey towards the lost land . . .'

The fact is that when I was about to go home to New Zealand I did not need reasons for returning; but others needed to know why, to have explanations. I could have said that, sitting at my sewing machine table looking out at the fields of East Suffolk, I had known a sensation of falseness, of surface-skimming . . . the feeling, perhaps, when after writing a letter and sealing it and writing the address on the envelope one might find that the stamp won't hold, there's nothing to glue it to the envelope, and no matter how hard one tries, the stamp keeps coming unstuck — so what use, except as a self-confirming exercise, was a letter that stayed with the writer?

Whatever my reasons for returning to New Zealand, I knew I would try to make them sound as elevated as possible; but I did experience this unease in Suffolk, knowing that thousands of miles away there was a cabbage tree or clump of snowgrass or a sweep of sky that I had not examined as carefully as I examined the ninety-foot lilac hedge; and a nation of people that I had never learned to know as well, as during my short stay in Suffolk — or in Ibiza or Andorra — I felt I knew the inhabitants, their landscape, their history and was beginning to know their language.

Now that writing was my only occupation, regardless of the critical and financial outcome, I felt I had found my 'place' at deeper level than any landscape of any country would provide. In New Zealand Frank Sargeson had saved my life by affirming that I could spend my time writing, although to him, I think, I was always the 'mad, sane' person; here in London writing had been affirmed as a way of life without psychiatric qualifications. I now felt, inhabiting my 'place', that day by day I could visit the Mirror City and ponder questions that only those trying to practise a form of art have time for: artists, monks, idlers, any who stand and stare. I could journey like a seasoned traveller to the Mirror City, observing (not always consciously), listening, remembering and forgetting. The only graveyard in Mirror City is the graveyard of memories that are resurrected, reclothed with reflection and change, their essence untouched. (A truthful autobiography tries to record the essence. The renewal and change are part of the material of fiction.)

Having advised against my returning to New Zealand, and accepting that I chose to return, Dr Cawley reminded me that I should live as I wished and not as others wished, that I had no obligation to 'mix', that he agreed with me that living alone was my ideal way of life if I chose it to be. And writing.

He did advise that I buy a return ticket.

I knew, finally, that leaving one's native land forever can be a strength or a weakness or both, depending on the artist, to be used to add to the store of material processed in Mirror City, and that for the writer of fiction being an exile may be a hindrance, especially if the writer is from a country just beginning its literary tradition. The writer (if there is ever such a person as 'the writer') may find herself spending a lifetime looking into the mists of a distant childhood, or becoming a travel writer who describes the scene, then leaves it, pocketing the uprooted vegetation, erasing the sea and the sky without hearing the cries of a world that has been torn from itself into the fictional world, from people whose very skin is left hanging in the centuries-old trees; the unmistakable cry of a homeland truthfully described and transformed.

I know that unless the writer embraces the language of the new land there are constant betrayals of language. (Language may betray the writer but the writer must not be the betrayer.) When I had returned to New Zealand and wrote *The Adaptable Man* set in Suffolk, a sharp-eyed critic noted my inaccurate reference to the *Orwell River* instead of the correct, *River Orwell*, my usage being the New Zealand idiom — the Rakaia River, the Waitaki River, the Clutha River — and not the English — River Thames, Humber, Orwell.

Wherever one lives, in the growing necessity for a 'world view', living or not living in one's native land may give equal advantages and insights, and from whatever land, the truth is always painful to extract and express whether it be the truth of fact or fiction.

I had written a few chapters of *Letters to a Sculptor*. Although my return fare to New Zealand had been guaranteed by 'an anonymous donor' whom I suspected (correctly, I think) to be Charles Brasch (the poet), I preferred to receive money from an institution rather than an individual. I had enough to pay my return fare and my proportion of the rent of the Kensington apartment, but there were no prospects of my being able to have funds in New Zealand. I therefore applied either for a Literary Fund Grant or for the Scholarship in Letters for 1964.

I booked my passage, a single cabin on the *Corinthic*, a one-class ship sailing from London through the Panama Canal to Auckland. I knew I had been advised never again to travel by sea but I was ever hopeful of becoming a good sailor.

Where had my London years gone? Why had I never been to Stratford-on-Avon? To the Brontë country? To Hardy country? Stonehenge, Tintagel Castle, Tintern Abbey? I had spent a week in the Lake District camping out for one night beside Sour Milk Force on the route through to Buttermere. I had roamed the Fells all day visiting places known to Wordsworth, Coleridge, Shelley.

I had absorbed much from living in London. I had seen the rise and strength of the Campaign for Nuclear Disarmament, the Easter Marches to Aldermaston; the Suez crisis; the Hungarian Revolution, the Parliamentary scandals. I had seen the arrival of the 'kitchen sink' playwrights and painters, the West Indian novelists, the North Country novelists and I had found my favourites to take their place beside those already there — I read the Beat Poets of City Lights Press; Ted Hughes, Sylvia Plath (recently dead); William Golding; Samuel Selvon; Iris Murdoch, Albert Camus, Sartre, Duras, Sarraute, Robbe-Grillet . . . I had seen *Last Year in Marienbad* and the new films from India. I had attended a performance of *Three Sisters* in Russian . . . I had listened in St Pancras Hall to the London Mozart Players, the Bach Players . . . and Kathleen Ferrier, dead. I had interesting correspondence with Bertrand Russell's first love. The librarian at the Kentish Town flat had sponsored me for a ticket to the British Museum Reading Room. Well, my London days were full of experience — museum, galleries, libraries, people; and underlying all was a gradual strengthening of me in my place through my talks with Dr Cawley as if he was a *bespoke* tailor helping to reinforce the seams of my life and now I was putting on my own garment to try it. And woven into the garment were my experiences in Ibiza and Andorra. (I'd had a loving postcard from the fur shop in the south of France, from El Vici Mario, but the address was illegible and I therefore excused myself from replying.)

There were many people I knew whom I do not describe here; they are living and I have tried to restrict myself to my own story without presuming to tell the stories of others. Writing of the dead is a different matter, for the dead have surrendered their story. There is a danger, however, in living at a distance from the source of one's fiction, for one so easily equates distance with death, and, rejoicing over the freedom of a story, one is suddenly faced with the curtailing effects of facts that have never undergone the necessary transformation in Mirror City; the writer has supposed that staying safe in this world and sprinkling a potion of distance-death upon a chosen ingredient of fiction, can result in the same transformation that occurs within the harsh lonely places of Mirror City. Instant fiction is as contradictory as instant future.

I said goodbye to London where living had been for me like living within a huge family with London our house. I looked forward to the terrible winters of frost, ice, chilblains. I watched the leaves turning and falling and drifting against the black iron railing of the parks. I saw the sun change to blood-red and stand on end upon the winterbeaten grass of the Common; I watched the people with a new urgency in their gait, hurrying to their homes, if they had homes to escape the dark and the cold; and those with no homes depending for warmth and shelter on the doorways of peopleless places like banks and insurance buildings and (before the great railway stations were demolished or remodelled and rebuilt without seating) on the seats of the railway stations and bus terminals and down from the Strand, by the river, underneath the arches. Then after dark the new life of London, the glitter, the people in taxis and dark polished cars . . . wandering misfits shouting at the sky . . . the dark January days . . . the appearance of spring . . . June, dusty July, August, the cycle again. The seasons in the city of millions became my relations as they had been in the countryside of New Zealand. Here there was the evidence of lives shared with the human power of destruction and creation; the irreparable mistakes that are part of the construction of a city, no matter how carefully it has been planned, the effect of the mistakes, some disastrous, the illumination of the way of human beings, shafts of light not originating in the sun; while the seasons, modified, damaged, but recurring, continue to regard the city, they too in a sense at home, acclimatised to themselves. The effect of London as a vast city gives only a hint of the complexity of Mirror City, yet it filled my life with thoughts and images that have stayed and will stay until I, as a season, accept inevitable change, when leaves of my own memory drift downward to become part of the rich earth of Mirror City.

My departure from London was sad and strange. With scenes in my mind of my journey from New Zealand, of my father, Uncle Vere and Aunty Polly waving goodbye from the shelter of the wharf sheds in Wellington; streamers, the ritual playing of *Now is the Hour*, the fearful apprehension that came over me when I watched the hills receding, the rising sense of adventure when I realised there was no turning back. I tried to imagine how it would be now, leaving London. The wharf, the embarkation, sailing down the Thames to the open sea . . . but where were the people to say goodbye in a city where my only family was the city itself?

I had spent seven years away from New Zealand with my past few years occupied entirely with writing, dividing my time between writing, solitary walking, dreaming in cinemas. I had no close friends who might wish to stand on a London wharf waving a sad goodbye. Unable to face a solitary departure I asked the librarian who had secured me a ticket to the Reading Room, would she mind 'seeing me off'. She agreed. The literary agent, Patience Ross, farewelled me at Victoria Station, and when the train arrived at the East London docks there was Millicent the librarian, who had taken an extended lunch hour to say goodbye. We had afternoon tea on board ship. I thanked her. She returned to her work. And as the engines started and the last farewells were made, and the ship began to move down the Thames, I looked about me at the sober, subdued passengers. There had been no band playing, no streamers. Some of the passengers had the air of being about to sail to their doom; many, no doubt were emigrants who had said last goodbyes and would never return; faces showed anxiety rather than anticipation, a certainty of a journey away from rather than a journey towards.

Recovering from my own brief self-pity (all those years in London and I need to ask someone to say goodbye to me!) I looked with interest at the dock buildings and the dark dampness of 'dockside' and I thought of my father and his Sexton Blake paperbacks, half-sized pocketbooks on mottled paper, and their scenes of crime in London's dockland; and the character, Tinker's, 'Right, guv.' I thought how much Dad would have relished a description of the docks, and how grateful he would have been like one who feels the movement of a telephone wire although there is no distinct message, had I written to say that I could just imagine Tinker and Sexton Blake at the docks meeting some unsavoury character, a 'nark' who would give them the 'tip-off'.

And so it was not the buildings of London, the Tate Gallery, the new literature, the excitement of living in London, that I thought of as the ship sailed towards the open sea, it was the girlhood sharing with my father of the cheap, poorly written detective stories with their pulp-soaked racist sterotypes, Tinker and Sexton Blake and their 'guvs' and 'm'lords' and 'm'luds' who were yet fictional characters whatever their literary deficiencies; and it was not even Dickens or Lamb or Samuel Pepys, it was Sexton Blake and Tinker, his faithful servant, who farewelled me from London while I, in my turn, was waving goodbye for the last time to my father, he too perhaps sheltering in fiction, huddled by the docks in the company of Tinker and Sexton Blake of Baker Street.

22 The Return

The seasickness that began as soon as we pitched and rolled on the open sea did not appear so hopeless from a deck cabin with a fresh breeze blowing in or from a deckchair outside. I was sitting quietly in a deckchair, trying to work out a way of having meals and avoiding the terrible weakness when a young man came out on deck.

'Would you like a slice of my birthday cake?' he asked. 'My mother made it for me.'

'Oh thank you.' I said. We were now two days out of London and I'd had no food, except the biscuits I'd brought with me.

The young man sat beside me. His name was Albert, he said, and he was a nuclear physicist travelling to take up a post in a New Zealand university where he hoped to concentrate on geophysics, volcanoes and earthquakes.

He was a mild, shy, pale young man in his late twenties, and from that day whenever I took up my place in the deckchair outside my cabin, sooner or later he would appear, sit beside me and talk to me. He brought me food from the dining room, and it was not long before he was bringing a small meal on a tray, enough for me to survive without increasing the sickness by making the journey to the dining room in the depths of the ship.

I told him I was a writer returning home after seven years away, but when he asked about the titles of my books my almost primitive shyness about naming prevented me from telling him. If, as is often said, the role of a poet is to name, then I understand my diffidence in naming titles, my reluctance to reduce or drain into speech the power supply of the named.

Albert became my attendant and companion throughout the voyage. His conversation was interesting. He was curious about the nature of the world, and I was an eager listener. He had spent his life asking questions and answering some of them. It is dismal to be alone and ill on land but the misery increases on board ship if one can't walk to the dining room to eat the meals enticingly displayed in the shipping brochure, nor see the films, nor take part in the games or the dancing, but can only lounge in a deckchair and not even travel into a poem or dream. Albert, full of information, brought news of life on board ship and of the world of science. I remembered how in my university days when I pored over the university calendars reading the science curriculum, I felt the excitement and mystery of the subject, 'Heat, Light and Sound', and I thought, 'Surely this is the province of poets, painters, composers of music, as well as of scientists, and why is it reserved exclusively for a handful of students?' And I remembered how, lured by the mystery and the magic, I borrowed books on physics and, opening them, I was faced with a wall of figures and symbols far beyond my Scholarship mathematics and chemistry: sentences that I could not understand, that roused the same feeling of frustration I'd had when I tried to read my father's bagpipe music as if it were simply another book, and it *was* a book. How could Heat, Light, Sound belonging to everyone, so remove itself from us? And I felt the frustration of the limits of my mind, curiosity and eagerness turning to dull fury and a surrender to myself as myself and not as I dreamed I might be, because I, living always with heat, light, sound, was excluded from its secrets.

It was thus a rare gift for me to have for thirty-one days the company of a 'real' physicist, this quiet shy man, a member of the Society of Friends, a great nephew of a famous poet, a pacifist and campaigner for nuclear disarmament who had worked at an atomic station and whose life was the study of violent earth movements, upheavals of fire and ashes, and whose recent invention had been a *safety detonator*: like his subject, Heat, Light, Sound, he was a living contradiction.

When the ship berthed at various ports my seasickness disappeared as soon as the ship stopped moving, and Albert and I went ashore and I listened eagerly while he described the formations of earth, water, sky, and asked and answered How, What, Where. And at the end of the voyage I felt that Albert's presence on board ship, through luck, coincidence or mysterious providence, had enabled me to survive.

At last we entered the Hauraki Gulf sailing slowly past the Bays with their unexpectedly colourful houses like rows of boiled sweets (ten years earlier I would have said 'lollies') in pink, yellow, blue, green, with some striped — set against the vivid green grass (leaf green? viridian?) and the darker green where stands of native bush remained. I'd forgotten about the confectionery housepaint and the drowning depths of the blue sky, not distant, but at hand, at head, a shared sky.

'Isn't Auckland pretty?' someone said.

'Isn't it?'

And there again was the Auckland light, not forgotten, like mountain light in a city without mountains, yet softer, full of currents of buoyant blue and purple and grey, and, moving, one waded effortlessly through the light.

When the Customs and Health launch arrived, members of the press also came on board, and I was surprised that they asked to talk to me. I had not realised that in the seven years I had been absent, the publication overseas and in New Zealand of several books had built a reputation known as an *overseas reputation* and therefore valued apparently more than a reputation *within New Zealand* — the reputation of excellent writers living in New Zealand was usually qualified by the phrase *known within New Zealand only*. (The growth of jet planes and the building of airports known as *international* resulted in the decline of *overseas* as an adjective of prestige and its replacement with *international* — an *international reputation*.) Also, as I'd been absent there had been no visible person to fasten this reputation upon, and with my arrival home, a dam of opinion and speculation burst over me. I had been quite unaware of this. I came home to find that I was looked on, variously, as famous, rich, a woman of the world, sane, insane, inevitably different from the shy unknown who had departed. Had I not lived and worked *overseas*? Had not my books been noticed *overseas*? Why, I was asked, as if there were no possible reason, should I want to return to New Zealand?

Perhaps we are a lazy people; the literary world is lazy too, preferring to pick up reputations from overseas rather than risk their own judgment within New Zealand.

The ship berthed. Albert's former colleague at the atomic station who had promised to meet him had sent his daughter. Her father was dying of cancer, she said. I wondered about the atomic station and its safety, for other colleagues had died.

My sister, her husband and children met me and drove me across the new Harbour Bridge ('see, there's our Harbour Bridge') to Northcote where they had hired a small caravan for me to stay until I travelled south to Oamaru and Willowglen. Where the Gordons had once lived surrounded by bush with tall kauris there were now rows of houses and acres of concrete, while the once wet wooded roadsides were treeless. The Gordon children, now teenagers, with Pamela at Intermediate School, filled the tiny house as they took up their places to watch *Ponderosa* or *Wagon Train* on television.

Later when I began to walk to Frank Sargeson's place in Esmonde Road, I discovered that except for a stand at Northcote by the harbour, all the bush had vanished and the country road to Takapuna where cows, horses, swamphens had once stared at the solitary walker, now was lined on each side by a ribbon of houses from Northcote to Takapuna, while the end of

Frank's road, once secluded with mangroves, swamp, sea, had been extended, the swamp filled in, the land 'reclaimed', and the approach road to the Harbour Bridge built upon it. Suddenly thrust into a world where there was much talk of 'reclaimed' land, 'desirable' property, the price of sections, sections with and without views, I felt I was seeing a new kind of greed for whatever could be touched, measured, seen, and priced. I was in a new city that looked outward and hoped and prayed for and paid for a *view*. And no one was saying what or whom the land belonged to before the famous reclamation.

Frank's bach had been almost surrounded by 'units' built upon what was now expensive 'real estate'. I felt sad as I bent forward to clear the ever-growing hedge with the honeysuckle as its sweet parasite, and trod the path that was now set with concrete paving stones, like stepping stones from one world to another, towards the back door with its empty upturned jar clamped upon the familiar message scribbled on the scrap of green paper. *Janet. Back at three-thirty.* With a cross for a kiss.

I pushed open the door. I felt very much like the Traveller returning. The bulk of manuscripts and books had increased while a huge bookcase (recognised as once belonging to the aunts who had died) divided the corner bed from the kitchen counter. There was a new large wooden chair used like a deckchair, the back adjusting with a wooden rod into several reclining positions. A writing-board, a pile of ink-written manuscripts upon it, was set beside another wooden chair by the counter. The rows of fruit, groups of peppers, seeds, were still there along the windowsill and on the counter. The circle of damp in the pinex ceiling had spread, still in a circle, with scalloped edges. The wood of the counter, the built-in desk (its surface covered with books), the chairs, the mantelpiece, the door, the bed-base, the windowsills and frames, had a more mellowed, worn appearance as if each day had passed across the surface, leaning on and fingering and even striking blows on the now golden wood.

I heard the swish of the overgrown vegetation as Frank came around the corner of the bach. I sensed that he was as apprehensive as I about our meeting after seven years. I could see his nervousness, but when we saw each other we each knew we were as we had been in that we were recognisable to each other after seven years. The tension eased.

Frank, preparing a cup of tea behind the counter, said hurriedly, 'You know, I'm not jealous. I'm not jealous.'

I was surprised that he, too, had been trapped by the words 'overseas reputation', and that he had expected to see someone different from the scared J.F. who stayed in the hut seven years ago.

Then, 'Have you seen it?' he asked.

'Seen what?'

'The hut. I had to have it demolished. It was overrun with rats and falling to pieces. You don't have to see it if you don't want to. I know it will distress you.'

I was touched by Frank's everlasting concern, and I felt ashamed of my lack of feeling for the hut. We went down the overgrown garden ('that's all gone,' he said sadly) by the tall flourishing pawpaw tree, its already gnarled trunk and twisted branches recording experience of direction, time, weather, unknown to the stripling new tree I had last seen in Frank's garden. We came to the heap of rubble that had been the hut where I lived and wrote, and now it was hidden by grass, paspalum and wild-seeded sweetcorn. I could see the burned circle of earth where I used to destroy all but the last version of manuscripts. I felt no regret, although careful of Frank's feelings and expectations, I sighed. 'Well, it's sad,' I said, and I felt sad then, but I knew that although I had lost the hut when I left Takapuna, I had kept within myself the memory of the time I spent there, knowing it was one of the cherished times of my life: the material vanishing now was nothing.

Frank then showed me the room he'd had built for Harry, with its separate entrance a grape arbour where already the white grapes hung in clusters.

'Taste them,' he said, tugging at a laden stalk. 'I give them to the paperboy.'

They were small, hard, bitter.

Frank then cooked a meal while he gave news of our friends, acquaintances, visitors, and the bodgies and widgies who had invaded his bach.

'And Karl and Kay Stead?'

He gave their news.

'Maurice and Barbara Duggan?'

'Jess and Ernest Whitworth? Jack? Harry? Reece Cole and Christine? Tony Stones? Kevin Ireland? Ian Hamilton? Werner and Greville? Odo Strewe? That small dark woman, you remember she came here only once and you said that if you'd ever been the marrying kind you would have married her?'

'Mrs Ansell?'

He gave news of her. He had news of everyone. Bob Lowry, Glover, Curnow, Shadbolt, Nigel Cook, Jimmy, Clarrie, Ted Middleton, Dennis McEldowney . . . everyone. Frank Haig? . . . on and on. 'And Charles Brasch?'

He gave all news, out-of-town and Auckland news, the out-of-town news having suffered a certain dilution, especially if it had crossed Cook Strait.

He told of the new writers, too, many of them. 'You may have an international reputation,' he said, 'but do you know, Janet, you and I are *passé*.'

I thought that perhaps he was right.

In my memory I hold this sheaf of pages labelled *The Return*; some pages are faded, some still starkly printed. When Frank asked where I would be living, saying there was always a bed for me at 14 Esmonde Road, I told him of my application for the Scholarship in Letters for 1964. I'd be returning to Willowglen, I said, to tidy affairs there, then I'd find a room in Auckland or the North Shore to live and write. In the meantime I had use of the eight-foot caravan at my sister's place in Northcote.

The visit to Willowglen was urgent. My brother had written that the house had been broken into several times: the new pair of double blankets had been stolen, he said. Other possessions were missing. I could feel the intensity underlining the reference to household goods and I knew with the wonder of recognition that I still had my passport to Mirror City, that it was my true home no matter how small my talent might be, how clumsy my sentences; each day and night I was in touch with the unalterable human composition that is the true basis of fiction, the great events of everyone's life and death — the returns, the losses, the gains, and now, anticipating my visit to my old home, the long pursuit of and flight from the dead and the goods of the dead. The news that the Kaiapoi blankets, soft white woollen blankets never known but now precious, had gone or been stolen, encompassed a cry to bring back the dead.

The next day I booked my seat on the overnight train to Wellington and the express across the Canterbury plains and the salmon river, to Oamaru.

23   *Willowglen*

Arriving in Oamaru, I went at once to the motor camp where I had rented a unit for the night. I bought supplies from the dairy and I stared curiously at the dairy owner, Mr Grant, who had been named next-of-kin when my father collapsed outside the shop. I looked searchingly at the goods I bought as if they and Mr Grant and my father were now in possession of a death I had come too late to share.

When I walked back to my cabin I saw a young man hiding in the bushes and peering out at me. He came towards me. He was a reporter, he said, from the local newspaper and he hoped I would give him first chance to talk to me as the provincial paper was also looking for me. He too had been fed the diet of 'overseas reputation' causing him to form an unreal image of me. He'd been sent to find the New Zealand author who was now jewelled with *overseas*, to gaze on her and share the jewels; and I, in my paste glitter, felt embarrassed. Although the reporter soon discovered that I did not carry the riches he expected, he was pleased to be first with his story, *Oamaru Author Returns*. We walked in the Gardens where he photographed me sitting in the Japanese garden, and I was remembering how as children wearing our Aunty-Polly-made puffed-sleeve summer-breeze dresses, we had been photographed or 'snapped' near the same bridge.

That day also, I collected the Willowglen key from the lawyer who asked what my plans were for Willowglen. My brother was getting married and needed a home, he said. The place was worth little, he was sure no one would buy it, and so there was little prospect of a division of money from any sale. He advised me to sell my share and not give it away as I had suggested. My father had wanted me to have it, he said. I had already made up my mind to give my brother my share for I knew he had little money and I also knew that throughout his life he had not been as lucky as I.

First, however, I must visit Willowglen in its springtime. Oamaru, as much as ever the kingdom by the sea, had now been declared a city as its population was up to ten thousand, but it was the sea that still clamoured to be heard, making the city like a shell singing in everyone's ears. My return alone to the deserted Willowglen was softened by the green of the leafy trees, and the sight of the once slender pine trees 'down on the flat', startling at first, as they were now a dark forest almost as formidable as the 'second planny' on the hill of Eden Street, and by the sound of the distant roar of the surf pounding at the breakwater on the shore. The driveway of Willowglen was overgrown with cocksfoot and littered with rusting parts of old cars, old stoves, and remnants of a dray. The shed where the pictures and the heavier furniture had been stored after the move from Eden Street was collapsed upon itself, open to the sky, with picture frames and table-legs still angled among the ruins. The cowbyre, the fowlhouse, the old pigsty overgrown with hemlock, the apple shed were all gradually falling apart, boards hanging, swinging to and fro as if the months and years had passed with such violence as to rip them apart like useless limbs. A wild black cat, perhaps one of Siggy's families, lurked in the hawthorn hedge. Siggy had recently died, aged eighteen.

I walked up the path under the old 'ghost' tree, that huge pine with the drooping dark branches. I walked in the porch, the lean-to against the hill,

treading on last year's squashed pears and seeing even among the pear blossom a few, shrivelled and shrunken, still clinging to the tree with no one to gather them any more. The old iron boot-last was still there, just outside the back door; Dad's fishing bag, as I remembered it in Kensington, fishy-stink and scabbed inside with old dried fish scales; and there were his thigh gumboots for wading in the shingle beds of the Waitaki, Rakaia, Rangitata. I opened the back door and walked in. I had not expected it would be as I found it, yet how else could it have been? My father's pyjamas hung over a chair. His long cream-coloured Mosgiel underpants with a faint brown stain at the crotch lay on the floor; even his last cup of tea sat in its saucer, a swill of tea in the bottom of the cup, making an old brown ridge against the china. The latest — two-and-a-half-months old — newspaper folded to present the crossword half filled in with the stub of the ink pencil beside it, lay by the cup of tea. There were ashes in the kitchen range with the ashpan half drawn out ready for emptying, while above on the brass rack, neatly folded pyjamas lay ready for the night.

The old sofa where Tittups the cat had peed and we tried to absorb the smell with our Christmas carnation scent, where the headmistress of Waitaki sat the day she came to give her sympathy over my sister Isabel's drowning, still took the length of the wall facing the shadowing hill beyond the lean-to where the bank was thick with cocksfoot, periwinkle, and small broadleaf plants sheltering in their own clay bed beneath the parent tree. In the kitchen, the curtains were new, a bright pattern of teapots and cups and saucers, the kind of pattern mother would never have chosen. I drew aside the curtains by 'Dad's seat' and looked out along the path to the cypress tree and the old dunny with its dunny roses spilling in a mass of white buds over the corrugated tin-hat roof.

I walked into the middle bedroom where I hoped to sleep. Books, linen were scattered everywhere. The two front rooms were also strewn with books, newspapers, old clothes, with the room that used to belong to our parents appearing tidier. There, the bed had some bedclothes and the pink eiderdown bought years ago on account from Calder Mackay, and there was a strange-looking electric heater like a copper pipe in front of the dis-used fireplace. I opened the front door and looked out at the grassy slope to the old orchard, the creek, and part of the 'flat' where my brother had transported an old house and where, I'd been told, Uncle Charlie, Dad's youngest brother, lived from time to time. I stood at the front door. The grass was growing on the doorstep. I remembered the time the cow had come to the front door and looked in. An owl in the tall macrocarpa tree by the old wash-house, startled by a human presence, fluttered from its sleeping perch to the paddock beyond.

My homecoming was as sad and desolate as I knew it would be, yet I relished its importance to the Envoy from Mirror City, that watching self, who was already waiting to guide me to my fictional home. Many times in my life I have received and cherished these gifts of fiction. From my home now in Mirror City I can only keep trying to parcel these gifts in language that satisfies the ear and the heart and the demands of truth. (It is the events of living that are not easily recognised as legends and part of myths that are the test of the value of lifelong tenancy in Mirror City; and it is the discovery of the new legends and myths that keeps building, renewing the city.)

As I explored the house I realised that I had forgotten or never knew about practical matters like turning on electricity, water, arranging a telephone, and I was reduced at once from the glory of my 'overseas reputation' when I received a bill for having the water switched on, and I was questioned by the power board about my ability to pay. I had forgotten in the midst of apparent kindness shown to me on my return home, that the world is still a cruel place, and Oamaru was no exception, and in all the abundance of Oamaru's giving and taking through water — the reservoir, the sea, the baths, the loved creeks and ponds, even the water-race known to us as the 'rolldown sea' by the post office, everything and everyone must be paid for.

I built a fire down on the flat to burn the rubbish collected in the house — old newspapers, receipts going back many years. I read everything before I burned or saved it. I burned family letters. I saved documents that I thought might be wanted by my sister and brother or myself, some that might be looked on as keepsakes — Isabel's athletic and academic certificates, her funeral receipt, other receipts that still bore the anguish of receiving the account so vividly that I said to myself, I remember when that bill came and Mum cried wondering how we could possibly pay it, but now it's paid and gone; how could a sheet of paper headed 'Dr To' (we had always thought of it as *Doctor*) cause so much anguish? I found the Star-Bowkett Building Society book with its detailed payments on the loan that bought Willowglen, and I heard again the anxiety in Mum's or Dad's voice — 'Where's the Star-Bowkett book? Have we paid the Star-Bowkett this month? When we pay the *Star-Bowkett* . . .' There were the Calder Mackay receipts, too, everything paid. And the local receipts — MacDiarmids, Builleids, the Polytechnic, Hodges, Kerrs, Jeffery and Smith, Adams . . . all the tradespeople that inhabited without knowing it our house, our daily conversation, and determined the mood of the family.

I found a pile of letters in a handwriting I did not recognise, and I began to read. The letters were from Dad's woman friend living in another town.

I had only recently heard about her from my sister who had said they planned to marry. The new curtains and pillowcases had been bought by her. She and Dad had been good company for each other, for apparently she had stayed often at Willowglen and attended to various household chores, and they had enjoyed themselves over a few drinks, as the numerous empty bottles disclosed. Her letters expressed concern over the house and its furnishings. She also wrote of the presents my father had given her, some of which she asked for in her letters.

As I read, I found myself slowly assuming the role of my mother, feeling the shock of knowing that 'Curly' who never 'touched a drop of drink' had left empty *liquor bottles* in the house, that the love that so steadfastly bound him over the years had been cast aside for this 'cheap' relationship with someone obviously in search of a 'sugar daddy'. I then became the outraged daughter — how dare our father abandon us for this woman? How dare she try to replace our mother? And why had Dad never told me? Not a word in all his letters with their detailed times, dates, costs, journeys, and the state of the government. I suddenly felt lonely, an outsider in my family.

Then as the last of the letters flared and died in the ashes I saw my father as he had been — widowed, living alone, troubled by bouts of undiagnosed sickness, still dosing himself with his 'chalk' to ease the pains in his stomach, coping with the physical effort of cycling each day along that bleak sea-exposed road out past the Boys' High to attend the boiler at the Presbyterian Home, returning wearily to an unlit cold house that escaped from the shadow of the hill only twice during the day, in the early morning when the sun trod briefly on the front doorstep and glanced in the window of the side bedroom, and later when it lay a hand along the front windowsill, then withdrew it, disappearing behind the trees. The frost in that all-day shade was as cruel as ever; and even the glorious seafoam wave of pear blossom at the back door could not atone for the awful chill laying all winter outside and inside the draughty, flimsy wooden house.

I prepared the middle bedroom for myself. I lifted the mattress from the floor and found a gaping hole in the cover and, snuggled within the kapok, a nest of bald pink baby rats. I don't recall how I disposed of them.

I washed the available bed linen and hung it to dry on the wire clothes-line that stretched from the top of the hill to the apple shed on the flat. I hoisted the line further in the air with the old manuka-stick prop and heard the familiar squeak-squeak as the stretched line pulled at the tree support, the old oak by the apple shed near where mother used to rest before she 'tackled' the steep sloping path to the house. I saw again in my mind my father's hunched figure, the sugar sack of railway coal on his back, his knees bent to ease the strain as he too struggled up the slope that became steeper

year by year.

And that night with the house cleaned and the bedclothes dried, I slept in the middle room. I was wakened by the wind in the many trees, by the silence, by the searchlight glare of the midnight express train as it turned the corner past the Gardens towards the railway crossing. The trees heaved and rocked in the rising wind; moreporks and the little 'German' owls called from the macrocarpa. And in the morning I was wakened by the gurgling, gargling magpies.

I decided I would not stay at Willowglen. I would walk into town that morning to book my return passage to Auckland, and when I had chosen those possessions I thought of as 'keepsakes' for members of the family, I would leave Oamaru.

Although the retraced path is a factual and fictional cliché, I'm not beyond indulging my memory. It was a delight to walk down Chelmer Street to the town while remembering other, not happier, times. Chelmer Street, too, with the hilly side of the street facing north, lived in perpetual shade on the north side, with occasional rays of afternoon sun touching the 'Gardens' side of the street. The street was so clearly divided in its share of sun and shade that it was like a street that had suffered a stroke and was left paralysed on one side, with the shade and the frost as the paralysing agents.

At the end of the street I passed the Town Baths and felt again, held within the dull red colour of the rows of seats and their spindly uncomfortable slats, the sense of the old glory of 'being at the Baths', and then I remembered after my sister Myrtle's drowning, the deliberate disentangling, the excision of the baths from my life and the way I then looked on the site as a strange hateful place as if it had been a friendly neighbour who was now an enemy sitting there unpunished for its crime. Now, remembering the succession of feelings towards the Baths, I felt only the sadness of the dull red colour of the seats, that iron-roof, railway-hut, railway-wagon, railway-station red that was painted through my life as part of my childhood rainbow.

I walked through Takaro Park where the circus used to pitch its tent and the sixpenny zoo was held in a row of cages under separate canvas; and there was the old building we used to call the Middle School, used for teaching technical subjects, and always apparently empty during the day. I remembered how I used to walk past it and feel a shiver of curiosity and strangeness at its emptiness and brownness and the tall windows with their cords hanging untouched during the daytime; it was a neutral kind of school, it had fairness, it was middle ground, between the fierce rivalries of the North and the South Schools. I walked by the Oamaru Creek and what

I still thought of as the 'Morgue', that small stone hut; and by the green water-race that reminded me of a *weir*, of Maggie Tulliver and *The Mill on the Floss*.

And as I stood in the queue at the post office people spoke to me, welcoming me home to Oamaru; some I knew, others were strangers who had seen my photo in the paper. One woman said she'd been at Waitaki when I was there. I stared at her. 'Oh yes,' and the former rigid classifications came to mind — good at maths; stodgy; not much good at phys. ed. Lives in the country, on a sheep station with a fancy name. Teachers talk with deference of the sheep station. We all turn our heads, envious.

We talked a while. She gave me news of others in the school class. 'Oh? That's interesting, I didn't know. Yes. Oh.'

I walked by the small telegraphic office next to the post office and there was the Social Security Department, and now I remembered my horror and shame as I used to sneak in to present my medical certificate with its telltale writing, *Schizophrenia*, and cash my sickness benefit during my brief stays in Oamaru. I remembered how I used to emerge from that office feeling as if all delight had gone from the day, knowing that I was a 'funny' peculiar person, and wanting to hide forever. I felt dirty, my clothes felt like the clothes of a mental patient, and my shoes looked clumsy.

I allowed myself the luxury of remembering these feelings and knowing that in the magic language of the world of racing — *this time* — everything was different. I need not go to the Social Security Department where the man behind the grille peered at me to see if my schizophrenia were showing.

I returned to Willowglen walking through the Town Gardens with its *Oamaru Beautifying Society* plaques. I passed the fern house and saw the ferns with their hair leaning against the milky windows, and I thought of how as children we used to go to the fern house just to feel the experience of wetness and greenness and the smell of being in the earth with the world above and around. I walked from the Gardens, past Lovers' Lane, the hideaway walk with its tree-enclosed paths, past the children's playground with its seesaws and boat swings and merry-go-round that used to make me so sick I could never play on them. And there was the paddling pool and the murky pond where the ducks and the swans lived, the big white swan with the orange beak and the fierce hooded eyes, and I remembered how I used to think of the Seven Brothers who were changed into swans but there was not enough magic for the youngest who had only one wing and could not fly. And I'd always thought that magic was magic, without limit.

Later that day I searched for keepsakes. I sat among the strewn books that were family books, history books bought by my brother who was always interested in history, 'rogue' books from nowhere, prizes from

431

Waitaki. I chose my sister Isabel's school prizes, Christmas books, London, my Training College *David Copperfield* and school prizes; Isabel's collection of native plants. For June and her family, Dad's book of fishing flies, the polished rod and case won in a fishing competition and never used because he preferred to make his own; various books; dishes, table covers, and the old kitchen clock with the dragons around the glass face. For myself, a pair of old blankets, the eiderdown, Dad's paintings, leaving some for my brother, Aunty Polly and Aunty Isy's paintings, the bagpipe chanter, the bedcover sewn by Dad from the collection of blazer material from throughout New Zealand, used by Aunty Isy at the Ross and Glendinning Mills. There was little more that I could take in my luggage. I had no place of my own to live in. My brother could make good use of the rest of the family 'treasures'.

Sitting there choosing and rejecting from the pathetic remnants of a family's life, I could still feel the value of them, my need for them, the need of others to have them as keepsakes. Each object was alive with its yesterdays. I wanted to embrace them, even the books; and when I finally packed them, I looked regretfully at those I had been forced to leave behind: the long kauri form where we used to sit for meals and where my father and his brothers and sisters had also sat, and, like us, had used the upturned form as a canoe. The dining table had been used only on special occasions at Eden Street, but at Willowglen it would fit only into the small kitchen: it had been the Christmas and New Year table, the Sunday Bible-reading table, the table-when-visitors-came; Dad's leather workbag which he always sewed while we watched fascinated as he trimmed the raw leather, cut the bag to shape, stained it, and finally sewed it, first drawing the thread through a lump of beeswax. I pocketed a few of his salmon spoons and sinkers only because we had shared, too, in their making, watching (seen and not heard) while Dad leaned over the stove with the sinkers in their small pan, and the dreaded 'spirits of salts'.

Having a last look over the house I opened the sewing machine drawer where the bullets used to be kept and there they were, two or three, shining with a point at the end like bronzed rockets. 'Don't you touch the bullets,' our parents would say. Curious, we often touched them, and played school with them, marshalling them along the mottled brown varnished machine-stand.

And so with my bundle of treasures from Willowglen I took the train and ferry north to Auckland.

24   Only to Please the Envoy

Treasures dreamed of and seen in their home are different when they are homeless. I arrived at the Gordon's place in Northcote with a heap of apparent rubbish — a bundle of frayed linen, an old broken kitchen clock, a chipped ivory chanter without a reed, a stained flybook that clearly wanted to be in no other place but clasped in my father's hand or thrust like a wallet in the outer pocket of his fishing bag; a golden cut glass dish where mother used to make the Christmas and New Year jellies that we would hold up to the light and look through, to see the gold; a small dark blue china shoe that used to be on the mantelpiece at home and held an assortment of needles, buttons, clips. The only items of worth was the unused fishing rod in its new varnished case, and the red fan heater. In the Gordon's smart new house ('designed by an architect') with its 'cedar weatherboards' and 'cantilever terrace' and 'peep of Rangitoto', the treasures looked pathetic. Except for the cut glass dish, the china shoes, and the heater (which with the bedcover of blazer cloth I gave to Frank Sargeson), they were thrust under the house by the garage where one of my suitcases of possessions had been left while I was away overseas. Returning, opening the mouldy case, I had felt the fumes of past misery rising from the dark blue and dark green remnants of skirts and jerseys, the everglaze summer dress (again dark blue with pattern of exploding stars), the typed pages of old poems and stories wedged into a ravine of yesterdays.

The kitchen clock with the dragons on the glass, the old bedcovers lay homeless among the bits and pieces until one or two found a place in the playhouse of my niece, Pamela, where they revived, briefly at home among fantasy teas and conversations. I remember my anger and shock when I perceived that the treasures I had rescued were being treated carelessly, ill used, not given their pride of place; and then I smiled to myself at my concern as I realised that even in my journeys to Mirror City I had abducted treasures from their homeland, placed them in strange settings, changed their purpose, and in some cases destroyed them to make my own treasures even as my niece was doing in her playhouse. And here was I being trapped also within one of the great themes of fiction — the gift, the giver, the receiver and the thing received, a theme so basic it is embedded in the grammar and syntax of the language where it lies like a trap or a shaft of light.

In writing this autobiography I have been returning to each year of my life to collect the treasures of my experience, and I have set them down in their own home, their own place. In my record I have returned to New Zealand where I am awarded the Scholarship in Letters for 1964 that enables me to write without financial worry for a year, and in 1965 I become a Burns Fellow at the University of Otago where I can buy a cottage for twelve hundred pounds . . . my writing continues, living and expressing. In trying to secure and bring home to their place the treasures of my recent past I find that, like Pamela with her playhouse of fantasy, carpeting her floor with old treasures, pouring her teas out of cups and saucers removed from their home but transformed in their new setting, I prefer to take my treasurers to my home, my playhouse, Mirror City. I have the pressure of the Envoy to do this, and even as I write now the Envoy from Mirror City waits at my door, and watches hungrily as I continue to collect the facts of my life. And I submit to the Envoy's wishes. I know that the continued existence of Mirror City depends on the substance transported there, that the waiting Envoy asks, 'Do you wish Mirror City to thrive? Remember your visit there, that wonderful view over all time and space, the transform-ation of ordinary facts and ideas into a shining palace of mirrors? What does it matter that often as you have departed from Mirror City bearing your new, imagined treasures, they have faded in the light of this world, in their medium of language they have acquired imperfections you never intended for them, they have lost meaning that seemed, once, to shine from them and make your heart beat faster with the joy of discovery of the matched phrase or cadence, the clear insight. Take care. Your recent past surrounds you, has not yet been transformed. Do not remove yet what may be the foundation of a palace in Mirror City.'

I plead, 'Let me write of further travel, of the way of life of a writer in New Zealand, of my return to Dunedin and the University, of books written and books planned, of friends made and kept. Quick, just once, let me look out at the clouds travelling along the North-East Valley sky in Dunedin, that immense sky sprawled above the hills, with every cloud going somewhere in a trail of white or black smoke pursued by storm and wind and sun. And let me describe how . . .'

'There is much to do,' the Envoy says, looking over my shoulder as I see in my mind the clouds in the Dunedin sky. 'And what is that city shining across the valley?' the Envoy asks.

I look triumphant.

'That's Dunedin. I was born there. Let me write of my life there, how I made friends and wrote books, how I went north to live by the sea, how I moved to other cities with other clouds and skies.'

'You say it's Dunedin? It's Mirror City. You know it's time to pack this collection of years for your journey to Mirror City.'

I stare more closely at the city in my mind. And why, it *is* Mirror City, it's not Dunedin or London or Ibiza or Auckland or any other cities I have known. It is Mirror City before my own eyes. And the Envoy waits.

ACKNOWLEDGMENTS

To the Is-Land
Grateful acknowledgment for the continuing support of the New Zealand Literary Fund, my friends and publisher.
Grateful acknowledgment is also made to the following for permission to reprint selected verse passages:
Extract from 'I Met at Eve' by Walter de la Mare, reprinted by permission of the Literary Trustees of Walter de la Mare and the Society of Authors as their representative;
Extract from 'Old Grey Squirrel' by Alfred Noyes, reprinted with the permission of William Blackwood & Sons Limited and the author's estate.

An Angel at my Table
Grateful acknowledgment is made to the following for permission to reprint selected passages.
Extract from 'The Stares Nest by My Window' by W. B. Yeats reprinted by permission of Michael B. Yeats, Macmillan London Ltd. and Macmillan Publishing Company, New York from *The Poems* by W. B. Yeats, edited by Richard J. Finneran, copyright 1928 by Macmillan Publishing Company, Inc., renewed 1956 by George Yeats.
Extracts from 'Great Sea, Kona Coast, Hawaii' and 'A View from Rangitoto' by Charles Brasch reprinted by permission of Mr Alan Roddick and the estate of Charles Brasch.
Extract from 'Time' by Allen Curnow reprinted by permission of the author.
Extracts from 'Lamentation' from *Poems* by Lynette Roberts reprinted by permission of Faber and Faber Ltd., London.
Extract from 'Five Minutes More' by Jule Styne and Sammy Cahn used by permission of Morley Music Inc.
'All or Nothing at All'. Words and music by Arthur Altman and Jack Lawrence © copyright 1939, 1940 by MCA Music, a division of MCA Inc., New York, N.Y. Reproduced by kind permission of MCA Music Australia Pty. Ltd.
'Don't Get Around Much Anymore'. Music by Duke Ellington, lyrics by Bob Russell. © 1942 Robbins Music Corp. USA. Reproduced by permission of EMI United Partnership Ltd. London WC2H 0EA.

The Envoy from Mirror City
Grateful thanks to John Money (John Forrest) of Baltimore, Maryland, John and Rose Marie Beston of Pittsford, New York, and Bill Brown and Paul Wonner of San Francisco, for the hospitality that enabled me to complete my manuscript.
Extract from 'In Memory of W. B. Yeats' from *W. H. Auden: Collected Poems*, edited by Edward Mendelson reprinted by permission of Random House Inc., New York, and Faber and Faber Ltd., London.
Extracts from *Notebooks* by Albert Camus translated from the French by Philip Thody reprinted by permission of Hamish Hamilton Ltd., London and Alfred A. Knopf, Inc., New York. French edition copyright Editions Gallimard 1962.
Extract from 'Oh No Work of Words' from *Collected Poems 1934-52* by Dylan Thomas reprinted by permission of J. M. Dent and Sons Ltd., London, and the literary executors of the Dylan Thomas Estate.